·THE SEDUCTION OF UNREASON·

THE SEDUCTION ·OF UNREASON·

THE INTELLECTUAL ROMANCE WITH FASCISM · FROM NIETZSCHE TO POSTMODERNISM ·

· RICHARD WOLIN ·

PRINCETON UNIVERSITY PRESS · PRINCETON AND OXFORD

Copyright © 2004 by Princeton University Press

Published by Princeton University Press, 41 William Street, Princeton, New Jersey 08540

In the United Kingdom: Princeton University Press, 3 Market Place, Woodstock, Oxfordshire OX20 1SY

All Rights Reserved

Library of Congress Cataloging-in-Publication Data

Wolin, Richard.

The seduction of unreason : the intellectual romance with fascism : from Nietzsche to postmodernism / Richard Wolin.

p.   cm.

Includes bibliographical references and index.

ISBN 0-691-11464-1 (cl : alk. paper)

1. Fascism.   2. Political science—Philosophy.   3. Ideology.   I. Title

JC481.W65 2004

335.6—dc22   2003057955

British Library Cataloging-in-Publication Data is available

This book has been composed in Dante Typeface

Printed on acid-free paper. ∞

pup.princeton.edu

Printed in the United States of America

3   5   7   9   10   8   6   4   2

For EMMA, SETH, *and* ETHAN

May you stay forever young

Thinking begins only when we have come to know that Reason, glorified for centuries, is the most stiff-necked adversary of thought.

—Martin Heidegger, "The Word of Nietzsche: 'God is Dead'"

All knowledge rests upon injustice; there is no right, not even in the act of knowing, to truth or a foundation for truth; and the instinct for knowledge is *malicious* (something murderous, opposed to the happiness of mankind).

—Michel Foucault, "Nietzsche, Genealogy, and History"

Reason must in all its undertaking subject itself to criticism; should it limit freedom of criticism by any prohibitions, it must harm itself, drawing upon itself a damaging suspicion. Nothing is so important through its usefulness, nothing so sacred, that it may be exempted from the searching examination, which knows no respect for persons. Reason depends on this freedom for its very existence. For reason has no dictatorial authority; its verdict is always simply the agreement of free citizens, of whom each one must be permitted to express, without let or hindrance, his objections or even his veto.

—Immanuel Kant, *The Critique of Pure Reason*

· CONTENTS ·

Hitler has compelled humanity to accept a new categorical imperative:
orient your thinking and acting so that Auschwitz would never
repeat itself, so that nothing similar would recur.

—THEODOR W. ADORNO, *Negative Dialectics*

THIS IS A BOOK about skeletons in the closet. It reexamines the checkered relationship between intellectuals and right-wing politics during the 1930s, and the implications of this relationship for the political present.

It would be comforting to think, as some have argued, that fascism was an anti-intellectual phenomenon attractive only to criminals and thugs. Today, however, we know better. Many of the continent's intellectual leading lights were clamoring to mount the fascist political bandwagon. After all, following the Great War and the Crash of '29, democracy's credibility had sunk to unprecedented depths. An enumeration of fascism's literary and philosophical sympathizers—a list that would include Ernst Jünger, Gottfried Benn, Martin Heidegger, Carl Schmitt, Robert Brasillach, Pierre Drieu La Rochelle, Louis-Ferdinand Céline, Paul de Man, Ezra Pound, Giovanni Gentile, Filippo Marinetti, Gabriele d'Annunzio, W. B. Yeats, and Wyndham Lewis—points to the tip of a sizeable iceberg. Moreover, now that Marxist explanations, focusing on fascism's economic origins, have broken down, the question of the intellectual origins of far-right politics must be seriously rethought.

This historical nexus between intellectuals and the extreme right has shaped contemporary political discourse in numerous respects. During the 1990s, far-right parties, such as Jörg Haider's Austrian Freedom Party and Jean-Marie Le Pen's National Front, made sweeping gains among European voters. Political parties with analogous ethnocentric, nativist leanings also made great strides in

Scandinavia, Belgium, and a number of the recently emancipated nations of eastern Europe. Inevitably, commentators have felt compelled to enquire whether fascism's ghosts were making an uncanny comeback.

In academic quarters, postmodernism has been nourished by the doctrines of Friedrich Nietzsche, Martin Heidegger, Maurice Blanchot, and Paul de Man—all of whom either prefigured or succumbed to the proverbial intellectual "fascination with fascism." Consequently, the troubling prospect arose that an antidemocratic orientation popular during the 1930s was making an eerie comeback—this time, however, under the auspices of the academic left. Such filiations, provocative and unsettling in many respects, seemed to confirm a time-honored political maxim: *les extrêmes se touchent.*

Today the postmodern juggernaut seems to have run aground. Outside of the parochial climate of contemporary academe, its program of a "farewell to reason" failed to take root. Its bold proclamation concerning the end of "metanarratives" of human emancipation also failed to gain widespread acceptance. Moreover, the eastern European dissidents whose words and actions inspired the "revolutions of 1989" successfully relied on the discourse of "human rights" to undermine totalitarianism. In this way, a political orientation predicated on the values of Western humanism that the cultural left had denigrated as a tool of American hegemony made a meaningful comeback.

During the 1980s and 1990s the academic left attempted to replace the discourse of democratic legitimacy with the avowedly anti-universalistic concept of "identity politics." But this approach was fraught with contradictions and difficulties. Identity politics— the anti-politics of cultural self-affirmation—seemed plausible and attractive among polities where basic constitutional and legal guarantees remained firmly in place. Such provisions secured a political space—a "magic wall" of governmental noninterference, so to speak—in which the parameters of cultural identity could be safely explored in ways that stopped short of riding roughshod over competing identity claims. Yet where such assurances were lacking—the cases of Bosnia, Rwanda, and Algeria immediately leap to mind— identity politics engendered unspeakable tragedy. These experiences affirm one of the central precepts of political modernity: the formal guarantees of procedural democracy remain an indispensable prerequisite for the values of toleration and mutual recognition to flourish. Or, to express this insight in the idiom of contemporary political theory, such experiences confirm the priority of the "right" over the "good."

In retrospect, postmodernism's contention, most pointedly expressed in Michel Foucault's work, that the institutionalization of "reason" and "progress" leads to enhanced domination rather than emancipation seems overtly cynical and empirically untenable. The "Third Wave" of democratization that swept across eastern Europe, South America, and (more tentatively) Asia during the 1980s and 1990s has demonstrated that the legacy of democratic humanism harbors considerable staying power. Conversely, as the cases I have examined from the 1930s show, principled enmity toward democratic values can easily lead to disastrous political outcomes.

It is one of the supreme ironies of the contemporary period that postmodernism's demise has been most rapid and extensive in contemporary France, its putative philosophical birthplace. During the 1970s and 1980s the values of humanism were perceived as the most effective bulwark against the excesses of "revolutionism," whose catastrophic consequences—in eastern Europe, Mao-tse-tung's China, and the Cambodia of (Paris-educated) Pol Pot—had become undeniable. French intellectuals quickly realized that a slack postmodernist relativism lacked the moral and conceptual resources necessary to stand up to the inequities of tyranny both abroad and at home. A renewed emphasis on human rights as the unsurpassable political horizon of our time resulted.

Hence, the current disaffection with postmodernism is in no small measure attributable to recent political circumstances. Humanism's return spells postmodernism's demise. Totalitarianism was the twentieth century's defining political experience. Its aftermath has left us with a new categorical imperative: *no more Auschwitzes or Gulags*. We now know that an ineffaceable difference separates democratic and totalitarian regimes. Despite their manifest empirical failings, democratic polities possess a capacity for internal political change that totalitarian societies do not. A discourse such as postmodernism that celebrates the virtues of cultural relativism and that remains ambivalent, at best, vis-à-vis democratic norms is inadequate to the moral and political demands of the contemporary hour.

Although the present study probes the nexus between intellectuals—several of whom figure prominently in the postmodernist pantheon—and fascism, I do not intend it as an exercise in guilt by association. Whereas, historically, fascism flirted with the values of a strong state, postmodernist political thought leans toward a philosophical anarchism. As a rule it views almost all political institutions—democratic ones included—with endemic suspicion. From a practical standpoint, this attitude has meant an adieu to real-world politics in favor of airy and speculative discussions of "the political."

The critique of postmodernism in the pages that follow has a different aim. My concern is that at a certain point postmodernism's hostility towards "reason" and "truth" is intellectually untenable and politically debilitating. Often its mistrust of logic and argumentation are so extreme that its practitioners are left dazed and disoriented—morally and politically defenseless. When, in keeping with the practice of a neo-Nietzschean "hermeneutic of suspicion," reason and democracy are reduced to objects of mistrust, one invites political impotence: one risks surrendering the capacity for effective action in the world. Esoteric theorizing—theory tailored to an audience of initiates and acolytes—threatens to become an ersatz praxis and an end in itself.

As a result, the postmodern left risks depriving democracy of valuable normative resources at an hour of extreme historical need. In times of crisis—such as the current global war on terrorism in which basic rights and liberties have been manifestly jeopardized—that the elements of a "democratic minimum" be preserved is imperative. Postmodern political thought, which devalues coalition building and consensus in favor of identity politics and political agonistics, prematurely discounts this heritage. It thereby inherits one of the most problematic traits of "leftism": the cynical assumption that democratic norms are little more than a veil for vested interests. Of course, they *can* and *do* serve such purposes, but they also offer a crucial element of ethical leverage by means of which dominant interests may be exposed and transformed. The political gains that have been registered during the last three decades by previously marginalized social groups (women, gays, ethnic minorities) testify to a logic of political inclusion. They demonstrate capacities for progressive political change that remain lodged in democratic precepts and institutions. To surrender entirely these potentials means abandoning progressive politics altogether.

Note on Postmodernism

A basic terminological clarification concerning the concept of "postmodernism"—undoubtedly, one of the most overused and, hence, potentially confusing terms in scholarship—would seem in order.

Discussions of postmodernism developed from postwar transformations in architecture and the arts. They suggest that the key concepts of aesthetic modernism—formalism, difficulty, depth, the artist qua "genius"—have exhausted themselves. As such, postmodernism heralded a new exoteric, pragmatic, and populist spirit in the arts—a spirit that was reflected in Andy Warhol's pop iconography and the architect Robert Venturi's rediscovery of the American vernacular ("Learning from Las Vegas"). In the visual arts, postmodernism signaled the transition from the involutions of abstract expressionism to the "new immediacy" of the 1960s art scene: op art, conceptual art, performance art, happenings. In architecture, it connoted a rejection of the "international style," as represented by the stifling uniformity of the "glass and steel box" (Bauhaus functionalism), in favor of an often random and ad hoc borrowing of bygone, traditional approaches. In literature, postmodernist orientations often toyed with the lures of "metafiction": literature that explores or places in question its own raison d'être.

At a later point, under the impact of "poststructuralism" or French "theory," postmodernism encompassed a much broader assault on the epistemological and historiographical presuppositions of modernity: objective truth and historical progress. Circa 1980 the doctrines of postmodernism (in the arts) and poststructuralism (in philosophy) became fused in the North American academic-intellectual imaginary.

When postmodernism is at issue in the text that follows, I am primarily referring to the last-named phenomenon: the rejection of the intellectual and cultural assumptions of modernity in the name of "will to power" (Nietzsche), "sovereignty" (Bataille), an "other beginning" (Heidegger), "différance" (Derrida), or a "different economy of bodies and pleasures" (Foucault).

New York City, April 2003

·ACKNOWLEDGMENTS·

EARLIER VERSIONS of chapters 2 and 3 appeared in *The New Republic,* and both benefited immensely from literary editor Leon Wieseltier's discerning eye for intellectual clarity and narrative coherence. An earlier rendition of Political Excursus II first appeared in *Fascism's Return,* edited by Richard Golsan. I am grateful to the University of Nebraska Press for their permission to reprint.

A number of chapters experienced a trial run as lectures at various North American and European universities: the University of California, Berkeley, the New School University, New York University, Reed College, the University of British Columbia, Simon Fraser University, Lisbon's Intituto Piaget, and the Central European University in Prague. I presented chapter 6, "Down by Law: Deconstruction and the Problem of Justice," as the 2003 Baldwin-Dahl Lecture in Comparative Literature at Yale University. I am particularly grateful to my Yale hosts, Alison Weiner and Hiba Hafiz, for their kind invitation and gracious hospitality.

I would like to express my sincerest gratitude to my editor at Princeton University Press, Brigitta van Rheinberg. Once again Brigitta demonstrated an unerring eye for how best to turn an inchoate manuscript into a focused book. CUNY Graduate Center Provost Bill Kelly, the paragon of the enlightened administrator, generously granted me a one semester leave during which much of the writing was completed.

I also benefited greatly from the illuminating criticisms proffered by two outstanding intellectual historians, Jeffrey Herf and Jerry Seigel. Undoubtedly, the end result would have been far inferior had it not been for their valuable and constructive input. For a long time now another excellent historian, Martin Jay, has been a patient and insightful critic of my ideas—even (or, perhaps especially) when he disagrees with them. William Scheuerman, from whose work on "rule of law" I have learned much, generously offered a variety of helpful comments on chapter 6 ("Down By Law"). During the final stages of composition, graduate students Martin Woessner and Brian Fox contributed a number of timely suggestions.

Last, but certainly not least, I'd like to thank my wife, Melissa, for her patience, good cheer, and unstinting support.

Chirico, Giorgio de (1888–1978) The Song of Love, 1914 © 2003 Artist
Rights Society (ARS) New York/SIAE, Rome. Oil on canvas, 28¾ x 23⅜".
Nelson A. Rockefeller Bequest (950.1979) The Museum of Modern Art,
New York, NY, U.S.A. Digital Image © The Museum of Modern Art/
Licensed by SCALA/Art Resource, NY.

I HAVE SELECTED an early painting from Giorgio de Chirico's so-called metaphysical period, "The Song of Love," as *The Seduction of Unreason*'s graphic template. In many respects, the painting's imagery is germane to the theme implied by my title: that "unreason" has an uncanny power to fascinate and seduce.

De Chirico, of course, became an icon among the Surrealists. Breton adjudged him one of the first genuinely Surrealist painters: the artist who was responsible for initiating a revolutionary break with the unpardonable prosaism of representational art. (At a later point, when de Chirico abandoned metaphysical painting for the assurances of neo-realism, he fell out of favor with his one-time champions.)

The iconography of this image is both simple and inexhaustibly rich. According to scholarly lore, much of it derives from the artist's boyhood in Volos, Greece: the wall, the green cloth ball, and the smoking locomotive—a de Chirico fixture.

But the painting's most striking imagery concerns the provocative juxtaposition of the Apollo Belvedere and the rubber surgical glove. In light of Apollo's status as a god of illusion and appearance—an interpretation famously codified by Nietzsche in *The Birth of Tragedy*—de Chirico's painterly tribute to him is fitting and unremarkable. Moreover, the visage of Apollo—also the god of love—gives the painting its title.

Yet the image of Apollo presented here is a fragment—a lifeless and oversized bust. As such, de Chirico's tribute is both reverential and irreverent. The painting purveys a sense of "transcendental homelessness": de Chirico's homelessness as an émigré, as well as our own irreducible alienation from the classical tradition. The tradition still speaks to us, but it does so in a language we do not immediately understand. Out of this loss, de Chirico is trying to forge new meaning—a new, post-classical iconography, a symbology "after the fall," as it were. At the same time, the painter knows that the new symbolism is destined to be non-classical: a symbolism condemned to fragmentation. As a painter, de Chirico's bravado lay in the fact that he accepted this condition and made it the subject matter of his art.

But, undoubtedly, the painting's most disconcerting image is the gigantic rubber glove, nailed to the wooden partition next to the Apollo bust. Before de Chirico had had a chance to incorporate it into the painting, this glove-fetish caught the attention of Guillaume Apollinaire. Writing in the July 1914 issue of the *Paris Journal*, Apollinaire announced:

> Mr. de Chirico has just recently acquired a glove of pink rubber, one of the more extraordinary objects that one can find. It is destined, once copied by the artist, to render his future works even more striking and disconcerting than his past ones. If one asks him as to the terror that this glove is capable of inciting, he will speak to you immediately of the still more terrifying toothbrushes just invented by the dental art, the most recent and perhaps the most useful of all the arts.

Why the "terrifying" glove? Was de Chirico merely heeding Baudelaire's maxim that the "painter of modern life" must lionize the everyday? Is the glove de Chirico's humble contribution to the creation of a "modern mythology" (Aragon), a mythology the disenchanted denizens of the modern urban life so desperately crave? In any event, the glove and the Apollo Belvedere represent a genuinely striking juxtaposition; they are living proof of the Surrealist insight (borrowed from Lautréamont) about the "marvelous" nature of a "chance encounter of a sewing machine and an umbrella on a dissecting table." In point of fact, de Chirico's glove happens to be a *surgical* glove. In this way, nine years before the publication of Breton's "Manifesto of Surrealism," de Chirico anticipated the Surrealist doctrine of "objective chance." Thereby, both de Chirico and the Surrealists put the intoxicating powers of "unreason" to productive use.

·THE SEDUCTION OF UNREASON·

Answer to the Question: What Is Counter-Enlightenment?

IN HONOR of the Enlightenment the eighteenth century was commonly known as the century of *lumière,* or light. Its advocates viewed themselves as the "party of humanity": they sought to represent the "general will" rather than the standpoint of particular interests, estates, or castes. The champions of Enlightenment counterposed reason as an analytical solvent to dogma, superstition, and unwarranted social authority. Their compendium of political grievances culminated in the *cahiers de doléances* submitted to Louis XVI in conjunction with the summoning of the Estates General in 1788—a damning indictment of the injustices and corruptions that prevailed under the absolute monarchies of Louis and his predecessor, Louis XV. With one or two notable exceptions (e.g., Jean-Jacques Rousseau), the *philosophes* were political moderates. They confidently believed that the monarchy could be progressively restructured, and, consequently, put their faith in piecemeal political reform from above. As such, most were proponents of either "Enlightened Despotism" or, in the case of the so-called Anglomaniacs, English-style constitutional monarchy. Yet, time and again, monarchical intransigence pushed them in the direction of democratic republicanism. When on June 27, 1789, the deputies representing the Third Estate—whose members had been bred on Enlightenment precepts—took their seats in the National Assembly on the *left* side of the hall, the modern political left was born.[1]

Of course, the same sequence of events precipitated the birth of the modern political right, whose adherents elected to sit on the opposite side of the Versailles assembly hall on that fateful day in 1789. But in reality the political battle lines had been drawn decades earlier. By mid-century defenders of the *ancien régime* knew that the cultural momentum lay with the "party of humanity." A new breed of anti-philosophe emerged to contest the epistemological and political heresies proposed by the Party of Reason—the apostles of Counter-Enlightenment. Relying mainly on theological arguments, the anti-philosophes cautioned against the spirit of critical inquiry, intellectual hubris, and the misuse of reason. Instead, they emphasized the need to preserve order at all costs. They viewed altar and throne as the twin pillars of political stability. They believed that any challenge to their unquestioned primacy threatened to undermine the entire social edifice. They considered self-evident the view—one in effect shared by many of the philosophes themselves—that men and women were fundamentally incapable of self-governance. Sin was the alpha and omega of the human condition. One needed both unquestioned authority and the threat of eternal damnation to prevent humanity from overreaching its inherently fallible nature. Unfettered employment of reason as recommended by the philosophes was an invitation to catastrophe. As one of the leading spokesmen of the Counter-Enlightenment, Antoine de Rivarol (one of the major sources for Edmund Burke's *Reflections on the Revolution in France*), remarked in 1789, "From the day when the monarch consults his subjects, sovereignty is as though suspended . . . When people cease to esteem, they cease to obey. A general rule: peoples whom the king consults begin with vows and end with wills of their own."[2]

Rivarol and company held "philosophy" responsible for the corruption of morals, carnal licentiousness, depravity, political decay, economic decline, poor harvests, and the precipitous rise in food prices. The social cataclysms of revolutionary France—mob violence, dechristianization, anarchy, civil war, terror, and political dictatorship—convinced the anti-philosophes of their uncanny clairvoyance.

In a much-cited essay Isaiah Berlin contended that one could trace the origins of fascism to Counter-Enlightenment ideologues like Joseph de Maistre and Johann Georg Hamann.[3] Indeed, a certain plausibility marks Berlin's claim. For one of fascism's avowed goals was to put an end to the Enlightenment-derived nineteenth-century worldview: the predominance of science, reason, democracy, socialism, individualism, and the like. As Goebbels pithily observed a few months after Hitler's rise to power, "The year 1789 is hereby erased from history."[4] Maistre and his contemporaries were horrified by the specter of radical change. As such, they preferred the "contrary of revolution" (reform from above) to the specter of "counter-revolution," which would merely perpetuate the cycle of violence.

The fascists, conversely, crossed the Rubicon and never looked back. They knew that, in an age of total war, a point of no return had been reached: there could be no going back to the tradition-bound cocoon of the *ancien régime*. They elected to combat the values of the French Revolution with revolutionary means: violence, war, and total mobilization. Thereby, they ushered in an alternative vision of modernity, one that was meant to supersede the standpoint of the philosophes and the political champions of 1789.

Who's Afraid of Enlightenment?

Surely, one of the more curious aspects of the contemporary period is that the heritage of Enlightenment finds itself under attack not only from the usual suspects on the political right but also from proponents of the academic left. As one astute commentator has recently noted, today "Enlightenment bashing has developed into something of an intellectual blood-sport, uniting elements of both the left and the right in a common cause."[5] Thus, one of the peculiarities of our times is that Counter-Enlightenment arguments once the exclusive prerogative of the political right have attained a new lease on life among representatives of the cultural left. Surprisingly, if one scans the relevant literature, one finds champions of postmodernism who proudly invoke the Counter-Enlightenment heritage as their own. As the argument goes, since democracy has been and continues to be responsible for so many political ills, and since the critique of modern democracy began with the anti-philosophes, why not mobilize their powerful arguments in the name of the postmodern political critique? As a prominent advocate of postmodern political theory contends, one need only outfit the Counter-Enlightenment standpoint with a new "articulation" (a claim couched in deliberate vagueness) to make it serviceable for the ends of the postmodern left.[6] Yet those who advocate this alliance of convenience between extreme right and extreme left provide few guarantees or assurances that the end product of the exercise in political grafting will result in greater freedom rather than a grandiose political miscarriage.

One of the crucial elements underlying this problematic right-left synthesis is a strange chapter in the history of ideas whereby latter-day anti-philosophes such as Nietzsche and Heidegger became the intellectual idols of post–World War II France—above all, for poststructuralists like Jacques Derrida, Michel Foucault, and Gilles Deleuze. Paradoxically, a thoroughgoing cynicism about reason and democracy, once the hallmark of reactionary thought, became the stock-in-trade of the postmodern left.[7] As observers of the French intellectual scene have frequently noted, although Germany lost on the battlefield, it triumphed in the seminar rooms, bookstores, and cafés of the Latin Quarter. During the 1960s Spenglerian indictments of "Western civilization," once cultivated by leading representatives of the German intellectual right, migrated across the Rhine where they gained a new currency. Ironically, Counter-Enlightenment doctrines that had been taboo in Germany because of their unambiguous association with fascism—after all, Nietzsche had been canonized as the Nazi regime's official philosopher, and for a time Heidegger was its most outspoken philosophical advocate—seemed to best capture the mood of *Kulturpessimismus* that predominated among French intellectuals during the postwar period. Adding insult to injury, the new assault against *philosophie* came from the homeland of the Enlightenment itself.

One of the linchpins of the Counter-Enlightenment program was an attack against the presuppositions of humanism. By challenging the divine basis of absolute monarchy, the unbelieving philosophes had tampered with the Great Chain of Being, thereby undermining morality and inviting social chaos. For the anti-philosophes, there existed a line of continuity between Renaissance humanism, Protestant heresy, and Enlightenment atheism. In *Considerations on France* (1797) Maistre sought to defend the particularity of historical traditions against the universalizing claims of Enlightenment humanism, which had culminated in the Declaration of the Rights of Man and Citizen of August 20, 1789. In a spirit of radical nominalism, the French royalist observed that he had encountered Frenchmen, Italians, Russians, and even *Persians* (if only in the writings of Montesquieu). But "humanity" or "man in general," he claimed, was a figment of a feverish and overheated philosophe imagination. "Man" as such did not exist.[8]

An assault on humanism was also one of French structuralism's hallmarks, an orientation that in many respects set the tone for the more radical, poststructuralist doctrines that followed. As one critic has aptly remarked, "Structuralism was . . . a movement that in large measure *reversed* the eighteenth-century celebration of Reason, the credo of the *Lumières*."[9] In this spirit, one of the movement's founders, Claude Lévi-Strauss, sought to make anthropology useful for the ends of cultural criticism. Lévi-Strauss famously laid responsibility for the twentieth century's horrors—total war, genocide, colonialism, threat of nuclear annihilation—at the doorstep of Western humanism. As he remarked in a 1979 interview, "All the tragedies we have lived through, first with colonialism, then with fascism, finally the concentration camps, all this has taken shape not in opposition to or in contradiction with so-called humanism . . . but I would say almost as *its natural continuation*."[10] Anticipating the poststructuralist credo, Lévi-Strauss went on to proclaim that the goal of the human sciences "was not to constitute, *but to dissolve man*."[11] From here it is but a short step to Foucault's celebrated, neo-Nietzschean adage concerning the "death of man" in *The Order of Things*.[12]

For Lévi-Strauss, human rights were integrally related to the ideology of Western humanism and therefore ethically untenable. He embraced a full-blown cultural relativism ("every culture has made a 'choice' that must be respected") and argued vociferously against cross-cultural communication. Such a ban was the only way, he felt, to preserve the plurality and diversity of indigenous cultures.[13] His strictures against cultural mixing are eerily reminiscent of the positions espoused by the "father of European racism," Comte Arthur de Gobineau. In *The Origins of Inequality Among Human Races* (1853–55) the French aristocrat claimed that miscegenation was the root cause of European decline. The ease with which an antiracism predicated on cultural relativism can devolve into its opposite—an unwitting defense of racial separatism—was one of the lessons that French intellectuals learned during the 1980s in the course of combating the ideology of Jean-Marie Le Pen's National Front.[14]

Lévi-Strauss's polemical critique of Western humanism represents a partial throwback to J. G. Herder's impassioned defense of cultural particularism at the dawn of the Counter-Enlightenment in *Yet Another Philosophy of History* (1774). For Herder, a dedicated foe of universal Reason's leveling gaze, it was self-evident that "Each form of human perfection is . . . national and time-bound and . . . Individual. . . . Each nation has its center of happiness within itself, just as every sphere has its center of gravity."[15] While Herder's standpoint may be viewed as a useful corrective to certain strands of Enlightenment thought (e.g., the mechanistic materialism of the High Enlightenment; La Mettrie, after all, sought to view "man as a machine"), in retrospect his concerted defense of cultural relativism ceded too much ground vis-à-vis the political status quo. To achieve their ends, the advocates of political emancipation required a more radical and uncompromising idiom. Unsurprisingly, they found it in the maxims of modern natural right as purveyed by philosophes such as Voltaire, Rousseau, Diderot, and Condorcet.

During the 1960s among many French intellectuals cultural relativism came to supplant the liberal virtue of "tolerance"—a precept that remained tied to norms mandating a fundamental respect for human integrity. When combined with an antihumanist-inspired Western self-hatred, ethical relativism engendered an uncritical Third Worldism, an orientation that climaxed in Foucault's enthusiastic endorsement of Iran's Islamic Revolution.[16] Since the "dictatorship of the mullahs" was antimodern, anti-Western, and antiliberal, it satisfied *ex negativo* many of the political criteria that Third Worldists had come to view as "progressive." Similarly, Lévi-Strauss's unwillingness to differentiate between the progressive and regres-

sive strands of political modernity—for instance, between democracy and fascism—suggests one of the perils of structuralism. By
preferring the "view from afar" or the "longue durée," the structuralists, like the anti-philosophes of yore, denigrated the human
capacities of consciousness and will. Instead, in their optic, history
appeared as a senseless fate, devoid of rhyme or reason, consigned
a priori to the realm of unintelligibility.[17]

The parallels between the core ideas of Counter-Enlightenment
and postwar French thought have been shrewdly analyzed in a
recent study of Maistre's intellectual legacy. With tact and discern-
ment, Owen Bradley phrases the problem as follows:

> Maistre's absence from current debates is a yet much greater sur-
> prise given the uncanny resemblance between his work and the
> dominant trends in recent French thought. Bataille on the sacred as
> the defining feature of human existence . . . Blanchot on the . . . vio-
> lence of all speech and writing; Foucault on the social function of
> punishment in pre-Revolutionary Europe; Derrida on violence and
> difference . . . all of these themes . . . were anticipated and exten-
> sively elaborated in Maistre's writing.[18]

In many respects, these suggestive remarks concerning the strangely
underresearched affinities between Counter-Enlightenment and the
postmodernist credo form the core of the study that follows.

"The Sovereign Enterprise of Unreason"

In the concluding pages of *Madness and Civilization* Foucault praised
the "sovereign enterprise of Unreason," forever irreducible to practices that can be "cured." Foucault's contrast between the exclusionary practices of the modern scientific worldview, whose rise was
coincident with Descartes's *Discourse on Method,* and the noncon-
formist potentials of "madness" qua "other" of reason, would help
to redefine the theoretical agenda for an entire generation of French
intellectuals. Even in the case of Derrida, who formulated a powerful critique of Foucault's arguments, there was little disagreement
with the Foucault's central contention that Reason is essentially a

mechanism of oppression that proceeds by way of exclusions, constraints, and prohibitions. Derrida's own indictment of "logocentrism," or the tyranny of reason, purveys a kindred sentiment: since the time of Plato, Western thought has displayed a systematic intolerance vis-à-vis difference, otherness, and heterogeneity. Following the precedents established by Nietzsche and Heidegger, deconstruction arose to overturn and dismantle Reason's purported life-denying, unitarian prejudices.

In a similar vein, Jean-François Lyotard attained notoriety for his controversial equation of "consensus" with "terror." The idea of an uncoerced, rational accord, argues Lyotard, is a fantasy. Underlying the veneer of mutual agreement lurks force. This endemic cynicism about linguistically adjudicating disputes is another one of poststructuralism's hallmarks. Yet one cannot help but wonder how Lyotard expects to convince readers of the rectitude of his position if not via recourse to time-honored discursive means: the marshaling of supporting evidence and force of the better argument. If, as Lyotard insinuates, "force" is all there is, on what grounds might we prefer one position to another? One cannot help but suspect that, ultimately, there is something deeply unsatisfying about the attempt by Lyotard and his fellow poststructuralists to replace the precepts of argumentation with rhetoric, aesthetics, or agonistics.[19]

The Seduction of Unreason is an exercise in intellectual genealogy. It seeks to shed light on the uncanny affinities between the Counter-Enlightenment and postmodernism. As such, it may also be read as an archaeology of postmodern theory. During the 1970s and 1980s a panoply of texts by Derrida, Foucault, Deleuze, and Lyotard were translated into English, provoking a far-reaching shift in American intellectual life. Many of these texts were inspired by Nietzsche's anticivilizational animus: the conviction that our highest ideals of beauty, morality, and truth were intrinsically nihilistic. Such views found favor among a generation of academics disillusioned by the political failures of the 1960s. Understandably, in despondent times Nietzsche's iconoclastic recommendation that one should "philosophize with a hammer"—that if something is falling, one should give it a final push—found a ready echo. Yet, too often, those who rushed to mount the Nietzschean bandwagon downplayed or ignored the illiberal implications of his positions. Moreover, in retrospect, it seems clear that this same generation, many of whose representatives were comfortably ensconced in university careers, had merely exchanged *radical* politics for *textual* politics: unmasking "binary oppositions" replaced an ethos of active political engagement.[20] In the last analysis it seems that the seductions of "theory" helped redirect formerly robust political energies along the lines of acceptable academic career tracks. As commentators have often pointed out, during the 1980s, while Republicans were commandeering the nation's political apparatus, partisans of "theory" were storming the ramparts of the Modern Language Association and the local English Department.

Ironically, during the same period, the French paradigms that American academics were so busy assimilating were undergoing an eclipse across the Atlantic. In France they were perceived as expressions of an obsolete political temperament: *gauchisme* ("leftism") or "French philosophy of the 1960s."[21] By the mid-1980s French intellectuals had passed through the acid bath of antitotalitarianism.[22] Under the influence of Solzhenitsyn's pathbreaking study of the Gulag as well as the timely, if slick, anticommunist polemics of the "New Philosophers" such as André Glucksmann and Bernard Henri-Lévy, who were appalled by the "killing fields" of Pol Pot's Cambodia (the Khmer Rouge leader had been educated in Paris during the 1950s) and the Soviet invasion of Afghanistan, French intellectuals began returning to the indigenous tradition of democratic republicanism—thereby leaving the 1960s leftists holding the bag of an outmoded philosophical anarchism. The tyrannical excesses of Third Worldism—China's Cultural Revolution, Castro's Cuba, Idi Amin's Uganda, Mobutu's Zaire, Duvalier's Haiti—finally put paid to the delusion that the "wretched of the earth" were the bearers of a future socialist utopia. Suddenly, the nostrums of Western humanism, which the poststructuralists had emphatically denounced, seemed to merit a second look.

During the 1960s the poststructuralists sought to supplement Marx with more radical critiques of "civilization" set forth by Nietzsche and Heidegger. Their indictments of Western humanism seemed well-suited to the apocalyptical mood of the times, framed by the war in Vietnam and the reigning superpower nuclear strategy of "mutually assured destruction." The experience of totalitarianism, however, which remained a reality in Eastern Europe until 1989, suggested that the idea of human rights had become the sine qua non of progressive politics. In another one of history's profound ironies, during the 1970s and 1980s *marxisant* French intellectuals were reinstructed in the virtues of civic humanism by their Eastern European counterparts: courageous dissidents such as Vaclav Havel, Adam Michnik, George Konrad, and Andrei Sakharov. At this point "French philosophy of the 1960s" ceded to the neohumanism of "French philosophy of the 1980s."[23]

Another reason for poststructuralism's demise related to a series of embarrassing political scandals that dated from the 1930s but only came to light in the course of the 1980s. The first concerned revelations that during the 1930s French literary critic Maurice Blanchot, one of deconstruction's seminal forebears, had published a number of compromising articles in the profascist, anti-Semitic journal *Combat*. In 1936 Blanchot, referring to the Popular Front government, bemoaned "the detestable character of what is called with solemnity the Blum experiment . . . a splendid union, a holy alliance, this conglomerate of Soviet, Jewish, and capitalist interests."[24] At the time, the opprobrious litany associating communists, Jews, and capitalists (in defiance of rudimentary considerations of political logic) was the standard fare of French rightists, whose watchwords were "France for the French" and "better Hitler than Blum."

Although efforts to limit the fallout associated with Blanchot's youthful political transgressions were largely successful, the same cannot be said for two subsequent scandals, bearing on the compromised pasts of Heidegger and deconstruction's American ambassador, Paul de Man. Since both of these "affairs" have now been rehearsed *ad nauseum* in countless books and articles, I will refrain from discussing them at length.[25] Nevertheless, the damaging revelations about the compromised intellectual pedigree of French "theory" raised a number of troubling questions that poststructuralism's defenders never seem to answer satisfactorily. The deliberative ineptitude of poststructuralism's champions when it came to proffering a credible defense has been as injurious as the facts themselves. Thus, at a pivotal moment in the debate over de Man's fascist past, Derrida "deconstructed" one of the young Belgian's articles from the early 1940s that enthusiastically endorsed the deportation of European Jews—at the very moment the Nazi Final Solution was being implemented—by claiming, counterintuitively, that it demonstrated de Man's status as a closet *résistant*.[26] Similarly, in the debate over Heidegger's Nazism, several poststructuralists argued implausibly that the German philosopher had succumbed to Nazism's allure owing to a surfeit of humanism. It was the later Heidegger, they claimed—the avowed "antihumanist"—who was the genuine antifascist.

The poststructuralists may be distinguished from their predecessors, the structuralists, by virtue of having rejected the concepts of "totality" and "totalization." According to Derrida, poststructuralism's basic lesson teaches that the idea of a textual coherence is a chimera. Poststructuralism demonstrates that the "center does not hold"; attempts to achieve epistemological "finality" or "closure" are unsustainable. Language is inherently polysemic and plurivocal. As such, its fissures and slippages militate against the Hegelian ideal of Absolute Knowledge. By glorifying the ideal of "scientific closure," by trying to limit the free play of signification, the structuralists merely repeated the errors of Western metaphysics. By succumbing to the foundationalist urges of traditional metaphysics, structuralism reveals itself to be "logocentric"—merely another species of "first philosophy."

According to the conventional wisdom, both poststructuralism and postmodernism are movements of the political left. One of the goals of the present study is to challenge this commonplace. After all, historically, the left has been staunchly rationalist and universalist, defending democracy, egalitarianism, and human rights. One of the hallmarks of the political left has been a willingness to address questions of "social justice," systematically calling into question parochial definitions of liberty that sanction vast inequalities of wealth, demanding instead that proponents of formal equality meet the needs of socially disadvantaged groups. Time and again, the left has forced bourgeois society to live up to democratic norms, challenging narrowly individualistic conceptions of rights as well as the plutocratic ambitions of political and economic elites.[27] Thus, if one examines the developmental trajectory of modern societies, one discerns a fitful progression from civic to political to social equality.

On almost all of these questions, postmodernists remain out of step with left-wing concerns. Since their approach has been resolutely "culturalist," questions of social justice, which have traditionally preoccupied the left, have remained imperceptible. Since postmodernists are self-avowed "post-Marxists," political economy plays a negligible role in their work. Yet in an age of globalization, when markets threaten to become destiny, this omission proves fatal to any theory that stakes a claim to political relevance.[28]

From latter-day anti-philosophes like Nietzsche and Heidegger, poststructuralists have inherited a distrust of reason and democracy. The ideas they have recommended in their stead—"*différance*" (Derrida), "transgression" (Foucault), "schizophrenia" (Deleuze and Guattari)—fail to inspire confidence. Their denunciations of reason's inadequacies have an all-too-familiar ring: since the dawn of the Counter-Enlightenment, they have been the standard fare of European Reaction. By engaging in a neo-Nietzschean assault on "reason" and "truth," poststructuralists' criticisms remain pitched at a level of theoretical abstraction that lets capitalism off the hook. Ultimately, their overarching pessimism about prospects for progressive political change—for example, Foucault contended that the idea of emancipation is a trap laid by the forces of "governmentality" to inscribe the "subject" in the clutches of "power-knowledge"— seems conducive to resignation and inaction. After all, if, as Foucault claims, "power" is everywhere, to contest it seems pointless. Instead of challenging domination practically, postmodernists prefer to remain on the relatively safe terrain of "metapolitics"—the insular plane of "theory," where the major risks are "conceptual" and concrete politics are rendered ethereal.

But "culturalist" approaches to power leave the structural components of domination untouched—and, ultimately, unchallenged. The complacency of this approach surfaces in Foucault's recommendation in *The History of Sexuality* that, in the place of traditional left-wing paradigms of social change, which he considers discredited, we seek out a "different economy of bodies and pleasures."[29] One thereby runs the risk of substituting a narcissistic "lifestyle politics" for "movement politics." "Identity politics" usurps the traditional left-wing concern with social justice. To be sure, differences need to be respected—but not fetishized. An uncritical celebration of "difference" can readily result in a new "essentialism" in which questions of group identity are elevated to the rank of a first principle. Since efforts to achieve consensus are a priori viewed with derision and mistrust, it seems virtually impossible to restore a meaningful sense of political community. Historically, the end result has been the cultural left's political marginalization and fragmentation. Instead of spurring an attitude of active contestation, a narrow-minded focus on group identity has encouraged political withdrawal. As one astute commentator has pointed out, today the apostles of "cultural politics"

> do not even bother to pretend to be egalitarian, impartial, tolerant, or solidary with others, or even fair. In its worst guise, this politics has turned into the very opposite of egalitarian and democratic politics—as the emergence of virulent forms of nationalism, ethnocentrism, and intolerant group particularism all over the world witness. One begins to wonder whether the [new culturalist approaches] have played into the hands of the antidemocrats by depriving us of the language and conceptual resources indispensable for confronting the authoritarian assertions of difference so prevalent today.[30]

Identity is not an argument. It represents an appeal to "life" or brute existence as opposed to principles that presuppose argumentative give-and-take. As a European friend once put it: "identity politics—that's what they had in Germany from 1933–45." The failures of cultural politics mirrors the decline of the New Left as chronicled by Christopher Lasch and Richard Sennett: the renunciation of an oppositional, public sphere politics in favor of an inner-directed and self-absorbed "culture of narcissism."[31]

That postmodernists rely unwittingly on arguments and positions developed by proponents of Counter-Enlightenment does not mean they are conservative, let alone reactionary. The study that follows is not an exercise in guilt-by-association. Nevertheless, such reliance suggests that their standpoint is confused, that the disjunction between their epistemological radicalism and their political preferences (supposedly "progressive," though often difficult to pinpoint) results in a fundamental incoherence. Nor are postmodernists, as their right-wing detractors maintain, particularly "dangerous." Despite their antipathy to democracy and their radical political longings, they, too, are the beneficiaries of a modern political culture in which tolerance has been enshrined as a fundamental value.

In his *History of Structuralism,* François Dosse remarks that the poststructuralist aversion to democracy represents an expression of intellectual self-hatred.[32] He points out how, ironically, this hostility has become pronounced in the homeland of Rousseau, modern republicanism, and the "ideas of 1789." Although it was the French Revolution that put democracy on the map of European political culture, of late it seems more a source of embarrassment than an index of national pride.[33] Paradoxically, whereas a visceral rejection of political modernity (rights of man, rule of law, constitutionalism) was once standard fare among counterrevolutionary thinkers, it has now become fashionable among advocates of the cultural left. Postmodernists equate democracy with "soft totalitarianism." They argue that by privileging public reason and the common good, liberal democracy effectively suppresses otherness and difference. Of course, one could very easily make the converse argument: historically speaking, democracy and rule of law have proved the best guarantors of cultural diversity and political pluralism. During the 1980s the debate on "difference" would take an insidious turn as the European New Right, led by France's Jean-Marie Le Pen, embraced the "right to difference" as a justification for racial separatism.[34] The shock of recognition resulting from Le Pen's electoral successes pushed the European left firmly back into the democratic republican camp.

Although Derrida has recently professed a sly interest in a nebulous "democracy to come" (*"democratie à venir/avenir"*), what he might have in mind by this metapolitical decree—long on rhetoric and short on empirical substance—is anybody's guess. By denying the basic emancipatory potentials of democracy, by downplaying the significant differences between it and its totalitarian antithesis, the postmodern left has openly consigned itself to the political margins. For, whatever their empirical failings, states predicated on rule of law contain a basic capacity for internal political change fundamentally absent from illiberal political regimes. Over the last forty years, the qualified successes of the women's, antiwar, ecological, civil, and gay rights movements have testified to this political rule of thumb.

Poststructuralism arose at a peculiar juncture in French political history, one marked by the depredations of civil war (the Algerian conflict and its aftermath), a delirious Third Worldism, a Gaullist regime that had gained power via extraconstitutional means (and which many observers viewed as a dictatorship), and the eclipse of a viable political left. At the time, all inherited theoretical and political options seemed bankrupt, and the need for a total break with tradition desirable. But attempts to translate the élan of this unique intellectual moment beyond the circumstances of its origination seem dubious. One of the major problems with the North American encounter with French "theory" is that its reception has been radically decontextualized. Little attention has been paid to the peculiarly French conditions of its genesis. Consequently, especially among acolytes, its reception has been distinctly uncritical. By filling in these historical and intellectual gaps, the present study hopes to expand significantly the parameters of debate.

Part I, "The German Ideology Revisited," reexamines the legacy of three German thinkers who have exerted a major influence on contemporary intellectual life. One of my main concerns is the enduring influence German *Existenzphilosophie* (existentialism) has had on postwar French thought. In this respect Nietzsche's work represents an indispensable point of reference. The landscape of contemporary French thought would be unrecognizable without his momentous and controversial impact. Moreover, the "French Nietzsche"—

the antifoundationalist, literary stylist, and proponent of aesthetic self-fashioning—has in turn become canonical for North American postmodernism.

But the appropriation of Nietzsche for the ends of postmodernism raises a number of troubling interpretive dilemmas. To begin with, there is the important question of periodization. After all, Nietzsche was a contemporary of Flaubert, Mallarmé, and Dostoevsky, all of whom were classical "modernists." In what sense, then, can he justifiably be appropriated for the ends of postmodernism, which, at the very earliest, dates from the post–World War II period?

Moreover, upon closer inspection, the attempt to pass Nietzsche off as an aesthete appears selective and arbitrary. This interpretive gambit was clearly adopted to put as much distance as possible between Nietzsche and the Nazis, among whom he enjoyed the status of "court philosopher." One of the major questions that surfaces in the postmodernist reception of Nietzsche is, When so much of the original doctrine is intentionally left to one side, to what extent can one claim one is still dealing with Nietzsche?

With the advent of postmodernist feminism, Jung's theories began to make significant inroads in the academy.[35] Jung's doctrines proved attractive insofar as they supplanted Freud's scientism with elements of fable and myth. Among the broader public, Jung's influence on popular psychology and New Age thought has long been prodigious. Whereas among both of these constituencies Freud has been perceived as a conservative advocate of Victorian morality, Jung stood out as someone who was willing to take risks. In vintage Enlightenment fashion, Freud sought to subject the unruly forces of the unconscious to the pacifying balm of analytical Reason. Jung, conversely, displayed a willingness to confront the irrational on its own terms—hence, his manifest affinities with the postmodernist devaluation of Reason. Unlike his Viennese mentor, Jung felt the need to reestablish psychoanalysis as a vehicle of personal salvation—as a new religion. Thus, in keeping with the irrationalist vogue of his day (the rise of Theosophy, Anthrosophy, and so forth), Jung experimented freely with the mysteries of Aryan religion, from which his core doctrines—the theory of archetypes and the collective unconscious—derive.

Yet, like a modern-day Faust, Jung would pay the price for this fascination with forbidden wisdom. When the Nazis came to power in 1933, brandishing swastikas and advocating neopaganism, it seemed like an instance of preestablished harmony: Jung thought he was witnessing his own theories come to life. Since the break with Freud, Jung had been convinced of the phylogenetic superiority of Aryan archetypes. Having rejected reason as an inferior mode of cognition, he found the National Socialists' recourse to Aryan symbols and myths highly congenial. Hitler, he was convinced, was Wotan reincarnate, a modern-day shaman. From his safe haven in Switzerland, Jung jumped aboard the Nazi bandwagon with alacrity.

For a long time the career of Hans-Georg Gadamer (1900–2002) seemed to be one of the Federal Republic of Germany's unequivocal success stories. Unlike his mentor, Heidegger, Gadamer never joined the Nazi Party. In an era marked by totalitarian extremism, he seemed to possess an uncanny knack for remaining above the political fray. During the Nazi years, Gadamer allegedly sought refuge in "inner emigration." But a closer look at his orientation during this period demonstrates how difficult it was both to achieve professional success and to steer clear of compromises with the reigning dictatorship.

During the early 1940s Gadamer proved a willing propagandist on behalf of the regime, traveling to Paris to present a lecture on "Volk and History in Herder's Thought," which explicitly justified the idea of a Nazi-dominated Europe. Enlightenment ideals were bankrupt, argued Gadamer. Germany's battlefield triumphs reflected the superiority of German *Kultur*. In the New Europe, the Volk-Idea, as set forth by Herder and his successors, would predominate. This dubious chapter of Gadamer's political biography represents a paradigmatic instance of the ideological affinities between Counter-Enlightenment and the forces of political reaction.

Philosophically, Gadamer remains one of the leading representatives of hermeneutics, a view that stresses the situated and partial nature of all truth claims as well as the irremediably contextual basis of human knowledge. The traditionalist orientation of Gadamer's thought—his stress on the "happening of tradition"—would seem unambiguously *un*postmodern. Yet in American pragmatist circles, his "anti-foundationalism" (his rejection of "first principles" and universal morality à la Kant) has been widely viewed as an important harbinger of the postmodernist rejection of objective truth.[36] Thus, the postmodernist embrace of hermeneutics may not be as strange as it might seem on first view.

In "Fascism and Hermeneutics: Gadamer and the Ambiguities of 'Inner Emigration,'" I suggest that Gadamer's acquiescence vis-à-vis the Nazi dictatorship possesses a philosophical as well as a biographical basis. Hermeneutics' skepticism about Enlightenment reason made the Nazi celebration of German particularism—the ideology of the German "way"—seem unobjectionable, and, in certain respects, politically attractive. The German mandarin tradition had long held that the sphere of politics was corrupt. From this vantage point, to make a devil's bargain with Hitler and company seemed no worse than the compromises required by other political regimes. At this juncture, relativist conceptions of ethics and politics begin to unravel and cry out for an unmediated dose of cognitive and moral "truth."

In *L'Idéologie française*, Bernard-Henri Lévy took note of a phenomenon that the majority of his countrymen had been unwilling to explore until quite recently: modern French history, far from demonstrating the progressive triumph of Republican ideals, betrays a well-nigh constant preoccupation with the regressive temptations of "integral nationalism"—the redefinition of citizenship in accordance with the illiberal values of "blood" and "soil." From the Boulanger and Dreyfus Affairs of the 1880s and 1890s, to the proto-fascistic "leagues" of the 1930s, to the authoritarian paternalism of Pétain's Vichy and de Gaulle's Fifth Republic, the lure of a "revolution from the Right" has proved a constant seduction among French intellectuals.

Part II, "French Lessons," explores this lure in the case of Georges Bataille, one of poststructuralism's key intellectual forebears. Until recently, Bataille was perhaps best known as the founding editor of *Critique*, one of France's most prestigious literary reviews. Conversely, during the 1930s he belonged to a series of avant-garde cultural groupings, several of which were avowedly anti-Republican. For this was an age of political "non-conformism": an era of boundary-crossers and taboo-breakers, of intellectuals and politicians in search of a "Third Way" between communism and liberalism. Acting under the assumption that democracy had been discredited by the Crash of '29 and the political uncertainty that followed, large strata of the French intelligentsia succumbed to the proverbial "fascination with fascism." The fascist regimes of Mussolini and Hitler seemed to restore a measure of social cohesion that, in liberal democracies, remained in distinctly short supply. Perhaps, reasoned many, the idea of a fascism à la française was worth a closer look.

It was in this context that Bataille and his associates at the College of Sociology assumed the role of "sorcerer's apprentices": a self-appointed elite capable of restoring the elements of myth, charisma, and community, the absence of which seemed to be one of the most debilitating features of modern society. The members of the college thought of themselves as a secret society, akin to the medieval Knights of the Templar or a monastic order, ready to lead should political conditions prove ripe. They viewed the Ordensburgen of Nazi Germany—the elite training centers for the SS—as a contemporary equivalent. In 1939, the College's final year, Bataille presented a lecture on "Hitler and the Teutonic Order," whose title betrays the intellectual risks that he and his fellow nonconformists were willing to take in the name of a "Third Way" between communism and liberalism.

One of the recurrent themes of postwar French thought concerns the deficiencies of "representation": the ontological gap separating our linguistic capacities from reality. In his Course on General Linguistics, Saussure famously proclaimed the arbitrariness of the signifier, implying that no necessary correlation existed between the phonemes we employ and the concepts or "signifieds" they designate. For a subsequent generation of French intellectuals influenced by structuralism, Saussure's insight seemed akin to a revelation. When one thinks of the intellectual traditions that dominated French intellectual life during the previous two hundred years—Cartesian rationalism, Enlightenment materialism, Comtean positivism, and neo-Kantianism—one can begin to appreciate the distance that post-modern French intellectuals have traveled.

In "Maurice Blanchot: The Use and Abuse of Silence," I suggest, via an examination of Blanchot's strange career and "double life" (right-wing political journalist during the 1930s, and one of postwar France's premier literary critics thereafter), that the critique of representation is itself historically conditioned. The loss of faith in traditional intellectual paradigms is attributable, at least in part, to a series of real historical and political traumas: the setbacks of war, defeat, occupation, and decolonization robbed the French intelligentsia of their traditional confidence in the supremacy of Reason. As a result, a strange process of inversion occurred whereby the intellectual values traditionally held in high esteem by the French intellectual mandarinate—lucidity, certainty, and objectivity—suddenly became objects of opprobrium. This new generation of thinkers valorized indeterminacy, relativism, and flux.

Jacques Derrida is one of Bataille's—and Blanchot's—spiritual progeny. Several of his early essays appeared in *Critique* (founded by Bataille), and his first book, *Writing and Difference,* contained an extended meditation on Bataille's theory of "general economics"—an approach to exchange that transcends the utilitarian orientation of political economy. Bataille's concern with "otherness"—phenomena that escape the economic and logical imperatives of bourgeois society—would also become one of the signatures of Derridean *"écriture"* or "writing." Lastly, both Bataille and Derrida are known for generating "texts" that flaunt the traditional genre distinction between literature and philosophy.

One of Derrida's most cited maxims has been: "there is nothing outside the text" (*"il n'y a pas de hors texte"*). Few would disagree that deconstruction's forte has been its "close readings" of demanding literary and philosophical works. Conversely, its undeniable weakness has been its lack of effectiveness in dealing with the "nontextual" spheres of history, politics, and society. Hence, by the early 1990s deconstruction had been surpassed by a number of more politically engaged paradigms: "cultural studies" and the Foucault-inspired model of "new historicism."[37]

Over the last ten years Derrida has made a concerted effort to redress this perceived weakness, writing widely on questions of justice, ethics, and politics. But have these forays into the realm of "the political" in fact made a "difference"? When all is said and done, one suspects that discussions of "the political" are merely a metapolitical pretext for circumventing the realm of "real" politics.

Endemic to Derrida's perspective is the problem that, early on, he attained renown by reiterating a "total critique" of the West that derived from Heidegger's antihumanism. According to this view, humanism culminates in the Cartesian "will to will." The twentieth century's political horrors—genocide, totalitarianism, nuclear war, and environmental devastation—are merely the logical consequences thereof. The dilemma besetting Derrida's approach to politics is that once one accepts the frameworks of "antihumanism" and "total critique," it becomes extremely difficult—if not impossible—to reconcile one's standpoint with a partisanship for reasonable democracy. In "Down By Law: Deconstruction and the Problem of Justice," I reassess Derrida's theoretical legacy, concluding that the shortcomings of "really existing democracy" cannot be remedied by recourse to the antidemocratic methods recommended by Heidegger and Nietzsche.

Derrida is by no means a Counter-Enlightenment thinker. Nevertheless, in the lexicon of deconstruction, "reason" is identified as a fundamental source of tyranny and oppression. An analogous prejudice afflicts Foucault's concept of "discursive regime." Here, too, "discourse" is primarily perceived as a source of domination. Whatever deconstruction's methodological intentions may be, its pragmatic effect accords with the anti-intellectual orientation of the anti-philosophes. By the time deconstruction gets through with the history of philosophy, very little remains. One is tempted to seek refuge in myth, magic, madness, illusion, or intoxication—all seem preferable to what "civilization" has to offer. The end result is that deconstruction leaves its practitioners in a theoretical no-man's land, a forlorn and barren landscape, analogous to one described by Heidegger: an "age of affliction" characterized by the flight of the old gods and the "not yet" of the gods to come.

Following Part I and Part II, I have included two political excurses. Both chapters may be understood as cautionary tales concerning the dangers of Counter-Enlightenment orientations in modern politics. They illustrate that the Counter-Enlightenment program is not merely a thing of the past. The European New Right has inherited the counterrevolutionary critique of modern natural law; it privileges the values of ethnicity (*ethnos*) over democracy (*demos*). According to this optic, the prerogatives of cultural belonging trump considerations of "right." Thereby, New Right politicians seek to advance a type of *parliamentary ethnic cleansing*. As with the proponents of interwar fascism, today's antidemocrats seek to exploit the openness of the constitutional state to undermine democratic norms. Postmodern political philosophy plays into their hands by suggesting that human rights are a logocentric atavism: a discourse of pseudo-emancipation that serves to conceal our entanglement in "power."

The first excursus treats the rise of the German New Right, whose advocates viewed reunification as an occasion to purvey revisionist canards about the German past. That these attempts failed is a tribute to the strength of German democracy. For the first time, democracy in Germany has become a matter of heartfelt conviction rather than mere lip service.

The second excursus discusses a parallel phenomenon in contemporary French politics: the rise of the French New Right (*Nouvelle Droite*) in conjunction with the political success of the National Front's Jean-Marie Le Pen. Over the last two decades authoritarian national populist parties, such as Jörg Haider's Austrian Freedom Party, have registered disconcerting electoral gains across the European political landscape. More seriously, in an era of intense global competition and economic retrenchment, they have been able to steal the political thunder from the mainstream parties and reframe public discourse in keeping with their own xenophobic, anti-immigrant agenda.

The conclusion, "'Site of Catastrophe': The Image of America in Modern Thought," examines "anti-Americanism" as an enduring component of Counter-Enlightenment and postmodernist discourse. Legitimate criticism of America, directed toward the excesses and miscalculations of its foreign and domestic policy, is welcome and indispensable. One might even argue that, in the context of the post-1989 New World Order, in which American power reigns virtually unchecked, such criticism has become an imperative. Yet, in the discourses in question, rarely is the "real" America at issue. Instead, these discourses address an imaginary or metaphorical America—the New World as a projection of European fears concerning progress, modernity, democracy, and an escalating rate of social change.

Traditionally, dystopian views of America have been the stock-in-trade of counterrevolutionary writers such as Maistre, Arthur de Gobineau, and Oswald Spengler. More recently, they have made inroads among champions of the postmodern left, such as Jean Baudrillard and Slavoj Zizek. In their theories, America represents the epitome of a postmodern, technological Moloch: a land devoid of history and tradition in which the seductions and illusions of a media-dominated mass culture have attained unchallenged hegemony. The postmodernists allege that the traditional orientations of family, community, and politics have ceded to the febrile delusions of "hyperreality." Today, we experience the reign of "simulacra": media-generated copies, shorn of originals, that circulate autonomously. This attitude helps explain the enthusiasm with which Baudrillard greeted the September 11 attacks: a "dream come true." According to Baudrillard, although terrorists committed the actual deed, it was something that, given the conceit of American power, the whole world had wished for.[38]

· PART I ·

The German Ideology
Revisited

·1·

Zarathustra Goes to Hollywood: On the Postmodern Reception of Nietzsche

If you should ever get around to writing something about me . . . have the good sense, which unfortunately no one has yet had, to characterize me, to "describe" me—but not to "evaluate" me. . . . It is not at all necessary, not even desired, that one thereby take sides for me; on the contrary, a dose of inquisitiveness, as if before a strange plant, with an ironic resistance would seem to me to be an incomparably more intelligent stance toward me.[1]

—NIETZSCHE, letter to Carl Fuchs, July 29, 1888

In truth, we are relativists par excellence, and the moment relativism linked up with Nietzsche, and with his Will to Power, was when Italian Fascism became, as it still is, the most magnificent creation of an individual and a national Will to Power.

—MUSSOLINI, "Relativismo e Fascismo"[2]

Crossing the Rubicon

In 1888 the breakthrough Nietzsche had long been searching for at last seemed at hand. It had been a remarkably productive year in which he completed five books: *The Case of Wagner, Twilight of the Idols, The Antichrist, Ecce Homo,* and *Nietzsche contra Wagner.* The public acclaim he had long sought finally began to materialize. The Danish scholar Georg Brandes gave a series of lectures on Nietzsche's philosophy—the first of their kind in any land—that met with resounding success: over three hundred listeners regularly crammed the tiny lecture hall. Suddenly, Nietzsche's name was on the lips of all Copenhagen. At about the same time, Nietzsche began a lively exchange of letters with the Swedish dramatist, August Strindberg, who took to signing all his correspondence with the injunction, "Read Nietzsche!" Inquiries about his philosophy began pouring in from all corners of the globe. A princess from St. Petersburg—described by Nietzsche as "one of the foremost women of Russian society"—displayed a keen interest in his work.[3] An American journalist proposed writing a detailed essay on his philosophy. Even Nietzsche's publishing fortunes, which had been consistently atrocious (his books rarely sold more than one hundred copies, and often Nietzsche himself had to underwrite publication costs), began to take a turn for the better.

Corresponding to this unexpected upturn in his fortunes, an eerie euphoria began to pervade Nietzsche's letters. Berated and scorned throughout his productive life, Nietzsche felt his genius had been belatedly recognized. In his mind, minor details of his daily life in Turin began to take on world-historical meaning. Turinese from all walks of life responded to him, he claimed, with the utmost reverence and solicitude. When Nietzsche dined out, waiters ensured that he received only the finest cuts and the largest portions—at a discount! Nietzsche's growing megalomania—simultaneously moving and pathetic—is well captured in a December 1888 letter to his mother:

> All in all, your old creature is now an immensely famous person. . . . I have real geniuses among my admirers—today no other name is treated with so much distinction and reverence as mine. You see that is the best trick of all: without a name, without rank, without wealth, I am treated here like a little prince, by everyone, down to my peddler woman, who will not rest until she has found the sweetest of all her grapes for me.[4]

Shortly thereafter, the floodgates burst and Nietzsche's delusions of grandeur knew no bounds. In a letter to his sister, he claimed to hold "quite literally, the future of mankind in the palm of my hand."[5] To the musicologist Carl Fuchs he declared that since the old God had abdicated, "I shall be ruling the world from now on."[6]

To his longtime friend and former University of Basel colleague Franz Overbeck he wrote, "I am working on a memorandum for the courts of Europe, with an anti-German league in view. I mean to sew up the Reich in an iron shirt and to provoke it to a war of desperation."[7] On New Year's Eve 1888 he wrote to the composer Peter Gast, unambiguously alluding to the state of his sanity, that he had crossed "the famous Rubicon."[8] There followed a postcard to Strindberg in which Nietzsche declared he was ordering a convocation of princes in Rome and having the young German emperor shot. (Strindberg's response, "Dear Doctor! It is a joy to be mad!")[9] Partly cognizant of his own dementia, Nietzsche signed these final delusory missives, "Dionysus" and "The Crucified."

Then came the dramatic final breakdown. On the morning of January 3, 1889, Nietzsche left his Turin apartment to find a cab driver mercilessly beating his horse in the Piazza Carlo Alberto. Nietzsche shielded the horse, swooned, and crumpled to the pavement. Overbeck, who had just received another outlandish letter from Nietzsche (in this one, Nietzsche declared that he was having all anti-Semites shot), rushed to Turin to retrieve his deranged friend. Arriving by train, he found Nietzsche hunched in a corner of his apartment, clutching the proofs to *Nietzsche contra Wagner,* trembling uncontrollably. Nietzsche rose to embrace his friend, began sobbing hysterically, and then collapsed, at which point, Overbeck, profoundly shaken by the manifest deterioration of his friend's condition, also lost his composure.

What was it that pushed Nietzsche over the brink? Contemporary diagnoses suggested he was suffering from tertiary syphilis. But at the time symptoms such as Nietzsche's were often misinterpreted, and the original diagnosis has never been definitively confirmed. There may well have been compelling physiological reasons for Nietzsche's "crossing the Rubicon," as he insightfully put it. But Nietzsche was also a victim of his own megalomania. In the end his lifelong persecution complex—he once prophesied that his teachings would be understood only fifty years later—simply metamorphosed into delusions of grandeur.

Nietzsche thought of himself as a new prophet or savior in an entirely literal sense. He perceived his writings not as "literary works" but as "declarations of war" directed against Europe's reigning spiritual crisis. He viewed himself as a "battlefield" on which the next two hundred years of European history would play themselves out. To him the figures of Zarathustra and Dionysus were not mere metaphors. He *was* Zarathustra and Dionysus, the prophets of the "Superman" and "eternal recurrence." Even the god-complex to which Nietzsche succumbed during his final days in Turin (as he wrote to Burckhardt: "Actually I would much rather be a Basel professor than God, but I have not ventured to carry my private egoism so far as to desist from creating the world on his account") was only one step removed from his typically exaggerated self-characterizations of the 1880s.[10] To be misunderstood, pilloried, and crucified was a fate he expected—even if, in the end, such clairvoyance made that fate no easier to bear. Ultimately, this enormous tension between his own grandiose expectations and the benign neglect of his work ("They all talk of me . . . but no one *thinks* of me! This is the new silence I learned; their noise about me spreads a cloak over my ideas.") proved insupportable. It broke his spirit and, tragically, pushed him to the breaking point.

Anyone who has seriously examined Nietzsche's reception in recent decades cannot help but be struck by the strange occlusion of the political dimension of his thought. Instead, we have Nietzsche the aesthete: a *Kulturmensch* and dedicated stylist, the contemporary of Baudelaire, Flaubert, and Mallarmé. That on several occasions he vigorously renounced *l'art pour l'art* as a form of warmed-over romanticism seems to have mattered little. In this way, the myth of the "unpolitical" Nietzsche was born—a strange development in the case of a thinker who, during the last five years of his life, plotted the outlines of a major work entitled *The Will to Power.*

A fascination with "power" (*Macht*) was Nietzsche's way of bidding adieu to the *juste milieu* of European liberalism. Whereas Tocqueville, despite his aristocratic prejudices, believed that democracy was inevitable and that, consequently, the best course of action was to adapt, Nietzsche fought against this eventuality tooth and nail. His training as a classicist convinced him that greatness was the province of an elite and that meritocracy was synonymous with mediocrity.

In *Ecce Homo,* Nietzsche famously described himself as "the last antipolitical German," yet this phrase has often been misconstrued.[11] It was Nietzsche's way of rejecting the vulgar *Machtpolitik* pursued by the statesmen of contemporary Europe, Bismarck included. Yet it left Zarathustra's alter ego with other options. Thus in the 1880s his political thinking would culminate in the notion of "Great Politics," a doctrine he associated with the empires of Rome, Athens, and Napoleonic France. Nietzsche was an apostle of cultural grandeur, but he was also a dogged defender of power, cruelty, and the warrior ethos as personified by several of history's more sanguinary tyrants: Alexander the Great, Julius Caesar, and Napoleon. The problem for interpreters who seek to aestheticize (and thereby, as it were, anesthetize) Nietzsche's doctrines is that, as the following quote from the *Nachlass* shows, in his mind conquest and cultural flourishing went hand in hand: "The new philosopher can arise only in conjunction with a ruling caste, as its highest spiritualization. Great Politics, rule of the earth, are at hand."[12]

Of course Nietzsche was anything but a systematic thinker, and the result has been the predictable hermeneutic feeding frenzy that has always surrounded his work. Nevertheless, "will to power" and "great politics" were mainstays of his later thought. Any attempt to interpretively brush these concepts aside risks distorting Nietzsche's central philosophical intentions.

From Machtpolitiker *to Aesthete*

One might readily debate the high point of Nietzsche's cultural influence. Most of the twentieth century's great philosophers— Heidegger, Jaspers, Foucault, and Habermas—have felt compelled to take a stand, pro or contra, in relation to his thought. But there can be no debating the low point. On November 2, 1933, Germany's new chancellor, Adolf Hitler, paid a ceremonial visit to the Nietzsche Archive in Weimar. There to receive Hitler was the administrator of the estate, Nietzsche's sister Elisabeth, who had systematically altered its contents, suppressing documents and forging others, to make Nietzsche out to be the German nationalist and anti-Semite he was not. (In 1885 Elisabeth married the anti-Semitic publicist Bernhard Förster, whom Nietzsche loathed. A year later the couple emigrated to Paraguay to found an Aryan utopia, Nueva Germania. Four years later Förster was accused of embezzling funds from his fellow colonists and promptly took his own life.) *Mein Kampf* never mentions Nietzsche's name. Nevertheless, following Hitler's visit, he was posthumously canonized as the philosophical inspiration behind Nazism. Unlucky in life, Nietzsche was in many ways even unluckier in death. In his 1952 book, *The Destruction of Reason,* the Marxist philosopher Georg Lukács confidently asserted, "Nietzsche foreshadowed in the most concrete fashion possible Hitler's fascist ideology."[13] In 1981 the influential German news magazine *Der Spiegel* ran a cover story, featuring pictures of both Nietzsche and Hitler, with the provocative headline: "Hitler Perpetrator, Nietzsche Thinker."

After the war, efforts to ensure Nietzsche's rehabilitation commenced. The English-speaking world will long be in the debt of philosopher Walter Kaufmann, whose skillful editions and translations made Nietzsche's writings widely accessible. Yet, ultimately, Kaufmann's Nietzsche is remarkably un-Nietzschean. In his translations and commentaries, we are presented with a Nietzsche who is a cultured European, rather liberal and uncontroversial—all in all, a Nietzsche who resembles a mildly dyspeptic Voltaire. Missing in this account is the Nietzsche who "philosophized with a hammer," who proudly described his works as "assassination attempts," the apostle of "active nihilism" who believed that if contemporary Europe was collapsing, one should give it a final shove.[14]

In the wake of Kaufmann's liberal Nietzsche, a different rehabilitation strategy began to take hold. The new approach—the "postmodern Nietzsche"—could not have been more different than the Nazi understanding of Nietzsche as an apostle of power politics. According to this new interpretative tack, Nietzsche's work was emphatically apolitical. In this reading Nietzsche appeared as a detractor of metaphysics, a convinced relativist, and something of an aesthete. Thus emerged what one might call the "perspectivist" Nietzsche: the Nietzsche who once proclaimed that "there are no facts, only interpretations," that "there is only a perspectival seeing, only a perspectival knowing"[15]; the Nietzsche who, in *The Will to Power*, famously mocked the idea of objective truth with the assertion that "Truth is a kind of error without which a certain species of life could not live."[16]

Allied with this image of the perspectivist Nietzsche is the view of Nietzsche as an aesthete preoccupied with questions of "style." As Nietzsche remarks in *The Gay Science: "One thing is needful.—*To 'give style' to one's character, a great and rare art! It is practiced by those who survey the strengths and weaknesses of their natures and then fit them into an artistic plan."[17] Here, Nietzsche advocates "self-overcoming": to the world-weary "last men" of the fin-de-siècle (who remained, in his view, "human, all too human") he counterposed the Superman—resolute, high-minded, and, if necessary, cruel. In the aesthetic or literary understanding of Nietzsche, however, self-overcoming is detached from its usual context in his work, the theory of "the will to power." Instead, it becomes independent, emphasizing life as a process of incessant and directionless self-transformation. Since the self is inherently a fiction, the only genuine end of self-transformation is aesthetic: to perpetually overlay the groundless self with "style" for the sake of making it ever more attractive and interesting. It is in this spirit allegedly that Nietzsche, in *The Will to Power*, characterizes the world "as a work of art that gives birth to itself." "We possess art," Nietzsche goes on to say, "lest we perish of truth."[18]

In the postmodern reading, Nietzsche is reduced and reconfigured to suit the needs of a blasé, post-philosophical (post-humanist, postindustrial, post-Freudian—take your pick) culture, in which rarely is anything momentous or important at stake. We are offered a domesticated and "presentable" Nietzsche, who would perhaps make for a good companion on a long train ride. Here is a Nietzsche whom even Richard Rorty, a self-described "postmodern bourgeois liberal," could wholeheartedly embrace.

In recent years the postmodern reading of Nietzsche has become canonical. Correspondingly, more substantive, less trivial approaches to his philosophy have become anathema. We owe these developments primarily to the influence of the French Nietzsche. The enthusiastic reception of Nietzsche's work has been perhaps the singularly most important development of postwar French intellectual life. In *Modern French Philosophy*, Vincent Descombes describes the momentous shift in French intellectual life from Marx to Nietzsche. "Burning the idol venerated until now, this generation denounced the dialectic as the supreme illusion, from which it sought to free itself through recourse to Nietzsche."[19] Within a period of ten years—the 1960s—an intellectual community whose philosophical mainstays had been Descartes, Kant, and a Hegelianized Marx converted en masse to a Zarathustrian standpoint of "active nihilism." Only recently, with the emergence of a robust and indigenous neoliberalism—a perspective well-represented in Luc Ferry and Alain Renaut's *Why We Are Not Nietzscheans*—has the intellectual tide begun to turn.

In one of the great ironies of modern European intellectual life, at the precise moment Nietzsche had become persona non grata in his native Germany, he was anointed and apotheosized by French poststructuralism. The reasons for Nietzsche's sudden and remarkable currency are complex. In part they pertain to the rapid delegitimation of France's traditional philosophical models, associated with a Cartesian "philosophy of the subject," following the ignominious collapse of the Third Republic. In the postwar period the paradigm of existential Marxism, as propagated by Sartre and others, seemed to offer hope for intellectual and political renewal. Yet following the 1956 Soviet invasion of Hungary—and Sartre's apologetics on behalf of the regime (although Sartre vigorously condemned the invasion, he insisted that the Soviet Union's socialist character remained essentially unaffected)—these hopes quickly disintegrated. Thereafter, French intellectuals perceived both existentialism and Marxism as politically and intellectually compromised, expressions of a bureaucratic world society whose twin ideological expressions, capitalism and communism, were viewed merely as two sides of the same coin.

As a credo, Nietzscheanism allowed French intellectuals to maintain a stance of uncompromising philosophical radicalism while avoiding all questions of direct moral or political commitment (Foucault's intermittent interventions on behalf of human rights issues constitute something of an exception). It offered an ideal standpoint from which to ruthlessly criticize a Fifth Republic that did not seem to stand for much other than its own survival: the fading glories of Gaullism, consumer affluence, and that emblem of French virility, the *force de frappe*. After Marxism had been unmasked as merely another ideology of class oppression (and throughout the postwar period, no Western communist party was more rigidly Stalinist than the French), where else was one to turn for an unrelenting critique of modern mass society than to Nietzsche? Marxism offered the idea of a dialectical critique, ever-brandishing the Hegelian prospect of renewed wholeness or synthesis. French Nietzscheanism made a conscious and wholesale break with all such blandishments. Selectively seizing on a number of Nietzsche's more provocative formulations (one favorite from *Twilight of the Idols:* "What must first be proved is worth little"[20]), it proudly embraced an epistemological nihilism in which the differences between fiction and reality, truth and illusion, were deconstructed and then effaced outright. The idea of truth, the French Nietzscheans asserted, had been appropriated and instrumentalized by grandiose philosophies of history—be they of a Marxist or a bourgeois stripe. In the future such seductions could be avoided, they concluded, by simply rejecting the notion of truth in toto.

Klossowski's Nietzsche

The *éminence grise* of the French Nietzsche renaissance was Pierre Klossowski. Speaking of Klossowski's influential study, *Nietzsche and the Vicious Circle,* Michel Foucault observed, "It is, along with Nietzsche himself, the greatest book of philosophy I have read."[21] The world of French letters has certainly had its share of intellectual mavericks. Klossowski need take a back seat to none of them. The older brother of the neofigurative painter Balthus, Klossowski was born in Paris in 1905. In 1936 he translated into French Walter Benjamin's landmark essay, "The Work of Art in the Age of Mechanical Reproduction." (Klossowski's own theory of "simulacrum"—the aesthetic embodiment of an imaginary construct—was inspired by Benjamin's thesis that in a technological age, copies become more important than so-called originals.) In the late 1930s Klossowski gravitated toward two celebrated avant-garde cultural groups animated by Georges Bataille, Acéphale and the College of Sociology. When these efforts came to naught, he entered a Dominican monastery from which he would reemerge in 1947. Following the war, Klossowski published a well-received study of the Marquis de Sade and achieved renown as a novelist. Circa 1970 he abandoned literature for a successful career as a graphic artist.

Acéphale (headless) was conceived as a secret society modeled after Sade's Society of the Friends of Crime. Though its initiation rites were a carefully guarded secret, for a time Bataille and his followers entertained the idea of performing a ritual human sacrifice. Inspired by the anthropological theories of Marcel Mauss and Georges Dumézil (Mauss, Durkheim's nephew and author of the classic study, *The Gift,* would disavow their reckless appropriation of his ideas), Acéphale's neoprimitives hoped to stimulate a rebirth of the sacred and of myth to combat the materialism, secularism, and individualism of contemporary European society. The more exoteric College of Sociology (1937–39) inherited Acéphale's neopagan designs.

One of the bonds that united Bataille and Klossowski was a common interest in the philosophy of Nietzsche, whose unrelenting iconoclasm, visceral critique of reason, and rehabilitation of the forces of instinct and will made his thought uniquely serviceable for the ends of radical criticism. The movement from Marx to Nietzsche during the 1930s presaged an analogous, more far-reaching philosophical shift during the 1960s. Klossowski was a key participant during both phases, the crucial intergenerational link, so to speak.

As the title—*Nietzsche and the Vicious Circle*—indicates, Klossowski's interpretation concentrates on Nietzsche's doctrine of eternal recurrence. In Klossowski's view, Nietzsche's "great thought"— an epiphany the philosopher experienced in 1881 while hiking in the Swiss Alps— was the psychic manifestation of a somatic disturbance. During the 1870s Nietzsche was chronically ill—so ill that in 1878 he was forced to resign his Basel professorship. He suffered from (among other ailments) incapacitating migraines that for days at a time prevented him from either reading or writing. The only treatment that alleviated these headaches was sitting motionless in a dark room for hours on end. Whereas earlier critics unjustly sought to dismiss Nietzsche's philosophy as an expression of illness, Klossowski claims that his "delirium" was emblematic of his greatness. Rather than signifying a debility, Nietzsche's dementia was a sign of divine possession, indicating that he was privy to the hidden mysteries of the universe. His body had assumed the form of a "medium," his ailments and "moods" were a form of "channeling."

For Klossowski, Nietzsche's greatness lay in his use of "total obscurity"—insight into the essential Chaos underlying all Being—to "attack the very notion of lucidity."[22] The Regime of Reason, buttressed by a conspiracy of psychiatrists and experts, sought to cure Nietzsche. In truth, however, they wished to silence him to suppress his disturbing truths and disconcerting visions.

According to Klossowski, Nietzsche's thoughts could no longer be communicated via reason or language. His madness expressed the fact that the philosopher had "reached the limit of the principles of identity and reality." Consequently, for the last eleven years of his life, he simply lapsed into muteness. The obscure teachings that he left behind—above all, the doctrine of eternal recurrence—embodied the ultimate rejection of all inherited structures of culture and authority. As Klossowski explains:

> Nietzsche's *declarations* transferred the muteness of his [physiological] *mood* into thought, insofar as the mood came up against the resistance of culture from without (that is, the *speech* of universities, scientists, authorities, political parties, priests, doctors). . . . Culture (the sum total of knowledge) . . . is the obverse of the soul's tonality, its intensity, which can neither be taught nor learned.[23]

Whereas culture prattles and dissimulates endlessly, Nietzsche, by lapsing into silence, spoke the truth. Klossowski does not pretend he is providing a faithful account of Nietzsche's views. On the very first page of *Nietzsche and the Vicious Circle*, he confesses to having written a *"false* study." In an earlier essay, he claimed that all interpretations of Nietzsche are inevitably "parody."

In Klossowski's view, Nietzsche's doctrine of eternal recurrence negates and surpasses all of his previous ideas. Before his 1881 vision Nietzsche's thought remained "idealistic": he still believed in the virtues of "culture." Only with the idea of eternal recurrence, claims Klossowski, did Nietzsche abandon idealism and embrace the fundamental Chaos that subtends all existence. His other precepts, such as the "will to power," were teleological: they remained wedded to the illusion that there existed worldly values and ends worth pursuing. Only with eternal recurrence did Nietzsche definitively relinquish such delusions. Once Nietzsche realized the illusory character of all language and human ends, *silence* became the only viable and honest response. Recourse to "consciousness" and "reason" would only falsify this profound realization.

The "vicious circle" Klossowski alludes to in his title expresses this dilemma. The act of turning the eternal return into a "doctrine" risks falsifying it, risks translating an unfathomable insight into the hackneyed terms of linguistic convention or "culture." The theory of eternal recurrence embodies a new "lucidity"; yet, paradoxically, this lucidity must remain inexpressible.

> For if such a lucidity is impossible, what the doctrine of the vicious Circle tends to demonstrate is that "belief" in the Return, adherence to the non-sense of life, in itself implies an otherwise impracticable lucidity. We cannot renounce language, nor our intentions, nor our willing; but we could evaluate this willing and these intentions in a *different* manner than we have hitherto evaluated them—namely, as subject to the "law" of the vicious Circle.[24]

The vicious circle expresses the fundamental paradox of the human condition: *"the only way we can overcome our servitude is by knowing we are not free."*[25] We cannot escape the essential determinism of all being. Nevertheless, insight into this condition permits a measure of tragic superiority for a spiritual elite, the "lucid few."

The anti-intellectual implications of Klossowski's "parody" of Nietzsche are stunning. They are tantamount to a willful abandonment of reason, history, and freedom. Taken by themselves, Klossowski's views are beguiling and provocative. Yet when one reflects on the fact that his understanding of Nietzsche as an "enemy of culture" would become an article of faith for an entire generation of French thinkers—analogous arguments would suffuse the work of

Deleuze, Derrida, Foucault, and Lyotard; all credit Klossowski as an indispensable source—a less kind perspective emerges. How, then, did it come to pass that such a resolutely nihilistic perspective gained acceptance among so many of France's leading philosophers and intellectuals?

Here, a number of historical considerations are absolutely central. The generation of French intellectuals that came of age circa mid-century was exposed to a series of shattering historical traumas: the fall of France, the ignominies of occupation and collaboration, the existential uncertainties of the Cold War and the nuclear age, humiliating defeat in Indochina, and a colonial uprising in Algeria that precipitated the end of the Fourth Republic and brought the nation to the brink of civil war. The social and cultural changes France experienced during these years were equally profound. France was transformed from predominantly rural to primarily urban. Traditional cultural values seemed threatened by a rising tide of mass culture. Formerly one of the Europe's leading powers, France was forced to accustom itself to a new role as a bit player on the stage of world politics.

For French intellectuals, these events proved nearly unassimilable. One common response was a radical mistrust, bordering on rejection, of the very concepts of language, culture, and reason. Such notions, some French intellectuals claimed, were fully implicated in the recent historical catastrophes and disasters. Only a thought that was as far removed as possible from the Western tradition and the disasters it had wrought—a "thought from outside," as some referred to it, a paradoxical "language of silence"—was deemed adequate to the new historical situation. Such themes and tropes became the stock-in-trade of postwar French intellectual life; they were manifest in a variety of cultural settings, from theater of the absurd to the *nouveau roman* to Roland Barthes' notion of "writing zero degree." If one is searching for the origins of French philosophical nihilism—the avidity with which French intellectuals deconstructed and sent packing the concepts of the individual, reason, and truth—this historical sequence constitutes the indispensable subtext and background.

Reason's Return

In *Why We Are Not Nietzscheans* Ferry and Renaut reconstruct their intellectual itinerary as follows:

> For most of the students of our generation—the one that began its course of studies in the 1960s—the ideals of the Enlightenment could not but be a bad joke, a somber mystification. That, anyhow, was what was taught to us. The master thinkers in those days were called Foucault, Deleuze, Derrida, Althusser, Lacan. Merleau-Ponty, the humanist, was old hat, and most of us no longer read Sartre. From the rue d'Ulm to the Collège de France, we discovered the philosophers of suspicion: Marx, Freud, and Heidegger of course, but, above all, Nietzsche.[26]

Beginning with this neo-orthodox characterization of the Enlightenment as a "bad joke," one can retrace the route that winds from the intellectual pieties of French poststructuralism to the self-immolating platitudes of American postmodernism.

Nietzsche certainly was a radical critic of reason. He wished to show that the modern West, by emphatically opting for the values of instrumental rationalism, had systematically precluded other, more distinguished value options. Nietzsche forcefully sought to demonstrate the opportunity costs of—the one-sidedness and partiality of, as well as the losses entailed by—"cultural rationalization" (Max Weber). He once lamented that the modern West suffered from a "hypertrophy of the intellect," to the detriment of other venerable and worthy human faculties—and on this point who would disagree? Yet in the rush to radicalize Nietzsche, to enlist his services in a series of bitter, internecine intellectual disputes, the Gallic reception willfully suppressed the subtleties and nuances of his position. In French hands Nietzsche was transformed from a principled critic of reason into a devout foe of the same.

Beginning with Socrates and culminating with the Enlightenment, the critical employment of reason highlighted the tension between the claims of reason and the unreasonable character of existing social institutions. As such, reason's claims were always inimical to illegitimate social authority. Reason sought to illuminate the cleft between unjustifiable claims to authority and its own more general, "universal" standpoint. If, as later historians contended, the collapse of the ancien regime was a foregone conclusion, its demise had been precipitated by the labor of criticism undertaken by *lumières* and philosophes, the so-called party of reason.

In Foucault's eyes Nietzsche's singular virtue was to have radicalized the Enlightenment notion of critique, to have succeeded in turning the acid bath of criticism against reason itself. Reason, argued Nietzsche, was constitutionally opposed to all metaphysical dogma and fixed ideas. Ironically, though, one unexamined dogma yet remained: *reason itself.* Reason remained convinced of its own impartiality, whereas all completing claims to truth were allegedly tainted by interest. It was Nietzsche, according to Foucault, who delivered the coup de grace to the naïve self-understanding of reason. It was he who, as it were, unmasked the unmaskers by showing how reason willfully concealed its own intrinsic prejudices and partisanship.

"Truth is a thing of this world," proclaims Foucault in "Truth and Power." Far from being disinterested and neutral, it must be understood "as a system of ordered procedures for the production, regulation, distribution, circulation, and operation of statements." As such, truth is "linked in a circular relation with systems of power which produce and sustain it, and to effects of power which it induces and which extends it."[27] In other words, the traditional assumption that truth and power are opposed to one another is illusory. Truth is instead merely a disguised emissary of power. Viewed from this perspective, truth is even more insidious—and more dangerous—than outright claims to power, insofar as, under the guise of objectivity, it systematically strives to mask and conceal its biases.

Foucault's quasi-Nietzschean, wholly cynical reinterpretation of the relationship between truth and power suggests that, in essence, no difference separates the terms. "Truth" is merely the guise that power assumes under the reigning "episteme" of the modern West. In the pre-Christian era, there was no need for power to disguise its will-to-domination by characterizing itself as "moral." But as Nietzsche shows in *The Genealogy of Morals*, following the Judeo-Christian "slave revolt in morals," all power must legitimate itself by calling itself "moral" or "just."

"Power-knowledge" has become the battle cry of Foucault's American disciples. Foucault was never more frank concerning this cynical, pseudo-Nietzschean reduction of knowledge to power than in "Nietzsche, Genealogy, History," his most sustained meditation on Nietzsche's import as a critic of truth. As Foucault observes, "The historical analysis of this rancorous will to knowledge reveals that all knowledge rests upon injustice; that there is no right, not even in the act of knowing, to truth or a foundation for truth; and that the instinct for knowledge is *malicious* (something murderous, opposed to the happiness of mankind)."[28]

Let there be no mistake: the claims Foucault makes against "knowledge" are simply astonishing. To characterize knowledge as such—rather than, say, particular manifestations of knowledge—as "malicious," to argue, presumably in good faith (by what standard, one would rightfully demand to know), that it is "something murderous, opposed to the happiness of mankind," is dishonest and, ultimately, anti-intellectual. This claim, gleefully parroted by numerous American acolytes, has in its various versions and forms probably wreaked more intellectual havoc, has been responsible for more pseudo-scholarly feeblemindedness, than one could possibly recount. In essence, Foucault's position countenances subsuming all claims to "right" or "justice" under claims of power. In his work the idea of power is grotesquely over-generalized: it assumes the status of a metaphysical *fundamentum inconcussum,* analogous to medieval theologians' talk about God or Heidegger's invocation of the omnipotence of "Being."

Vincent Descombes points out that in their approach to knowledge, the French Nietzscheans fatally confuse questions of "genesis" with questions of "validity." As Descombes convincingly demonstrates, once we have discovered *who* is speaking and *why,* we have as yet said nothing about the propositional content of the utterance or assertion in question. As Descombes explains:

If a distinction is to be maintained between the history of ideas and philosophy, it is so that we can make a distinction between an argument's success and its content. The distinction passes between two meanings of what is called an argument's *force:* (1) the power it has, under certain conditions, to mobilize the mental forces of the public it is presented to (power which is precisely, its "psychological moment"); and (2) the power it has to logically generate diverse consequences (the power that its "meaning" consists of, in the philosophical use of the term).[29]

The rules of argumentation suggest that "force of the better argument"—which derives from the logical cogency of an assertion—should not be confused with the (contingent) psychological and empirical circumstances of an argument's acceptance—precisely the trap to which Foucault succumbs. As Ferry and Renaut warn, "The hatred of argumentation means, principally, the return of authority."[30] In other words, once the notion of truth has been rejected in favor of considerations of power, one is thrown back into a Hobbesian world, a war of all against all, where, as the author of *Leviathan* maintained, "Auctoritas, non veritas, facit legem"—"authority rather than truth makes the law."

The Imperatives of "Style"

In the United States the high water mark of the postmodern, literary interpretation of Nietzsche was Alexander Nehamas's *Nietzsche: Life as Literature.* For Nehamas, Nietzsche's emphasis on "style" was a direct outgrowth of his epistemological perspectivism, his denial of objective truth. Once traditional ideals of truth have been discarded, nothing remains but to reconstruct the self on an aesthetic basis: that is, as a work of art or a literary work. As Nehamas remarks at the outset of his well-executed study, "Nietzsche's effort to create an artwork out of himself, a literary character who is a philosopher, is then also his effort to offer a positive view without falling back into the dogmatic tradition he so distrusted. . . . His aestheticism is, therefore, the other side of his perspectivism."[31] Generations of Nietzsche interpreters have been (rightly) baffled by the philosopher's kaleidoscopic alternations in authorial personae—classicist, Wagnerian, French moralist, nihilist, prophet, madman. Nehamas's claim that these various literary guises were part of a conscious plot to transcend philosophy with literature— that is, an attempt by Nietzsche to turn his oeuvre as well as his life into a vast literary endeavor—is highly suggestive. It is also "economical" insofar as in a stroke of hermeneutic bravado it consigns to irrelevance a number of theoretical conundrums that have plagued Nietzsche interpretation for decades. For if Nietzsche's chameleonic changes in standpoint are best understood as part of a vast literary charade, then, ingeniously, the various normative incongruities besetting his work become matters of indifference: in the last analysis, they are part and parcel of an immense novelistic enterprise in which "style" counts more than "truth." Nehamas suggests that once we have surrendered traditional conceptions of truth, which Nietzsche time and again unmasks as so many manifestations of the "will to power"—hence, as anything but "objective" and "disinterested"—the only orientation left standing is the *aesthetic standpoint*. Nietzsche's fortitude as a thinker is that he unflinchingly defended a conclusion that exposed the totality of Western philosophy as vacuous—a search for nonexistent metaphysical first principles or "things-in-themselves." If truth is, as Nietzsche famously claimed, an "illusion without which a certain species could not live," then "appearance" (*Schein, Erscheinungen*) is all there is.[32] The aesthetic leap of faith evident in Nietzsche's later writings shows that he possesses the courage of his convictions.

One of the ingenious aspects of Nehamas's study is that he, too, has the courage of his convictions. In his introduction Nehamas readily admits that "whole books very different than mine could be written about the very same texts on which I have decided to concentrate"—a claim that leaves one wondering why one should accept his views rather than the interpretations set forth in innumerable competing studies.[33] By making this argument, Nehamas is trying to act as a consequential perspectivist. Yet there is no doubt that in promoting the idea of Nietzsche qua littérateur or aesthete,

Nehamas believes he is on to something essential that other interpreters of Nietzsche's work have failed to grasp—that he has in fact discerned the *genuine* nature of Nietzsche's philosophical project in a way that has escaped the attention of his intellectual rivals.

In the last analysis Nehamas's position leaves too many questions unanswered about Nietzsche's profound and enduring fascination with the rudiments of philosophical questioning—a fascination that persisted until his final, tragic descent into madness. Above all, it suggests paradoxically that if Nietzsche's philosophical intentions are primarily aesthetic and that his texts are best understood as literary exercises, then the weighty moral and cosmological injunctions of his later works should not be taken seriously. They are rather merely a token of literary gamesmanship that, as with all his nonaesthetic claims, are best interpreted *cum grano salis*.

Nehamas's reliance on perspectivism as Nietzsche's last word on epistemological questions also presents a problem, a problem with which Nietzsche interpreters have long been familiar: that of self-reference. For if all truth claims are merely perspectives, if, as Nietzsche contends, "there is only a perspectival seeing, only a perspectival knowing," then perspectivism itself is merely one among other perspectives, thereby forfeiting its claim to nonrelative truth. Of course, Nietzsche could maintain without the risk of succumbing to self-contradiction that perspectivism represents merely a value preference rather than a deeply rooted cognitive insight about the nature of reality as such. But there is no getting around the fact that in the pronouncements concerning perspectivism that animate his later work, Nietzsche has in mind something greater than an offhand subjective preference.[34] Instead, his refutation of the Parmenidean biases of Western metaphysics (a preference for the "one" over the "many," "sameness" over "difference," "substance" over "accidents") appears to be predicated on his vindication of the competing theory of knowledge embodied in the doctrine of perspectivism.[35] Nehamas himself seems to recognize this problem early on in his study, remarking: "it is not clear how one can argue for a position, as Nietzsche often clearly wants to do, and yet not suggest that this position is, to use the only possible term in this context, true."[36]

Did questions of aesthetics and style really occupy such a central niche in Nietzsche's worldview? Or does this view merely foist the contemporary postmodernist aversion to strong evaluative claims back upon Nietzsche? Is it accurate to read Nietzsche's philosophy, in consequence of his perspectivism, as closely allied with the aims of literary modernism? After all, although the consolations of aesthetic illusion certainly occupied a central position in Nietzsche's work, he was hardly an uncritical champion of modern art. Never one to mince words, in *The Will to Power* Nietzsche describes art for art's sake unflatteringly as the "virtuoso croaking of shivering frogs, despairing in their swamp."[37] And what about Nietzsche the classicist who praised Attic tragedy for having had the audacity to confront the deepest truths of human existence?[38] Still under the influence of his youthful mentor, Schopenhauer, in his magisterial *Jugendschrift,* the *Birth of Tragedy,* Nietzsche argued that the ancient Greeks' singular achievement was to confront life's existential meaningless via the Apollonian consolations of form. Could it be that the mature Nietzsche, who went on to embrace portentous cosmological doctrines such as the "will to power" and "eternal recurrence"—thereby returning unambiguously to the pre-Socratic origins of his thought—merely jettisoned such concerns in favor of comparatively trivial questions of "style"? To be sure, as postmodernists claim, Nietzsche was a strident critic of the epistemological "subject." Yet, ironically, in the work of his mature period he supplants the "subject" of Descartes and Kant with the doctrine of the *Übermensch* or Superman—a virtual "mega-Subject" whom he deems "beyond" questions of good and evil. Whereas postmodernists are energized by the nihilism and fragmentation of our fin-de-siècle, the point of Nietzsche's Superman was to stem the rising tide of decadence. It is highly doubtful whether the historical Nietzsche—who was, after all, a proponent of "manliness" and "will"—would have had many affinities with the flaccid, postmodern representations of his legacy, in which cognitive indeterminacy, moral relativism, and an effete aestheticism predominate.[39] For when Nietzsche claimed that his work heralded a "Transvaluation of All Values" he had in mind not a playful reshuffling of traditional moral judgment, but, as the *Genealogy of Morals* makes clear, the restoration of a virile and, if needs be, cruel Homeric-aristocratic ethos that had been subverted some two thousand years earlier by the Judeo-Christian "slave revolt" in ethics. For this reason Nietzsche describes the Superman as a "synthetic, summarizing, justifying man," the prelude to a *higher form of being.*"[40] Whereas postmodernists take delight in the dissolution of inherited value paradigms, openly reveling in nihilism, Nietzsche's Zarathustra, conversely, is a lawgiver of the classical stamp whose raison d'être is to bring decadence to a halt.

Both Peter Berkowitz's *Nietzsche: The Ethics of an Immoralist* and John Richardson's *Nietzsche's System* were written to offset the proliferation of modish, postmodern readings of Nietzsche. Both studies are learned, well argued, and thorough. Both books may be described (to use one of Nietzsche's pet terms) as "untimely," insofar as, by treating Nietzsche as a serious thinker rather than as a glib antiphilosopher, they go against the grain of current opinion. Nietzsche emerges not as an intractable foe of truth but as a thinker who relentlessly criticized his philosophical predecessors because they failed to take truth seriously enough. It is precisely in this spirit that Nietzsche, reviewing his life's work in *Ecce Homo,* affirms that "Zarathustra is more truthful than any other thinker. His teaching, and his alone, upholds *truthfulness as the supreme virtue.*"[41]

Berkowitz's study is guided by a profound awareness of the extent to which even the mature Nietzsche remained true to his training as a classicist. To be sure, Nietzsche belittled classics as an academic discipline that practiced a mummified "antiquarianism"; that is, it failed to appreciate antiquity's use-value for life in the historical present. At Basel he even tried unsuccessfully to wriggle free of his classics appointment since he felt that his seriousness of purpose could only be realized within a department of philosophy proper—hardly the mark of an "antiphilosopher." Whereas it is customary to view Nietzsche as an archenemy of Plato and all he represented, Berkowitz's book breaks new ground by demonstrating how Nietzsche's guiding theoretical concerns remained continuous with those of the Socratic school. Of course, Nietzsche was hardly a Platonist. Yet Berkowitz correctly recognizes that Nietzsche was in the first instance a philosopher of virtue or human excellence:

"[Nietzsche's] view, reduced to a formula, is that the highest type must engage in right making based on right knowing."[42]

Nietzsche never renounced the tasks of serious philosophical inquiry. Instead, his prodigious philosophical musings are informed to the core by two fundamental Socratic precepts: the unexamined life is not worth living, and virtue is knowledge. Admittedly, Nietzsche emphatically rejected Plato's response to such moral philosophical conundrums (the theory of ideas, which taught that all earthly occurrences are merely pale copies of disembodied, celestial "forms"). Nevertheless, throughout his life Nietzsche remained passionately convinced that wisdom or truth represented the key to human flourishing—a quintessentially Socratic conviction. His unsparing indictment of European modernity was not in itself nihilistic, nor did his perspectivism approximate a shallow relativism. Instead, Nietzsche intended his "transvaluation of all values" as a way station on the path to a set of higher, more robust and affirmative value-ideals. The same impassioned concern for the welfare of the "soul" that one finds in Socrates and Plato one also discovers in Nietzsche. The paramount Aristotelian distinction between "mere life" and the "good life"—that is, a life lived according to the prescriptions of virtue as opposed to a life that, devoid of higher ends, merely "subsists"—motivated his philosophy at every turn. As Berkowitz aptly observes, "One will have squandered a golden opportunity if one passes by Nietzsche's thought without observing the love of truth, the courage, and the yearning for the good that animate his magisterial effort to live an examined life by giving an account of the best life."[43]

Not only did Nietzsche never abandon his interest in "first philosophy," he approached metaphysical problems in a manner that was remarkably consistent and rigorous. To be sure, Nietzsche's stylistic preference for the aphorism and the philosophical fragment places a systematic interpretation of his thought at risk. Nevertheless, at nearly every turn Nietzsche embraced the fundamental questions of metaphysics and sought to provide them with compelling and original answers. At times Nietzsche's philosophical concerns appear to be inordinately traditional, even "conservative"—a view that, given Nietzsche's impassioned rejection of political and cultural modernity, merits our full attention. After all, were not Nietzsche's doctrines of "eternal recurrence" and the "will to power" attempts to come to grips with the essential nature of Being, and, as such, metaphysics at its purest? What was his theory of the Superman if not an earnest attempt to redefine "virtue" or the "best life" in an era where cultural baseness and intellectual philistinism seemed to gain the upper hand? And what motivated Nietzsche's perspectivism if not a desire to arrive at a less limited, more robust understanding of the nature of truth in all its richness and multiplicity? As Richardson remarks:

> [Nietzsche] invites us to learn to overcome [our] mistakes, thereby encompassing and rising above those [inferior psychological] types and tracking truth better than they. So his critiques presume that perspectives can become truer, in particular by encompassing more perspectives, and by the self-clarity of health or activeness. . . . Similarly, when Nietzsche denies that his truths are "for everyone," his principal suggestion is not that others will have equal truths of their own but that others can't or won't bear so much truth, and such truth.[44]

After all, could Nietzsche, who in *The Gay Science* proclaims that "it is still a metaphysical faith upon which our faith in knowledge rests—that even we knowers today, we godless anti-metaphysicians still take our fire from the flame lit by a faith that is thousands of years old, that Christian faith which was also the faith of Plato, that God is truth, that truth is divine"—could this Nietzsche be other than a "lover of wisdom," a philosopher?[45]

Superman vs. Amor Fati

Nietzsche's historically oriented studies—*The Birth of Tragedy, The Use and Abuse of History,* and *The Genealogy of Morals*—sketch an evaluative framework brought to consummation in his more systematic works of the 1880s. The underlying theme of each of these texts is the fragility of virtue, the evanescence of human greatness. Inevitably, the pinnacles of human achievement—Attic tragedy, the aristocratic spirit, and life-enhancing historical knowledge—prove fleeting; they can be sustained only with great difficulty. Nietzsche spent his entire creative life pondering what it would mean to recapture such precarious exemplars of virtue in a modern age dominated by social leveling and mass conformity—the triumph of the "herd."

Nietzsche considered *Zarathustra* his masterpiece. He told Lou Andreas Salomé that *Zarathustra* had been conceived as an artistic substitute for the son he would never have, as "an explosion of forces that have been building up over the course of a decade." And upon completing it, Nietzsche characteristically succumbed to almost uncontrollable euphoria: "I fancy that with this Zarathustra I have brought the German language to its full realization. After Luther and Goethe a third step had to be taken—tell me . . . whether there has ever been such a combination of strength, resilience and euphony."[46]

Zarathustra is also Nietzsche's most self-consciously literary work. The saga of Nietzsche's star-crossed eremite overflows with uncanny portents and mysterious parables. It shows Nietzsche at his most misanthropic, even his most grotesque. In one disturbing scene, Zarathustra encounters a young shepherd "writhing, choking, convulsed, his face distorted; a heavy black snake was hanging out of his mouth." "Its head off! Bite!" yells Zarathustra. Then it is revealed that the snake—"all that is heaviest and blackest"—stood for "man," who must be "overcome." The men and women who inhabit the book's pages are all a sorry lot. The only beings capable of understanding Zarathustra's prophecies are his faithful animals: a snake and an eagle. Stylistically, the book parodies the Gospels to subvert the ethos of early Christianity: meekness, pity, love of one's neighbor. In their stead, Zarathustra proposes the values of a new lawgiver, the "Superman," who refuses to shun violence and cruelty when they are called for: "He who has to be a creator in good and evil, truly, has first to be a destroyer and break values. Thus the greatest evil belongs with the greatest good. . . . For evil is man's best strength. 'Man must grow better and more evil'—thus do *I* teach. The most evil is necessary for the Superman's best."[47]

It is in *Zarathustra* that Nietzsche develops his doctrine of "eternal recurrence." In *The Gay Science* (1882), under the heading "The

Greatest Weight," Nietzsche offers a trial formulation of this controversial motif:

> What if some day or night a demon were to steal after you into your loneliest loneliness and say to you: "This life as you now live it and have lived it, you will have to live once more and innumerable times more; and there will be nothing new in it, but every pain and every joy and every thought and sigh and everything unutterably small or great in your life will have to return to you, all in the same succession and sequence—even this spider and this moonlight between the trees. . . . The eternal hourglass of existence is turned upside down again and again, and you with it, speck of dust!"[48]

Nietzsche celebrates the thought of eternal recurrence as an affirmative, "yea-saying" ideal that only the strongest spirits are able to bear. It expresses a profound and unreserved embrace of life that Nietzsche commonly referred to as *amor fati,* love of fate.

The plausibility of Nietzsche's theory has been called into question insofar as it apparently enters into direct conflict with his doctrine of the "will to power." Brusquely put, whereas the theory of eternal recurrence implies a cosmological fatalism, the doctrine of the will to power suggests the indomitable nature of human will. In an important section of *Zarathustra,* "Of Redemption," Nietzsche hints at the paradoxical incommensurability of these two basic ideals:

> To redeem those who lived in the past and to recreate all "it was" into a "thus I willed it!"—that alone I would call redemption! Will—that is the name of the liberator and joy-bringer; thus I taught you, my friends! But now learn this, too: the will itself is still a prisoner. Willing liberates; but what is it that puts even the liberator himself in fetters? "It was"—that is the name of the will's gnashing of teeth and loneliest melancholy. Powerless against what has been done—it is an angry spectator of all that is past. The will cannot will backward; and that it cannot break time and time's covetousness—that is the will's loneliest melancholy.[49]

It would seem that the contradiction between these two standpoints is insurmountable. According to Nietzsche, the Superman, the highest embodiment of the will to power, is "lion-willed," insofar as he countenances no obstacles to the realization of his will. He is a supreme legislator, "judge and avenger and victim of his own law."[50] Conversely, Nietzsche describes European nihilism primarily in terms of a paralysis of will. Characterizing the will to power in *Zarathustra,* Nietzsche at times speaks as though the will could rectify the past and its "it was": "The will is a creator. All 'it was' is a fragment, a riddle, a dreadful accident—until the creative will says to it, 'But thus I will it; thus shall I will it.'"[51] But as we have seen, this claim flatly contradicts other passages where Nietzsche contends that "the will cannot will backward."

Karl Löwith suggests—correctly, in my view—that the theory of eternal recurrence is inherently contradictory. Nietzsche oscillates between two essentially incompatible versions of the doctrine: first, a voluntarist, "anthropological" version compatible with the theory of the will to power, according to which, the idea of eternal recurrence expresses a new categorical imperative: live every moment so that you could will that moment over and over again eternally; and second, a more literal, "cosmological" version, according to which the cosmic cycle of recurrence is indifferent to all human willing.[52]

Great Politics

In some accounts Nietzsche's philosophy ultimately founders insofar as it underwrites a "radical devaluation of political life."[53] Nietzsche, the self-described "last antipolitical German," was a relentless critic of European politics. In *Zarathustra* he famously describes the state as "the coldest of all cold monsters." "A death for many has been devised that glorifies itself as life," observes Nietzsche; "I call it the state." Thus, if "great souls" and "free spirits" are to prosper, this will occur only outside of the political sphere. "Only there, where the state ceases," proclaims Nietzsche, "does the man who is not superfluous begin: does the song of the necessary man, the unique and irreplaceable melody, begin."[54] Moreover, since Nietzsche views cultural excellence as superior to political ends, he seems patently indifferent to political injustice. More odious still, according to Nietzsche's Olympian ethical calculus, the suffering of the masses is a necessary precondition for the engendering of a handful of "Higher Men." "Mankind in the mass sacrificed to the prosperity of a single stronger species of man—*that* would be an advance," declares Nietzsche in *The Genealogy of Morals*. In *The Will to Power*, he expresses an analogous sentiment: "A declaration of war on the masses by *higher men* is needed. . . . A doctrine is needed powerful enough to work as a breeding agent: strengthening the strong, paralyzing and destructive for the world-weary. The annihilation of the decaying races. . . . Dominion over the earth as a means of producing a higher type."[55]

Ironically, whereas an earlier generation of critics took Nietzsche's philosophy to task for its repugnant political message, the postmodern approach is fond of celebrating his apoliticism. But no special interpretive talent is needed to see that the remarks just quoted, far from being "apolitical," are fraught with political directives and implications. The postmodernists exaggerate Nietzsche's status as an aesthete and systematically downplay the components of his work that are politically consequential. Nietzsche was, admittedly, an unrelenting critic of contemporary European politics, which in his estimation wreaked of mediocrity and conformity. But that hardly makes him an apolitical thinker. Instead, Nietzsche's unabashed embrace of hierarchy, violence, and the virility of the "warrior type," combined with his visceral distaste for the values of altruism and political egalitarianism, suggests that his doctrines foreshadowed *nolens volens* some of the more unsavory dimensions of twentieth-century *Machtpolitik* cum total war.

Any serious attempt to reassess Nietzsche's philosophical legacy must ultimately confront the distasteful character of his moral and political views. Conversely, any discussion of Nietzsche that focused exclusively on this aspect of his thought would be extremely limited. Nietzsche's influence on modern thought and literature has been incalculable. Writers as diverse as Rilke, Yeats, Valéry, D. H. Lawrence, and George Bernard Shaw embraced his teachings. In *Doctor Faustus* Thomas Mann used Nietzsche as the model for the composer Adrian Leverkühn. For a period of five years during the late 1930s Martin Heidegger lectured exclusively on Nietzsche. Perhaps the writer Gottfried Benn said it best when in the late 1940s he observed to a friend, "Really, you know, [Nietzsche] has anticipated and formulated everything, absolutely everything we poke around in—what else have we done these last fifty years but trot out and vulgarize *his* gigantic thoughts and suffering."[56]

His stylistic brilliance aside, no other writer articulated the spiritual disorientation of fin-de-siècle Europe as consummately as Nietzsche. As a cultural analyst, a diagnostician of European moral collapse, his acumen was unparalleled. A self-described "good European," he sensed, in a manner that was almost uncanny, the abyss toward which Europe was uncontrollably heading. Who could deny the preternatural clairvoyance of the following prophetic claim from *Ecce Homo:*

> When the truth enters into a fight with the lies of millennia, we shall have upheavals, a convulsion of earthquakes, the like of which has never been dreamed of. . . . The concept of politics will have merged entirely with a war of spirits; all power structures of the old society will have been exploded. . . . There will be wars the like of which have never yet been on earth. It is only beginning with me that the earth knows *great politics.*[57]

No one gave voice to the dilemmas of European nihilism with as much force and clarity as Nietzsche. He realized that the religious, moral, and political values that had been the mainstay of the old Europe were moribund and that the new values destined to supplant them had not yet arisen. Nietzsche viewed himself as the midwife of these new values. But he was also aware that he was a man ahead of his time. As a prophet of nihilism, Nietzsche recognized that Europe had lost its moral compass, that it was ethically adrift. In the opening sections of *The Will to Power,* he offered a succinct definition of nihilism, "The highest values devaluate themselves. The aim is lacking; 'why?' finds no answer." With the advent of the modern age, condemned to labor in the shadow of Zarathustra's chilling proclamation concerning the death of God, Europe had seemingly begun an irreversible course of existential meaninglessness. In Nietzsche's view, its only salvation lay with the birth of the Superman. As Nietzsche proclaims in *The Will to Power:*

> In opposition to the dwarfing and adaptation of man to a specialized utility, a reverse movement is needed—the production of a synthetic, summarizing, justifying man for whose existence the transformation of mankind into a machine is a precondition, as a base on which he can invent his higher form of being. . . . A dominating race can grow up only out of terrible and violent beginnings. *Where are the barbarians of the twentieth century?*[58]

The answer to Nietzsche's provocative question would soon materialize.

Was Nietzsche really apolitical? Though he mercilessly criticized the dominant political movements of his day, he was also a tireless advocate of "great politics," a veritable leitmotif of his later writings. For Nietzsche, cultural and political greatness were necessary corollaries. Not only was he an enthusiast of Homer, Goethe, and Wagner; he was also a profound admirer of Julius Caesar, Cesare Borgia, and Napoleon. In many respects, his reflections on "great politics" were as coherent and systematic as his musings on cultural and philosophical themes. "The time for petty politics is over," Nietzsche confidently announces in *Beyond Good and Evil;* "the very next century will bring the fight for the dominion of the earth—the *compulsion* to great politics." Here, too, Nietzsche's orientation was shaped by his training in the classics. Surveying the world of antiquity, the West's unsurpassed cultural pinnacle, he concluded that a hierarchical organization of society and politics was entirely natural. He fully subscribed to his University of Basel colleague Jacob Burckhardt's opinion that the rise of democracy had precipitated Athens' downfall. One of the most felicitous descriptions of his political orientation was provided by his Danish admirer, Georg Brandes, who spoke of Nietzsche's "aristocratic radicalism"—a characterization that Nietzsche fully approved of. Aristocracy means "rule of the best." In Nietzsche's view, it was only natural that "the best"—the strongest and most powerful natures—should rule—and rule ruthlessly. As he remarks in *The Genealogy of Morals*, "To expect that strength will not manifest itself as strength, as the desire to

overcome, to appropriate, to have enemies . . . is every bit as absurd
as to expect that weakness will manifest itself as strength. . . . No act
of violence, rape, exploitation, destruction, is intrinsically 'unjust,'
since life itself is violent, rapacious, exploitative, and destructive."[59]
Only the Judeo-Christian "slave revolt" in ethics had dared to
assume otherwise, insidiously turning the tables on the masters by
declaring that strength was evil and weakness good. Nietzsche
viewed democracy as merely the political corollary of the pusillani-
mous Christian view that all persons were equal in the eyes of God.

How might one translate the conviction that hierarchy is bene-
ficial and equality symptomatic of weakness—beliefs Nietzsche
held—into the terms of a consistent political ethos? This was the
dilemma confronting Nietzsche as a political philosopher, and the
solution he found was an endorsement of "great politics." His belief
in the necessity of hierarchy had profound political implications,
which found expression in his conviction that the "well-being of the
majority and the well-being of the few are opposite viewpoints of
value." If one were passionately committed to greatness, as was
Nietzsche, one couldn't shy away from drawing the necessary conclusions, harsh as they might seem from a humanitarian point of
view. Nietzsche, of course, was anything but timorous in this regard.
As he observes in *Schopenhauer as Educator*, "A People is a detour of
nature to get six or seven great men."[60] And in the notes for *The Will
to Power*, he flirts seriously with the idea of a "master race":

> From now on there will be more favorable preconditions for more
> comprehensive forms of dominion, whose like has never yet
> existed. . . . The possibility has been established for the production
> of international racial unions whose task will be to rear a *master race*,
> the future "masters of the earth"—a new, tremendous aristocracy,
> based on the severest self-legislation, in which the will of philosoph-
> ical men of power and artist tyrants will be made to endure for
> millennia.[61]

In *Ecce Homo* Nietzsche openly speculates on what a "successful"
realization of his doctrines ("my attempt to assassinate two millennia of antinature and human disfiguration") might mean. The sce-

nario he envisions cannot but make one shudder: "That higher Party of Life which would take the greatest of all tasks into its hands, the higher breeding of humanity, *including the merciless extermination* [Vernichtung] *of everything degenerate and parasitical,* would make possible again that excess of life on earth from which the Dionysian state will grow again."[62] So pronounced was Nietzsche's contempt for Enlightenment doctrines of "progress" that as a philosopher of history and prophet he felt compelled to stand these ideas on their head. Massive cataclysms and exterminations alone, and not the philosophes' naïve faith in the "infinite perfectibility of man," would create fertile soil for the proliferation of Dionysian Supermen, who, in Nietzsche's view, represented humanity's sole raison d'être.

A *Lust nach Untergang* (aesthetic fascination with catastrophe) was a characteristic trope of reactionary German *Kulturkritik,* as well as a concept that the Nazis—whether they derived it directly from Nietzsche's doctrine of amor fati or from his influential heirs such as Oswald Spengler or Ernst Jünger—sought to put into practice. After all, the National Socialists viewed the doctrine of "total war" and the unprecedented genocide and carnage it had unleashed in quintessentially Nietzschean terms: as a *Götzendämmerung* or "twilight of the idols," a macabre aesthetic spectacle of the first order. Documentary evidence corroborates the extent to which the SS (*Schutz Staffel*) adopted as its credo—and thereby found ideological inspiration to carry out the "Final Solution"—Nietzsche's admonitions to "live dangerously" and to practice "self-overcoming."[63] As French fascist Marcel Déat remarked at the height of World War II, "Nietzsche's idea of the selection of 'good Europeans' is now being realized on the battlefield, by the LFV and the Waffen SS. An aristocracy, a knighthood is being created by the war which will be the hard, pure nucleus of the Europe of the future."[64] The Nazis found Nietzsche's self-understanding as a "good European" eminently serviceable for their bellicose, imperialist ends: as an ideological justification for continental political hegemony. The Third Reich's ideology planners considered only three books fit for inclusion at the Tannenberg Memorial commemorating Germany's World War I triumph over Russia: *Mein Kampf,* Alfred Rosenberg's *Myth of the Twentieth Century,* and Nietzsche's *Zarathustra.*[65] Although the Nazis also tried to render German poets such as Goethe and Schiller serviceable for their cause, their attachment to the traditional ideals of European humanism represented a formidable hurdle. In Nietzsche's case, however, no such obstacles existed. As Steven Aschheim observes in *The Nietzsche Legacy in Germany*:

> Here was a German thinker with what appeared to be genuinely thematic and tonal links, who was able to provide the Nazis with a higher philosophical pedigree and a rationale for central tenets of their weltanschauung. As Franz Neumann noted in 1943, Nietzsche "provided National Socialism with an intellectual father who had greatness and wit, whose style was beautiful and not abominable, who was able to articulate the resentment against both monopoly capitalism and the rising proletariat."[66]

Was it really so far-fetched, as Nietzsche's defenders have claimed, that a thinker who celebrated Machtpolitik, flaunted the annihilation of the weak, toyed with the idea of a Master Race, and despised the Jews for having introduced a cowardly "slave morality" into the heretofore aristocratic discourse of European culture—was it really so far-fetched that such a thinker would become the Nazis' court philosopher? Reflecting on Nietzsche's fascination with breeding, extermination, and conquest—all in the name of a "racial hygiene" designed to produce superior Beings—the historian Ernst Nolte speculates that the scope and extent of the wars envisioned by the philosopher might well have surpassed anything Hitler and company were capable of enacting:

> What Nietzsche had in mind was a "pure" civil war. Yet when one thinks the idea through to its logical conclusion, what needs to be annihilated [*vernichtet*] is the entire tendency of human development since the end of classical antiquity . . . .: Christian priests, vulgar champions of the Enlightenment, democrats, socialists, together with the shepherds and herds of the weak and degenerate. If "annihilation" [Vernichtung] is understood literally, then the result would be a mass murder in comparison with which the Nazis' "Final Solution" seems microscopic.[67]

These facts should give pause to supporters of the contemporary cultural left who believe they can appropriate the radical trappings of Nietzsche's doctrines without succumbing to their distasteful political debilities.

Of course, with the advantage of historical hindsight, it is difficult not to read such Nietzschean prescriptions as a direct harbinger of Nazi practices. To do so, however, would be partly misleading. The Nazis gave no thought to the cultural flourishing that was Nietzsche's foremost concern. Moreover, the aristocratic radical in Nietzsche would undoubtedly have been repulsed by the movement's petty bourgeois, volkisch histrionics—its ultrakitsch "strength-through-joy" celebrations and so forth.

Instead, those in search of Nietzsche's genuine political heirs—the proverbial "barbarians of the twentieth century"—might do better to look toward Mussolini's Italy. The prefascist theorists of political elites Gaetano Mosca and Vifredo Pareto were well-versed in Nietzsche's aristocratic views. The manifestos of the Italian Futurists— soon to become the artistic handmaidens to Mussolini's "New Rome"—were awash in Nietzschean rhetoric and imagery. "We want to glorify war—the only cure for the world—and militarism, patriotism, the destructive gesture of the anarchists, the beautiful ideas which kill," Marinetti would declare in his 1909 *Futurist Manifesto*.[68]

One of the best kept secrets of twentieth-century intellectual history is the extent to which the Duce himself was a Nietzsche connoisseur and admirer. Seduced by the German philosopher's exaltation of vitality and will, Mussolini as a young socialist valued Nietzsche almost as much as he did Marx. As a grade school dropout and autodidact, Mussolini's approach to Marxism always had a distinctly heterodox cast, which is in part attributable to Nietzsche's influence. In Nietzsche, Mussolini found a virile alternative to the pacifist and reformist mentality of his fellow Italian Socialists. In Mussolini's eyes, Italian liberals of the Giolitti stamp were simply beneath contempt.

During his "wilderness" years in Switzerland (1902–4), Mussolini imbibed Bergsonian vitalism, which he found a welcome alternative to the timorous Enlightenment rationalism that was the dominant credo among contemporary European socialists. One may also date his first encounter with Nietzsche from this period: Mussolini had begun learning German and read *Beyond Good and Evil* and *The Genealogy of Morals*. If the European working class had suffered the maiming effects of capitalist mechanization, was not vitalism a doctrine well suited toward restoring its lost sense of mission and spirit? In 1908 he read Sorel's Nietzsche-inspired *Reflections on Violence,* which he greeted as an epiphany. In Sorel Mussolini discovered a bellicose rhetoric of combat, will, and force—a lexicon requisite, he believed, to elevate backward Italy into a European power equal to England, France, and Germany. After all, before Engels and Kautsky scientifically codified Marxism, it had been a doctrine of revolution, awash in the rhetoric of violence and struggle as its leading theorists admonished the impoverished masses to rise up in a decisive, sanguinary battle and "expropriate the expropriators." In short, as a result of reading Nietzsche, Mussolini was on his way to becoming an unorthodox socialist, laying the intellectual groundwork for his future political "conversion." By reevaluating socialist precepts through a Nietzschean lens, "Mussolini was moving toward an original theory of revolution, distancing himself from Marxism in order to emerge finally as an anti-Marxist fascist."[69]

Was a marriage between Nietzsche and Marx, then, so entirely far-fetched? The writings of the young Mussolini reveal that such an alliance was hardly unimaginable. "I have a *barbaric* concept of socialism," Mussolini once remarked. "I understand it [socialism] as the greatest act of negation and destruction. . . . Onward, you new barbarians! . . . Like all barbarians you are the harbingers of a new civilization."[70] In opposition to pacifists and parliamentarians, Mussolini insisted that socialism meant "movement, struggle, and action."[71] In his writings, one of the slogans the future dictator was most fond of citing was Guyau's saying that "To live is not to calculate, but to act!"[72]

Given these momentous early encounters with the vitalist doctrines of Bergson and Sorel, a confrontation with Nietzsche seems to have been a foregone conclusion. One of the elements of Nietzsche's thought that Mussolini prized unreservedly was the philosopher's impassioned hatred of Christianity. In Mussolini's eyes Church-spawned religious indoctrination was one of the leading factors responsible for maintaining the revolutionary masses in a passive and quiescent state—a condition that served the interests of the capitalists and their ideological allies. In this respect, Mussolini believed he could reconcile Nietzsche's sensualism—his idea that one should philosophize with one's instincts—with Marx's anthropological materialism.

For analogous political reasons, Mussolini was early on attracted to the elitist implications of Nietzsche's doctrines. After all, despite the decennial economic crises afflicting fin-de-siècle Europe, the promised land of socialism prophesied by Marx seemed nowhere in sight. In Mussolini's eyes—as well as those of many other socialist leaders—the revolution's failure to materialize signified a crisis of Marxism. Traditional socialist methods and strategies' failure to produce the desired result required radical innovation. Not only had Nietzsche astutely diagnosed the role played by Christianity in creating pliable and docile "masses," but the contemporary proletariat approximated the philosopher's unsparing portrayal of the herd morality in the *Genealogy of Morals:* meek, conformist, and risk-averse.

How, then, was one to turn these indolent peasant and factory hands into the revolutionary shock troops demanded by Marx's philosophy of history? As Ernst Nolte has shown, at this juncture the thinking of Nietzsche and Lenin began to merge in Mussolini's syncretic worldview.[73] If the proletariat in its current state was incapable of making a revolution, it needed of a dose of Nietzschean "self-overcoming": it would have to turn itself into a "Superman." As Mussolini observed in a 1908 essay, "The plebs, who are excessively christianized and humanitarian, will never understand that a higher degree of evil is necessary so that the Superman might thrive. . . . The Superman knows revolt alone. Everything that exists must be destroyed."[74] According this new scenario, given the proletariat's political backwardness, the Leninist vanguard party must become the "Superman" in its stead. The party assumes a nihilistic attitude toward bourgeois institutions that the proletariat qua timorous "herd" proves incapable of transcending. When World War I broke out and the European socialist parties exchanged internationalism for patriotism (the Italian party being, at least temporarily, a noteworthy exception), Mussolini rapidly and astutely calculated the political consequences: in the future nationalism rather than socialism would hold the key to revolutionary struggle. The fascist idea was born.[75]

Walter Benjamin famously identified the aestheticization of violence as one of fascism's distinguishing features.[76] What Marx treated as the means to an end—the sanguinary imperatives of revolutionary struggle—fascism viewed as an end in itself. In passages such as the following that betray a strong Nietzschean influence, one has little trouble glimpsing the future fascist *in statu nascendi:* "One must view revolutions as the revenge of madness against the healthy human understanding," claims Mussolini. "For revolutions are insane, violent, idiotic, bestial. They are like war. They set fire to the Louvre and throw the naked bodies of princesses on the street. They kill, plunder, destroy. They are a man-made Biblical flood. Precisely therein consists their great beauty."[77]

During the interventionist crisis of 1914, it may well have been the Nietzschean values of heroism, myth, and martial glory that ultimately convinced Mussolini to break with his fellow socialists and join the Fasci d'Azione Rivoluzionaria—a precursor of his own postwar National Fascist Party. To show that he took his intellectual debts seriously, in 1931 Mussolini donated some twenty thousand lira to the Nietzsche Archive in Weimar.

Nietzsche's status as a prophet of twentieth-century power politics should neither be exaggerated nor sidestepped. In confronting the issue directly, one learns a lesson that has become familiar from the annals of literary modernism (Pound, Wyndham Lewis, Gottfried Benn, Paul de Man, and Ernst Jünger): one can be both a towering writer and thinker *and* politically a fascist—or, in Nietzsche's case, a protofascist. This lesson challenges our customary notions of intellectual greatness, which makes it all the more worth contemplating.

·2·

Prometheus Unhinged: C. G. Jung and the Temptations of Aryan Religion

The Jewish race as a whole . . . possesses an unconscious which can be compared with the Aryan only with reserve. Creative individuals apart, the average Jew is far too conscious and differentiated to go about pregnant with the tensions of unborn futures. The Aryan unconscious has a higher potential than the Jewish; that is both the advantage and the disadvantage of a youthfulness not yet fully weaned from barbarism. In my opinion it has been a grave error in medical psychology up till now to apply Jewish categories . . . indiscriminately to Germanic and Slavic Christendom. Because of this the most precious secret of the Germanic peoples—their creative and intuitive depth of soul—has been explained as a morass of banal infantilism.

—C. G. JUNG, "The State of Psychotherapy Today"

Our society sees as one of its principal assignments to call out to doctors, educators, and all fellow-countrymen who are concerned with human guidance, not lastly to those in the armed forces and the economy: Do not forget the unconscious! *Do not think that you are grasping the whole man when you close your eyes to the unconscious.*

—M. H. GÖRING, Director of the Third Reich's German Institute for Psychological Research and Psychotherapy (1940)

Progenitor of Postmodernism

For many years in the aftermath of World War II, Jung's doctrines had trouble catching on. Jung's willingness to assume a position of leadership among Nazi psychologists—shortly after the war, there was even talk among the Allies about prosecuting him as a war criminal—constituted an irremediable taint, as did his numerous public declarations in favor of German and Italian fascism. The approval Jung bestowed upon the Nazis confirmed the suspicions of many concerning the peculiarities of his "analytical psychology." Since his demonstrative break with Freud in 1914, Jung's approach increasingly flirted with the theosophical doctrines that had nourished the Nazi *Weltanschauung* its early stages.[1] Whereas Freud had always proudly asserted his Enlightenment patrimony, Jung's voluminous theoretical writings denounced the failings of Western civilization in a proto-Spenglerian idiom. The Enlightenment and its defenders had promoted the concept of autonomous subjectivity as a cognitive and ethical ideal, but in Jung's opinion this approach embodied an intellectualist orientation capable only of yielding depthless and superficial personality types—T. S. Eliot's "Hollow Men."

During the 1930s the Nazis denigrated psychoanalysis as a Jewish science. To escape persecution, Freud's followers emigrated to Anglo-Saxon lands, where they proceeded to reestablish themselves professionally with considerable success. For Jung's followers, the battle for acceptance would be an uphill climb.

The differences between Freud and Jung manifested themselves most clearly over the status of the unconscious. In Freud's view the unconscious represented a repository of disturbing, hence repressed, experiences. As such, it was a potential source of neurotic and psychotic discomfort. The key to a healthy personality lay in bringing this substratum of buried experience to the light of consciousness. Like the philosophes of yore, Freud held that rational self-awareness—the goal of the analytic process—was the key to emancipation.

Jung's approach to the unconscious could not have been more different. In many ways he appropriated Freud's precepts and stood them on their head. According to the strictures of analytic psychology, the rational ego represents an *obstacle* to the goal of individual self-realization rather than an asset. In Jungian terms "Enlightenment" is a question of putting the Self in touch with a more primordial bedrock of human experience: the collective unconscious. Thus, if Freudians seek to reacquaint analysands with their "inner child," Jungians seek to reconnect them with their "inner Fatherland." According to the doctrines of metempsychosis, individuals lead numerous lives. Only by reconnecting with their prior, archaic, mythological Selves can they attain spiritual fulfillment. Civilization had embarked on a false path when the Enlightenment sought to place science and religion on separate tracks. Jung never tried to conceal that his ultimate desideratum was to transform analytic psychology into a new religion—not a religion for everyman but one suited for a new spiritual elite. As a contemporary of Jung and Freud remarked during the 1930s, "It is interesting how the fascisticization of science had to change precisely those elements of Freud which stemmed from the enlightened, materialistic period of the bourgeoisie . . . For these friends of darkness, Freud does not go nearly far back enough. . . . Jung skips this enlightened disenchantment and . . . seeks the primeval right of the artistic imagination, of religious myths . . . precisely in the unconscious."[2]

A similar argument could be made for their contrasting employment of "myth." Freud was wont to use myths as parables or as literary illustrations of his doctrines, as he did most famously in the case of the Oedipus legend. Jung, conversely, unabashedly accorded myth and legend a superior epistemological status. In the case of the myths he favored, such as Mithraism, symbolic lavishness testified to their greater cognitive majesty.

As memories of the war faded, analytical psychology began to make inroads among the denizens of the "affluent society." Freud's vaunted *Kulturpessimismus,* which had been honed in the precarious calm of interwar Europe, dovetailed poorly with the ever-rising expectations of a society of abundance. As the age of commitment—the 1960s—ceded to the "culture of narcissism," a cultural breach emerged, which Jungians managed to fill with a vengeance. An era of rising social expectations suggested that the id no longer needed to be feared but could now be safely explored. Amid the hunger for meaning provoked by the consumer society's spiritual void, it seemed that Jung's pseudo-religiosity had infinitely more to offer than the dour sobriety purveyed by the champions of psychoanalysis. Jungianism became the alternative religion of choice for New Agers with 401(k)'s and disposable incomes.

Still, until quite recently in academic circles, "resistances" to analytic psychology remained considerable. Even psychology departments—hardly bastions of Freudian orthodoxy—seemed loath to accord Jung a place in the canon. After all, his methodology was avowedly mystical and obscurantist. As the anthropologist Rodney Needham once observed, Jung's findings were a "veritable farrago of imagery, parallelisms, patterns, visions and symbolic formulations."[3] To subject his insights to the customary scholarly solvents of critical discourse and analytical reason—approaches that Jung had openly renounced—made little sense. As with most mystics, for Jung the fact that the truths of analytical psychology remained inaccessible to the criteria of "public reason" became a point of honor. In this sense, his insights and claims were frankly "unfalsifable"—impervious to conventional standards of reason and truth. Instead, they required a suspension of disbelief.

Yet all of these hesitations and misgivings seemed to wilt in the face of the postmodernist onslaught of the 1980s, when Jung's stock rose semi-miraculously, like a phoenix from the ashes. The editors of the recently published *Cambridge Companion to Jung* give voice to the consensus view when they observe, "Many of [Jung's] ideas anticipate the intellectual and socio-cultural concerns of our current 'postmodern' period."[4] Since Jung had early on become a decided antagonist of that quintessential modernist, Sigmund Freud, the parallels between Jung and postmodernism seemed eminently worth exploring. After all, Jung's contention that the cognitive potentials of scientific reason were grossly inferior to those embodied in mythical and religious experience seemed to jibe broadly with postmodernism's generalized disillusionment with the Enlightenment project as well as its search for "alternative" sources of knowledge. The scathing indictments of Western reason purveyed by Foucault, Derrida, and Lyotard make Jung's criticisms seem tame by comparison.[5] Feminists who were convinced of reason's "masculinist" and "phallocratic" biases came to view Jung as a kindred spirit. For Jung's doctrine of "anima"—the archaic, female "inner self" possessed by both sexes—seemed to qualify as a genuine harbinger of the concerns of gynecological or "difference" feminism. As Susan Rowland writes in *Jung: A Feminist Revision,*

"Jung's anima as signifier of the unknowable unconscious is his incarnation as postmodern Jung."[6]

Lastly, in recent years psychoanalysis has experienced its share of crises. Far from the closely-knit guild-mentality that earlier predominated, it has gradually opened itself up to new methodologies: object relations, ego psychology, and humanistic approaches.[7] Amid this pluralistic intellectual climate, it has been more difficult to deny Jung and his theories a place at the table.

Prodigal Youth

By all accounts Carl Gustav Jung was a peculiar youth. Alienated from his parental milieu in late nineteenth-century Basel, he took to introspection. At the age of eight he invented a game whereby he would sit on a stone and ask himself whether he was Jung or the stone. "The answer was totally unclear," he would later confess. Two years later he engaged in a ritual with a ruler whose top half he had carved into the figure of a mannequin. During moments of emotional insecurity, Jung would present the totem, which he scrupulously kept hidden under a floorboard in the attic, with small scrolls written in a secret language. He would later describe these rites as a "very powerful formative influence," the "climax and conclusion of my childhood."[8] Intensely disliked by his classmates ("I had never come across such an asocial monster before," one would later recall), Jung would, to the dismay of his parents, habitually feign fainting spells to escape their sadistic torments.[9] In adolescence, he became preoccupied with the thought that he was really someone else; thus began Jung's search for what he would call his "No. 2" personality. In accordance with family lore, which held that Jung's paternal grandfather was the illegitimate son of Goethe, Jung came to the conclusion that this shadow self was indeed the great German poet. Later he became convinced that he was in fact Goethe reincarnate.

But the key event of Jung's youth was his celebrated "cathedral fantasy." As he would declare in his autobiography, "My entire youth can be understood in terms of this secret."[10] At the tender age of twelve, Jung experienced a prophetic vision. Returning from school on a bright summer day, he took note of the town's majestic cathedral and envisioned God seated above it on a golden throne. But his desire to further revere this beautiful and imposing structure was beset by an intense conflict that pursued him for days. The inner crisis was finally resolved by another hallucinatory image: an "enormous turd" dropped from God's throne shattering the cathedral to bits, at which point Jung reported feeling a great sense of "relief," even bliss.

Jung's father was a Protestant minister. To his son he had always been the embodiment of indecision and petty bourgeois conformity. Hence, in later life the cathedral fantasy came not only to symbolize Jung's Oedipal break with paternal authority and ecclesiastical convention, but also appeared as a sign sanctioning his obsessive pursuit of unorthodox, paranormal spiritual truths. Thus, in retrospect, Jung's vision seemed to give license to the heretical mystical quests that we now commonly associate with his name and legacy, quests that pertain to the murky realm of primal images or "archetypes" buried deep within humanity's collective unconscious.

For a time Jung himself seemed destined for a brilliant and eminently bourgeois career in the field of clinical psychology. In 1900, upon finishing medical school at the age of twenty-five, he became a resident at one of the world's most prestigious clinics, the Burghölzli in Zurich, where Jung apprenticed under the renowned Eugen Bleuler. It was here that Jung discovered Freud's writings. In 1906 he began to make a name for himself by inventing a word association test inspired by Freud's theory of the unconscious. That same year the two titans of the early psychoanalytic movement began corresponding. Their friendship would peak in 1909, when Freud and Jung traversed the Atlantic together to deliver lectures at Clark University. As their ship approached New York, Freud is alleged to have turned to Jung and said, "Don't they know we're bringing them the plague?"[11]

In retrospect, it is safe to say that the Jung-Freud affiliation was dominated by feelings of profound mutual transference. At the turn of the century the Burghölzli was one of the world's most vaunted psychiatric facilities. Freud, conversely, was marooned in Vienna, and the "psychoanalytic movement"—which at this point consisted of the Master and a handful of Jewish disciples who attended his Wednesday Night meetings—sorely lacked an institutional base. In his correspondence Freud made no secret of the fact that he viewed Jung and Bleuler—the "Zurich School"—as the ideal emissaries to purvey the psychoanalytic gospel to the non-Jewish world and thereby reap the international acclaim that was its (and his) due. In this way, the commonplace castigation of psychoanalysis as a "Jewish science" might be surmounted. Moreover, Freud held his Vienna associates in relatively low regard. In Jung—tall, handsome, brilliant, and, last but not least, a genuine "Teuton"—the fifty-year-old Freud believed he had found a worthy successor, the crown prince of the psychoanalytic movement. "You really are the only one capable of making an original contribution [to psychoanalysis]," he remarked to Jung in a 1908 letter.[12] Three years later Freud would confide to the Swiss psychologist Ludwig Binswanger, "When the realm I have founded is orphaned, no one but Jung shall inherit it all."[13] Thus, when the International Psychoanalytic Association was established in 1910, Jung, with Freud's benediction and to the great dismay of the Viennese contingent, was elected President, a post he would retain until their ultimate break four years later.

In Freud, who was Jung's senior by nearly twenty years, Jung believed he had found both the father figure he lacked as a child ("father-son" rhetoric permeated their correspondence), as well as a source of the professional recognition he sorely craved. Jung never attempted to conceal the homoerotic nature of his attachment to Freud—he speaks frankly of its "undeniable erotic undertone"—a veneration that Jung likened to a "religious crush." Freud countered—prophetically, as it turns out—that such religious adulation could only end in apostasy.

To speak of "love at first sight" may be hyperbolic, but we do know that upon their first meeting in Vienna in 1907 the two men talked for thirteen hours straight. His traumatic break with Fliess fresh in mind, in correspondence Freud frequently pressed for reassurances of Jung's loyalty. On most occasions, the younger man dutifully complied. Freud was particularly uncertain about the extent to which Jung accepted his theory of the sexual origins of neurosis—his so-called "libido theory," which had become the linchpin of psychoanalytic doctrine. His Oedipal fears seemed confirmed as the two men were about to board a steamship for the Clark University conference. At dinner after a glass or two of wine, Jung began prattling incessantly about the discovery of some prehistoric archaeological remains, "peat-bog mummies," that had been recently unearthed in Belgium. Freud tried to change the topic of conversation, but Jung plowed ahead undeterred. Perceiving Jung's unrelenting fascination with this theme as a death-wish against him, Freud fainted straight away.[14]

During their transatlantic voyages the two men entertained themselves by analyzing one another's dreams until the early morning hours. It was during one of these sessions that a fundamental breach in their relationship occurred. While deciphering one of Freud's dreams, Jung asked him to supply some details of his private life to complete the interpretation. Freud demurred, claiming that to do so would be to place his authority at risk. According to Jung, Freud's refusal represented a point of no return, insofar as it demonstrated that the founder of psychoanalysis valued authority more than truth.

Freud had invested nearly everything in Jung as his handpicked heir to the psychoanalytic throne. Hence, for a time he quite naturally did everything within his power to keep his Swiss colleague within the movement's orbit. To little avail. Circa 1911, as Jung commenced work on a bizarre and convoluted treatise whose focal point was the relationship between the unconscious and classical mythology (*Transformations and Symbols of the Libido*), their communications took a decisive turn for the worse. Undeniably, at this juncture the intellectual paths of the two men had permanently diverged. Freud had always insisted that psychoanalysis was in the first instance a science. His intellectual ethos was firmly rooted in the Enlightenment tradition. By making what had previously been unconscious conscious, psychoanalysis sought to release individuals from the dead weight of the past and thereby restore their autonomy. Or, as Freud with elegant pith once described the telos of the analytic process, "Where id was, there ego should be."[15]

As Freud would soon learn, Jung, conversely, had acquired a different set of intellectual allegiances and values. For Jung, it was not enough for psychoanalysis to be a science. Science was the epitome of Western rationalism: an arid intellectualism conducive only to libidinal stultification and mass neurosis. In many ways it was directly responsible for the widespread social pathologies of modern man—part of the disease rather than the cure. Instead, if psychoanalysis were to measure up to the immense spiritual challenge of the modern age, it would have to become something more: *a new religion,* a worldview that was capable, à la Nietzsche, of supplanting the nihilistic values of the moribund Christian West.

In response to a 1910 query by Freud as to whether the psychoanalytic movement might benefit by aligning itself with an ethical fraternity, Jung unabashedly tipped his hand:

> I imagine a far finer and more comprehensive task for [psychoanalysis] than alliance with an ethical fraternity. I think we must give it time to infiltrate into people from many centers, to revivify among intellectuals a feeling for symbol and myth, ever so gently to transform Christ back into the soothsaying God of the vine, which he was, and in this way absorb *those ecstatic instinctual forces of Christianity for the one purpose of making the cult and the sacred myth what they once were—a drunken feast of joy where man regained the ethos and holiness of an animal.* That was the beauty and purpose of classical religion.[16]

Freud, taken aback by his protégé's boldness, vigorously protested Jung's equation of psychoanalysis and religion: "But you mustn't regard me as the founder of a religion. My intentions are not so far reaching. . . . I am not thinking of a substitute for religion; this need must be sublimated."[17] But his cautionary words were destined to fall on deaf ears.

Of course, Jung's suggestion that one must "transform Christ back into the soothsaying God of the vine" was less a prescription for the regeneration of Christianity than a recipe, in the spirit of Nietzsche and German romanticism, for a new paganism. The "soothsaying God of the vine" was none other than Dionysus, whose mythological status was synonymous with intoxication and libidinal-orgiastic frenzy. Such were the iconoclastic terms in which Jung had reinterpreted Freud's libido theory. It no longer referred merely to the "sexual origins of neurosis." Instead it came to designate a repressed stratum of pre-Christian mythological symbols and practices whose release, via the Jungian technique of "active imagination," would facilitate modern man's reattunement with his lost primal self. Here, Jung's future status as the high priest and intellectual guru of the New Age movement—*Iron John, Women Who Run With Wolves, Denial of the Soul*—is plain for all to see. The distortions of "civilization," as promoted by rational intellectuals and, often enough, *Jews*—something that, as the chapter's epigraph indicates, Jung was never averse to pointing out—only served to mask and mutilate this vital phylogenetic-mythological heritage.

"The Jews Do Not Have This Image"

The issue of Jung's anti-Semitism has been much discussed over the years. His supporters are quick to point to his many Jewish associates and disciples. Moreover, that Jung was profoundly attracted to Jewish women is well-known—though most would agree that it is questionable whether this can be adduced as unequivocal evidence of a superordinate philo-Semitic streak. In an early paper he went so far as to refer obliquely to his "Jewess complex."[18] During his Burghölzli years Jung had an impassioned, on-again off-again affair with a Jewish patient, Sabina Spielrein, who would herself later go on to become Freudian analyst. A few years later he would engage in a similar arrangement with another Jewish patient, Toni Wolff, who would continue as Jung's coworker and mistress until her death in 1953. Thus Jung, who had openly flaunted his "polygamous tendencies" in letters to Freud, and who would at one point claim, "The prerequisite for a good marriage, it seems to me, is the license to be unfaithful," showed he could also walk the walk.[19]

It is also well known that the theory of archetypes had a strong Aryan-racial component. As Jung would insist, the archetypes deposited in the collective unconscious of Aryans were of a qualitatively different (read: superior) variety than those that could be uncovered in the collective unconscious of Jews. As Richard Noll observes in *The Jung Cult,* "Semitic cultures were not regarded by

Jung as based as directly on the same natural sources of Ur-religion as the ancient Aryans and therefore did not have 'mysteries' in the sense of a direct experience of the divine through initiation rituals."[20] Indeed, one of the key sources that Jung used in *Transformations and Symbols of the Libido,* Albrecht Dieterich's *A Mithra Liturgy,* makes this standpoint unequivocally clear. Referring to the central Aryan/pagan motif of rebirth through ritual initiation, Dieterich observes, *"The Jews do not have this image."*[21]

In Jung's 1934 essay on "The State of Psychotherapy Today," his rejection of psychoanalysis as an essentially "Jewish science" reached fever pitch. (Moreover, while publishing such diatribes Jung was safely tucked away at his home in Küsnacht, Switzerland; thus, there were no thugs from the SS forcing his hand.) Jung begins the essay by claiming that "Freud took his stand with fanatical one-sidedness on sexuality, concupiscence—in a word on the 'pleasure principle'. . . . It almost looks as if man's desire and greed have been made the cardinal principle of psychology."[22] By leveling these charges, Jung was merely reiterating the standard litany of anti-Semitic insinuations against Freud and his doctrines: that psychoanalysis, as a Jewish science and like Jews in general, was excessively concerned with sex, that Jews by nature were predominantly driven by greedy and lascivious motivations. That Jung made these accusations just as the Nazi dictatorship had begun to entrench and extend its brutal rule, makes them especially damnable. Jung would conclude the essay with an even more devastating characterization of Jews and their debased phylogenetic heritage:

> The Jews have this peculiarity in common with women; being physically weaker, they have to aim at the chinks in the armour of their adversary, and thanks to this technique which has been forced on them through the centuries, the Jews themselves are best protected where others are most vulnerable. . . . As a member of a race with a three-thousand-year-old civilization, the Jew, like the cultured Chinese, has a wider area of psychological consciousness than we. Consequently it is *in general* less dangerous for the Jew to put a negative value on his unconscious. The Aryan unconscious, on the other

hand, contains explosive forces and seeds of a future yet to be born, and these may not be devalued as nursery romanticism without psychic danger. The still youthful Germanic peoples are fully capable of creating new cultural forms that still lie dormant in the darkness of the unconscious of every individual—seeds bursting with energy and capable of mighty expansion. The Jew, who is something of a nomad, has never yet created a cultural form of his own and as far as we can see never will, since all his instincts and talents require a more or less civilized nation to act as host for their development.[23]

According to Jung's warped conception of racial archetypes, the Jews, as an older people, had been subjected to the repressive and debilitating influences of monotheism—Nietzsche's "slave morality"—for a longer duration than had the Aryans. Thus, though Jewish "intellect" and "consciousness" remained acute (from a Jungian standpoint, this was certainly a dubious compliment), their "unconscious," the source of all creativity, energy, and life, was hopelessly impoverished. As far as the urgent tasks of cultural regeneration were concerned, therefore, one could expect precious little from the Jews. The Aryans, conversely, remained a "youthful" people insofar as they had endured the Judeo-Christian yoke for only a thousand years. Their unconscious was consequently much richer. From them there was still much to hope.

Given that the centerpiece of Jungian psychology—the doctrine of the collective unconscious—was so thoroughly beholden to contemporary racial thinking (in *Transformations and Symbols of the Libido,* Jung approvingly cited H. S. Chamberlain's *The Foundations of the Nineteenth Century,* which would later become a Nazi bible) that Jung found himself quite at home during the early years of the Third Reich, is not surprising. Thus, Jung eagerly cooperated with the Göring Institute for Psychological Research and Psychotherapy, accepting the presidency of the Nazi-run General Medical Society for Psychotherapy and serving as editor for its journal, the *Zentralblatt für Psychotherapie.* Although Jung always claimed that he undertook these responsibilities with the intention of protecting Jewish colleagues—a possibility one can certainly not rule out—such professions of philo-Semitism are, as we have seen, belied by his public statements on the rigid phylogenetic differences between Aryans and Jews. Already in a 1932 address, Jung celebrated the triumphs of Italian fascism with the claim, "The huzzahs of the Italian nation go forth to the personality of the Duce, and the dirges of other nations lament the absence of strong leaders." In the 1934 published version of the same lecture, he would add: "Since this sentence was written, Germany too has found its Führer."[24]

Nor are positive references to Hitler uncommon in his addresses during this period. The Nazis always suspected that psychology, because of its inordinate focus on the individual, was ultimately incompatible with the collective goals of the racial community. In a 1933 Berlin radio interview (reprinted in *C. G. Jung Speaking*), Jung went to great lengths to demonstrate the synchronicity between his own "analytic psychology" and the Nazi revolution. As he would remark at one point, "Only the self-development of the individual, which I consider to be the supreme goal of all psychological endeavour, can produce consciously responsible spokesmen and leaders of the collective movement. As Hitler said recently, the leader must be able to be alone and must have the courage to go his own way." In the same interview, he praises the principle of "leadership" ("The need of the whole always calls forth a leader, regardless of the form a state may take") and denigrates democratic institutions ("Only in times of aimless quiescence does the aimless conversation of parliamentary deliberations drone on") in an unmistakably National Socialist idiom.[25] Then, in a January 1939 interview published in *Hearst's International-Cosmopolitan*, Jung would characterize the German Führer in the following glowing terms:

> There is no question but that Hitler belongs in the category of the truly mystic medicine man. As somebody commented about him at the last Nürnberg party congress, since the time of Mohammed nothing like it has been seen in this world. This markedly mystic characteristic of Hitler's is what makes him do things which seem to us illogical, inexplicable, curious and unreasonable. . . . So you see, Hitler is a medicine man, a form of spiritual vessel, a demi-deity or, even better a myth.[26]

As Geoffrey Cocks has shown in *Psychotherapy in the Third Reich*, Jungian psychology's emphasis on the unique collective experiences of various races and cultures garnered for its theories an especially favorable reception during the Nazi years. To many in the Third Reich, the intellectual affinities between the two worldviews seemed compelling and undeniable. Thus, at a time when Freud's theories were banned and his books publicly burned, Jung's ideas enjoyed a definite renaissance. And Jung himself was hardly averse to the renewed attention his doctrines were receiving. In 1946 the British Foreign Office went so far as to consider trying Jung as a war criminal. A damning compilation of documents, "The Case of Dr. Carl G. Jung: Pseudo-Scientist and Nazi Auxiliary," attests to their findings. In the end, however, they decided there were bigger fish to fry.[27]

Certainly, as time passed, Jung came to appreciate the diabolical fanaticism that was endemic to the regime and began to take his distance. But in many respects it was too late. True to the Faust legend he so much admired (whose best known version, moreover, had been authored by his reputed great-grandfather), Jung had sold his soul to the devil. Thereafter, he would have to pay the price for his transgression, at least in the court of public opinion. Though Jung was never an outright Nazi, his status as a fellow traveler, and, more importantly, the marked intellectual affinities between many of his key ideas and the National Socialist worldview, remain troubling to this day.

As a result of two recent and dramatic archival findings, the balance of the evidence on the question of Jung and anti-Semitism seems to have tipped decisively against the Swiss psychologist. First, a 1913 letter written by Jung to a Swedish colleague has recently been uncovered suggesting that the falling out with Freud was a major stimulus in the development of his own anti-Semitic attitudes and outlook. As Jung baldly declares toward the end of the letter, "Until now I was no anti-Semite, but now I'll become one, I believe."[28] Second, as Noll reveals in *The Jung Cult*, the "Aryans-only path to redemption that Jung envisioned in 1916 is supported by a 'secret appendix' to the by-laws of the Analytical Psychology Club of Zurich."[29] According to this clandestine provision, Jewish membership in the Club was tightly "restricted": there was a ten percent quota on regular Jewish membership and a twenty-five percent quota on Jewish guest membership. Jung finally did away with the quota only in 1950, as voluble public debate over his collaboration with the Nazis threatened to harm his global psychotherapeutic empire. Noll views this evidence as "confirmation of Jung's long-standing covert anti-Semitism."

Close Encounters with Otto Gross

Circa 1911 Jung repeatedly declared that he was being tormented by the "hydra of mythological fantasy."[30] What sinister forces had come to possess C. G. Jung—the mild-mannered assistant to Bleuler and rising star in the psychoanalytic firmament, suddenly caught in the grip of hallucinatory delusions and Dionysian sensual excess? To understand this development—one of the decisive turning points in Jung's career—we must turn to his fateful encounter with sexual immoralist and renegade psychoanalyst Otto Gross.

In the early years of psychoanalysis, Otto Gross seemed to be destined for greatness. Few who knew him ever doubted either his genius or his innate charisma. To Ernest Jones, Gross was "the nearest approach to the romantic idea of genius I have ever met."[31] Freud once claimed that, along with Jung, Gross was one of the few persons "capable of making an original contribution [to psychoanalysis]."[32]

But Gross was also, to put it mildly, a deeply troubled soul. His father, Hanns Gross, was the founder of modern criminology. Though Austrian by birth, the elder Gross was by all accounts the incarnation of Prussian patriarchal intolerance. Thus, a good deal of Otto's rebelliousness had profound Oedipal roots. He was incurably addicted to both cocaine and morphine. Furthermore, his combined reading of Nietzsche and Freud had taught him that sexual monogamy was the primary source of contemporary civilization's ills. Thereafter, he became a prophet of unrestricted libidinal gratification. After Otto's debauchery had spun out of control in the 1910s, his father had him declared legally incompetent. A warrant for his arrest was circulated, and an international manhunt ensued. Gross was captured and incarcerated, and an impassioned "free Otto" movement sprang up among central Europe's Bohemian intelligentsia. After he was freed, Gross resettled in Prague, where he and Kafka became friendly. Undoubtedly, the two frequently commiserated about the injustices of paternal despotism. Some scholars maintain that Gross's legal travails were the model and inspiration for *The Trial*'s Josef K.

Gross was a fixture on the Munich-Zurich-Ascona counterculture circuit, where vegetarianism, free love, and pagan spirituality were the reigning credos. Gross's habitudes, however, were deemed a bit too outré even for this milieu of fin-de-siècle progressives, and he was reportedly expelled from Ascona's Monte Veritá settlement for engaging in orgies. In 1907 Gross carried his message of libidinal redemption north to the cerebral Mecca of Heidelberg, home of the celebrated Max Weber *Kreis*. There Gross encountered the von Richthofen sisters, Else Jaffe and Frieda Weekly. Both were married—so was Gross—but he seduced each of them in turn. Later that year both Else and Otto's wife, also named Frieda, gave birth to sons by Gross, and both women named their sons Peter. A few years later Frieda Weekly would elope with D. H. Lawrence in one of the century's most celebrated itinerant literary romances. Via Frieda, Gross's influence on Lawrence was profound. When all is said and done, he was probably one of the major subterranean influences on twentieth-century European literature. Gross met an untimely if foreseeable end on the streets of Berlin, where he was discovered starving to death and homeless in 1920.[33]

In 1908 Gross had again hit rock bottom. Strung out and penniless, he sought out Jung at Freud's suggestion at the Burghölzli for a last-ditch psychoanalytic cure. Despite Jung's initial hesitancies, the two men hit it off famously and would take turns analyzing each other in marathon sessions of twelve hours or more. As Jung would report to Freud, "Whenever I got stuck, he analyzed me. In this way my own psychic health has benefited."[34] Jung, it seems, couldn't praise Gross highly enough: "In spite of everything he is my friend, for at bottom he is a very good and fine man with an unusual mind. . . . In Gross I discovered many aspects of my true nature, so that he often seemed like my twin brother—*except for the Dementia praecox.*"[35] As it turns out, this would prove to be quite a weighty exception.

Gross would ultimately "terminate" the analysis by jumping over the Burghölzli walls and fleeing toward Munich. Nevertheless, it appears that, at a certain point in the analysis, Jung and Gross essentially traded roles: Gross became the analyst and Jung the patient. As a result of this role reversal, Gross liberated Jung from the strictures of bourgeois monogamy and converted him to the doctrine of untrammeled libidinal hedonism. Indeed, not long after Gross's disappearance, positive references to Jung's own "polygamous components" began appearing in his letters. In *Transformations and Symbols of the Libido,* Jung would write, in the spirit of Otto Gross, "The existence of a phallic or orgiastic cult does not indicate *eo ipso* a particularly lascivious life any more than the ascetic symbolism of Christianity means an especially moral life."[36] According to Noll, moreover, "Jung's relationship to [Sabina] Spielrein took a sudden erotic turn due to the encounter with Gross."[37]

Spielrein would provide telling evidence to this effect in an entry from the diary she kept during her treatment by Jung:

> I sat there waiting in deep depression. Now he [Jung] arrives, beaming with pleasure, and tells me with strong emotion about Gross, about the great insight he has just received [i.e., about polygamy]; he no longer wants to suppress his feeling for me, he admitted that I was his first, dearest woman friend, etc., etc., (his wife of course excepted), and that he wanted to tell me everything about himself.[38]

"Poetry" seems to have been the code word she used to describe their many intimate encounters and trysts during these years.

According to Noll, the upshot of Gross's analysis with Jung was that the analyst rather than the analysand emerged permanently transformed:

> Gross captivated Jung with his theories of sexual liberation, his Nietzscheanism, and his utopian dreams of transforming the world through psychoanalysis. Jung must have heard stories about a world that he had been too afraid to venture into, a bohemian realm that was antithetical to everything he thought he valued. During these

long hours he learned of Gross's sexual escapades in Heidelberg. He heard of the seductions of the von Richthofen sisters, of illegitimate children, of vegetarianism and opium and orgies. He learned of the Schwabing to Zurich to Ascona countercultural circuit and listened, amazed, as Gross informed him of colonies of neopagans, Theosophists, and sun worshipers who had formed their own colonies in Jung's Switzerland.[39]

From this point hence, Jung began to abandon the bourgeois world of scientific sobriety and social respectability. Thereupon commenced his headlong plunge into a hallucinatory world of neopagan mystery cults and occult practices. In this way Jung willingly succumbed to the "hydra of mythological fantasy" he had alluded to in his letters to Freud. Such themes and influences would become a staple of his writing and teachings during the crucial decade between 1910 and 1920 when the formative concepts of Jungian "analytical psychology"—anima and animus, persona, collective unconscious, and archetypes—were conceived and elaborated.

At this point Jung reconceived the analytic project in an avowedly Counter-Enlightenment spirit. For Jung this meant overcoming the strictures and inhibitions of the conscious mind (the "persona") and engaging in a confrontation with phantoms of the archaic past that lay sedimented deep within the collective unconscious—the analysand's "inner Fatherland," as it were. As Noll observes, "The iron cage of 'civilization'—Judeo-Christian beliefs and other political and value systems—had to be cast off in order to recover true culture, the primordial ground of the soul, the Volk. There was only one solution: recover the 'archaic man' within, allowing a rejuvenating return to the chthonic powers of the Edenic, Aryan past."[40] In this way the doctrine of "Aryan psychoanalysis" was born. Thereafter, Jungian analysis would serve its own ends of reenchantment and myth rather than the Freudian ends of maturity and autonomy. At the same time, it is important to recognize that the völkisch-neopagan epiphanies that Jung was experiencing at this time (the second part of *Transformations and Symbols of the Libido* offers ample evidence) were far from unique. Instead, they dovetailed with a much broader

German rejection of modern cultural "decadence" in favor of the life-enhancing values of Aryanism, archaic religion, spiritualism, and sun worship.

Aryan Religion

Jung recounts his purported experience of self-deification—a veritable turning point both in Jung's life and in the history of his movement—in the course of a 1925 seminar, the transcript of which has only recently come to light. There Jung tells the story of a series of delusional, self-induced trances he underwent in 1913. During these reveries Jung claims to have encountered a gallery of mythological demigods. Prominent among them was Philemon-Elijah, a figure from Mithraic lore with a long white beard and the wings of a kingfisher. There was also Salomé, whom Jung would come to identify as his "anima" or female inner self. Convinced Jung could cure her blindness, Salomé began to worship him. In response to Jung's question, "Why do you worship me?" she replied simply: "You are Christ." Then, the following scene occurred:

> Then I saw [a] snake approach me. She came close and began to encircle me and press me in her coils. These coils reached up to my heart. I realized as I struggled that I had assumed the attitude of the crucifixion. In the agony and the struggle, I sweated so profusely that the water flowed down on all sides of me. Then Salomé rose, and she could see. While the snake was pressing me, I felt that my face had taken on the face of an animal of prey, a lion or tiger.[41]

Thus transpired Jung's experience of pagan self-apotheosis via initiation into the cult of ancient Mithraic mysteries. In the course of this visionary quest he had become the legendary Deus Leontocephalus, or lion-headed god, of Mithraic-Aryan lore. Only individuals with the most profound capacity for "active imagination" were capable of experiencing this *ur*-stratum of the Indo-European ancestral-archetypal past. As Jung would recall, "The important part that led up to the deification was the snake's encoiling of me.

Salomé's performance was deification. The animal face which I felt mine transformed into was the famous [Deus] Leontocephalus of the Mithraic Mysteries."[42]

Mithraism was a dualistic religion that flourished in late antiquity, though its roots may be traced to Persian Zoroastrianism. Its liturgies included secret initiation rites that counted seven levels. Key aspects of Mithraic ritual—sacramental feasts during which bread and water were consecrated, ceremonies in which priests sang hymns and rang bells—seem to have anticipated Christian liturgy. The most sacred moment of the ceremony came with the unveiling of an image of Mithras slaying a bull—Mithraism's celebrated "tauroctony." Mithraism would figure prominently in Jung's *Transformations and Symbols of the Libido*. As an indication of its importance to him, Jung would reproduce an image of Mithraic tauroctony in its pages. Indeed, the text is brimming with allusions to Aryan-Mithraic imagery and ritual.

Little wonder that shortly after reading *Transformations*, Freud would offer the following comments about the phylogenetically expanded concept of libido with which Jung and his Swiss cohorts were experimenting at the time: "They are now doubting the influence of infantile complexes and are at the point of already appealing to racial differences in order to explain the theoretical disparity." And further: "Jung must now be in a florid neurosis. . . . [My] intention of amalgamating Jews and goyim in the service of [psychoanalysis] seems now to have gone awry. They are separating like oil and water."[43]

Jung's 1913 experience of self-deification would subsequently become the cornerstone and inspiration for Jungian psychoanalysis in general. Thus, Jung's own primal confrontation with illustrious mythological forbears or "archetypes"—his personal transfiguration qua Mithraic Deus Leontocephalus—would become the model of his own analytic approach. In this way, Jung sought to effect a synthesis among the diffuse currents of heretical knowledge preoccupying him at the time—Aryan religion, sun worship, spiritualism, ancient mystery cults—integrating them within his own analytic psychology. In *The Jung Cult*, Noll offers the following account of the ideological intentions underlying Jung's professed "phylogeny of the human soul":

> In the individual psyche there are strata that comprise the sediment of two thousand years of Christianity. Two thousand years of Christianity makes us strangers to ourselves. In the individual, the internalization of bourgeois-Christian civilization is a mask that covers the true Aryan god within, a natural god, a sun god, perhaps even Mithras himself.... In society, too, Christianity is an alien mask that covers our biologically true religion, a natural religion of the sun and the sky. The scientific proof are cases of patients with dementia praecox documented by Jung and his Zurich School assistants that demonstrate that there is a pre-Christian, mythological layer of the unconscious mind. It is archaic and corresponds to the thought and especially to the souls of our ancestors.[44]

Thus, Jungian analysis

> became an initiatory process, a descent into the unconscious mind in order to spark a process of individual transformation through a direct encounter with the transcendental realm of the gods.... For those that survived an encounter with the god or gods, Jung promised rebirth as a true "individual," free from all repressive mechanisms of conventional beliefs about family, society, and deity.[45]

At the same time, it appears that Jung's account of his own Mithraic self-deification was substantially, even fatally, flawed. Clearly, Jung's description of Mithraic rites is taken from a well-known contemporary source: Belgian scholar Franz Cumont's two volume study, *The Mysteries of Mithra*. Cumont's work was translated into German in 1903, and Jung cites it in *Transformations and Symbols of the Libido*. Jung's entire knowledge of Mithraism derived essentially from a single chapter of Cumont's work: "The Mithraic Liturgy, Clergy, and Devotees." Needless to say, if Jung's familiarity with Mithraism is primarily derived from contemporary textual sources, then his claims to have experienced a genuine Mithraic initiation ritual via the procedure of "active imagination" are groundless.

Either such claims were an outright fabrication on his part, or they were the result of "cryptomnesia"—hidden memories that Jung had forgotten or repressed, which then resurfaced in the course of his self-induced trance. Either way his reputed self-apotheosis qua Mithraic Deus Leontocephalus—the foundational experience upon which Jungian analytical psychology in its entirety is predicated— stands as little more than a phantasm or chimera. There are more polite ways of putting it, but Jung was a fraud. As Noll remarks, "the collective unconscious may still be said to exist, but only on the shelves of Jung's personal library."[46]

But there is a further problem with Jung's over-reliance on Cumont as a source: as a result of subsequent archaeological findings, many of Cumont's speculations about the actual meaning of Mithraic liturgy and iconography have either been disproved or seriously called into question. For example, doubt has been cast on the Persian origins of Roman Mithraism, as well as the purported soteriological significance of the tauroctony, the cult's central image. In fact, contemporary scholars now speak freely of a "breakdown of the old Cumontian consensus" and of the "mythical" aspects of Cumont's own reconstructions and interpretations. Hence, not only were Jung's visions of neopagan rebirth based on contemporary literary sources, they were also based on historically fallacious analyses and interpretations.

Of course, Jung and his Swiss colleagues claimed to have discovered significant evidence of kindred Aryan-Mithraic imagery while analyzing neurotic patients. Jung contended that such clinical testimony constituted irrefutable proof of a collective unconscious as a repository of primal images from the Indo-European past. How, then, is one to account for these corroborating archetypal visions among Jung's patients?

The answer is simple. On the Munich-Zurich-Ascona circuit from which Jung and company recruited the majority of their patients, such pagan-mythological motifs were all the rage. Many of these patients had easy access to a wealth of contemporary publications—pamphlets, journals, books—celebrating neopagan spirituality. Undoubtedly, then, the "recovered memories" of Jung's patients revealed much more about the contemporary cultural psyche than about Indo-European prehistory. Finally, given the passionate nature of Jung's new mythological interests, his assistants were most likely instructed to press with particular zeal when it came to unearthing such themes in the course of their analyses. No doubt, the power of suggestion itself can account for a good number of such pseudo-instances of phylogenetic recollection.

Solar Phallus Man

At several points in his career Jung recounted the story of one of his landmark cases: the patient who in Jungian lore came to be known as Solar Phallus Man. In a famous BBC television interview in 1959, two years before his death, Jung credits this case as having first convinced him of the reality of the collective unconscious.[47] Similarly, Jung scholar Sonu Shamdasani has maintained that the Solar Phallus Man "carried on his shoulders the weight and burden of proof of the Collective Unconscious."[48] But with the particulars surrounding this celebrated case, Jung's trail of intellectual charlatanry begins to glow red hot.

Jung's first discussion of the case appeared in *Transformations and Symbols of the Libido*, where he describes a psychotic patient who had visions of an erect phallus swaying from the sun. As the phallus moved, the wind would blow. In the 1911 version of *Transformations*, Jung identified his assistant, J. J. Honneger, as the attending physician in the case. "This strange hallucination remained unintelligible to us for a long time until I became acquainted with the Mithraic Liturgy and its visions," Jung claimed.[49] He went on to cite a 1907 text by G.R.S. Mead, *A Mithraic Ritual*, as his source for the link between the solar phallus imagery and ancient Mithraic liturgy.

Honneger committed suicide in 1911. In Jung's subsequent references to the case, Honneger's involvement is excised from the official record, which he began falsifying with a 1930 essay, "The Structure of the Psyche," in which he personally takes credit for having discovered the case; Honneger's name is also missing from the 1952 edition of *Transformations*. Instead, Jung simply claims that the Solar Phallus Man was his patient, as he would also maintain in the aforementioned 1959 BBC interview. Moreover, in discussions of the case dating from the 1930s, Jung would backdate it to 1906—even though Honneger had not started working at the Burghölzli clinic until 1909, which would thus have been the earliest date the Solar Phallus man could have been treated by him.

It seems that Jung backdated the case to avoid the suspicion that the Solar Phallus Man's reminiscences could have been derived from contemporary literary sources rather than from the depths of the collective unconscious. Since Mead's book on Mithraic liturgy appeared in 1907, one way of deflecting skepticism would be to claim that the patient's hallucinations predated its publication—hence, the decision to date the case to 1906. Yet once Jung made the decision to falsify the date for the case, then Honneger's pivotal role in its discovery would also have to fall by the wayside, since he had only begun treating patients in 1909.

At some point Jung became aware that a 1903 book by Albrecht Dieterich (Jung himself at times relied on the 1910 edition of Dieterich's work) contained a detailed description of Mithraic Liturgy. Now the story changed yet again: Jung's editors, in an attempt to cover for the master, alleged that the patient in question had been institutionalized long before 1903 and, hence, could not have been familiar with the text. Yet, as Noll convincingly shows numerous other popular publications were available at the time that could have been the source of such knowledge, even had the editors' claim been true:

> Even an institutionalized mental patient could pick up a Theosophical journal and ingest an occultist interpretation of the latest scholarship on Greek Magical Papyri (including the Mithraic Liturgy), the Hellenistic mystery cults, polytheistic Greco-Roman religion, Zoroastrianism. . . . The likelihood that Honneger's patient . . . could have come into contact with such publications is quite high. The myriad publications of the Theosophical Society provided more than enough material to fill any personal unconscious with the sort of mythological material that Jung and his associates claim was from a nonpersonal source.[50]

Honneger's papers, which mysteriously went missing for eighty years, have recently been deposited in the Library of Congress. Though they are known to contain Honneger's notes to the Solar Phallus Man case, the Jung estate has apparently forbidden access to them.

Conclusion

Today Jungism is a worldwide industry generating hundreds of millions of dollars in annual revenue. C. G. Jung Educational Centers may be found in most major cities around the globe. They serve to attract converts, patients, trainees, and benefactors; more generally, they function as an institutional basis to propagate the faith. Over the years, wealthy patrons have endowed the Bollingen Foundation, which has overseen the publication and translation of Jung's collected works throughout the world. In *The Aryan Christ*, Noll recounts the fascinating tale of one such patient-benefactress, Rockefeller heiress Edith Rockefeller McCormick, whose wealth and influence were instrumental in facilitating Jung's success during the tenuous early years of his movement. Since the 1970s Jung's influence on spiritualistic currents of the New Age movement has been enormous. It may be only a slight exaggeration to say scratch a witch and underneath you will find a Jungian.

How might one account for the astonishing success of Jung and Jungism in the contemporary world? Simply put, Jung's doctrines satisfy a spiritual hunger among a privileged elite for whom the answers of traditional religiosity have long sounded hollow and antiquated. Jungism thereby provides an antidote to what Hegel once called the "prose of the world": to the radical secularism of a modern society for which questions of salvation have increasingly become a matter of indifference. In this respect, Jungism is capable of providing something that Freud—the immovable secular humanist—shunned like the plague: a promise of redemption. The basic terms of Jungian psychology—anima, persona, archetype, and collective unconscious—may well boil down to so much verbal hocus pocus and intellectual chicanery. Little matter. For true believers, they do the trick. They claim to put the individual in touch with mysterious powers that transcend his or her own atomized and spiritually impoverished existence. They offer a promise of wholeness and meaning in an acosmic universe where prospects for salvation seem to exist at an infinite remove. Jungian psychology offers to reintegrate members of the lonely crowd within the great chain of being.

Nevertheless, there is something deeply disturbing about all this. In many respects Jungian psychology seems like the postmodern equivalent of the medieval Christian practice of selling indulgences. If much about Jung and Jungism is conceptually and historically flawed, what can be the real-world value of the mystical consolations that the Jung industry is so ready to dispense—albeit, for the right price? History has repeatedly shown that in times of acute turmoil and stress, nations and individuals are willing to rely on the most extravagant mythological means to endow a confusing world with order and meaning. Perhaps it is to this pervasive existential need that Jungism in the first instance speaks.

· 3 ·

Fascism and Hermeneutics: Gadamer and the Ambiguities of "Inner Emigration"

The Germans are unique perhaps in the ardor with which they pursue
ideas and attempt to transform them into realities. Their great
achievements, their catastrophic failures, their tragic political history are
all impregnated with this dangerous idealism. If most of us are the
victims of circumstances, it may truly be said of the Germans as a whole
that they are at the mercy of ideas.

—E. M. BUTLER, *The Tyranny of Greece Over Germany*

A Copernican Turn in Scholarship

Over the course of the last decade, a number of taboos about exploring the role of German scholars during the Third Reich have been lifted. Correspondingly, the longstanding diversionary myths of the "other Germany" and "inner emigration" have, it would seem, suffered a lethal blow.

Already in the late 1980s, in a groundbreaking study of so-called *Ostforschung*, Michael Burleigh uncovered the critical role played by historians in the colonization and enslavement of the peoples of eastern Europe.[1] We now know that these historians—few of whom may be described as "convinced Nazis"—furnished the SS with indispensable logistical and demographic information that facilitated the planning and execution of the Final Solution. As such, they fall under the rubric of "Vordenker der Vernichtung"— "prophets of annihilation." Similarly, at the 1998 annual meeting of German historians (Deutscher Historikertag) the profession was rocked by fresh revelations concerning the extensive role played by

historians in legitimating the Nazi ideology of genocidal imperialism.[2] But as the research of Burleigh and others has made clear,
intellectual justifications for German political hegemony, far from
being of exclusively Nazi provenance, were widely purveyed by
nationalistically inclined German scholars of varying political
persuasions.

In the context at hand it is important to recognize that when it
came to Germany's imperialist geopolitical designs, Nazis and German conservatives genuinely disagreed on few points. Instead, what
is striking about the recent scholarly findings is the remarkable ease
with which more traditional German nationalists such as the
philosopher Hans-Georg Gadamer embraced Nazi policies. In light
of these discoveries, to proceed with a rigid dichotomy between
Nazis and national conservatives like Gadamer would be misleading. To do so would be to misunderstand the nature of the political
coalition that facilitated Nazism's success.

In *Deutsche Geisteswissenchaft im Zweiten Weltkrieg: die "Aktion
Ritterbusch," 1940–1945* (German Humanities During the Second
World War), Frank-Rütger Hausmann has convincingly portrayed
the eagerness with which scholars from the humanities—art history, classics, *Germanistik* (German studies), history, and philosophy—jumped on the Nazi bandwagon. Fearing they would be left
behind by more immediately practical fields such as law, medicine,
and engineering, German humanists sought to demonstrate that
the Third Reich's claims to European political hegemony were justifiable on the basis of German cultural superiority.[3] Thus, under
the direction of Kiel University professor of law Paul Ritterbusch,
the "Kriegeinsatz der Geisteswissenschaften" program was born. Its
avowed aim was "to organize spiritual opposition to the spiritual
and value-world of [Germany's] opponents." To this end, Ritterbusch and his colleagues organized a series of high-profile academic
conferences and published an ambitious monograph series. In a parallel vein, throughout occupied Europe during the 1940s the Nazis
established pseudo-scholarly "German Institutes." Centers for the
dissemination of Nazi propaganda, the institutes were supported
and staffed by major scholars of the pre-Nazi period.[4] Their aim was

to grease the wheels of the Nazi occupation by convincing vanquished European elites of Germany's cultural superiority.

The case of Gadamer's mentor, Martin Heidegger, has received the greatest measure of attention. Documents recently made available in volume 16 of his *Gesamtausgabe* show how profoundly the philosopher had internalized then-fashionable Nazi racial ideology. In his capacity as rector of Freiburg University, Heidegger actively lobbied the provincial minister of culture for a chair in "Race Studies and Genetics." The "command structure [Befehlskraft] of the new German reality," argued Heidegger, should be based on principles of "inheritance" and "health," which are in turn dependent on the historical and political development of a Volk. To preserve the health of the state, continues Heidegger, questions of euthanasia should be seriously contemplated.[5] Such remarks make clear that the customary attempts to establish an absolute thematic disjunction between Heidegger's own "fundamental ontology" and Nazi racial doctrines no longer hold water.

Additional facts concerning Gadamer's involvement in Third Reich politics have also come to light. In his autobiography Gadamer grudgingly admits to having signed an internationally circulated petition of support for Hitler, organized by German university professors in November 1933. (The occasion for the petition was Hitler's referendum on Germany's withdrawal from the League of Nations—the first step on a long road to international lawlessness.) Petitions of this nature conferred an invaluable measure of legitimacy upon the regime in the eyes of Germany's educated elite (the proverbial *Bildungsbürgertum*) during the initial tenuous months of the regime's existence. Three years later Gadamer voluntarily enrolled in a Nazi camp for political "reeducation" for the sake of furthering his career. But the philosopher selectively avoids mentioning that he had joined the National Socialist Teachers' Association (Nationalsozialistschen Lehrerbund)—also in 1933—suggesting the possibility of a deeper commitment to the politics of the regime than his autobiographical retrospective indicates. (Remarkably, in his recently published, five-hundred-page biography of Gadamer, Jean Grondin also neglects to mention this fact, thereby remaining faithful to the selective memory of his protagonist.)[6]

Amid such sensational recent findings concerning the role of the humanities during the Third Reich, one moment in particular stands out. During the heated discussions at the aforementioned 1998 German *Historikertag,* an impassioned Hans Mommsen stepped to the podium to urge his fellow historians once and for all to set aside their customary rationalizations and defense mechanisms. For decades German scholars had relied on a wide range of circumlocutions and half-truths to avoid a direct confrontation with their guild's misdeeds. In light of the new disclosures, argued Mommsen, to speak euphemistically of mere "affinities" to National Socialism would no longer suffice. The scholars in question had, to all intents and purposes, made the Nazi worldview their own.[7]

As a result of these new discoveries, one would be justified (to invoke a famous metaphor) in speaking of a "Copernican turn" in our awareness concerning the relationship between German scholarship and National Socialism. Intellectual collaboration, once thought to be the exception, has turned out to be the rule. Just as the myth of the "apolitical," ideologically impervious Wehrmacht has in recent years come to grief with the controversial Wehrmacht exhibit sponsored by the Hamburg Institute for Social Research, the allegation that the German professions remained immune to the Third Reich's ideological blandishments has proved equally untenable.

One concrete result of the new case studies of intellectual collaboration across the disciplines has been the realization that our traditional interpretive paradigm no longer suffices. In the past, researchers investigating the parameters of scholarly collaboration adhered to an overly narrow definition and concept of what it meant to "participate." Thus, unless it could be proved that an individual was a dyed-in-the-wool Nazi—becoming a Party member as well as having internalized the Nazi worldview in its most extreme manifestations—support for the regime could be discounted as qualified, partial, or insincere. Given the fundamentally syncretic and protean character of Nazi ideology, however, adherence to an overly restrictive definition of Nazism was bound to lead investigators astray.[8] Hence, for decades a common "strategy of exoneration" among a politically compromised German professorate has been the time-honored refrain, "But he wasn't a *real* Nazi." But, if it has demonstrated anything, recent research concerning the participation of German scholars in the Nazi experiment has shown time and again not only that one did not need to be a "genuine Nazi" to play a significant role in the regime's misdeeds, but also that the notion of a narrowly circumscribed definition of what it meant to be a Nazi is a red herring. Thus, throughout its twelve-year existence, the regime manifested a certain ideological pluralism: traditional German nationalists, radical conservatives, racists, and anti-Semites of all stripes combined to form an alliance that proved responsible for its stunning domestic and foreign policy triumphs. Yet, as Allied troops discovered to their surprise shortly after the German collapse of May 8, 1945, suddenly no "genuine Nazis" could be found in the whole of Germany. For twelve years, the entire scholarly community had subsisted in a state of "inner emigration."

Predictably, scholars with political ambitions who actively tried to usurp or influence the regime's ideological orientation (the cases of Heidegger, Carl Schmitt, and Ernst Krieck come to mind) met with strong resistance, and in some cases censure, from Party higher-ups. In essence, as long as scholars refrained from openly criticizing the regime, endorsed the ideological superiority of German Kultur, and unequivocally rejected both communism and liberalism, political interference from above remained minimal. Ironically, scholars like Gadamer who lacked strong political convictions and who were able nevertheless to meet the regime's basic ideological criteria halfway, often stood a better chance of prospering than those who harbored more dogmatic political beliefs.

Moreover, especially among scholars, the threshold of "belonging" was never very high. The regime quickly realized that it would have been foolhardy and self-defeating to tolerate the participation of ardent Nazis alone. This quasi-pragmatic orientation was one that the National Socialist leadership also applied to other strategic branches of German society such as the Wehrmacht and the civil service. Had a narrow standard of political allegiance been invoked, the attendant disruptions to the German university system (including, presumably, sweeping dismissals on ideological grounds) surely

would have been massive. As in many other cases, in the sphere of
higher education the Nazis often valued considerations of stability
over absolute ideological rectitude—whose terms proved difficult
to define in any event. Thus, "in lieu of a [central] institution capable
of declaring certain [ideological] positions obligatory, thereby providing conformist scholars with clear guidelines, a thoroughgoing
Nazification of pedagogy and scholarship was hardly conceivable."[9]
This malleable, ideological "gray zone" was especially characteristic
of the *Geisteswissenschaften,* where "the borders between a traditional, national-conservative orientation, with its inclination toward
nationalism and its penchant for 'Deutschtümelei,' and an unequivocal National Socialist orientation" remained fluid.[10]

Those who attempt to account for the success of the Nazi dictatorship in narrowly ideological terms misconstrue the nature of the
phenomenon they seek to explain. After all, in Germany's last free
elections prior to the advent of one-party rule (November 1932),
the Nazis garnered a mere 33.1 percent of the vote (a decline of
4.3 percent from their July 1932 high water mark). Since the Nazis
could not rule by terror alone, where did the rest of their support
come from? One of the indispensable keys to their political triumph
lay in the cooperation of traditional German conservatives—the
segment of German society with which Gadamer identified politically. Although conservative nationalists might have had serious
reservations about Nazi methods—the SA's uncouth brutality and
Hitler's rabid anti-Semitism—like the Nazis, they were fundamentally convinced of the bankruptcy of the liberal "system" and of the
need for an authoritarian resolution of Germany's political instability. In the last analysis, they found a sufficient number of common-
alties with the Nazi platform to make common cause with the
regime. Had this not been the case, the regime's lifespan would
have undoubtedly been far briefer. As Hans-Ulrich Wehler observed
in his classic study of the German *Sonderweg,* it was the *traditional
German elites*—the army, Prussian Junkers, major industrialists, and,
not least of all, the mandarin "spiritual reactionaries" who had
become influential antidemocratic "opinion leaders"—who in 1933
helped place Hitler in the saddle. As Wehler observes, under Nazi

rule, "since continuity in the imperial bureaucracy and the army, in the education system and the political parties, in the economy and its pressure groups was largely preserved, one thing at least was assured: the traditional power-elites were able to depute the stirrup-holders for Hitler."[11]

Marburg Days

By all accounts the career of Hans-Georg Gadamer was an unambiguous success story. An encomium written on the occasion of his ninety-fifth birthday fittingly identified him as "the most successful philosopher of the Federal Republic."[12] Born at the century's turn in Marburg, Gadamer's autobiography recounts a tranquil boyhood punctuated by convulsive technological change: "the transition from gas to electric lighting, the first automobiles . . . the first Zeppelin over Breslau, the sinking of the Titanic." When his father, a chemistry professor, compared the fabled aquatic catastrophe to the devastation of an entire village, the worldly youth responded (by his own admission, insensitively), "Oh well, just a bunch of farmers."[13] A contrite apology to the family housekeeper, who had been listening in the wings nearby, was promptly mandated.

But the most influential event of his boyhood would clearly be his intellectual pilgrimage to Marburg, the legendary bastion of neo-Kantianism. Yet, two events of the 1910s combined to shatter the neo-Kantian trust in the trinity of reason, science, and progress: the advent of war and the philosopher Hermann Cohen's death in 1918. Among German youth it was imperative that the mindset responsible for the European conflagration be surmounted. A full-fledged Nietzschean "transvaluation of values" took hold. Thus, in 1919, as the young Gadamer established his new philosophical base, a variety of iconoclastic cultural influences permeated the otherwise subdued corridors of university life, ideas and orientations that were far removed from the arid intellectualism of Marburg neo-Kantian stalwarts Cohen, Paul Natorp, and their followers. In "Reflections on My Philosophical Journey," Gadamer describes the mood of cultural tumult:

Under the influence of a new reception of Kierkegaard in Germany, the claim to truth at that time called itself "existential." Existentialism dealt with a truth which was supposed to be demonstrated not so much in terms of universally held propositions or knowledge as in the immediacy of one's own experience and in the absolute singularity of one's own existence. Dostoevsky, above all others, seemed to us to have known about this. The red Piper editions of his novels glared on every writing desk. The letters of van Gogh and Kierkegaard's *Either—Or,* which he wrote against Hegel, beckoned to us, and of course behind all the boldness and riskiness of our existential engagement—as a still scarcely visible threat to the romantic traditionalism of our culture—stood the titanic figure of Friedrich Nietzsche with his ecstatic critique of everything, including the illusions of self-consciousness. Where, we wondered, was a thinker whose philosophical power was adequate to the powerful initiatives put forward by Nietzsche?[14]

Some four years later the students' prayers for a Nietzsche *redivivus* were answered with the arrival of Martin Heidegger.

According to Gadamer, Heidegger—"this guy from the Black Forest who had grown up on skis"—cut quite a figure in Marburg, holding lectures and seminars in the suspenders and knee-breeches of his native Schwarzwald (dubbed by his students the "existential outfit") instead of the customary black coat and tie.[15] To his credit, Gadamer's reminiscences of the Marburg Heidegger cenacle from time to time interject the appropriate measure of irony. For Heidegger was an adept seducer of youth—his lectures had a "narcotic" effect on students—and the faithful engaged in a good deal of intellectual mimicry and posturing. At one point during a seminar, Heidegger singled out a provocative statement by Schelling—"The fear of life itself drives human beings out of the center"—then declared, "Name for me one single sentence from Hegel that measures up to this sentence in depth!" "Everywhere," recollects Gadamer, "there were students who had learned a thing or two from the Master— mostly the way he cleared his throat and the way he spit." Heidegger's followers frequently imitated their mentor's trademark variety of "radical questioning" and penchant for philosophical "Destruction." Yet, as Gadamer freely avows, their pompous rhetoric could barely conceal their own "substantive emptiness." While listening to Heidegger's lectures during the 1930s, Gadamer himself occasionally wondered whether the philosopher's new pagan-combative idiom consisted of "expressions of thought or announcements of a neo-heathen mythology." Heidegger, for his part, was once compelled to break off a convoluted train of thought in mid-sentence, declaring in frustration: "This is all Chinese!" In Gadamer's own case, friends fondly coined a new unit of scientific measurement, the "Gad," to designate the number of unnecessary complications marring a philosophical explanation.[16]

Given the mood of apocalypse and catastrophe that prevailed amid the political upheaval and civil unrest following World War I, it was as though Heidegger's ponderous philosophical discourse had a tailor-made audience among postwar German youth. While Germany's mandarin podium-philosophers persisted in their traditional highly formalized and scholastic manner, Heidegger's lexicon was littered with terms suggestive of the "experience" that German youth of the day craved: "anxiety," "care," "authenticity," and, of particular relevance to the front generation, "Being-toward-Death." But equally important was that when Heidegger read "classic" texts, such as those of the Greeks, he viewed them as anticipations of contemporary questions and problems; for these reasons, above all, German youth turned to Heidegger for philosophical guidance. His courses were suffused with questions about "existence" and "life" that his fellow philosophy professors seemed too timid to raise. In the end it was this spirit that motivated Gadamer to become a classicist. As Gadamer observes:

> What a contrast to the bloodless academic philosophizing of the time, which moved within an alienated Kantian or Hegelian language and attempted once again either to bring transcendental idealism to perfection or else to overcome it! Suddenly Plato and Aristotle appeared as co-conspirators and comrades in arms to everyone who had found that playing around with systems in academic philosophy had become obsolete. . . . From the Greeks one could learn that thinking in philosophy does not, in order to be

responsible, have to adopt as system-guiding the thought that there must be a final grounding for philosophy in a highest principle; on the contrary, it stands always under the guiding thought that it must be based on primordial world experience, achieved through the conceptual and intuitive power of the language in which we live. The secret of the Platonic dialogues, it seems to me, is that they teach us this.[17]

Under the tutelage of the Marburg classicist Paul Friedländer, Gadamer successfully defended a habilitation study on "Plato's Dialectical Ethics" in 1928. He now awaited a "call" to a professorship, but it would be a while in coming, not least of all because of Germany's rapidly declining political fortunes. Gadamer diligently busied himself with his teaching duties and his antiquarian philological interests, by his own avowal oblivious to the gathering political storm. When asked by a friend whether he had read a book on current events, he responded demurely, "I basically read books that are at least only two thousand years old."[18] When 1933 rolled around, Gadamer, like so many other privileged Germans, simply failed to take seriously Nazi bombast and histrionics:

> It was a terrible awakening, and we could not absolve ourselves of having failed to perform adequately as citizens. We had underrated Hitler and his kind. . . . Not one of us had read *Mein Kampf*, although I had paid attention to Alfred Rosenberg's *The Myth of the Twentieth Century* . . . the intellectual basis of National Socialism. . . . It was a widespread conviction in intellectual circles that Hitler in coming to power would deconstruct the nonsense he had used to drum up the movement, and we counted the anti-Semitism as part of this nonsense. We were to learn differently.[19]

Within weeks of Hitler's accession to power, German university politics changed dramatically. Jewish and left-leaning professors were dismissed en masse. The *Gleichschaltung* of the German university system was in full gear, with Gadamer's mentor, Heidegger, leading the way in Freiburg. In keeping with the Nazi conception of "political science," political criteria had become one of the keys to university advancement. One by one Gadamer's esteemed Jewish friends and colleagues were forced to emigrate. "When [Karl] Löwith went abroad to an uncertain future," Gadamer recalls, "one felt ashamed to remain. . . . It remained difficult to keep the right balance, not to compromise oneself so far that one would be dismissed and yet still to remain recognizable to colleagues and students." That this juggling act would prove impossible soon became apparent: in 1934, when Richard Kroner, a Hegel scholar and long-time friend, was dismissed from the University of Kiel on racial grounds, Gadamer stepped in with alacrity to fill his position. Gadamer's retrospective gloss on the situation seems remarkably oblivious to the dire political context at hand. "For me this was a rich teaching period," he blithely opines.[20]

Since the Kiel position was temporary, Gadamer was compelled to find other mechanisms for self-advancement. Or, as he characterizes his professional dilemma at the time, "So in the 1930s my little ship had run aground. How I was to get it afloat again was a difficult question." But a solution was forthcoming. In 1936 he voluntarily attended a political "rehabilitation" camp run by the National Socialist *Dozentenbund* (University Lecturers Association). All in all, the situation proved none too demeaning and, in the end, it produced the desired result, securing Gadamer professorial appointments at Marburg (1937) and Leipzig (1938). During an excursion to Tannenberg that interrupted the daily routine ("morning gymnastics, competitive games, marches with nationalistic singing, and all that kind of paramilitary nonsense"), the young philologist was able to glimpse the Chaplinesque figure of the Führer himself: "He impressed me as being simple, indeed awkward, like a boy playing at being a soldier."[21]

Gadamer's successful march through the German university system was a tribute to his own Schweikian resilience. Political regimes would come and go, but Gadamer would abide, his reputation relatively unscathed. As the doctrine of "total war" took hold following the 1941 invasion of the Soviet Union, Nazi higher-ups seemed somewhat less concerned with questions of ideological fidelity in the rarefied sphere of university life. As Gadamer explains in a 1990 interview, "The real Nazis had no interest in us [philosophy professors] whatsoever."[22] Having never joined the party, after the war he was one of the few professors whose conduct was deemed entirely beyond reproach. Initially, Leipzig was occupied by American troops, and Gadamer became dean of the philosophy faculty. In fall 1945 the Soviets moved in. When his predecessor was deemed politically unacceptable, Gadamer became university rector. In the ensuing years he witnessed a series of political purges of university personnel—this time made in the name of the political left—that he found as repugnant as those that had occurred under the Nazis. One colleague's timely protest, "We didn't take off the brown straitjacket in order to put on a red straitjacket," predictably fell on deaf ears.[23] Gadamer spent a good deal of his time as rector arranging for more talented colleagues to find positions at universities in the West. Clearly, his own days in Leipzig were numbered. He thus seized the first available opportunity to flee to the Allied zone, accepting a post in Frankfurt in 1947. Two years later he resettled permanently in Heidelberg, which became the seat of his postwar renown.

Tradition and "Positive Prejudice"

In 1960 Gadamer published, to wide acclaim, *Truth and Method,* the treatise that would establish his a reputation as the doyen of "philosophical hermeneutics": an approach to understanding texts that emphasized the irreducible situatedness of the interpreter's standpoint. The modern discipline of hermeneutics began in the early 1800s with the theologian Friedrich Scheiermacher, who realized that authoritative texts, such as the Bible, no longer spoke to us in an unmediated and unproblematic way. Instead, owing to the passage of time as well as series of "dogmatic" interpretive distortions (largely at the hands of clerical authority), our comprehension of such texts was enshrouded in a palimpsest of misunderstanding. Thus, Schleiermacher defined hermeneutics as the art of *avoiding misunderstanding* to gain access to the unadulterated original meaning of texts. Schleiermacher thereby displayed an intrinsically positive orientation toward "the past"—in contrast with the presumptions and distortions of "modernity"—that was characteristic of German romanticism. Yet, for Gadamer, Schleiermacher's one-sided emphasis on "avoiding misunderstanding" precipitated him into a "objectivistic delusion" that would become one of the defining features of all subsequent hermeneutics: the delusion that one could conceivably gain access to the definitive truth of a text or an historical epoch in immediate, pristine fashion. According to Gadamer, this new hermeneutic premium on "method" itself represented a deformation, one that was perpetuated by Schleiermacher's successors among the German historical school. The hermeneutic desire to recapture the past as such echoed in Leopold von Ranke's famous methodological prescription: to recover the past "the way it really was"—that is, without a trace of subjective input by the historian. Gadamer correctly perceived the inordinate naiveté of this belief: so little removed were Ranke and his cohorts from contemporary traditions that their approach became paradigmatic for German nationalist historiography as a whole, with its glorification of the "great man," the state, *Machtpolitik,* and so forth. In his *Introduction to the Human Sciences* (1883) Wilhelm Dilthey stressed the methodological incommensurabilities between the natural sciences and the human sciences (Geisteswissenschaften)—whereas the former sought airtight, law-like explanations, the latter sought empathetically "to understand" manifestations of human life (Verstehen). Yet Dilthey ultimately succumbed to a similar delusion: while correctly criticizing the objectivistic approach of the natural sciences, he, too, believed that Verstehen entailed the denial of one's own historical standpoint for the sake of remaining faithful to the being-in-itself of the object of historical study.

It was Gadamer's encounter with Heidegger in Marburg during the 1920s that revealed the possibility of how one might surmount the methodological failings of the historicist tradition. Heidegger's characterization of Dasein as a "Being-in-the-world" governed by a series of unsurpassable existential modalities—"thrownness," "care," "discourse," "Angst," "everydayness," and so forth—represented a fundamental challenge to the scientific pretensions of modern thought. Whereas the Cartesian tradition held that all aspects of human finitude should be swept away in favor of the ideal of "absolute certainty," Heidegger stood this desideratum on its head by claiming that such traces of finitude served as the indispensable means by which the world and everything in it were revealed to us. Thus, what the philosophy of "method" interpreted as a hindrance, Heidegger took to be fundamental. As Gadamer puts it in *Truth and Method,* "What appeared first to be simply a barrier that cut across the traditional concept of science and method, or a subjective condition of access to historical knowledge, now becomes *the center of fundamental inquiry.*"[24] Whereas the historicists had sought to efface all aspects of their own historical situatedness, Gadamer, following Heidegger, argued instead that historicity was an indispensable feature of our Being-in-the-world. Instead of trying to escape it, we should acknowledge it in order to set the stage for a fruitful dialogue with the historical past.

> History does not belong to us, but we belong to it. Long before we understand ourselves through the process of self-examination, we understand ourselves in a self-evident way in the family, society and the state in which we live. The focus of subjectivity is a distorting mirror. The self-awareness of the individual is only a flickering in the closed circuits of historical life. That is why the prejudices of the individual, far more than his judgments, constitute the historical reality of his being.[25]

Thus, while earlier philosophers had viewed "objectivity" as a methodological desideratum, Gadamer insisted that the quest for absolute criteria did more harm than good. Instead, he argued that the essence of historical understanding lay in a never-ending process of dialogic interchange between interpreter and text, a "fusion of horizons," as it were, between past and present.

One of the more controversial features of *Truth and Method* concerned Gadamer's rehabilitation of the notion of "prejudice." Whereas the Enlightenment idea of truth as objectivity belittled prejudice as little more than "false consciousness," Gadamer reconceived it as an essential component of our intellectual situatedness or Being-in-the-world. "It is not so much our judgments," he remarks, "as *our prejudices* that constitute our being. This is a provocative formulation, for I am using it to restore to its rightful place *a positive concept of prejudice* that was driven out of our linguistic usage by the French and English Enlightenment. . . . Prejudices are not necessarily unjustified and erroneous, so that they inevitably distort the truth. In fact, the historicity of our existence entails that prejudices, in the literal sense of the word, constitute the initial directedness of our whole ability to experience."[26] This impassioned defense of the productive power of prejudice—one that, admittedly, sounds strange to contemporary ears—forms a crucial link between Gadamer's thought before and after World War II.

Yet another disputed aspect of *Truth and Method*—and one very much related to the justification of prejudice just discussed—concerned Gadamer's ardent vindication of the authority of tradition as opposed to the analytical (and hence, tradition-destroying) capacities of Enlightenment. Another one of the Enlightenment's baleful prejudices, argues Gadamer, was its endemic antipathy toward authority—a disposition that was historically responsible for unleashing an omnivorous political radicalism. "Thus," claims Gadamer, "the recognition of authority is always connected with the idea that what authority states is not irrational and arbitrary, but can be seen, in principle, to be true. This is the essence of the authority claimed by the teacher, the superior, the expert. The prejudices they implant are legitimated by the person himself. Their validity demands that one should be biased in favor of the person who presents them. . . . Thus the essence of authority belongs in the context of a theory of prejudices free from the extremism of the Enlightenment." "We owe to romanticism," he continues, "this correction of the Enlightenment, that tradition has a justification that is outside the arguments of reason and in a large measure determines our institutions and our attitudes."[27]

The Heideggerian origins of Gadamer's vaunted defense of "authority" and "tradition"—a defense that was, moreover, especially suspect in a German ideological context—came through in his discussions of the "happening of tradition," which suggested that we were more or less passively fated to accept what was transmitted by tradition. In essence, tradition "befalls us," and our job is to acquiesce by recognizing its superior power. As Gadamer puts it, "Not what we are doing, not what we ought to be doing but *what happens with us beyond our wanting and doing,* is at stake. . . . Understanding itself should be thought of not so much as an action of subjectivity but as *entering into the happening of tradition* in which past and present are constantly mediated."[28]

Suffice it to say that an imperative concern for social justice or human rights was not prominent features of Gadamer's storied and voluminous treatise. The chief defect of Gadamer's hermeneutics, then, is its uncritical veneration of the powers of tradition. His denigration of the capacities of "insight" and "reflection" are cornerstones of the Counter-Enlightenment worldview: since human insight is intrinsically untrustworthy, the best course is to limit its use as much as possible. Should a confrontation between authority and reason arise, it is always safer to err on the side of authority. But this is a recipe more appropriate for errant schoolchildren than for mature citizens. In the last analysis, and though Gadamer himself might be loath to admit it, *Truth and Method* purveys many standard components of the "German ideology." Thus, the main concepts of "philosophical hermeneutics" harbor an eerie affinity with worldview of German particularism. As Jürgen Habermas pointed out in an important review of Gadamer's tome, Gadamer belittles the legacy of philosophical "reflection" bequeathed by German idealism "because he has taken over an undialectical concept of Enlightenment from the limited perspective of the German nineteenth century; and with it he has adopted an attitude which vindicated for us Germans a dangerous pretension to superiority separating us from Western tradition."[29]

The "Political Plato"

The foregoing sketch more or less recapitulates the official version of Gadamer's philosophical autobiography, as recounted by the philosopher himself in *Philosophical Apprenticeships* and "Reflections on My Philosophical Journey" (the featured introductory essay in *The Philosophy of Hans-Georg Gadamer*). The official version is, as far as it goes, "true," although it is also radically incomplete. And as we will see, this incompleteness ultimately undermines the accuracy of Gadamer's account, its claim to being "true."

In his autobiographical jottings and in interviews, Gadamer always portrays himself as having been a "liberal."[30] In a German context, this means being a "national liberal," a supporter of rule of law and parliamentary process, though someone who is not opposed to the realization of national aims via the traditional methods of power politics. (Max Weber, who, following Germany's declaration of war in August 1914, showed up to his famous Sunday seminar in full military dress, was an exemplar of National Liberalism). Attention to Gadamer's few published writings during the 1930s and 1940s, however, yields a different portrait of his political orientation. And whereas he never displayed much outright sympathy for the Nazis, with their petty bourgeois, "strength through joy" histrionics—unlike Heidegger, Gadamer's own refined family background seems to have barred this option—there is little doubt that the philosopher bought into more of the German ideology than he was willing to avow in retrospect.

In this regard, two texts he published during the Nazi years are crucial. The first, a seemingly scholarly study of one of the most controversial episodes of Plato's *Republic,* the banishment of the poets in Book II, "Plato and the Poets," appeared in 1934, one year after the onset of the Nazi dictatorship. The second text, a 1941 lecture presented at the German Institute in Paris (and the only monograph Gadamer published during the Nazi years), is suggestively titled *Volk and History in Herder's Thought.*

To appreciate the argument of "Plato and the Poets"—a remarkably forceful vindication of Plato's decision to send the poets packing—some background concerning the political orientation of the German classics profession is in order.

Under the tutelage of Johann Winckelmann, German scholars conceived the discipline of modern classics in the eighteenth century. Winckelmann's celebrated definition of Greek art—"noble simplicity and calm grandeur"—sounded the clarion call for the neoclassical revival, liberating art from the convolutions of the baroque and rococo. But Winckelmann's characterization, ingenuous in many respects, failed to survive the onslaught of German romanticism, which took the measurelessness of the inner self as its standard. Yet it was Nietzsche who, in the *Birth of Tragedy* (1872), delivered the coup de grace to the harmonious, Winckelmannian understanding of the Greek temperament, by revealing a frenzied, Dionysian dimension of Greek art that earlier accounts had essentially repressed.

Nietzsche's insight into the demonic side of the Greek spirit had enormous influence on fin-de-siècle philosophy and literature, but, at the time, his iconoclastic findings, effectively parried by Wilamowitz-Moellendorf, left the staid discipline of classical philology more or less unmoved. Instead, the preponderance of German Hellenists were content to pursue their antiquarian passions and maintain their traditional, Olympian professional bearing.

Such mandarinesque detachment would quickly unravel following the dislocations of the Great War. Like their brethren in other disciplines (e.g., the sociologist Werner Sombart in "Traders and Heroes," the philosopher Max Scheler in "The Genius of War and the German War"), German classicists, intoxicated with the "ideas of 1914," hazarded their own reflections on the war's meaning and import from a *national* point of view (it was at this point, moreover, that National Liberalism ceased to be "liberal"). Study of the classics had reached a point of no return. In the 1920s the discipline would undergo a powerful ideological transformation that made the transition to a brown-clad *Volksgemeinschaft* fifteen years hence more or less fluid.

All along the classics profession had administered a good dose of mythologizing. Its widespread, if unofficial, credo had been that modern Germany was ancient Hellas *redivivus*. In the end, such delusions proved far from innocent, since they were frequently coupled with a series of unwholesome geopolitical assumptions: as Greece reborn, Germany represented the salvation for a post-revolutionary Europe in the throes of accelerated cultural decline. Moreover, this German claim to uniqueness was polemically directed against those "decadent" Latin nations that, two thousand years earlier, had diluted Greek greatness by Romanizing it. In this way, German classicists perpetuated and nurtured the unsavory ideology of German singularity.

Retracing the discipline's national-authoritarian reconfiguration during the 1920s and 1930s, one finds that one of the worst offenders was the renowned Hellenist Werner Jaeger. Shortly after the Great War's end, Jaeger offered the following reflections on the continuities between "Arminius" (the legendary conqueror of the Roman legions in the Teutoburger forest) and General Ludendorff: "Only centuries later would the German spirit come into its own. . . . The previously assimilated elements of antiquity gradually sank into the unconscious to become the substratum of our material culture. But in the bright light of conscious creation that the German race now undertakes [i.e., in the war effort] antiquity is reborn, now in a much higher, more spiritual sense as the leader and stimulus of the new Volk-culture [Führerin und Anregerin der werdenden Volkskultur]."[31] Jaeger's remarks are indicative of the extent to which considerations of "race" began to supplant more traditional notion of spirit (Geist) in German cultural discourse.

In the 1920s Jaeger initiated an influential movement within classics called the "Third Humanism." The first two humanisms were ancient Greece and the Renaissance; modern Germany purportedly embodied the third. With the help of like-minded classics scholars, Jaeger was enormously successful in promoting an ideological reconfiguration of Plato studies: whereas, heretofore, classicists had concentrated on Plato's cosmology and metaphysics, Jaeger's "New Humanism" (as it was occasionally called) redirected attention to the "political Plato"—above all, to *The Republic,* often tellingly translated into German as *Der Staat.*[32] The stated goal of the Third Humanism was to highlight the contemporary *political* relevance of antiquity and thereby force the antiquarians in the discipline to the sidelines. In *The Republic,* with its celebration of Spartan virtues such as "breeding" and "rank," along with its characterization of the "guardians" as a biologically superior warrior caste, the Third Humanists thought they had discovered a virtual blueprint for a new authoritarian state to replace the widely despised Weimar Republic. Among the political Platonists, Socrates' vivid portrayal of the follies of democratic rule in *The Republic,* book VIII—a state of political anarchy in which the appetites that govern the nether realm of the human soul consume men and women, thereby rendering "virtue" and a well-ordered polis impossible—now appeared as an uncanny anticipation of the political chaos into which Germany's fledgling republic had recently descended.[33] Plato's Seventh Letter, in which the philosopher movingly describes the necessity for lovers of wisdom to abandon spiritual pursuits and enter politics for the sake of the greater good of the polis that had nurtured them—despite the intellectual compromises thereby entailed—also took on special mystagogical import for the New Humanists. It was reconceived as a furtive commission for the German spiritual elite, who would succeed politically where Plato, in his ill-conceived efforts with the tyrant Dionysos at Syracuse, had failed. It was precisely in this sense that in 1933 Jaeger praised Plato as the "state-founder and lawgiver of our generation."[34]

Jaeger and his fellow Third Humanists, in conjunction with ideologically like-minded scholars from other disciplines, were remarkably successful in promoting an authoritarian reconceptualization of the hallowed educational ideal of *Bildung*—the German equivalent of the Greek *Paideia* (which was also the title of Jaeger's three-volume *chef d'oeuvre*). Dating back to the days of Goethe, Schiller, and Wilhelm von Humboldt, Bildung, in its traditional employment, stressed the notion of individual self-cultivation, culminating in the ideal of well-rounded, cosmopolitan subjectivity. Under the revisionist push of Jaeger and the political Platonists, however, Bildung was refashioned to suggest that individuals, if left to themselves, were powerless to attain such ends. Instead, according to the new "political" criteria promoted by Jaeger et al., the state now played an indispensable role in facilitating what was formerly a strictly individual achievement. Jaeger vigorously opposed the individualistic orientation of Enlightenment humanism, which he viewed as manifestly inferior to the Nazi ideal of state-fostered political Bildung. "Humanism," claimed Jaeger, "is an ideology whose roots date back to the rational cultural system of the eighteenth-century West European Enlightenment and is therefore incompatible with the intellectual historical presuppositions of National Socialism."[35]

Thus it would be only a slight exaggeration to say that the political *Gleichschaltung* (cooptation) of the German classics profession occurred before the Nazi seizure of power. Indeed, among Third Reich classicists the idea of *Staatsgesinnung*—a stress on the importance of a positive attitude towards the state—in stark contrast with the weakness and vacillation of state authority during Weimar, would become a commonplace.[36] As Plato-scholar Kurt Hildebrandt observed enthusiastically, "The Greek doesn't bind himself to God and the world as an individual; he becomes a man through and by virtue of his belonging to the State."[37] The notion that by themselves, individuals count for naught but only achieve fulfillment by virtue of the greater sense of purpose transmitted by the state encouraged classicists, as well as humanists of all stripes, to greet the advent of the Third Reich with open arms. This idea had been propounded not only by German radical conservatives but also by traditional conservatives like Hegel, whose *Rechtsphilosophie* famously celebrated the state as the repository of "ethical substance" (Sittlichkeit) lacking among individuals: "The state is the actuality of the Ethical Idea. It is ethical mind qua the substantial will manifest and reveled to itself. . . . The state is absolutely rational inasmuch as it is the actuality of the substantial will which it possesses in the particular self-consciousness [i.e., the monarch] once that consciousness has been raised to the consciousness of universality."[38] Hence, across the political spectrum of the German right, there was ample reason to greet the Nazi doctrine of Machtpolitik, vindicating the idea of a strong state, as both the realization of a political program with deep roots in German history and an indication of a teleological affinity between Germans and the ancient Greeks. That in *The Republic* eugenics plays a central role in maintaining a healthy body politic and in avoiding the chaos and disunity associated with political "degeneracy" seemed to certify a preestablished harmony between Plato and National Socialist racial policies and doctrines.

Predictably, following the consolidation of Hitler's dictatorship, the political Platonists proceeded to surpass the rhetorical bellicosity of their earlier efforts. The philosopher Hans Heyse declared that Plato's *Republic* was the "Ur-form of the idea of the Reich."[39] Among ancient historians, the notion that Pericles and Hitler led "parallel lives" became almost a commonplace.[40] Under Jaeger's tutelage, the Association of German Philologists proclaimed, "The goal of German education is *German man* as a member of the *Volks-gemeinschaft.*"[41] And Jaeger himself, writing in the Nazi organ *Volk im Werden,* exulted over the conquest and subjugation of traditional humanism, whose orientation, he claimed, had been excessively "individualistic." After fifteen years of the New Humanism, Jaeger continued, one has finally come to realize that "man of antiquity, in all the decisive aspects of his historical life, is a *political man,*" whose "humanitas" consists in his "membership in a political community."[42]

Finally, if one peruses *Paideia*—Jaeger's masterpiece, whose first volume appeared in German in 1934—one cannot help but notice the semantic affinities to the Nazi worldview. Under Alexander the Great, argues Jaeger, the Greeks began their push for "world-mastery" (Weltherrschaft), as the Nazis soon would; he contrasts Greek culture favorably with the racially and culturally inferior peoples of the Orient (it seems clear that the Jews were his intended target, even though Jaeger's second wife was herself Jewish); and he observes unabashedly that the superiority of the Greeks has its "deeper reason in the latent characteristics of race and blood."[43] (These semantic affinities with the Nazism survive only in dimly in Gilbert Highet's otherwise admirable English translation.)

Only against this sweeping ideological makeover of the German classics guild does the political subtext of Gadamer's 1934 article on "Plato and the Poets" become discernible. Although in a later interview Gadamer would characterize the field of classical philology as a "sphere of retreat" (Rückzugsgebiet) beyond the disruptions of contemporary politics, this description seriously misrepresents the facts.[44] Like most other academic disciplines in the Third Reich, classics, too, bent over backward to adapt itself to the Nazi ideal of "politicized science."[45] Gadamer's impassioned defense of Plato's expulsion of the poets places him squarely in line with the "Political Platonists" and their glorification of *The Republic* as a contemporary political model.

Gadamer was aware that given the traditional apolitical and humanistic bent of German classics, Plato's ostracism of the poets presented itself as one of the most unpalatable aspects of the philosopher's doctrine. In "Plato and the Poets" he seeks to portray this act as compatible with the needs of the contemporary "German spirit."[46] Gadamer's text is littered with a highly charged, Heideggerianized political rhetoric—"hour of decision" and "cleansing," as well as positive references to the tasks of "political guardianship"—that today comes through only dimly in English translation, but to his German contemporaries, the essay's basic political thrust would have been unmistakable. The text's repeated condemnation of Plato's intellectual foes, the Sophists, seems a clear rejection of Weimar's free-floating class of "chattering" intellectuals. (Weimar Germany, one might say, to continue the historical analogy, would be the modern equivalent of the "city of pigs" lampooned by Plato in *The Republic,* Book II). The members of Plato's academy, observes Gadamer, are "no apolitical community of scholars." Instead, they are united in their abhorrence of "the current sophistic paideia, with its encyclopedic instruction and arbitrary morals," as well as in their desire to promote *"the shaping of the political* [staatlichen] *human being."*[47] Taking an additional swipe at Weimar liberalism, Gadamer adds, "In Plato justice of the state is not founded negatively on the weakness of individuals whose prudence leads them into a contract. Instead the human being is political in a *positive* sense because he is capable of rising above his insistence on himself."[48]

Gadamer then concludes in the following vein:

> Plato's paideia is thus meant as a counterweight to the centrifugal pull of those forces of sophistic enlightenment exerted upon the state. . . . In opposition to this sophistic paideia, Plato advances a willfully and radically purified poetry, which is no longer a reflection of human life but the language of an intentionally beautiful lie. This new poetry is meant to express the ethos which prevails in the purified state in a way that is pedagogically efficacious.[49]

Clearly, "Plato and the Poets" is hardly a Nazi text. Nevertheless, Gadamer's willingness to entertain at length the precepts of "educational dictatorship" in the fateful year of 1934—the year in which Hitler was able to consolidate the gains of his first year in office (e.g., the Röhm purge, combining the offices of chancellor and president following von Hindenburg's death)—certainly gives pause.

Reflecting in 1977 on this *Jugendschrift,* Gadamer insisted that it testified to his staunch *opposition* to Nazism. To support this claim, he invokes a passage from Goethe he used as an epigraph, "He who philosophizes is out of step with the ideas of his time."[50] Yet, here, Gadamer actually misquotes himself, and in a manner that is all too revealing. Instead, the motto in full reads as follows: "Difficult though it might be to detect it, a certain polemical thread runs through any philosophical writing. He who philosophizes is not at one with the previous and contemporary world's ways of thinking of things. Thus Plato's discussions are often not only directed *to* something but also directed *against* it."[51] Given the essay's allegorical indictment of democratic cultural license, clearly, the thrust of the Goethe's maxim is directed not against the Third Reich but against its profligate predecessor, the Weimar Republic.

One of the greatest offenders in the Nazification of Plato was George-Kreis stalwart Kurt Hildebrandt. In 1920 Hildebrandt published an influential book on racial hygiene, *Norm and Degeneration of Man*. In the early 1930s he turned his attention to the Greeks with a book entitled *Plato: The Struggle of the Spirit for Power* (*Der Kampf des Geistes um die Macht*; titles of this nature were, sadly, all too typical of the times). The book is horrendous—the *Republic* is treated as a model of political dictatorship and allusions to the Nazis abound. Yet in 1935 Gadamer wrote a fulsome review of it in the *Deutsche Literarische Zeitung*, where he suggested that the book was a model of current Plato scholarship. In a later interview Gadamer offers an emphatic retrospective justification of the "political Plato" line: it derived from a "need for a model of the state in which there was a positive attitude toward the state [Staatsgesinnung]." "For this," he adds, "is something we didn't have in the Weimar Republic."[52] Moreover, when queried about the widespread reliance on racial concepts in German scholarship during the 1930s, Gadamer remains unrepentant: "Races have existed since the beginning of the world. . . . Interests in racial theory [are] absolutely legitimate." And when his interlocutor cautiously tries to steer him to safer shores—"Needless to say, one can treat cultural groups from the standpoint of the sociology of religion or cultural anthropology. . ."—Gadamer will have none of it. "All of these have racial foundations!" he insists. "Indians are not Japanese!"[53]

It is important to keep in mind that the ideological liaison between German classicists and Nazism was an entirely mutual affair. Hitler made no secret of his admiration for the Greeks, whose "monumentalism" he consciously sought to emulate in his architectural plans for the Thousand-Year Reich. "The struggle that arises today," he declared in Mein Kampf, "concerns far-reaching goals: a millennial culture is fighting for its life, one that encompasses both Greece and Germanness together."[54] And while Sparta, which he once enthusiastically referred to as "the most unsullied racial state in history," occupied a special niche in his historical thinking, he frequently singled out Athens for special praise.[55] Thus, an unpublished sketch entitled "Monumental World History" contains the subheading, "The German Revolution," followed by "Foreword: Athens–Rome."[56] In a 1920 speech, "Why Are We Anti-Semites?" he observes, with an eye to Germany's future, that the Greeks achieved their most glorious level of cultural triumph in the aftermath of their defeat of the Persians.[57] According to Albert Speer, Hitler was fond of drawing parallels between Pericles and himself: just as Pericles had built the Parthenon, he—Hitler—had constructed the Autobahns![58] In From Pericles to Hitler? the historian Beat Näf aptly summarizes the Third Reich's fascination with the ancients. "Monumental buildings, art, beauty, the sublime, racial purity, power politics, Pericles, and hero emulation—these were the ideas that connected Hitler to antiquity."[59] The philosopher Teresa Orozco, who has written the definitive study of Gadamer's political involvements during the Nazi years, takes Näf's claim a step further, "Without the ideological construction of the Greek-German axis the 'naked and the dead of the Third Reich' are inconceivable."[60]

"Volk and History in Herder's Thought"

Like classics, the field of German literary studies did its best to fall in line with the ideological requirements of the "German Revolution." Here, too, the transformation did not occur overnight. Instead, the völkisch-national tendencies prominent in German culture for 150 years merely gained the upper hand—albeit, with a new racially tinged stridency. Professors sought to highlight the purity and superiority of indigenous German literary traditions, which they were

fond of contrasting with the superficiality of "cosmopolitan" literature—so-called *Weltliteratur.* It would be foolish to underestimate
the inordinately positive roles these scholars played in legitimating
the Third Reich in the eyes of more tradition-oriented German
elites such as the *Bildungsbürgertum.*

In the search for authentic progenitors of the pan-German
worldview, a veritable industry arose around the thought of J. G.
Herder. As was true of the dominant interpretations of Plato, the
political readings of Herder's philosophy were highly selective.
Thus, whereas the early Herder had been a vociferous critic of the
Enlightenment and an advocate of cultural particularism, the
avowed cosmopolitanism of his later *Ideas for a Philosophy of History
of Mankind* was generally suppressed or ignored.[61] And although
Herder was a cultural pluralist rather than a chauvinist—in his view,
each culture was charged to develop a specific nature, and none was
intrinsically superior to any other—his German interpreters during
the 1930s and 1940s could not resist claiming his *Volk*-idea for the
National Socialist cause. For a worldview that revolved essentially
around the concept of "Volk" (*Volkstum, Volkheit, Volksseele,* and
Volksksindiviualität represent merely a partial list of the most common Nazi derivations), the union was perhaps far from unnatural.

Thus, for the German literary guild of the 1930s Herder was celebrated as a "prophet of Greater Germany," a "prophet of German
unity at the time of the Germany's tribal dispersion."[62] Since
Herder was deemed one of the spiritual "leaders" of the German
Volk (one observer referred to him as "the greatest spiritual leader
[Führer] of our nation"), comparisons with Hitler abounded.[63] In
his 1934 study, *The National Idea from Herder to Hitler,* the Germanist
Hans Dahmen summarized the reigning mood of Herder scholarship by declaring, "From Herder to Hitler—that is the fate-laden
path of the German spirit as well as the German state."[64] Scholars
frequently contended that what Herder meant by "tribe" or "blood"
(Geblüt) was a distinct harbinger of the Nazi concept of "race."[65]
Like everything else in the National Socialist state, literature, too,
had an order-preserving function—it gave expression to and solidi-
fied the life of the *Volk*—and Herder was purportedly one of the
first to realize this fact.

Gadamer's Herder monograph, *Volk and History in Herder's Thought*, fits squarely within the line of interpretation dominant during the Third Reich. Moreover, the circumstances of its composition and presentation—Gadamer wrote it in the aftermath of Germany's dramatic victory over France in 1940, and delivered it the following year as a lecture at the German Institute in Paris—raises additional questions. Such lecture trips were a common Nazi propaganda device to bolster the regime's intellectual respectability abroad. Moreover, the German Institute had been established in September 1940 according to the retrograde credo that "the 'moral renewal' of the defeated can only come from the conquerors."[66]

Gadamer's lecture openly basks in the glory of Germany's recent military triumphs. It suggests that Germany's battlefield successes are the expression of a manifestly superior culture; the French defeat, conversely, is indicative of a culture ("rationalistic" and "enlightened") clearly past its prime. As Gadamer phrases it in his opening remarks, "Only by breaking with the historical image and cultural ideal of the French [i.e., eighteenth] century could Herder attain the secret meaning for 'Volk' and 'State' of the Germans that we attribute to him today. . . . *Critique of the Enlightenment:* that was the passionate attitude that Herder shared with his great contemporaries."[67] By forsaking the "abstract shadow images" of the Enlightenment, Herder made his great discovery: that "'heart, warmth, blood, humanity, [and], life'" and not "ideas," are the "essence of history." [68] "In a century that was proud of its freedom from prejudice, Herder recognized the power of prejudice to produce happiness, insofar as it 'concentrates peoples around their respective centers.'"[69]

In this respect Herder's ideas were a stimulus to future "political will and thought." Although Herder was "no friend of the state," continues Gadamer, "neither did he have the free happiness of the individual foremost in mind." Instead, the animating idea of his thought was the *"genetic spirit and character of a Volk"*: "From Herder's new historical experience of reality there arises the idea of a living constitution that derives from the spirit of the nation. . . . His blindness to the order- and form-giving role of the absolutist state of his day turned him into a visionary of a new basic force in the sphere of the state: *the life of the Volk.* . . . . In this way the word 'Volk' gained . . . a new depth and power in Germany."[70]

Gadamer views Herder as the direct precursor of all that is significant in subsequent German intellectual life: German romanticism, Hegel's notion of the *Volksgeist,* the historical school of law. Although Herder never lived to see a unified Germany, his *völkisch* thought was a harbinger of Europe's political future. But in the end, muses Gadamer, perhaps Germany's belated development was a "precondition for the German concept of *Volk*—in contrast with the democratic shibboleths of the West—to prove its power [to form] a new social and political order."[71]

One can only imagine how Gadamer's concluding remarks were received by his (quite literally) captive audience: "Herder imparted to the German Volk . . . that which distinguishes it from all other European peoples: the depth and breadth of its historical self-consciousness." Whereas other nations have merely *one* formative, epoch-making event to their credit (in France's case, the revolution of 1789), Germany, conversely, "lives from the entire expanse of its world-historical heritage: from the passion of the Greek polis as well as the faith of early Germany, the medieval idea of the German Empire as well as the great moments of political and national unity in modern history." "In every German, whether he knows it or not," concludes Gadamer, "lives a part of Herder's soul."[72]

Gadamer's *Collected Works*—a definitive compilation of the philosopher's published writings—comprises ten volumes. *Volk and History in Herder's Thought,* however, has not been included. Although a revised version of the text was republished in 1967 as an afterward to Herder's *Yet Another Philosophy of History* (under the title "Herder and the Historical World"; it now appears in volume 4 of Gadamer's *Collected Works*), the offending passages have been struck without reference to the original text. The concept of "Volk," the intellectual focal point of the 1942 version—as well as the ceaseless encomiums to the virtues of German particularism—has been excised virtually without a trace. In the revised text, instead of celebrating "the great moments of political and national unity of modern [German] history," Gadamer speaks about the "crudest despotism" that has "burdened German history of the last two centuries."[73]

In retrospect Gadamer characterized his Herder monograph as a "purely scholarly study" that "avoided every hint of relevance to the historical present."[74] By publishing it, he even ran certain political "risks," he claimed, due to a brief discussion of the so-called "Slav chapter" in Herder's *Ideas,* in which Herder, in keeping with his belief in cultural pluralism, advocates the development of national sentiment among Slavic peoples—a taboo theme during the Nazi era. "There was trouble right away," Gadamer recalls, "because I objected to the predominance of the Nordic and Germanic races and argued in terms of the diversity of peoples, cultures, languages."[75] Yet, as we have seen, this contention is flatly contradicted by the published version of Gadamer's text, which is suffused with claims to German ideological and political superiority—hardly the work of a *résistant* or "inner emigrant." Gadamer's claims to having provided "spiritual resistance" against the regime are surely exaggerated.

In 1970 Claus Grossner, a journalist for the German weekly *Die Zeit* who had recently completed a long interview with Gadamer on the subject of contemporary politics, expressed shock upon encountering the Herder text with its plethora of politically compromising passages. "The problem is not [Gadamer's] personal integrity, concerning which I have no doubts," observed Grossner. "Instead it is the question of the extent to which a philosophy in the Heideggerian mold—that is, 'philosophical hermeneutics'—stands in a systematic relationship to social conditions that produced a totalitarian system like National Socialism."[76] Forced to comment on his fleeting involvement with the regime, Gadamer reacted defensively and, one must avow, dishonestly: while conceding that the passages in question were disreputable and that he now firmly renounced them, he added, "But have no illusions about the fact that thirty years from now all of us will renounce what's going on [politically] today."[77] In other words, things were bad with the Nazis, but things have always been bad—and always will be—so, why make a fuss? Yet from the nebulous (and extremely ahistorical) vantage point of "the eternal recurrence of catastrophe," which Gadamer seemingly adopts, the singularity of real historical events—such as the Nazi era and its crimes—vanishes into insignificance. The Third Reich becomes merely one in a never-ending series of unfortunate political circumstances, none of which, ultimately, is worth taking seriously. In this respect Gadamer's Olympian distance from day-to-day politics is typical of the entire German mandarinate, whose credo was immortalized in Thomas Mann's *Confessions of an Unpolitical Man* (1917). But the flip side of apoliticism is a potentially lethal dearth of *Zivilcourage*—one of the characteristic debilities of the Germany's educated elite or *Bildungsbürgertum*.

"Tradition Is Not An Argument"

The point of the foregoing exercise in philosophical archaeology has not been to bury Gadamer, nor, however, has it been to praise him. In part, its purpose has been to demonstrate the circumstantial complexity of the Third Reich: how difficult it was, even for well-intentioned spirits, to play along without seriously compromising themselves. As Klaus Mann shows brilliantly in his novel, *Mephisto,* too often a train of initial compromises escalates to the point where, soon, one has lost one's soul.

At the same time, our examination of Gadamer's wartime conduct cannot help but raise critical questions about his philosophy and its relationship to its times—both then and now. Gadamer's hermeneutics has never sought to conceal its fundamentally "conservative" bearing: its trust in the past as intrinsically worthy of transmission. Thus, as he remarks in a 1967 article, "The history-embracing and history-preserving element runs deep in hermeneutics, in sharp contrast to sociological interest in reflection as a means of emancipation from authority and tradition."[78] Or, as Jürgen Habermas once put it, "Hermeneutics bangs helplessly from within against the walls of tradition."[79]

The endemically "conservative" nature of the hermeneutic standpoint came across vividly in Gadamer's well-known debate with Habermas over the virtues of "ideology critique"—the so-called emancipatory interest in unmasking "false consciousness"—a standpoint that Gadamer systematically mistrusted. For Gadamer, ideology critique is redolent of the Enlightenment's "prejudice against prejudice." The French philosophes' arrogant confidence in the sovereign powers of human reason, he argued, proves destructive of history, tradition, and cultural particularity; in this respect, it is a recipe for social engineering and political disaster. As he suggests at one point in *The Philosophy of Hans-Georg Gadamer:* "A world revolution of pure reason" would be akin to the "stabilization of the world's climate . . . by means of global air conditioning."[80] From his stance in the debate over the merits of ideology critique, one sees how central certain ideological elements of the Herder monograph are to his mature thought. Herder's critique of the Enlightenment—his anti-Enlightenment willingness to "recognize the power of prejudice to produce happiness," as Gadamer puts it—is a standpoint that Gadamer has made his own.[81] In fact, a well-known article on Gadamer's thought bears the title "The Philosophy of Prejudice."[82] And in a famous chapter of *Truth and Method* Gadamer undertakes a "rehabilitation of prejudice" clearly inspired by Herder and the lineage of Counter-Enlightenment. As Gadamer unambiguously phrases the issue in his philosophical chef d'oevure, "There is one prejudice of the enlightenment that is essential to it: the fundamental prejudice of the enlightenment is *the prejudice against prejudice itself,* which deprives tradition of its power." And further: "The recognition that all understanding inevitably involves some prejudice gives the hermeneutical problem its real thrust."[83]

When all is said and done, however, one cannot help but wonder, Isn't the hermeneutical defense of "prejudice" and "authority" all too reminiscent of the "German ideology": of the familiar Counter-Enlightenment rejection of "reason," "modernity," and "autonomy" in favor of often oppressive local circumstances and traditions? As a number of commentators have suggested, "The hermeneutical change in twentieth-century philosophy . . . has led to consequences apt to reinforce those problematical features of German tradition that are opposed to Enlightenment."[84] In the face of this inflexible defense of prejudice and tradition, where indeed might one discover the critical resources necessary to combat dogmatic beliefs and extreme social injustice? From a philosophical perspective, by making inflated claims for the "universality of the hermeneutic standpoint," Gadamer has seriously confused the "validity" of norms with their "being" or "facticity." In other words, just because a norm or meaning has been transmitted to us from the past does not make it worthy of acceptance. But the ontological approach Gadamer inherited from Heidegger, one that emphasizes the "happening of tradition" as a type of inescapable "fate," predisposes one to accept meanings by virtue of their authority rather than insight. Why later generations must remain ontologically beholden the values and beliefs of previous generations is by no means clear.

In general terms, one might describe the "German ideology" as a betrayal of Kant's famous prescription that "the critical path alone is the only one available." By this maxim Kant expressed the quintessential Enlightenment conviction that inherited norms and traditions should be accepted only if they can be justified by appeals to public argument and reflection. Or, as Kant might have put it: *tradition is not an argument.* In *Critical Theory of Society,* the philosopher Albrecht Wellmer offered an appropriate riposte to Gadamer's relativistic glorification of the virtues of tradition and community when he observes:

> The Enlightenment knew what a philosophical hermeneutics forgets—that the "dialogue" which we, according to Gadamer, "are," is also a context of domination and as such precisely no dialogue. . . . The universal claim of the hermeneutic approach [can only] be maintained if it is realized at the outset that the context of tradition as a locus of possible truth and factual agreement is, at the same time, the locus of factual untruth and continued force.[85]

Examining Gadamer's case with the German catastrophe of 1933–45 in mind, one is compelled to observe that the philosopher exhibited a failure to learn. His political writings in the postwar period partake of the "metapolitical" genre: eloquent, if familiar, indictments of science, technology, and reason—of the forces of "modernity" that threaten the closedness of traditional life-worlds and the purity of the "hermeneutic situation." As he remarks in a 1966 essay, "Unavoidably, the mechanical, industrial world is expanding within the life of the individual as a sort of sphere of technical perfection. When we hear modern lovers talking to each other, we often wonder if they are communicating with words or with advertising labels and technical terms . . . of the modern industrial world."[86] To be sure, elements of this critical standpoint are necessary and important. Yet the content and direction of Gadamer's criticisms is all too reminiscent of those mandarineque indictments of bourgeois Zivilisation that were standard issue during the 1920s—unilluminating footnotes to the work of Oswald Spengler and Ludwig Klages.

When Gadamer finally descends from the terrain of metapolitics to engage the contemporary world, the results are hardly more convincing. In "The Universality of the Hermeneutic Problem," for example, he proffers a nostalgic look at the cozy relationship between "art" and "Volk" during the Nazi era: "Despite its misuse by the National Socialists, we cannot deny that the idea of art being bound to Volk involves *real insight*. A genuine artistic creation stands within a particular community, and such a community is always distinguishable from the cultured society that is informed and *terrorized* [sic!] by art criticism."[87] In one interview during the 1980s he laments (echoing Heidegger) the fact that Germany is "caught in a pincers between Russia and America"—a "choice between two evils," he calls it—and bemoans Bonn's status as a cultural giant and a political dwarf: "We are reduced to the status of a *Kulturnation*. Our goods are cultural goods, as was the case with Greece under Roman rule. . . . To come back to the theme of Europe caught in the 'pincers between Russia and America,' yes, there is a danger [in] the appeal of the American way of life. . . . And in that sense the United States is a danger to peace, because there is a sense of mission which equals that of Soviet Russia. . . ."[88] His historicist rejection of "human rights"—which are presumably too redolent of the Enlightenment search for first principles—culminates in a shortsighted endorsement of the "Soviet way," which, in the last analysis, he justifies in terms of a relativistic "right to difference": "One needs to be tolerant in the West toward the Soviet Union. Always insisting on human rights, insisting that they must accept parliamentary democracy in order to industrialize fully, that reveals only our own preoccupations, which do not reflect *their* history."[89]

In the end one sees all too clearly that the beautiful soul of the "hermeneutical consciousness" has, to its discredit, remained essentially immune to the lessons and virtues of a democratic political culture.

Conclusion

The question remains: how might one evaluate Gadamer's conduct during the Third Reich from an historical standpoint? How might one make sense of Gadamer's attitude in terms of the political spectrum of the 1930s and 1940s?

In "Der 'Führer' und seine Denker: Zur Philosophie des 'Dritten Reichs,'" (The Fuhrer and His Thinkers: On the Philosophy of the Third Reich), the philosopher Gereon Walters has suggested that philosophical collaboration with the regime fell into three main categories: Nazis, upstanding individuals (Aufrechte), and opportunists.[90] Using this classification in a suggestive article on Gadamer's activities during the Third Reich, the literary historian Frank-Rutger Hausmann is content to classify Gadamer simply as an "opportunist."[91] In many cases, however, the boundaries between these rubrics remained fluid. Individuals could (and often did) act in ways that were both opportunistic and sincere.

Moreover, in individual cases, commitment to the regime frequently fluctuated in light of its "achievements." Thus, as Walters shows, many philosophers, despite reservations about specific aspects of the Nazi program, enthusiastically greeted the 1933 *Machtergreifung* because of their basic antipathy to Western liberalism.[92] Another high tide of enthusiasm occurred in 1940, following Germany's stunning Blitzkrieg victory over France. At the time, Heidegger celebrated the German victory as indicative of both the bankruptcy of French metaphysics as well as the Nazi war machine's embodiment of the "form of mankind equal to modern technology and its metaphysical truth." The German triumph, insisted Heidegger, "is *a metaphysical act*."[93]

Gadamer penned "Volk and History in Herder's Thought" in 1940–41 amid the same outpouring of national enthusiasm. He, too, believed that the Nazi victory testified to the supremacy of the German "way" and to the inferiority of French "civilization." In retrospect, it is extremely implausible to adjudge the content of this text as "insincere." Instead, it is undeniably an expression of *conviction:* not the conviction of an ardent Nazi—which Gadamer never was—but of a genuine national conservative who had few reservations about seeing the aims of the traditional German right realized through brutal Nazi methods. (After all, "war is hell.") While Hausmann is undoubtedly correct to claim that Gadamer's professional conduct under the Third Reich (his adherence in 1933 to the Nationalsozialistschen Lehrerbund, for example) manifested opportunism, to do justice to an individual case such as Gadamer's, one must also undertake an attentive content analysis of his writings— an examination that, in an otherwise probing article, Hausmann omits. In this spirit I have concluded that "Volk and History in Herder's Thought" represents a classic vindication of the ethos of German particularism. Although it is, strictly speaking, a non-Nazi text, it exhibits the salient features of the German Sonderweg mentalité. Historically speaking, to proceed from this "mentalité" to making peace with the Nazi worldview is a relatively short step rather than an insurmountable "leap," as Gadamer's defenders have argued.[94] As historians have pointed out, the acclaim with which Hitler's *Machtergreifung* was greeted by scholars was anything but a momentary fad. Instead, it derived from intellectual tendencies that were deeply rooted in the anti-Western orientation of the German nineteenth century.[95]

Were we to proceed, as Hausmann and others have suggested, by assuming that Gadamer's conduct during the 1930s and 1940s could be accurately described as "opportunistic," this characterization still leaves us with a number of nagging, unanswered questions. How many "opportunists" does it take to stabilize a totalitarian regime? Is the moral status of "opportunism" qualitatively superior to that of "true believers" or of those who act out of conviction? What, moreover, are the ethical implications of cooperating with a regime that, in its initial months, had suppressed civil liberties and political pluralism, banned rival political parties, interned leading political opponents in concentration camps, and undertaken a series of harsh legal measures to de-emancipate its Jewish citizens? Under the circumstances does he who merely feigns cooperation in any way merit our approval? As commentators have noted, there are ethical compromises by philosophers (from Plato to Heidegger, the history of metaphysics is littered with such instances) that one is prone to forgive; yet there are other lapses that qualify as "unpardonable." In which category, then, do Gadamer's transgressions and misdeeds during the course of the Third Reich fall? After all, "A philosopher can be deceived regarding political matters; in which case he will openly acknowledge his error. But he cannot be deceived about a regime that his killed millions of Jews—merely because they were Jews—that made terror into an everyday phenomenon, and that turned everything that pertains to the ideas of spirit, freedom and truth into its bloody opposite."[96] In other words, participation in a regime whose very raison d'être was *criminal,* whose conduct was predicated on an openly avowed ideology of genocidal conquest, constitutes a "lapse" of a qualitatively higher order. What effect, then, might such an ethical lapse have on Gadamer's reputation as a thinker? On these and related questions, the majority of Gadamer's supporters, including Hausmann, are strangely silent.[97]

In "Untruth and Method: On Gadamer's Publications during the Third Reich," Hausmann undertakes a broad contextualization of Gadamer's activities during the Hitler years. To be sure, many German scholars committed more serious offenses than Gadamer, and no categorical imperative mandates that, faced with an oppressive political system, one must act heroically or become a résistant.

Nevertheless, Gadamer's major act of "enlistment" on behalf of the regime—his 1941 lecture at the German Institute in Nazi-occupied Paris—deserves closer scrutiny. What were the main ideological objectives of these institutes? To what extent did those who participated in their proceedings compromise their scholarly integrity or facilitate the Nazi goal of maintaining continental hegemony? Unless one addresses these questions head-on, the political context subtending Gadamer's cooperation with the regime will remain in obscurity.

Although the German Institutes were staffed and administered by reputable scholars (in the case of the Paris Institute, by respected "Romanists"), their objectives were purely propagandistic. By selectively celebrating the superiority of German spiritual traditions, they sought to provide a cultural justification for the Nazi drive to achieve European hegemony. Their main activities—high-level academic conferences, German language courses, prestigious guest lectures (such as Gadamer's 1941 address)—were designed to appeal to the cultural and intellectual elites of the occupied lands as an enticement to collaboration. For the Nazis firmly believed that if these opinion leaders could be won over to the German cause, the material costs and risks of occupation could be minimized.

German Institute cultural programs were intended to "soften" the image of the Nazi conquerors to detract from the sadistic realities of the German occupation. Moreover, under the cover of promoting "cultural cooperation" among apparent equals, they served as a mechanism designed to conceal the horrors to come. As Goebbels commented in a 1942 diary entry, "If the French knew what the Führer had in store for them, they would probably drop in their tracks. It's a good thing that for the time being such matters remain well hidden."[98]

Paris Institute director Karl Epting, a Romanist by training, believed that in a Nazi-dominated Europe the humanities occupied a position of supreme importance. As he observed, "Those national values the [Party] leadership is attempting to implement are most purely expressed in the Humanities [Geisteswissenchaften]."[99] In such insights and practices, the völkisch commonplace about the integral relationship between "language" and the "racial constitution of a people" found expression. Thus, the emphasis the Institutes placed on language training, far from being primarily "educational," was deemed an effective way of indoctrinating subject races in the superiority of German culture. For analogous reasons, the Paris branch also supervised a major translation project—331 titles were published—of authors deemed acceptable to the regime. The program seemed to achieve its goal, since during the occupation sales of German literature in translation increased threefold.[100]

Note, however, that the translation of works by ardent Nazis (e.g., Goebbels, Rosenberg) was actively discouraged. The architects of the German occupation believed that French opinion leaders would only skeptically receive the ideological stridency of their texts. Instead, works by mainstream German nationalists (e.g., Fichte, Hegel, Wagner, Treitschke, Weber, Sombart, and Heidegger) were preferred. Here, too, the tenor and direction of Gadamer's Herder-Schrift perfectly suited the Nazis' propagandistic aims.

The German Institute in Paris possessed a more elaborate and challenging mandate than its European sister institutions. Nazi ideology planners, from the "Amt Rosenberg" on down, felt that the major challenge to Germany's drive toward continental mastery lay with France. As the historian Eckhart Michels has observed, "The danger that France posed to National Socialist Germany's plans for European hegemony was viewed in the first instance as a *spiritual-cultural danger*."[101] Goebbels once expressed the opinion that during the next three to four hundred years Germany would occupy the vanguard cultural role that France had enjoyed during the previous 150 years. According to this vision, Berlin would become the cultural center of Europe and Paris would assume the character of a provincial town. According to one scenario for a Nazi-dominated Europe, France would be deprived of its heavy industry but allowed to produce agricultural and luxury goods to dissuade its citizens from rebelling against Nazi rule.

Yet, frequently, the Nazi brass despaired over their ability to compete with the generally perceived superiority of French culture. After all, when it came to the strategic gamesmanship of European colonialism, Germany was a perennial latecomer. Until the nineteenth century French had been the semi-official language of European diplomacy. And France's legendary "mission civilisatrice" had a pedigree dating back to the Napoleonic era. Studies commissioned by the Reich Ministry for Education showed that throughout Western Europe French remained the second language of choice. Thus, the vigorous propagandistic labors of the German Institutes undertook to convince European "hearts and minds" that, in light of the Nazis' recent victories, it behooved them to honor and respect the superiority of *German* spiritual traditions. Lastly, from a military and strategic perspective, that Germany ensured that a defeated France cast its lot with the Nazis rather than go over to the English side was essential.

The recurrent ideological leitmotif of the cultural programs sponsored by the Paris branch stressed the irreversible decline of French values such as "universal reason" and "cosmopolitanism," and the concomitant rise to prominence of the völkisch perspective embodied in the Nazi *Weltanschauung*. As Epting wrote in his introduction to one Institute publication, "One of the great sacrifices that France must make for the sake of the new Europe is the surrender of its universal cultural claims. France will no longer be thought of as a Universal Church, but rather as a particular *völkisch* unit, marked by the claims of blood and history."[102] Unsurprisingly, these were precisely the thematic concerns that Gadamer stressed in his lecture on "Volk and History in Herder's Thought." Thus, in Gadamer's choice of theme as well as his ideological orientation, the philosopher's presentation harmonized perfectly with the regime's central propagandistic intentions.

In evaluating the status of Gadamer's German Institute lecture, it is important to keep in mind the draconian nature of the Nazi occupation. This was by no means a peace among equals. According to an internal document circulated among the staff of the German Foreign Office, France's role in a future Nazi-dominated Europe was foreseen as that of an "enlarged Switzerland."[103] Needless to say, the fate that awaited the conquered nations of eastern Europe was even more sinister.[104] Though they might have minor quibbles concerning specific "tactics" and "methods," it could be presumed that scholars who agreed to participate in Nazi-sponsored cultural events in occupied Europe more or less approved of the Third Reich's basic geopolitical aims.

Wasn't this, after all, the none-too-subtle subtext of Gadamer's Herder interpretation, which, given the circumstances of its composition and delivery, was obviously written with a keen eye to the political present? The universalistic values of the Enlightenment were in a state of advanced decomposition. Increasingly, France had succumbed to political, cultural, and demographic stagnation—its humiliating defeat in June 1940 served as the ultimate confirmation of these trends—and had correspondingly forfeited its right to continental cultural prominence. Instead, a new system of particularistic, völkisch values—best incarnated in the victorious National Socialist state—appeared on the horizon. As Gadamer readily affirms, Herder's worldview represents the triumph of the principle of "völkisch life," although, as he goes on to observe, it would take over a century to realize the *political* consequences of Herder's cultural outlook: "This unpolitical intuition of and preparation for what is to come was above all the fate of Germany during his time, and perhaps the fate of such political belatedness is the reason why the German concept of 'das Volk'—in contrast to the democratic slogans of the West—proves to have the power to create a new political social order in an altered present."[105] Consequently, from an historical standpoint, Germany took its rightful turn to see if it could rescue a strife-torn Europe from its longstanding civilizational crisis. Only a willfully obtuse, studiously ahistorical reading of Gadamer's Herder-*Schrift* could fail to appreciate its status as an allegorical paean to Germany's recent battlefield triumphs.

·POLITICAL EXCURSUS I·

Incertitudes Allemandes: Reflections
on the German New Right

Just as ancient peoples lived their past history in their imagination, in mythology, so we Germans have lived our future history in thought, in philosophy. We are philosophical contemporaries of the present day without being its historical contemporaries.

—KARL MARX, "A Contribution to a Critique of
Hegel's *Philosophy of Right:* Introduction"

The history of the Germans is a history of extremes. It contains everything except moderation, and in the course of a thousand years the Germans have experienced everything except normality. . . . Nothing is normal in German history except violent oscillations.

—A.J.P TAYLOR, *The Course of German History*

IN JUNE 2000 the German public sphere was unsettled by another sensational outburst. Ernst Nolte, a senior German historian given to floating revisionist claims, was awarded the Konrad Adenauer Prize from Munich's famed Institute for Contemporary History. Journalists and historians immediately clamored for the resignation of director Horst Moeller (Moeller had been an adviser to Chancellor Helmut Kohl during the 1990s), who, they claimed, had permanently tarnished the institute's reputation.

Though there are few doubts about Nolte's academic qualifications per se, the political circumstances surrounding his receipt of the prize were highly fraught. For it was Nolte who, in 1986, unleashed the German Historians' Debate by claming that the Soviet Gulag was "more original" than Auschwitz—which, consequently, seemed to dwindle to the status of a "second order" crime—and that Hitler's actions in the east (Operation Barbarossa) constituted an act of self-defense in the face of a perceived threat.

During the 1990s, however, in a series of controversial interviews and articles, Nolte's views became increasingly strident, and his will to provoke seemed to become an end in itself. He has repeatedly insisted that Nazi anti-Semitism possessed a "rational kernel," implying that certain of Hitler's policies toward the Jews were, given the historical circumstances, far from unreasonable. And in a controversial biography of Martin Heidegger, he openly contended that National Socialism had been the "right course" for Germany in 1933. Many of his more outrageous claims were reiterated in an open exchange of letters with the French historian François Furet, recently published in English.[1]

Were Nolte's views widely shared? Is there a danger in contemporary Germany that the liberal political consensus, so painstakingly forged during the heyday of the Bonn Republic, might indeed crumble? Hardly. Instead, Nolte's recent excrescences (in his acceptance speech, he proudly reiterated verbatim his most contentious claims and theses) is better understood as the last gasp at a failed effort to halt the "Western drift" of German political culture. A chronicle of these efforts—largely unsuccessful but significant nevertheless—follows.

A Rightward Drift

In his 1922 essay on "The Ideas of Natural Law and Humanity" Protestant theologian Ernst Troeltsch reflected on the dilemma of German particularism as defined in opposition to the values of the cosmopolitan West. Troeltsch realized that in the course of World War I the ethos of Germanocentrism, as embodied in the "ideas of 1914," had assumed a heightened stridency. The subsequent peace, under the sign of the draconian Versailles Treaty, instead of muting the idiom of German exceptionalism that Troeltsch viewed with such mistrust, seemed only to fan its flames. Thus, though Germany was nominally and for the first time a republic, convinced democrats remained few and far between. Moreover, the emergence of a vociferous, revanchist-minded revolutionary nationalism, propounded by a group of oxymoronic "conservative revolutionaries," sounded an ominous note. Although the fledgling republic would successfully fend off right-wing coup attempts in 1920 (the Kapp Putsch) and 1923 (Hitler), the handwriting was on the wall. In his article, Troeltsch sought—in vain, as it turned out—to blunt the thrust of German particularism to thereby return Germany to the values of the universalist fold. A model of intellectual historical concision, his reconstruction of German exceptionalism remains instructive, even though today the *Geistesgeschichte* approach has fallen out of favor.

Troeltsch laments the fact that German cultural life had yet to shed its long-standing attraction to "counterrevolutionary" mores and habitudes. Tracing these attitudes back to what he identified as the "half aesthetic, half religious . . . spirit of antibourgeois idealism" characteristic of German romanticism, such trends have culminated, remarks Troeltsch, in a "curious mixture of mysticism and brutality." From the idea of "individuality," German romanticism developed "a new principle of reality, morality, and history." "Instead of ideas of the equal dignity of Reason everywhere and of the fulfillment of universal law, we have the conception of a purely personal and unique realization of the capacities of Mind in every direction, primarily in individual persons, but secondarily also in communities themselves." Instead of the ideas of the "dignity of Reason and of the fulfillment of universal law," one is offered the spectacle a "wealth of national minds all struggling together and developing their [separate] spiritual powers. . . ."[2] This approach, observed Troeltsch, was predicated on the assumption of the inequality of individuals. It encouraged a "deification of the state" and cynically entrusted leadership in the hands of "great men." "The political thought of Germany," Troeltsch concludes, "is marked by a curious dualism, which cannot but impress every foreign observer."

Look at one of its sides and you will see an abundance of remnants of Romanticism and lofty idealism: look at the other, and you will see a realism which goes to the verge of cynicism and of utter indifference to all ideals and all morality; but what you will see above all is an inclination to make an astonishing combination of the two elements—in a word, to brutalize romance, and to romanticize cynicism.[3]

Few observers of the contemporary German scene have failed to note the changed tenor of German political culture in the aftermath of reunification. At issue is a resurrection of specters and spirits, visitations from the German past, albeit in a political context distinctly marked by considerations of restraint and stability—as though Konrad Adenauer's 1950s motto, *"Keine Experimente"* ("No experiments"), had become the unofficial German equivalent of the American "E pluribus Unum." The leading spirits of Germany's conservative revolutionary movement of the 1920s—Carl Schmitt, Ernst Jünger, Oswald Spengler—have again become fashionable. The title of a recent book by the liberal CDU (Christian Democratic Union) parliamentarian Friedbert Pflüger, *Germany is Adrift: The Conservative Revolution Discovers Its Children,* captured the mood of the post-reunification Zeitgeist.[4]

This renewed fascination with German national revolutionary traditions from the 1920s is symptomatic of a broader sense of cultural disorientation. Today the German question has little to do with traditional issues of Macht- and Realpolitik; such questions have largely been settled by Germany's integration within the economic and political framework of the European Union. But it has everything to do with questions of German identity. In the aftermath of reunification, it has become permissible, even de rigueur, to raise the question, *"Was ist deutsch?"* (What is German?)—a question that, certain right-radical fringe elements notwithstanding, had remained taboo for much of the postwar period. "Why We Are Not a Nation and Why We Must Become One," proclaimed the German literary critic Karl Heinz Bohrer in a oft-cited essay from the early 1990s.[5] *The Nation That Does Not Want to Be One* reads the rueful title of a 1991 book by the conservative historian Christian Meier.[6] Belatedly, prominent German intellectuals have rediscovered identity politics.

Therein lies the dilemma. Historically, discussions of German identity have been beset with the ideology of German particularism described so well by Troeltsch. As a rule, they were explicitly formulated in polemical opposition to the ideas of universal human equality that emerged in the course of the French Revolution—the despised "ideas of 1789." Historically, such discussions conjure the specter of Germany going its own way. Thus, the problem of German identity politics is that the major historical and cultural reference points have been tainted with the ethos of German exceptionalism. Inevitably, when themes pertaining to the development of German national consciousness arise today, it proves difficult—if not impossible—to escape the ethnocentric and solipsistic phrasing of earlier debates over German identity. Since this was the idiom that Germans traditionally used to discuss questions of national identity, they unavoidably resurface in the present historical context—a preternatural return of the repressed.

Were such neonationalist longings confined to a fringe element—were they little more than the dyspeptic musings of isolated cultural malcontents—there would be no cause for alarm. Significantly, however, such trends have acquired an established institutional foothold in post-reunification German political culture. Conservative revolutionary positions on the state, foreign policy, national identity, geopolitics, and Germany's attitudes toward "the West" have gained a hearing among academics, publishing houses, newspapers, and political figures. In this respect one can safely say that say that, since reunification, the cultural parameters of the Federal Republic have distinctly shifted. Political and cultural themes that, owing to their proximity to the Nazi worldview, were formerly kept at arms length now occupy center stage.

Unlike previous eras, in the short run at least, Germany's neighbors have little to fear. The irredentist claims of German expellees (e.g., the politically influential League of Sudeten Germans) have, if anything, abated since the annus mirabilis of 1990. A firm acknowledgment of existing political boundaries was one of the essential preconditions for the successful outcome of the so-called two plus four negotiations leading to reunification. The misfortunes and horrors visited upon mid-century Europe by an expansionist Germany is a situation no one is anxious to repeat—least of all the Germans themselves, who, as is well known, have since the war's end largely sublimated their once robust political energies along economic lines. Belatedly, Walter Rathenau's celebrated dictum, "economics is destiny," has acquired a ring of truth. At the same time, an ethos of depoliticization has its perils.

Thus, while for the moment risks of European political instability remain few, knowing what in the long run the future may hold is difficult. The key question seems to be, Will the structure of German democracy remain unaffected by its strident neonationalist detractors—that is, by the representatives of the so-called new democratic right and their sympathizers? Will the rightward shift of Germany's political spectrum leave the institutional fabric of the Federal Republic unchanged? Or does the peculiar disjunction between culture and politics presage an unsavory, illiberal political realignment?

In the contemporary German political context to raise the specter of brown-clad ghosts remains irresponsible. Yet, such caveats should not obviate the demands of sober political assessment. There are two structural variables affecting the current political situation that bear consideration.

1. The recent shift of Germany's political capital from Bonn to Berlin is an event fraught with both historical and symbolic significance. It has tempted many observers to conclude that the Bonn Republic was an aberration in the long-term course of German historical development. Thus, with the emergence of a Berlin Republic, some say that one can hark back with impunity to hallowed traditions of the Second Empire—that is, to the traditions of "respectable" German conservatism that the Nazis, as petty bourgeois radicals, ruined. That the Second Empire, for all its "modern" features, was ill-disposed toward the values of pluralism, democracy, and rule of law is a fact that in most accounts remains conveniently omitted.

2. Throughout most of the important political debates of the 1990s the German left has been a negligible presence. To be sure, the left's enfeeblement has not been a phenomenon entirely of its own making. Following the collapse of the Berlin Wall, Helmut Kohl made sure that debate over reunification was defined in narrow terms that emphasized economic stability and political continuity—"Deutsche Mark nationalism."[7] These constricted political parameters precluded public debate on fundamental constitutional questions, ensuring that the left (as well as other critics) were essentially left out (reflections on the value and meaning of "the nation" have never been the left's forté in any event). Nevertheless, the German left has traditionally had its own love-hate relationship with democracy. Since Marx's "On the Jewish Question" (1843), its indictments of bourgeois society have usually gone hand-in-hand with a willingness to jettison basic rights and liberal safeguards. This ambivalent anti-parliamentarist legacy was perpetuated by the extra-parliamentary left of the 1960s (the so-called APO) as well as the peace movement in the 1980s. Finally, with the collapse of the German Democratic Republic, the ideological debilities of left-wing "antifascism"—a lukewarm attitude toward the values of liberalism combined with an ingrained reticence to speak out against the evils communism—were finally unmasked. Its dreams of an authentic German socialism at last exposed, the antifascist left was morally discredited.[8] Yet this swan song of the German left had debilitating consequences for German political culture. For it meant that the German right, deprived of its major ideological adversary, was left with the political field virtually to itself.

Who Are the New Right?

The summons to normalize the German past has been led by the so-called New Right, a loosely affiliated group of younger publicists and historians who, for a time, occupied positions of influence at *Die Welt* (a leading German daily) and the Ullstein publishing house. Although, as Josef Joffe has correctly pointed out, the intellectual influence of this group has waned considerably since 1995 (when the historian Rainer Zitelmann was dismissed from his position as editor of *Die Welt*'s Sunday supplement), to focus narrowly on the fate of individuals instead of larger political and cultural trends would be shortsighted.[9] The New Right's importance is as much *representative* as it is intrinsic: its aspirations toward a new German "normalcy" are symptomatic of attitudes toward German history and politics that are shared by a broader stratum of opinion-leaders: journalists, literati, and politicians.

The German New Right has appropriated a tack from its counterpart in France, the so-called Nouvelle Droite.[10] One of its chief aims has been to counter a perceived left-wing cultural dominance by implementing a "Gramscism of the right," thereby replacing left-wing intellectual hegemony with a right-wing hegemony. The New Right likes to portray itself as an up-and-coming "young" generation, thus playing on the myth of Germany as a "young nation"—historically, a standard trope of German nationalist discourse. Similarly, it styles itself as the "generation of '89," claiming that, unlike its predecessors (in particular, the senescent APO-OPAs of the 1960s), it is the first generation qualified to arrive at an unbiased evaluation of the key events of twentieth-century history.

One of the New Right's main strategies has been a tendentious rereading of National Socialism. Its exponents believe that the first step to making German nationalism respectable again is to relativize—for the sake of minimizing—the crimes of the Third Reich. In this respect, they are explicitly retracing paths tread by the revisionist camp in the German Historians' Debate of the 1980s: Ernst Nolte's contention that Auschwitz, far from being unique, was merely one among many twentieth-century genocides (moreover, compared to the Soviet Gulag, it was far from "original"); and Michael Stürmer's functionalist definition of history writing: "In a land without history, whoever fills memory, coins the concepts, and interprets the past, controls the future."[11] Thus, for example, Zitelmann's doctoral thesis and first book took pains to distinguish the "positive" aspects of Nazi rule from the "negative." Building selectively on earlier, mainstream historical literature, he sought to emphasize National Socialism's role as a "modernizing" force. "The National Socialist Party was the first German party to achieve a [political] integration that went beyond class. Modernity was the key to its success, and this modernity formed an essential moment of National Socialist social policy following Hitler's seizure of power."[12] Moreover, by attributing National Socialism's excesses to "modernization" as a type of uncontrollable process that "befell" Germany from on high, as it were, Germany's own responsibility for these excesses is implicitly discounted.

This selective reevaluation of the National Socialist past—systematically neglecting Nazi atrocities and disingenuously highlighting its "progressive" side—has become a standard tactic for the New Right historical revisionism. Moreover, this rereading of German history stands in polemical opposition to the left-liberal social scientific approach of the Bielefeld school (led by Hans-Ulrich Wehler), which predominated during the 1970s and 1980s. Whereas Wehler and company sought to stress the social origins of Nazism, Zitelmann and his followers wish to return to the (compromised) empathic traditions of German historicism: a positive emphasis on the role of the state and its leaders, coupled with a rigorous extrusion of moral judgment—a patently suspect demand in the case of a regime such as National Socialism that committed crimes of unprecedented magnitude.

One of the New Right's most sensational forays into the German public sphere came on May 8, 1995, the fiftieth anniversary of Germany's defeat in World War II. Traditionally, politicians and historians commemorated this date as Germany's emancipation from Nazism. But Zitelmann and friends had a different agenda in mind. In keeping with Stürmer's maxim "whoever interprets the past controls the future," they sought instead to portray the date as the onset of Germany's misfortune: the Red Army's triumphant occupation of eastern Germany, the beginning of the nation's political division, and the loss of sovereignty to the occupying Western powers. Employing a familiar strategy, they sought to portray Germany and the Germans as the real victims in World War II. To drive home this point, they launched a controversial nation-wide campaign in German newspapers—"Against Forgetting."[13] In a manner wholly in keeping with the parochial focus of neonationalism, claims about German suffering were disproportionately highlighted, whereas the massive and willful suffering Germany had inflicted on others was passed over in silence.

Borrowing a page from the Nouvelle Droite, members of the German New Right disingenuously described themselves as apostles of tolerance and free speech, as defenders of liberty. Conversely, they portrayed the representatives of the reigning left-liberal consensus as intolerant, even "totalitarian." Thus, in their introduction to *Westbindung,* Zitelmann and his fellow editors leveled the following accusation against post-1960s German political culture: "Allegiance to the 'western value community' has attained the status of a political utopia that has penetrated the whole of society *in totalitarian fashion. . . .* This utopia is totalitarian insofar as it is the specific feature of totalitarian systems to exercise total ideological influence over the population of a nation."[14] Zitelmann has gone so far as to equate the years 1933 and 1968: in his view, both dates represent disastrous turning points for the fate of the German nation. Just as in the Historians' Debate, Nolte accused those who questioned his revisionist historical agenda of attempting to stifle free speech and legitimate scholarly debate, defenders of the New Right, who make no secret of their authoritarian political longings, portray themselves as "liberal" and their left-wing antagonists as tyrannical. They repeatedly attempt to score points by playing up their antiestablishment credentials: *they* are the breakers of taboos and challengers of received wisdom, whereas representatives of the left are painted as the repressive guardians of political and historiographical orthodoxy.

The protest against left-wing "political correctness" was one of the New Right's major rallying points. Yet upon reflection their Schmittian search for a worthy foe was risible: in the aftermath of reunification the fortunes of the German left had plummeted, and the *Zeitgeist* turned sharply to the right—at least until the 1998 success of Gerhard Schroder's Red-Green coalition (even then, given Schroder's preoccupation with curtailing social spending, many were left wondering what was "socialist" about the Social Democrats). In particular, feminism—another contested legacy of the 1960s—was viewed as anathema, a dangerous ideological scourge.

Feminism represented a clear and present danger to German manhood, the constant threat of emasculation. In the words of one of the contributors to the popular New Right anthology, *The Self-Confident Nation,* feminism is "the sexist virus that splits our society"—a characterization that betrays a obsession with the attributes of masculinity and virility, classic *topoi* of fascist ideology.[15] (One will also note the recourse to the language of virology, a rhetorical staple of the discourse of biological racism.) According to fascist scribe Ernst Jünger, father figure and economic patron of the New Right, "The 'elemental,' toward which we strive, is for the first time perceptible in the jaws of war. Only when the play of perpetual emptiness of normal life is swept away will what is natural and elemental within us—a genuinely primitive dimension that is otherwise hidden—erupt with blood and seed."[16] Similarly, for Carl Schmitt, "The hallmark of authentic politics is the moment when the enemy emerges in concrete clarity as the enemy."[17] According to the conservative revolutionary worldview, the nihilism and decadence of contemporary Europe are a direct result of the triumph of liberalism, whose political values—discussion, compromise, egalitarianism—are in essence *effeminate.* Only a renewed social Darwinist emphasis on virility and risk, guaranteed by a strong and well-armed state, might redeem Germany and Europe from a fate of liberal vacillation and indecision.

The German New Right is fond of characterizing itself as the "democratic right." By strategically distancing themselves from the far right (e.g., neo-Nazis), its members are cleverly able to present themselves as intellectual and political moderates, thereby stealthily interjecting their revisionist views into cultural mainstream. If, as Jürgen Habermas has suggested, the singular accomplishment of the Federal Republic has been Germany's reorientation toward the civic political culture of the West, the German New Right has done all it can to call this value commitment radically into question.[18] Thomas Mann once remarked that the West needs a European Germany rather than a German Europe. As staunch antiuniversalists, the followers of the New Right are vehemently opposed to Germany's participation in the European Union, which they are fond of satirizing as the *"Monstrum vom Maastricht."* Instead, their political program draws on a standard arsenal of 1920s national revolutionary positions: ethnic homogeneity, the nation as a "community of fate" (Schicksalgemeinschaft), "geopolitics" (suggesting that Germany foreign policy is dictated by its geographical position in the European center), and a strong state that must be able to compensate for the centrifugal tendencies of (liberal) "society." In all these respects New Right intellectuals trace their spiritual pedigree back to the authoritarian political doctrines of Carl Schmitt.[19] As one New Right critic has observed, "Thus we can see a 'Schmittian' constellation extending from the *FAZ* [*Frankfurter Allgemeine Zeitung*] and conservative politicians like Edmund Stoiber, Peter Gauweiler, Wolfgang Schäuble, and Alfred Dregger, on the one hand . . . to the *Junge Freiheit* and Franz Schönhuber's 'Republican' ideology, on the other."[20] The ubiquitous appeals to Schmitt's legacy have facilitated a blurring of the traditional distinctions between extreme and center right, black and brown, democratic and antidemocratic conservatism.

The Ghost of Carl Schmitt

Post-communist political instability and refugee problems have in intellectual and political circles abetted a "fortress Deutschland" mentality. And as the restrictive immigration law passed by the Bundestag in 1993 demonstrates, such developments have facilitated a measure of permeability between the New Right and the political mainstream. Even intellectuals on the left, Hans Magnus Enzensberger, for instance, have jumped on the neoisolationist bandwagon, decreeing that, since cosmopolitan dreams of "perpetual peace" are dead, the best that one can do is to cultivate one's own garden by safeguarding national borders and interests.[21] The dramatist Botho Strauss shares Enzensberger's despair, which he purveys in apocalyptical terms appropriate to an Ernst Jünger novel. In his vitriolic diatribe, "Anschwellender Bockgesang" ("swelling song of the goat"), he duly enumerates the following "seismic indicators of great distress": "world historical turbulence, a celestially decreed powerlessness, the violation of taboos . . . the destabilization and deterioration of intimate life, the arrival of times of famine in the biblical sense."[22] Strauss's fatalistic ruminations on planetary catastrophe betray a characteristic conservative revolutionary fascination with the "emergency situation" (Ausnahmezustand). Extreme situations call for extreme political measures. The conservative revolutionary diagnosis of the times dovetails perfectly with its preferred antidemocratic political prescriptions.

The conservative revolutionary standpoint has made inroads among a wide spectrum of politicians and opinion leaders. The "mercy of late birth," coupled with the obvious political and cultural capital to be gained by playing the nationalist card, has given rise to a new insouciance about breaking taboos. Wolfgang Schäuble, a leading CDU politician, has shown few inhibitions about portraying the nation as a "community of protection and of fate" (Schütz- und Schicksalgemeinschaft).[23] Intended to appeal to the nether regions of German national sentiment, this characterization insinuates that the existential needs of the national community trump considerations of principle. Conversely, one of Kohl's favorite slogans was "A good German is a good European." In support of his attempts to reanimate a romantic definition of the Volk, Schäuble approvingly cites the following remarks from the poet Joseph von Eichendorff: "The Volk lives neither by bread nor concepts alone. It wants something positive to love and to care for, in order to reinvigorate itself. It wants above all to have a *Heimat* in the full sense, that is, its own sphere of basic ideas, inclinations, and disinclinations, which vitally penetrate all its relationships."[24] Thus, whereas a previous generation of political leaders based foreign policy on an unflinching commitment to anchoring Germany firmly within Europe and NATO, a new generation, represented by men such as Schäuble, "do not even bother to conceal their primary allegiance to German nationalism pure and simple."[25]

Perhaps nowhere has the rightward shift in German political culture been more evident than in the medium of print journalism. In 1993 *Der Spiegel*—before reunification, a bulwark of liberal opinion—incited an uproar by publishing Strauss's illiberal tirade "Anschwellender Bockgesang"—an event described by one critic as a "caesura in the political discourse of the Federal Republic."[26] The following year *Spiegel* editor Rudolf Augstein provoked renewed outrage by allowing the historian Ernst Nolte a platform to air his revisionist political views. In an interview entitled, "Was Hitler Right from a Historical Standpoint? Ernst Nolte on National Socialism, Auschwitz, and the New Right," Nolte bemoaned that Nazism's world-historical potential—that of a "third way" between communism and capitalism—still remained historically unrealized. Nor did Nolte hesitate to express his conviction that the so-called Auschwitzlie—the denial of the gas chambers—contained "a small kernel of truth." Even false ideas, Nolte continued, must be objectively researched, for they are "often helpful in bringing more truthful ideas to light."[27] Leaving no doubt that the piece had the imprimatur of *Spiegel*'s editor-in-chief, Augstein personally conducted interview.

Undoubtedly, the leading offender in recycling the clichés and nostrums of neonationalism has been Germany's most prestigious daily, the *Frankfurter Allgemeine Zeitung*. As John Ely has remarked, "Empirical observation of right intellectuals and their discourse reveals an overlap in themes and rhetoric between newspapers such as the *FAZ* and publications of the far right . . . from 'Prussian virtues' (Baring) and mythologies of Caesarism to the 'arcades of power' at Sans-Souci (Stürmer), Ernst Jünger, and right wing postmodernism."[28] Since reunification, the *FAZ* has moved steadily to the right: belittling the legacy of '68, pandering to the claims of historical revisionism, glorifying the virtues of national homogeneity, celebrating tainted literati such as Ernst Jünger, and pontificating about geopolitical imperatives of the German *Mittellage*. The *FAZ* has published—unremarked—lavish death notices for former Hitlerdeputy Rudolf Hess and irredentist letters from Sudeten Germans declaring that they, too, should have a say in determining the future of the Czech Republic. A Schmittian, anti-liberal, *étatiste* approach to politics has become commonplace. Thus, with a swipe at Habermas's theory of discourse ethics, an editorial from the early 1990s begins, "Some things in the German system of government appear almost as a caricature of a domination-free discourse: everything gets said, and nothing is decided."[29]

Increasingly, the *FAZ* has sought to rehabilitate a crude version of "national liberalism"—the proverbial "German idea of freedom"

(Leonard Krieger). Historically, the German idea of freedom accorded little weight to considerations of individual liberty. Instead, freedom was associated with the nation's autonomous capacity for action (one of Germany's traditional political deficits as a "belated nation"), which trumped the rights and interests of the individual. Since the idea of national liberalism mandated that the individual exists for the sake of the state rather than vice versa, an air of illiberalism constantly haunted the doctrine. In *Idealism and Nation* the Schmittian political philosopher Bernd Willms aptly describes the national liberal standpoint when he observes: "Insofar as the national idea is realized in the consciousness of every individual, the nation is the objective connection not only of state and people but also of individuals to one another." Thus, concludes Willms, "the national is also the presupposition of conscious freedom."[30]

Border-Crossers and Spiritual Reactionaries

One of the most significant aspects of 1990s German political culture has been the number of former left-wing intellectuals and writers who have crossed over to the right. This shift entails a conventional identification with the "the nation" and its existential prerogatives. Like many other aspects of post-reunification German political culture, this neonationalist awakening was already noticeable during the 1980s, especially during the course of the "peace movement" debates.[31]

In part, the left-right shift was predictable: once the totalitarian nature of "really existing socialism" was exposed (a process that predates 1989), intellectuals on the left were deprived of a utopian alternative. To many, the idea of "the nation" seemed like the best available means to achieve analogous ends.

What were those ends? Historically, the extreme left and extreme right have shared a visceral hostility to bourgeois society. For the revolutionary left the bourgeoisie was defined as the "class enemy." Conversely, the conservative revolutionary distaste for *Der Bourgeois* was always tinged with an aristocratic and aestheticist bent that, at a later point, resurfaced in the phrases of left-wing Kulturkritik (e.g., the Frankfurt School). The bourgeois was vulgar, unrefined, the stereotypical social climber or parvenu. Of course, a strong dose of "geopolitics" is always mixed in with this assessment: Germany's traditional political rivals England and France (and later, America) were perceived as the bourgeois nations par excellence. They were (to quote Werner Sombart) the nations of *Händler* (traders) rather than *Helden* (heroes). In *Confessions of an Unpolitical Man* (1917) Thomas Mann contrasts the bourgeois unfavorably with the artist. After the Great War, Ernst Jünger upped the polemical ante, lionizing the risk-seeking "warrior-type" in contrast with the timorous bourgeois, for whom security and material well-being were ultimate values.

The thesis of "fraternal enmity" between left and right suggests that, at certain pivotal ideational junctures, *les extrêmes se touchent*. Excoriated by both right and left as a carrier of the iniquities of modern *Zivilisation*, the bourgeoisie, in the discourse of both groups, assumes a negative totemic status: were one to eliminate its influence, the shortcomings of modern society would magically disappear. Since the worldviews of both the extreme left and extreme right harbor a deep-seated and fundamental antipathy to capitalist society qua "technological Moloch," one can interchangeably appropriate aspects of either position for the sake of reaching analogous critical and political ends. Perhaps the best-known historical instance of left-right ideological crossover is the case of the National Bolsheviks, who during the 1920s were convinced that Germany should ape the Soviet model of economic planning and political dictatorship to surmount the "crisis of liberalism."[32] Insofar as National Bolshevism's best-known exponent, Ernst Niekisch, was an ardent foe of Nazism (he was persecuted by the regime), this outlook—purportedly free of political taint—appears highly serviceable for the ends of New Right. That the national revolutionary standpoint was staunchly antidemocratic and bellicist seems to be no great stumbling block to its enthusiastic adoption among New Right intellectuals.

Among the German cultural potencies who have foresworn their allegiance to the political left to ally themselves with the post-reunification "national awakening," one may include filmmakers Edgar Reitz and Hans-Jürgen Syberberg, the novelist Martin Walser, dramatist and essayist Botho Strauss, the Germanist Karl-Heinz Bohrer, and the late DDR playwright Heiner Müller.[33] They have been collectively dubbed Germany's new "spiritual reactionaries," insofar as their interventions have centered on cultural as opposed to explicitly political themes. By and large they share the conservative revolutionary diagnosis of the age: Kultur and *Innerlichkeit,* Germany's traditional spiritual strengths since the age of romanticism, are under threat from the superficial blandishments of mass society—consumerism, advertising, Hollywood, and, more generally, the "culture industry"—in sum, "Americanism." As Botho Strauss observes in "Anschwellender Bockgesang":

> Whoever allows himself to be laughed at in a private conversation by millions of onlookers harms the wonder and dignity of dialogue, of face to face discourse, and should be punished with a lifelong proscription from the intimate sphere. The regime of telecratic publicity is the ultimate form of violent, if bloodless, domination and the most all-encompassing totalitarianism known to history. . . . The reign of the transient holds sway, against which all forms of protest remain impotent.[34]

Strauss's "Bockgesang" outburst had a long prehistory. Since the 1980s he has bemoaned the modern triumph of technology and reason; in their stead he has recommended a return to the values of the sacred and "myth." Strauss believes that culture not predicated on an aesthetic experience of the sacred is destined to disintegrate into formlessness—precisely the risk run by modern civilization. Whereas works of art, qua secular myths, place us in contact with the miraculous, reason never penetrates to the essence of things. "The self-determined individual," declares Strauss, "is the most blatant lie of reason."[35] Myth, conversely, provides us with an experience of the ineffable. Denigrating modernity's attempts to legitimate itself via Enlightenment ideals such as popular sovereignty and subjective "rights," Strauss wishes instead to promote an *aesthetic* justification of existence. "Life as a work of art that gives birth to itself," proclaims Nietzsche in the *Gay Science*.[36] Thereby Strauss seeks to revivify a political ideal first celebrated by the German romantics: the ideal of the "aesthetic state."[37] The aesthetic doctrines articulated in Strauss's 1992 work, *Beginninglessness*, inform the cultural politics of "Bockgesang." Against the backdrop of neo-Nazi violence, which during 1992–93 resulted in some 25 deaths, Strauss invoked René Girard's idea that violence founds the political community. According to Girard, "The rite is the repetition of an original spontaneous lynching which guarantees order in the community." Strauss glosses this claim as follows: "Racism and xenophobia are 'fallen' cult practices that originally had a sacred, order-establishing meaning." "The stranger, the traveler is captured and stoned," he continues, "when there is unrest in the city. The scapegoat as the target of violence is never just an object of hate, but also a thing of worship . . . a metabolic vessel."[38] Since scapegoating is intrinsic to the demands of social order—without it, the community would violently feed on itself and implode—Strauss in effect delivers a post facto justification of neo-Nazi racism. "In our liberal-libertarian self-enclosedness we no longer understand why a people is prepared to defend its way of life against others and is ready to perpetrate *blood-sacrifice;* we consider it false and objectionable."[39] The provocative discussion of sacrifice links seamlessly with Strauss's aesthetic and cultural views. For the flipside of Germany's mass media-induced stupefaction is its incapacity to experience tragedy (the "goat-song") as a violent aesthetic rite that binds the community.

Throughout the essay Strauss's fealty to the national revolutionary worldview, historical and contemporary, is to the fore. He complains that the Federal Republic's left-leaning cultural consensus has "mocked Heidegger and demonized Jünger." He laments the fact that "ten million German television viewers are unlikely to become Heideggerians [sic]" and openly endorses Jünger's Armageddon-tinged prophecy of a "return of the gods."[40] His identification with the thematics of New Right cultural politics could hardly be more explicit:

> *To be on the right with one's entire being* means . . . to experience the superior power of remembrance that seizes the individual, isolates

and confounds him in the midst of modern, enlightened society where he leads his customary existence. It is a question of an act of rebellion against the total domination of the present that robs the individual of every moment of fulfillment [*Anwesenheit*] contained in the unenlightened past, that seeks to cancel and eliminate historical becoming and mythical time.[41]

Were Strauss's violent reactionary musings the voice of a misanthropic loner, there would be little cause for concern. But he has been joined by a veritable chorus of dyspeptic German literati and *régisseurs,* transforming the fissure between culture and politics into a veritable chasm. Thus, in a remarkable treatise, *On the Misfortune and Fortune of Art in Germany After the Last War* (1990), the director Hans-Jürgen Syberberg bemoaned the familiar debilities of postwar German cultural life—Americanization, depthlessness, an insufficiently "national" focus, or, as Syberberg puts it, "art without *Volk.*" "We have been taken over by the plastic world," Syberberg protests. "When we climb into a car, a plane, aboard ship, when we purchase today's kitchen, let ourselves into today's TV world, from the studio and substance to the image of the world, we enter the world of artificial chemical universes. . . . Our thought, our memories [are] the simulation of life."[42] The German director thereby updates the paranoid idiom of Spenglerian Kulturkritik to suit the demands of the information society. His remarks illustrate how the discourse of spiritual reaction excels in exaggerating—and thereby exploiting— legitimate fears about globalization and mass culture. Whereas historically the left has criticized the same phenomena in the name of the precepts of democracy and autonomy, the spiritual reactionaries use them as a pretext to undermine liberalism in the name of the values of German particularism.

To the idiom of spiritual reaction Syberberg adds a sinister, though predictable, anti-Semitic twist: "One could make a career out of consorting with Jews or leftists, forming bonds that had nothing to do with love, or understanding, or even inclination. Jews must have put up with this since they wanted power."[43] Although Syberberg's distasteful remarks met with opprobrium in most quarters of respectable German society, in the words of one commentator,

"The chorus of protest . . . led to the suspicion that one of their own had simply come out into the open."[44]

In 1993, the year of Strauss's "Bockgesang" tirade, the novelist Martin Walser complained that skinhead violence was due to a deficit of national thinking rather than a surfeit of the same, or to a dearth of civic consciousness, as most observers would reasonably suppose.[45] The official political response to these neo-Nazi excesses, a draconian revision of the federal asylum law in July 1993, suggested that the foreigners themselves were to blame for their own persecution. In 1998 Walser created a scandal when accepting a literary award at the Frankfurt Book Fair. He complained of the instrumentalization of the Holocaust as a "moral cudgel" with which to beat down and intimidate Germany, thus echoing the familiar New Right trope of German victimization. Auschwitz, commented Walser, should not become a "routine threat, a tool of intimidation, a moral cudgel or just a compulsory exercise." He objected to plans for a Berlin Holocaust memorial as a "monumentalization of shame" in the heart of the German capital. One of the immediate targets of Walser's remarks seemed to be the rash of demands on the part of Holocaust victims and slave laborers for compensation. Yet, in the course of his speech, Walser displayed little concern with distinguishing between licit and illicit, genuine and false, appeals to historical memory. One came away from his speech instead with the sense that virtually *all* contemporary allusions to the fate of the Jews were misappropriations.

Walser's Book Fair tirade was one in a long line of voluble outcries demanding that post-reunification Germany be treated as a "normal nation" again. Rushing to Walser's defense, the writer Monika Maron proclaimed, "For me, young Germans are as little incriminated as young Danes or young French."[46]

A nation that must repeatedly and demonstratively declare itself "normal" inevitably raises suspicions. What might its denizens be trying to hide? As the historian Saul Friedländer has inquired, "Is a normal society a society without memory, one that tries to conceal tragedy, one that turns away from its own past in order to live only in the present and the future?"[47] That German "normalcy" would be so vigorously proclaimed at a time of escalating neo-Nazi extremism, along with worrisome electoral inroads of far-right parties such as the Deutsche Volksunion, cannot help but raise doubts with respect to motives. According to a recent Emnid poll, 43 percent of Germans believe that National Socialism had good and bad sides; 40 percent believe that without the war and the extermination of the Jews, Hitler would have been a "great statesman."[48] Since reunification, acts of violent right-wing extremism have mushroomed: between 1992 and 1993, nearly five thousand such acts were reported. Although since the high-water mark of the early 1990s, such incidents have declined, they still remain significantly above 1980s levels. Since the early 1990s, anti-Jewish incidents have risen sharply, from 627 in 1992 to 1,155 in 1995. During the same period, desecrations of Jewish cemeteries and synagogues have averaged over fifty per year—a 66 percent increase since the mid-1980s.[49] None of these trends inspire democratic confidence. As Habermas has appropriately remarked, the myth of German normalcy is the second "life-lie" of the Federal Republic:

> Anyone who replies to the signals of desolidarization with an appeal to the "self-confident nation" or by calling for a return to the "normality" of the reestablished national state, is using the devil to drive out Satan. For these unsolved global problems reveal precisely the limits of the nation-state. From the somber drumroll of national history emerge war memorials with limited vision. Only as a critical authority does history serve as a teacher. At best it tells us how we ought *not* to do it. It is from experiences of a negative kind that we learn. That is why 1989 will remain a fortunate date only so long as we respect 1945 as the genuinely instructive one.[50]

The debate over German normalcy has been mistakenly cast. Walser and his supporters claim that Germans who were born after the war (the so-called mercy of late birth) should no longer have to feel guilty concerning their forebears' misdeeds. But it is less a question of guilt than one of historical responsibility. Claiming that Germans today are somehow "guilty" is foolish. But it is also insincere to deny that present-day Germany continues to bear a measure of responsibility for a legacy of conquest and expansion whose exceptional brutality has, in the annals of modern history, acquired emblematic status. Insofar as these acts of aggression were international in scope, the parameters of remembrance, too, transcend national boundaries. They cannot be dictated by the functionalist imperatives of national identity formation. Germany's victims, too, deserve to have a say, for the dialectics of ethical life suggest that forgiveness is the prerogative of those who were wronged; it cannot simply be proclaimed unilaterally by the perpetrators or their heirs. An awareness of the way one is perceived by others is an indispensable self-correcting mechanism.

One of Walser's major misgivings concerns the alleged instrumentalization of the Holocaust for so-called ulterior ends. Here, the solution is relatively simple. Rather than drawing a curtain on the German past (the proverbial *Schlusstrich*) as the new nationalism suggests, concerned citizens should strive to ensure that the commemorations of the past are genuine and meaningful rather than merely perfunctory. The plans for a new Holocaust monument in Berlin, on a 4.9 acre site that will include a million volume library, point precisely in this direction.[51]

As Tocqueville once remarked, "As the past has ceased to throw its light upon the future, the mind of man wanders in obscurity."[52] Throughout the postwar era, German political culture has been distinguished by a remarkable capacity for enlightened self-criticism. It is disturbing that following reunification a new national consensus would emerge suggesting that this capacity for self-criticism was excessive, or that a new, less reflective posture—one more in step with the demands of "normalization"—is needed. It makes one wonder whether the earlier gestures of contrition were sincere.[53] After fifty years of democratic stability, it would be foolish to overreact by suggesting that Germany is at risk of regressing to dictatorship. Yet the new nationalism raises the specter of Germany going its own way: the rejection of a cosmopolitan-European identity in favor of a renewed German provincialism. It indicates the dangers of Germany's uncoupling itself from the West in favor of a new identity oriented toward the conservative precepts of realism, Machtpolitik, and the geopolitical demands of the German *Mittellage*.

· PART II ·

French Lessons

· 4 ·

Left Fascism: Georges Bataille and
the German Ideology

How does one keep from being fascist, even (especially) when one believes
oneself to be a revolutionary militant? How do we rid our speech and our
acts, our hearts and our pleasures, of fascism? How do we ferret out the
fascism that is ingrained in our behavior?

—MICHEL FOUCAULT, Preface to *Anti-Oedipus*

A *Fascism* à la Française

In an essay that became a touchstone for the vociferous debates
concerning the merits of postmodernism, Jürgen Habermas famously
identified poststructuralism as a type of "young conservatism." His
remarks—which are far from uncontroversial—read as follows:

> The young conservatives embrace the fundamental experience of
> aesthetic modernity—the disclosure of a decentered subjectivity
> freed from all constraints of rational cognition and purposiveness,
> from all imperatives of labor and utility—and in this way break out
> of the modern world. They thereby ground an intransigent antimod-
> ernism through a modernist attitude. They transpose the sponta-
> neous power of the imagination, the experience of self and affectivity,
> into the remote and the archaic; and in Manichean fashion, they coun-
> terpose to instrumental reason a principle only accessible via "evoca-
> tion": be it the will to power or sovereignty, Being or the Dionysian
> power of the poetic. In France this trend leads from Georges Bataille
> to Foucault and Derrida. The spirit [Geist] of Nietzsche that was
> reawakened in the 1970s of course hovers over them all.[1]

The epithet "young conservative" has often been misconstrued by observers and critics. Moreover, since Habermas's accusation occurred in the context of a discussion of political neoconservatism during the Reagan and Thatcher era, many assumed that he viewed the aforementioned French theorists as "neoconservative"—which is far from true.[2] Instead, his comparison refers to a group of right wing—in truth, proto-fascist—German intellectuals who played an influential, subversive role during the waning years of the Weimar Republic. Among their number one would have to include Ernst Jünger, Arthur Moeller van den Bruck, Ludwig Klages, Ernst Niekisch, Carl Schmitt, Oswald Spengler, and the members of the *"Tat"* ("The Deed") circle.[3] In the context at hand, it is important to note that Martin Heidegger's critique of modernity and political interventions during the 1930s suggests profound affinities with their doctrines.[4] One could best summarize the role played by Germany's oxymoronic conservative revolutionaries by saying that they contributed decisively to the "spiritual preparation" for German National Socialism. Their withering critique of modernity, their indictment of the purportedly "Western" ideas of reason, liberalism, individualism, and so forth—in sum, of a decadent and moribund bourgeois Zivilisation (forced unwillingly upon Germany by the victorious allies)—helped undermine the credibility of Germany's fledgling democracy during the late 1920s and early 1930s.[5]

Habermas is not alone in having perceived the conceptual affinities between the "critique of reason" fashionable during the concluding years of Weimar and postwar French theory. Tübingen philosopher Manfred Frank has also noted the thematic parallels between these two powerful intellectual currents. As Frank has remarked with polemical verve, "Postmodernism and antimodernism perfidiously join hands. This is also the case with 'logocentrism': [Ludwig] Klages and the new anti-intellectualism *[Geistfeindlichkeit]* of our day agree in the affect against the achievements of Western 'rationality.'"[6] By referring to Klages, Frank alludes to the telltale fact that the term "logocentrism"—the critique of which has become the hallmark of Derridean "deconstruction"—was itself coined by Klages in his portentous opus of the late 1920s and early 1930s, *Der Geist als*

Widersacher der Seele (The Intellect as Antagonist of the Soul). The theoretical position shared by poststructuralism and the German critics of Zivilisation in the 1920s, concludes Frank, was that rationality and reason, which the Enlightenment tradition perceived as a balm for the ills of humanity, were themselves responsible for the West's "decline."

To speak of intellectual affinities between Germany's young conservatives and the French postmodernists, while suggestive, as yet tells us relatively little. On closer inspection, more substantive differences might exist between these two groupings than similarities. Moreover, on first view, their respective political leanings could not be more opposed: while the proto-fascist orientation of the German critics of civilization is unarguable, their French counterparts would seem to be the philosophical heirs of May '68.[7] Their thought inclines toward a philosophical anarchism that is resolutely anti-statist. Allegiance to an authoritarian state, as practiced by the German Young Conservatives, would in their case be difficult to imagine.

Yet the intriguing parallels between German "right" and French "left" come into clearer focus if we consider the figure who is generally regarded as the intellectual precursor of poststructuralism, Georges Bataille (1897–1962). Bataille: by day the unassuming librarian at the Bibliothèque Nationale specializing in medieval collections; at night, mystic, occultist, heretic, novelist, libertine and champion of "erotism"; cofounder of a secret society ("Acéphale," or "headless") as well as of the posthumously celebrated College of Sociology; sworn foe of André Breton and the surrealists; member of the avant-garde anti-Stalinist group, "La Critique sociale," founded by former Bolshevik and Stalin biographer Boris Souvarine; and (of greatest import from the standpoint of the investigation at hand) cofounder of the short-lived anti-fascist group "Contre-Attaque," which made no secret of its desire to fight fascism via fascist means. Bataille, who, according to contemporary and kindred spirit Pierre Klossowski, wanted above all "to create a religion without god."[8]

The assimilation of Bataille's texts became a rite of passage for a generation of French intellectuals who wanted to break decisively with the "progressive" implications of Sartrean existentialism, especially with Sartre's antiquated "humanism"—his defense of "subjectivity," "reason," "freedom," and philosophy of history. This generation of structuralist thinkers included (among Sartre's contemporaries) Claude Lévi-Strauss and Jacques Lacan, as well as their radical literary heirs such as Foucault, Derrida, Roland Barthes, Gilles Deleuze, and Jean-François Lyotard. Both Derrida and Foucault bequeathed impassioned early texts demonstrating that their confrontation with the Bataille's legacy proved a formative experience of the highest order.[9] In sum, Bataille is the pivotal figure linking one generation of French radical cultural critics to the next.[10]

Like Germany's young conservatives, Bataille came of age during the interwar period, when a radical disillusionment with European cultural ideals predominated. For this generation—on both sides of the Rhine—the carnage of World War I had seemingly turned Nietzsche's apocalyptical prophecies concerning "European nihilism" into a palpable reality.[11] Germany's longstanding resistance to the values of a democratic political culture are well known.[12] Did an analogous set of historical conditions exist across the Rhine that might account for a similar antipathy among French intellectuals to the values of political liberalism?

Given the robust tradition of French republicanism, it would seem unwise to pursue such parallels too aggressively. Still, although the Third Republic spanned some seventy years (1870–1940), it could hardly be described as a model of political stability. The threat of a monarchist counterrevolution haunted the nascent republic until 1875, when a constitution was finally promulgated. The 1880s witnessed both the menace of Boulangism—a veritable precursor of the fascist mass movements of the twentieth century—as well as the publication of Edouard Drumont's *La France juive,* a *succès de scandale* whose anti-Semitic virulence rivaled anything that had been produced to date in central Europe. Although the Dreyfus affair of the 1890s seemed to conclude on a positive note (the reluctant captain was pardoned and the French left belatedly rallied around the Republic), it simultaneously set a fateful precedent for the political manipulation of anti-Semitic sentiment in modern politics. As Hannah Arendt remarks, "It [anti-Semitism] had been tried out previously in Berlin and Vienna, by Ahlwardt and Stoecker, by Schoenerer and Lueger, but nowhere was its efficacy more clearly proved than in France."[13]

Following the colonel's rehabilitation, Georges Sorel vented his political frustrations by converting from socialism to the proto-fascism of the Action Française, an oscillation in political loyalty that would prove prototypical for a great many twentieth-century political actors, Mussolini being the first and best known. In Sorel's estimation, once the French Socialists had rallied to the aid of the republic, their nonrevolutionary, reformist essence stood permanently unmasked. In the eyes of the legendary revolutionary syndicalist, the Socialists' timorous embrace of the parliamentary system was an act that stimulated nothing but disgust. Charles Maurras's Action Française followers greeted Sorel with open arms. Both they and the syndicalists (who in 1911 united to form the Cercle Proudhon) were convinced that "democracy was the greatest error of the last century," and that "if one wishes to preserve and to augment the moral, intellectual and material capital of civilization, it is absolutely necessary to destroy the democratic institutions."[14] Both the right and left viewed these institutions reductively as a political tool employed by the bourgeoisie to suppress working-class interests. The fluid alliance of Sorelians and Maurassians, of left and right, would become the prototype for many similar political crossovers of the interwar period. Although largely confined to intellectuals, the Cercle Proudhon purveyed the values of "national socialism" some ten years in advance of its better known German variant.

In France such tendencies would come to fruition in the avowedly "national socialist" (albeit, short-lived) Faisceau, founded by Georges Valois in the mid-twenties. The time for "action"—a keyword for French fascism—was now ripe, and Valois established the Faisceau to meet this challenge.[15] In its passion for avowedly fascist ideals and methods the Faisceau temporarily surpassed the Action Française (with its antiquarian monarchism and its quaint literary pretensions) among French rightists. Valois's political aims—a *"total revolution"* that would be *"a negation of the whole political, economic and social philosophy of the nineteenth century"*[16]—would a decade later culminate directly in the "fascist drift" of former leftists Gaston Bergery, Marcel Déat, and Jacques Doriot.[17] The Faisceau was one of the first political groupings to celebrate the essential kindredness of fascism and Bolshevism: both movements were reactions to the plutocratic spirit that had taken hold of Europe; both proclaimed a new ethos of militarism and struggle—in Valois's parlance, "the law of the combatant"—that would leave the languorous comforts of a decadent bourgeoisie far behind.

As Tony Judt has remarked, during the twilight of the Third Republic, "Left and Right alike felt a distaste for the lukewarm and were fascinated by the idea of a violent relief from mediocrity."[18] Yet the ideological groundwork for this entwinement of political extremes had been laid years before: "[Pierre-Joseph] Proudhon and [Charles] Péguy were icons for the syndicalist Left and the neo-monarchist Right alike because they had addressed, in their very different ways, the limitations and frustrations of parliamentary republicanism that had occupied the thoughts of earlier generations as well."[19]

It was the same ideological kindredness—one that well reflects the fundamental illiberal tenor of the period's European social thought—captured by Pierre Drieu La Rochelle's felicitously titled 1934 work, *Le Socialisme fasciste*.[20] An atomistic bourgeois polity, crippled by predatory economic competition and lack of patriotism, would be supplanted by an new authoritarian, corporatist regime—"fascism." "Socialism" would ensure that exploitative economic conditions, predicated on the dominance of Jewish finance capital, would be mitigated, thereby protecting the native lower middle classes. In the context at hand, Proudhon's petit-bourgeois socialism, lampooned by Marx, also forms a crucial precedent (thus it was hardly an accident that the 1911 merger of rightists and leftists decided on the name "Cercle *Proudhon*").[21] Viewed in this context, the parallels between interwar French fascists and their German contemporaries—Ernst Niekisch's National Bolshevism, the Schwarze Front led by the renegade-Nazi Strasser brothers (which, unlike Hitler, took the "socialist" component of National Socialism quite seriously), not to mention Jünger's fascination with the total state as embodied in the Soviet five-year plan—appear palpable and undeniable.

Transgression and "Anti-Ethics"

The 1930s were crucible years for Bataille as a writer and engaged intellectual, a period of maturation in which he displayed remarkable bursts of creative energy that found their way into novels such as *Bleu de Ciel,* essays that remain today exemplars of French cultural theory ("Theory of Expenditure," "The Psychological Structure of Fascism," "The Use Value of D.A.F. de Sade"), and the establishment of legendary avant-garde cultural groupings such as Contre-Attaque, Acéphale, and the College of Sociology. Yet unless one appreciates the extent to which the Third Republic and the Enlightenment ideals it embodied had been culturally and politically delegitimated—culminating in political challenges from both left and right—one will be hard pressed to evaluate the field of cultural-political options with which Bataille found himself confronted.

One of the intellectual traits that tied Bataille most closely to the German young conservatives was his aversion to Reason.[22] Heidegger once remarked, "Thinking begins only when we have come to know that Reason, glorified for centuries, is *the most stiff-necked adversary of thought,*" a statement that could be taken as emblematic for an entire generation of German "conservative revolutionary" intellectuals.[23] Profoundly influenced by *Lebensphilosophie,* the conservative revolutionaries endorsed "affect," "life," and experiential immediacy as opposed to mediation and reflection. More generally, these "anti-intellectual intellectuals" associated Reason with "calculative thinking" or "instrumental reason" *simpliciter.* They reject reason's status as an arbiter in the domains of political judgment, morality, and law as "hostile to life."

In Bataille's thought, reason promotes the values of a "homogeneous society": a social order that is totally standardized and regulated, that systematically represses the forces of vitality and risk whence nearly everything of cultural interest derives. As Bataille stated laconically during the 1930s, "It is time to abandon the world of the civilized and its light."[24]

Returning momentarily to the parallels between Bataille and his like-minded German contemporaries: for Spengler, too, the West's glorification of "theoretical thought" alienates humanity from the health of immediate life, as yet unsundered by the fateful and pernicious mind/body dualism. The cultural stakes at issue may be traced back to deformations of an "intellectualist" civilization that has succumbed to what the German prophet of decline refers to as the *"the unconditional monarchy of the eye."*[25] As Spengler, very much in the spirit of Bataille, observes:

> The animal microcosm, in which existence and consciousness are joined in a self-evident unity of living, knows of consciousness *only as the servant* of existence. The animal "lives" simply and does not reflect upon life. Owing, however, to the unconditional monarchy of the eye, life is presented as the life of a visible entity in the light. . . . Instead of straight, uncomplicated living, we have the antithesis represented in the phrase "thought and action."[26]

Only nonconceptual, ethereal modes of expression, such as music, might "break up the steely tyranny of light," continues Spengler, thereby perpetuating a legacy of German Kulturkritik going back to both Schopenhauer's and Nietzsche's privileging the ineffable qualities of song.[27] In lieu of a world historical cultural metamorphosis that would *reverse* the tyranny of the theoretical side of human existence over the sensual, we are condemned, Spengler proclaims, to endure the fateful hegemony of "visual thought," *"the sovereignty of the eyes."*[28]

The cultural attitudes of Spengler and Bataille are linked by an aesthetics of violence that is highly characteristic of the so-called front generation. In a key passage in *The Decline of the West,* Spengler, depicting the "life-world" of blood and instinct that had been repressed by the Faustian spirit of modernity, observes, "War is the primary politics of *everything* that lives, so much so that in their depths, battle and life are one, and being and will-to-battle expire together."[29] For Jünger, similarly, "War is an intoxication beyond all bonds. It is a frenzy without cautions and limits, comparable only to the forces of nature."[30] Bataille (in the context at hand, the meaning of his name in French should be recalled), too, is convinced that "Conflict is life. Man's value depends upon his aggressive strength. A living man regards death as the fulfillment of life; he does not see it as a misfortune.... I MYSELF AM WAR."[31] As Martin Jay has observed in an oft-cited article on Bataille, "On a deeper level, [World War I] seems to have exercised a certain positive fascination [on Bataille]. For it is striking that many of Bataille's obsessive themes would betray an affinity for the experiences of degradation, pollution, violence and communal bonding that were characteristic of life in the trenches."[32]

In the worldview of both Bataille and German young conservatives, war plays an indispensable, positive role. It dissolves the *principium individuationis:* the principle of subjectivity on which the homogeneous order of bourgeois society—a world of anomie and fragmentation—depends. According to Bataille, "the *general* movement of life is . . . accomplished *beyond the demands of individuals.*"[33] It is in this spirit that he celebrates the nonutilitarian nature of military combat as a type of aesthetic end in itself: "*Glory* . . . expresses a movement of senseless frenzy, of measureless expenditure of energy, which the fervor of combat presupposes. Combat is glorious in that it is always beyond calculation at some moment."[34] For similar reasons, Bataille praises unreservedly those premodern "warrior societies in which pure, uncalculated violence and ostentatious forms of combat held sway."[35] Under such conditions, war was not subordinated to the vulgar ends of enterprise and profit—as in the case of modern-day imperialism—but served as a glorious end in itself.

In the early 1930s Walter Benjamin viewed this aestheticist celebration of "violence for violence's sake" or "war for war's sake" as the essence of fascism. As he remarks in an well known passage:

> "*Fiat ars—pereat mundus,*" says fascism, and, as [Filippo] Marinetti admits, expects war to supply the artistic gratification of a sense perception that has been changed by technology.... Mankind, which in Homer's time was an object of contemplation for the Olympian gods, now is one for itself. Its self-alienation has reached such a degree that it can experience its own destruction as an aesthetic pleasure of the first order. This is the situation of politics which fascism is rendering aesthetic.[36]

In Bataille's thought war serves as the harbinger of a cultural transformation in which the primacy of self-posting subjectivity would be replaced by the taboo values of an "ecstatic" community: a community no longer governed by the identitarian prejudices of visual culture—by norms of transparency, sameness, self-equivalence—but instead by those of self-laceration, difference, and finitude. In fact, this Bataille-inspired program of an ecstatic community has been explicitly perpetuated in the political writings of Maurice Blanchot, Jean-Luc Nancy, and Jacques Derrida.

In *The Accursed Share* and other writings Bataille contrasts his own anthropologically derived theory of "general economics" with modern capitalism's "restricted economics," an instrumental orientation that remains indifferent to qualitative concerns or ends. (In this regard, one of Bataille's major influences seems to have been Max Weber's important distinction in *Economy and Society* between "value-oriented" [wertrationales] and "instrumental" [zweckrationales] action.) In a manner that parallels the approach of his German contemporaries, Bataille embraced a type of vitalism—he defends *"the exuberance of life"* or *"the exuberance of living matter as a whole,"* against the rational accounting methods that distinguish capitalism.[37] In his writings of the 1930s and 1940s, he sought to combine philosophy of life (Lebensphilosophie) with an "anthropological romanticism," projecting contemporary society's holistic longings upon premodern forms of life, thereby endowing the latter with a utopian normative status. Thus, in opposition to modern society as a prosaic sphere of "disenchantment," Bataille reveres premodern communities as historical models of "re-enchantment."

Bataille's theory of ecstatic community is integrally related to his theory of "waste" or "expenditure" (dépense). Taking his cue from Marcel Mauss's celebrated essay on *The Gift* (1925), Bataille identified the outstanding feature of premodern societies as their capacity for "non-productive expenditure" or "waste." As Mauss explains, in non-Western societies exchange represented much more than a vulgar economic transaction. Instead, it embodied a "total social phenomenon": an act of exchange was simultaneously a *religious, aesthetic,* and *social* act, as well as an *economic* one. Describing the nature of gift-giving and potlatch in tribal societies, Mauss affirms, "In these 'early' societies, social phenomena are not discrete; each phenomenon contains all the threads of which the social fabric is composed.

In these *total social phenomena* . . . all kinds of institutions find simultaneous expression: religious, legal, moral, and economic."[38]

Like other sociologists and anthropologists, Bataille feared that since the ritual-oriented, community-binding dimensions of social practice had been banished from modern life, social instability was on the rise. In his view, only a revival of such long-lost practices and rites—practices that had been anathematized by theorists of social evolution as "primitive"—could restore solidarity and avert potentially grave crises of social disequilibrium.

In "The Notion of Expenditure" (1933) Bataille insisted that "war" constituted only one among many possible sources of cultural transgression. Other prospects included "luxury, mourning . . . cults, the construction of sumptuary monuments, games, spectacles, arts, perverse sexual activity (i.e., deflected from genital finality)." In Bataille's view these phenomena represented social "activities which, at least in primitive circumstances, *have no end beyond themselves.*"[39] They presented a stark contrast with commodity exchange, the predominant value-orientation of homogeneous societies, which degraded all social action to the status of a means to an end—the accumulation of wealth.

At times Bataille's longing for community and his glorification of "transgression"—acts of excess that would disrupt the status quo—seemed to argue for mutually contradictory values. For the rituals of premodern communities aimed at ensuring stability, tradition, and the maintenance of social "norms"—above all, the norm separating the sacred and profane. Yet Bataille, the self-proclaimed apostle of "excess" and black sheep of the twentieth-century avant-garde, professed a credo mandating *profanation for profanation's sake*—an "ethos" or "anti-ethos" obsessed with violating taboos, disrupting norms, and transcending limits. While this orientation was certainly well-represented in his theoretical writings, it came through even more vividly in his Sadean novellas of the 1920s and 1930s, *The Story of the Eye* and *The Blue of Noon*. Both novels represent explorations of (as Bataille puts it in "The Notion of Expenditure") "perverse sexual activity i.e., deflected from genital finality." Taboos are violated on virtually every page. The missionary position is the only sexual posture that remains unexplored.[40]

In reexamining the religion of transgression propagated by Bataille, however, one encounters significant ethical gaps. Echoing Tony Judt's findings in *Past Imperfect: French Intellectuals, 1944–1956,* one senses that aspects of Bataille's thought are redolent of a more general and longstanding "vacuum at the heart of public ethics in France"—"the marked absence of a concern with public ethics or political morality."[41] In France during the 1930s this ethical void reached crisis proportions when antirepublican sentiment proliferated on both the left and right sides of the political spectrum, foreshadowing the nation's "strange defeat" of 1940. Yet this is also the context in which Bataille's role as a precursor of poststructuralism becomes critical. For in the manner of Heidegger, who famously forswore "ethics" in favor of "Fundamental Ontology," poststructuralism, too, has had a notoriously difficult time articulating an ethics. Thus, following the iconoclastic lineage established by Bataille and Nietzsche, Foucault later equated "norms" with "normalization," the production of pliable minds and "docile bodies." He perceived norms as little more than cogs in the mechanism of modern society qua disciplinary regime. As a result, in his diagnosis of the age, the dimension of "principle" evaporated, becoming mere grist for the mill of modernity qua "carceral society." Like Bataille and Nietzsche, Foucault sought to stand traditional morality on its head. Following Nietzsche's summons in *The Genealogy of Morals,* he heralded a "transvaluation of values." Norms retained value only insofar as they served as objects of "transgression" or "self-overcoming."[42]

In recent years denizens of the poststructuralist camp have begun meditating on how one might constitute a community immune to totalitarian temptation. Unsurprisingly, Bataille's meditations on the sacred, sacrifice, and transgression have served as an indispensable point of reference.[43] Following Bataille's lead, this "unavowable" (Blanchot) or "inoperative" community (J. L. Nancy) would be predicated on the values of "heterogeneity" and "difference" instead of those of "totality." This community would be subtended not by the values of social transparency but by the anticonventional mores of transgression. Bernard-Henri Lévy has rightly sounded an alarm concerning the anti-moral implications of this new, avowedly illiberal "communitarian" spirit.

Organicism. Naturalism. Refusal of universal values. Denial of values purely and simply. . . . It is on these bases, on this mute foundation, that one deploys a cover of horror that is more somber and infinitely more clamorous. . . . I will have attained my objective when I have succeeded in convincing that fascism is not in the first instance barbarism; that it is not essentially and to begin with the apocalypse; that it does not always and of necessity mean storms of iron and blood. Instead, it is in the first instance a type of society, *a model of community, a manner of thinking and of organizing the social bond.*[44]

Bataille's "ecstatic" model of community, the manner of "thinking and of organizing the social bond" he seeks to privilege, merits critical scrutiny, for it is a model that embraces an aesthetics of transgression as the norm for social action. Bataille's ecstatic community would also be an *aesthetic community:* a community in which the favored mode of social practice would be action that yielded "no return"; action that, in a manner reminiscent of art for art's sake, had no end beyond itself.

At times, Bataille's celebration of transgression for its own sake seems woefully simplistic. In lieu of a conceptual framework that would permit one to distinguish between constructive and retrograde instances of transgression, we are left with an ethos of shock, rupture, and disruption *simpliciter.* Bataille seeks to ground postmodern ethics in the attitudes of a cultural avant-garde (Acéphale and the College of Sociology) oriented toward precapitalist life forms that modernity has scorned. Yet the very idea of achieving a conceptual reckoning with Bataille-generated ideals such as "transgression," "heterogeneity," and "expenditure" would seem inimical to their very spirit. In his idiom, to rely on procedures of principled legitimation or a rational accountability would be to succumb to the logic and rhetoric of "productive consumption"—the values of a society predicated on instrumental reason and commodity exchange.

The Gift of Death

To appreciate the pivotal position Bataille occupies in the intellectual life of twentieth-century France, one must view his work in relation to the legacy of Mauss and Durkheim's theory of religion. Mauss's work incited Bataille's fascination with the notions of sacrifice and the gift. The practices of ritual sacrifice and gift-giving formed the basis for Bataille's own conceptual innovations during the 1930s and 1940s, innovations that culminated in his theories of "waste" and of the "accursed share" (*la part maudite*).

In his "Moral Conclusions" to *The Gift*, Mauss offers a plea on behalf of the world we have lost. He bemoans the fact that modern social relations have been impoverished "by the substitution of a rational economic system for a system in which exchange of goods was not a mechanical but a moral transaction, bringing about and maintaining personal relationships between individuals and groups."[45] The *moral* side of exchange had been decimated by the impersonal reign of commodity production in modern societies, lamented Mauss, whose work might be viewed as an anthropological pendant to the Marxian critique of political economy. In premodern societies, in which economics were not yet separate from religious life, exchange played an essential role in the maintenance and reproduction of group solidarity. Conversely, with the advent of capitalism arose a society of pure competition—an economic *bellum omnium contra omnes*—and the natural bases of social solidarity degenerated to the point of collapse. Donning the guise of cultural critic, Mauss observes,

> It is only our Western societies that quite recently turned man into an economic animal. . . . *Homo oeconomicus* is not behind us, but before us, like the moral man, the man of duty, the scientific man and the reasonable man. For a long time man was something quite different; and it is not so long now since he became a machine—a calculating machine.[46]

Mauss's Weberian lament concerning the fragmentation of modern life is accompanied by admiration for premodern communities in which life approximated a meaningful totality. In such communities economic activity was never specialized and one-sided. Instead, it was a "total social phenomenon," incorporating religious, aesthetic, legal, and moral aspects. Premodern societies exuded an "economic effervescence which has little about it that is materialistic; it is much less prosaic than our sale and purchase, hire of services and speculations."[47] Whatever their failings, these societies displayed a balance and wholeness entirely lacking in their modern counterparts, governed as they are by a single-minded pursuit of profit and gain. They manifested a well-roundedness absent in societies dominated by the division of labor. In a passage that would have significant repercussions for many subsequent French anthropological critiques of modernity (from Lévi-Strauss to Baudrillard and postmodern ethnography), Mauss stressed the *aesthetic* orientation that suffused premodern societies:

> the dances performed, the songs and shows, the dramatic representations given between camps or partners, the objects made, used, decorated, polished, amassed and transmitted with affection, received with joy, given away in triumph, the feasts in which everyone participates—all these . . . are the source of *aesthetic emotions* as well as emotions aroused by interest.[48]

Mauss's flamboyant descriptions of sacrifice, potlatch, gift-giving, and other nonutilitarian forms of ritual were undoubtedly the main sources for Bataille's theory of expenditure or nonproductive consumption. But Mauss's conclusions are unproblematic in a way that Bataille's are not. Mauss—who was politically allied with the French Socialist Party (SFIO)—merely sought to restore an element of balance in advanced industrial societies whose relation to nonutilitarian modes of social interaction had seriously atrophied. His critique represented as a welcome corrective to their potentially debilitating uniformity.

Bataille's stance was in fact quite different. His critique of modernity was intended neither as a palliative nor as a corrective, but, in keeping with the leitmotif of transgression, as a type of (non-Hegelian) supersession.[49] Bataille appeals for a total break with the modernity. He rejects not only its utilitarian predispositions and excesses but also its very status as a form of life: its cultural, political, legal, ethical, and aesthetic aspects. Thus, his theory inclines toward a totalizing indictment of modernity that shares marked affinities with the critique of civilization proffered by the German conservative revolutionaries. Their shared belief that the shortcomings of the modern age can be remedied neither piecemeal nor from within entails an ethos of total contestation.

Bataille's strengths as a critic of civilization come to light in his creative appropriation of Durkheim and Mauss. What civilization lacks is what premodern societies took for granted: proximity to the sacred, which accounts for the difference between life lived with *intensity* (or, to use the term favored by Durkheim and Mauss, "effervescence") and "mere life." The keywords Bataille uses to refer to this exalted state in which individuation collapses and individuals are able to transcend the fragmentation and isolation of the *condition humaine* are "immanence," "intimacy," and "inner experience"—hence, Bataille's fascination with those moments of experiential intensity that breach the traditional barriers between the sacred and the profane. Such moments are epitomized by the resolutely non-utilitarian acts of sacrifice and gift-giving.

They are not, however, limited to such acts. Bataille invokes other forms of violent pleasure as means of overturning the reign of instrumental reason. The utilitarian mentality yields only the moderate pleasures associated with the accumulation of wealth. According to Bataille, conversely, "Human society [has] an *interest* in considerable losses, in catastrophes that, *while conforming to well-defined needs,* provoke tumultuous depressions, crises of dread, and, in the final analysis, a certain orgiastic state." Such cataclysms and upheavals are paradigmatic instances of *nonproductive expenditure.* They permit "the satisfaction of disarmingly savage needs" that "subsist only at the limits of horror." In such instances, Bataille continues, "The accent is placed on a *loss* that must be as great as possible in order for that activity to take on its true meaning."[50] Prodigious loss could serve as a prophylaxis against the temptations of unlimited accumulation, the "productive consumption" of goods. As Bataille observes:

Everything that was generous, orgiastic, and excessive has disappeared; the themes of rivalry upon which individual activity still depends develop in obscurity, and are as shameful as belching. The representatives of the bourgeoisie have adopted an unobtrusive manner; wealth is now displayed behind closed doors in accordance with depressing and boring conventions. . . . Such trickery has become the principle reason for living, working, and suffering for those who lack the courage to condemn this moldy society to revolutionary destruction.[51]

"In trying to maintain sterility in regard to expenditure in conformity with a reasoning that balances *accounts*," concludes Bataille, "bourgeois society has only managed to develop a universal meanness."[52] In such passages, his proximity to Nietzsche's lament concerning the disappearance of "heroic" values in modern life—for instance, struggle, cruelty, and risk—becomes crystal clear.

But problems exist with Bataille's use of ethnographic literature on sacrifice and the gift. For in certain respects his naïve employment of Mauss's findings risks regressing behind his mentor's account. For Bataille, the glory of ritual lies in its gratuitousness: qua social practice, ritual is totally removed from utilitarian ends. And as such, it engenders privileged moments when society embraces loss qua loss. Sacrifice in particular involves a transfiguration of everyday life that verges on apotheosis: both victim and community temporarily cross the line separating the sacred from the profane. The victim becomes a demigod momentarily permitted to dwell among the gods and the community stands in enhanced proximity to the sacred. For Bataille, profane existence is a "thing-world," a sphere of life beholden to mundane considerations of use. Its denizens grapple fecklessly with the cycle of production and reproduction that constitutes "mere life." "Sacrifice," Bataille observes, "restores to the sacred world that which servile use has degraded, rendered profane." Religion is purely "a matter of detaching from the *real* order, from the poverty of *things*, and of restoring the *divine* order." When viewed from the Bataillesque standpoint of "nonproductive expenditure," acts of destruction—sacrifice, potlatch, war, and violence—*ennoble.*

Destruction emancipates both objects and persons from the profane considerations of use. As Bataille contends, "Destruction is the
best means of negating a utilitarian relation."[53]

The grandeur of sacrifice or gift-giving lies in their restoration of
"intimacy": a proximity to the sacred reminiscent of Heideggerian
"nearness to Being" *(Nähe)*. As Bataille explains:

> The victim is a surplus taken from the mass of *useful* wealth. And he
> can only be withdrawn from it in order to be consumed profitlessly,
> and therefore utterly destroyed. Once chosen, he is the *accursed
> share,* destined for violent consumption. But the curse tears him
> away from the *order of things;* it gives him a recognizable figure,
> which now radiates intimacy, anguish, the profundity of living
> beings. . . . This was the price men paid to escape their downfall and
> remove the weight introduced in them by the avarice and cold cal-
> culation of the real order.[54]

Yet insofar as they misconstrue the historical parameters of ritual
practice, these celebratory descriptions risk becoming glib. Ultimately,
Bataille's appreciation of these phenomena succumbs to a type of
"primitivism." He decontextualizes the cult practices he analyzes the
better to incorporate them within his own theoretical agenda: "an
anthropology that will itself provide a living—and orgiastic—myth
to overturn, through its experience on a collective level, 'modern'
sterile bourgeois society."[55]

Bataille understands sacrifice as gratuitous and nonutilitarian.
Acts of sacrifice, he claims, have "no ends beyond themselves." But
this contention is misleading. Although Bataille is correct in describing such practices as unrelated to the production of wealth, they are
very much oriented toward the reproduction of existing power relations. As practiced among the Aztecs, human sacrifice redounded to
the credit of the ruling caste (priests and aristocracy), providing
them with a quasi-divine power to preside over life and death. For
these reasons, it is deceptive to claim, as Bataille repeatedly does,
that sacrifice has no end beyond itself.

One could raise an analogous criticism of Bataille's treatment of
potlatch—the public, demonstrative destruction of wealth—as well

as gift-giving. In truth, only those who possess great wealth can afford to destroy it. Consequently, the option to engage in potlatch does not exist for society's lower classes.[56] Like sacrifice, potlatch is implicated in the reproduction of social hierarchy. Such acts reinforce the status and prestige of those who destroy their wealth. In nearly every case, the practitioners of potlatch belong to the upper strata of society. Those who are forced to passively endure the potlatch are in effect humiliated. Through such acts, their lowly social rank is reaffirmed.

The same is true of gift-giving. Gifts are not freely bestowed, shorn of ulterior ends. Bataille seizes on the aspect of gift-giving that serves his purposes. Gift-giving is not an economic transaction; it is neither an act of barter, nor does it aim at the enhancement of social wealth. Instead, in the first instance with gift-giving, *social relations* among persons are at issue. As with both sacrifice and potlatch, what is at stake with the gift are relations of power. When given in accordance with social ritual, gifts always come with strings attached: unless the gift can be returned in kind, its social function is to intimidate the recipient. The object of gift-giving as a social ritual is to derogate and shame the recipient by virtue of his or her inability to return a gift of equal value. Gift-giving, too, then must be classified as a ritual practice that is in no sense gratuitous or free. Far from being an end in itself, as Bataille claims, it is fully implicated in the production and reproduction of social power.

Such insights are amply confirmed in the writings of Mauss and other ethnographers:

> The motives of such excessive gifts and reckless consumption, such mad losses and destruction of wealth, especially in these potlatch societies, are in no way disinterested. Between vassals and chiefs, between vassals and their henchmen, *the hierarchy is established by means of these gifts*. To give is to show one's superiority, to show that one is something more and higher, that one is *magister*. To accept without returning or repaying more is to face subordination, to become a client and subservient, to become *minister*.[57]

Left Fascism

Bataille's conceptual orientation harmonizes with the "noncon-formist" credo rife in France during the 1930s: an excoriation of liberalism, parliamentarism, autonomous subjectivity, and Enlightenment reason, offering, in their stead, a commitment to the idea of ecstatic community.[58] It is an attitude increasingly sympathetic toward the goals of "fascist socialism" (Drieu La Rochelle) or "left fascism"—a political disposition with deep roots in French political culture.

Bataille had no personal truck with Vichy—nor was he a *résistant*. Instead, he spent the war years in "inner emigration," preoccupied with literary concerns (the novel *Madame Edwarda*) and composing his anti-Thomist *Summa Atheologica*. As one observer has remarked, "All the texts written [by Bataille] during the war years . . . translate into a profound need to disengage himself."[59] The causes behind this retreat from public life were both personal and intellectual. In the prewar years, he endured both the tragic death of his lover, Laure, as well as the sudden dissolution of the College of Sociology, the legendary gathering of French intellectuals that Bataille had founded in 1937 with Roger Caillois.[60]

If one scrutinizes the political positions espoused by Bataille during the 1930s, the theme of left fascism assumes a vivid and disquieting reality. Bataille's biographer, Michel Surya, has stated that when he began work on his book *(Georges Bataille: La Mort à l'oeuvre)*, many of his interviewees, most of whom were Bataille's contemporaries, assumed quite naturally that Bataille "was a fascist."[61] More damning still are the remarks of the left-wing anti-Stalinist, Boris Souvarine, in whose journal, *La Critique sociale,* many of Bataille's pathbreaking essays from the 1930s appeared. In his preface to the 1983 republication of the review, Souvarine claims that Bataille was a fascist sympathizer, and that, if he had had the courage of his convictions, he would have rallied to the cause.[62]

Undoubtedly, Souvarine overstates his case.[63] Yet the deeper one probes Bataille's political orientation in the 1930s, the more disconcerting the overall picture becomes.

Bataille's article on "The Psychological Structure of Fascism," often hailed as a breakthrough in our understanding of the mass psychological bases of political dictatorship, already gives cause for alarm. It features a barely veiled admiration for the energy and vitality of Europe's youthful fascist states, especially when contrasted with the decadence and inertia of democracy. In a number of passages Bataille purveys a critique of parliamentarism as zealous as anything one finds in Carl Schmitt.

Parliamentary democracy, claims Bataille, partakes wholly of the homogeneous order. It aims at the cooptation and the elimination of difference. Its function is to repress the heterogeneous elements that threaten to explode the normative bases of the given social and political order. As Bataille observes, "The reduction of differences in parliamentary practice indicates all the possible complexity of the internal activity of adaptation required by *homogeneity*."[64] In elaborating this critique, Bataille refuses to distinguish between political and economic aspects of democratic society. For example, it would be more accurate to argue that whereas economic action is goal oriented and utilitarian, the end of democracy is self-determination.[65]

Given the low esteem in which Bataille holds parliamentary democracy, that he glorifies fascism as a breakthrough of vital, heterogeneous forces is unsurprising. For Bataille, "the fascist leaders are incontestably part of heterogeneous existence. Opposed to democratic politicians, who represent in different countries the platitude inherent to *homogeneous* society, Mussolini and Hitler immediately stand out as something *other*."[66] What Bataille admires about the fascist leaders (here, he borrows a page from Nietzsche's doctrine of the Superman) is their "sovereignty": "a force that situates them above other men." He also esteems their aversion to "law": "the fact that laws are broken is only the most obvious sign of the transcendent, *heterogeneous* nature of fascist action."[67] Here, the parallels with Carl Schmitt's critique of bourgeois legality are profound. Both Schmitt and Bataille view law as the consummate embodiment of democratic rationalism. It symbolizes everything they detest about the reigning order: its unheroic longing for security, its opposition to revolution, its abhorrence of "transcendence," its aversion to vitality and intensity. For Bataille law merits derision insofar as it stands for a consecration of the profane order of existence that impedes proximity towards the sacred—"intimacy."

Bataille's endorsement of fascist politics culminates in the following glowing encomium: "*Heterogeneous* fascist action belongs to the entire set of higher forms. It makes an appeal to sentiments traditionally defined as *exalted* and *noble* and tends to constitute authority as an unconditional principle, situated above any utilitarian judgment."[68] Whereas bourgeois utilitarianism sanctifies "the prose of the world" (Hegel), fascism offers a new political aesthetic. It reintroduces an *aesthetic politics* that foregrounds the values of an ecstatic community prized by Bataille: charisma ("sovereignty"), violence, and martial glory. Bataille reveres fascism insofar as it cultivates an emotional cathexis between leaders and masses—a bond that has grown precariously weak in modern democracy. According to Bataille, fascism "clearly demonstrates what can be expected from a timely recourse to reawakened affective forces." It promises a measure of collective solidarity in a society otherwise suffused with fragmentation and anomie. In sum, fascism allows for the reprise of an ecstatic politics amid the forlorn and disenchanted landscape of political modernity.

Here, it is worth recalling Bernard-Henri Lévy's remark that "[fascism] is in the first instance a type of society, a model of community, a manner of thinking and of organizing the social bond."[69] For one of the prominent leitmotifs of Bataille's early work concerns the renewal of affective energies associated with the communitarian bond prevalent in premodern societies. His preoccupation with sacrifice, the sacred, and the prospects for political rebirth embodied in fascist "action" are comprehensible in these terms alone. As one commentator has aptly remarked concerning Bataille's interpretation of fascism as a form of the sacred or heterogeneous:

> The worship of Otherness which underlies [Bataille's] concept of the sacred inevitably leads to an acknowledgment of the attraction historical fascism exerts through the *mana* of its leaders. The category of the heterogeneous, as Bataille defines it, contains so much that is "nature" rather than "history" that its repeated application to

manifestations of fascist power quite clearly produce a mythification.[70]

In his study of the social-psychological origins of fascism, the philosopher Ernst Cassirer makes an analogous point. Basing his ideas on Malinowski's researches among the Trobriand islanders, he shows how for purposes of everyday problem-solving, the islanders use common sense and natural ingenuity. Under extraordinary circumstances, however, where empirical knowledge falls short, they invoke supernatural help: magic and rituals intended to influence higher powers to bring about the desired result. As Cassirer notes, "This description of the role of magic and mythology in primitive society applies equally well to highly advanced stages of man's political life." By this analogy, when modern societies experience grave crises in which the traditional means of problem-solving appear inadequate (Cassirer's historical point of reference is, of course, the demise of the Weimar Republic), they have recourse to the "irrational" means of political myth and charismatic leadership—in the German case, the myths of race and the charismatic leader who triumphs not by dint of intellect and skill but by virtue of having been endowed by destiny with superior powers. Following Durkheim, Cassirer explains such myths as a type of collective wish fulfillment: they represent the ideational projections of the community and thus a type of imaginary resolution of social problems that cannot be resolved via recourse to experience. As Cassirer concludes, "In all critical moments of man's social life, the rational forces that resist the rise of the old mythical conceptions are no longer sure of themselves. In these moments the time has come for myth again."

> The call for leadership only appears when a collective desire has reached an overwhelming strength and when, on the other hand, all hopes of fulfilling this desire, in an ordinary and normal way, have failed. At these times the desire is not only keenly felt but also personified. . . . The intensity of the collective wish is embodied in the leader. The former social bonds—law, justice, and constitutions—are declared to be without any value. What alone remains is the

mystical power and authority of the leader and the leader's will is supreme law.[71]

Cassirer's cautionary remarks shed light on Bataille's conviction that a revival of the charisma and myth would serve as a salutary counterweight to the centrifugal tendencies of modernity. The veneration of "unreason"—madness, myth, and the heterogeneous—that we have observed thus far is only enhanced in Bataille's work of the late 1930s. "Only myth reflects the image of a plenitude extending to the community in which men gather," remarks Bataille in 1937. He goes on to praise "the violent dynamic belonging to [myth which] has no other object than the return to a lost totality."[72]

The members of Acéphale—the secret society, modeled after a medieval religious order, Bataille cofounded in 1937—viewed themselves as a Nietzschean cultural vanguard charged with preparing the way for a more general political upheaval. Although its members were sworn to secrecy about its rites and practices, it is generally acknowledged that they practiced animal sacrifice and that the group seriously contemplated the idea of human sacrifice. The College of Sociology's program called for the return to various forms of premodern religiosity and community as an alternative to the impoverished spirituality of the West.

A rehabilitation of "virility"—a virtual obsession in the writings of the 1930s fascist literati (Drieu La Rochelle, Robert Brasillach)—figured prominently in the texts authored by Bataille and college cofounder Roger Caillois. Caillois concluded his 1937 inaugural lecture, "The Winter Wind," with the following fascistic prophesy: "an irreversible cleansing takes place in nature . . . there is a rising wind of subversion in the world now, a cold wind, harsh, arctic, one of those winds that is murderous . . . and that kills the fragile [and] the sickly, one that does not let them get through the winter."[73] In an era of concentration camps and goose-stepping troops, in which the Nietzsche's doctrine of "rank" (Rang) and "breeding" (Zuchtung) had come into its own—an era in which the Nazis laid the groundwork for the Final Solution via their winter-wind-like euthanasia program—such appeals quickly forfeit their innocence. In a similar spirit Caillois recommended to his fellow collegians that the new cultural vanguard "regard the rest of humanity less as their rightful equals than as the raw material for their ventures."[74] During his self-imposed Argentine wartime exile, Caillois would flirt with similar "dangerous" notions in the *Communion of the Strong* (Communion des Forts), in which he celebrates the "hangman" and the "sovereign" qua objects of horror and veneration. By virtue of their unquestioned social authority as well as their proximity to the "sacred," argues Caillois, these two figures ensure a level of social cohesion that liberal democracies have to their great detriment squandered. Yet, as Meyer Schapiro pointed out in an insightful review, by singing the praises of a "super-socialized" society predicated on the authority of a virile and sadistic spiritual elite, Caillois "contributes to the intellectual conditions for a reactionary political power," one in which intellectuals themselves would no doubt play an extremely "sinister" role.[75]

Bataille's own political prescriptions during this short-lived gathering of "sorcerer apprentices" (philosopher Alexandre Kojève's description of the college) were no less problematic. His sympathies for fascist Italy dated from a 1934 visit to Rome, where he viewed a famous Exhibition of the Fascist Revolution. In a letter to ex-Surrealist Raymond Queneau, he effusively praised Italian fascism's morbid iconography: black pennants, mortuary symbols, and death's heads. In "Power," a 1938 lecture presented at the college, Bataille glorified fascist Italy for the "fasces as seen on every locomotive's belly." (The lictor's axe or "fasces"—composed of a bundle of sticks—was an ancient Roman instrument for beheading subjects.) In Bataille's view, the lictor's axe was an effective instrument for the preservation of "sovereignty." Like Caillois, he believed in the need for a spiritual elite to restore the dimension of social solidarity that was wanting in modern society. A kindred admiration for the collective energies unleashed by fascism would play a key role in the concluding passages of his 1935 novel, *Bleu de Ciel*. Although, for the most part, Bataille scholarship has timidly tip-toed around these potentially compromising political themes, his "equivocal" attitude toward Europe's fascist dictatorships was already partly exposed back in the 1980s in an important essay by Carlo Ginzburg.[76]

In 1939 Bataille delivered a college lecture on "Hitler and the Teutonic Order." A society of orders—inspired by medieval knighthoods in which the values of hierarchy, glory, and conquest remained prominent—represented one of the ideals that Bataille and his colleagues sought to emulate. Of course, it was also a model that Europe's newly minted fascist regimes sought to revive.

Conveniently, and undoubtedly to the advantage of Bataille's intellectual legacy, the text of "Hitler and the Teutonic Order" has not been preserved. One can only speculate as its probable content. Denis Hollier, who single-handedly rescued the college from literary oblivion, suggests a link with Alphonse de Chateaubriant's 1937 pro-Nazi text, *La Gerbe des Forces,* in which Chateaubriant speaks admiringly of the new German elite paramilitary *Ordensburgen.* Patterned after the ancient orders of chivalry, they produced "the strong men whom the world, as much as Germany, needs today" to revolutionize contemporary society.[77]

In a 1971 interview Caillois described the mission of the college as follows: "It was concerned with conducting philosophical research, but philosophy was in a way only a facade or a form, the real project being to recreate the sacred in a society that tended to reject it. We thought of ourselves as sorcerer-apprentices. We had decided to unleash dangerous movements."[78] But the program collapsed dramatically with the onset of war, for it was then that the folly of a cultural program based on a "return of the primitive" became undeniably apparent. In the eyes of Bataille, Caillois, and company, the Nazis had in effect brought such primitive energies directly to bear on modern European societies, and the result was disastrous. As Caillois observes, "The war showed us the inanity of the attempt of the College of Sociology. The dark forces that we had dreamed of unleashing had been freed on their own, and their consequences were not those that we had expected."[79]

Contre-Attaque

There remains one chapter in the saga of Bataille's forays into the heady world of the Parisian cultural avant-garde that bears recounting. The episode is crucial, for it illustrates Bataille's transition from the left to the right side of the political spectrum. In the aftermath of his three year involvement with Souvarine's *La Critique sociale,* Bataille formed an alliance with former antagonist André Breton. A few years earlier, Bataille had dismissed Breton and the surrealists as "decadent aesthetes utterly incapable of even the possibility of contact with the lower classes."[80]

In the fall of 1935 Bataille founded a new group, Contre-Attaque, in which Breton had agreed to participate. To be sure, the intellectual differences separating these two titans of the cultural avant-garde remained cavernous. Breton had concluded his "Second Manifesto of Surrealism" with a cursory dismissal of Bataille as an "excremental philosopher," owing to the latter's obsession with scatological themes.[81] Breton, who was medically trained, went on to add that Bataille suffered from a pathological disorder and was in need of a cure. But this was, after all, the era of the Popular Front, which served as the pretext for many reconciliations among former political antagonists.

In light of this background, it will perhaps come as no surprise to learn that the lifespan of Contre-Attaque proved mercifully brief. Its manner of dissolution, however, is of no small interest. In the spring of 1936, Breton and the surrealist wing withdrew abruptly from the group, accusing Bataille and his supporters of embracing a "sur-fascisme"—a "superfascism" paralleling Nietzsche's advocacy of a "surhomme" or "Superman."

Bataille's unabashed admiration of fascist methods—for example, their aesthetics of violence—had surfaced in a manner that proved profoundly embarrassing to Breton and his allies. In Bataille's view, only the fascist revolutions in Italy and Germany had been successful in challenging liberal democratic decadence. They alone had replaced the decrepit value system of bourgeois society with a new collective mythology, a restoration of myth so avidly desired by the belief-starved masses.

This telltale flirtation with a "left fascism"—the advocacy of fascist methods for left-wing political ends—was apparent from the group's inaugural manifesto of October 1935, "Contre-Attaque: Union de lutte des intellectuals révolutionnaires." A sanguinary fascination with revolutionary violence suffused the manifesto, in which Bataille's views played a formative role. Thus, one of the group's resolutions emphasized that "public safety" ("le salut publique") required an "uncompromising dictatorship of the armed people." Europe's political destiny would be determined by "the creation of a vast network of disciplined and fanatical forces capable of exercising one day a merciless dictatorship." In conclusion, Bataille and his confrères explicitly praised fascist methods: "The time has come for all of us to behave like masters and to physically destroy the slaves of capitalism. . . . We intend to make use of the *weapons created by fascism,* which has known how to make use of the fundamental human aspiration for *affective exaltation and fanaticism.*"[82]

The stress on revolutionary violence, the endorsement of "sovereignty" and "mastership," the celebration of "affective exaltation and fanaticism"—the emotional side of mass politics that fascism had excelled in exploiting—represent key aspects of the ethos of left fascism as propagated by Bataille. In the context at hand, it is of more than passing interest to note that the notion of a "revolt of the masters" ("Herren-Aufstand") was one of the key ideas of Ernst Jünger's prophetic 1932 fascist manifesto *Der Arbeiter* (The Worker).[83]

A heuristic definition of left fascism suggests the idea—extremely widespread in 1930s French politics—of appropriating fascist methods for the ends of the political left. But this approach ran up against an insoluble methodological dilemma. At a certain point it became impossible to define the magic line or point of no return where the assimilation of fascist means had become indistinguishable from the fascist cause. As Allan Stoekl has remarked, "Effervescence, the subversive violence of the masses, the baseness of their refusal to enter into boring discussions—all these things, then, without a clear and correct theory behind them, could easily be reversed into fascism, as Bataille quickly became aware."[84]

Henri Dubief, a former member of Contre-Attaque, has described Bataille's political thinking circa 1935 in the following terms:

Persuaded of [fascism's] intrinsic perversity, Bataille affirmed its historical and political superiority to a depraved workers' movement and to corrupt liberal democracy. . . . There is an inevitable movement from anguish to intoxication over fascism. At this moment there were reflections of the fascist experience among Georges Bataille and his friends. Later, the influence of Hitler's neopaganism was patent in the case of Acéphale.85

The publication of a one-page manifesto, "Sous le Feu des Canons Français" ("Under the Fire of French Canons"), precipitated the break between the factions dominated by Bataille and Breton. Breton had been listed as a signatory to the document without prior consultation. The tract began with a condemnation of the Soviet Union, whose counterrevolutionary nature had been exposed as a result of its willingness to enter into an alliance with the corrupt bourgeois democracies, the "victors of 1918." (Under the auspices of Léon Blum's Popular Front government, the Franco-Soviet cooperation treaty had recently been signed.) The declaration concluded with the following provocative claim: "We are against rags of paper, against the slavish prose of the chancelleries. . . . We prefer to them, *come what may,* the anti-diplomatic brutality of Hitler, which is more peaceful than the slobbering excitation of the diplomats and politicians."86 Such forthright praise for Hitler came as a major embarrassment to the surrealist faction (which, in addition to Breton, included Benjamin Péret and Paul Eluard), which promptly resigned.

Although in his "Manifesto of Surrealism" Breton, in a Dadaist spirit of "épater le bourgeois," had openly celebrated the virtues of random violence—"The simplest surrealist act consists of dashing down into the street, pistol in hand, and firing blindly, as fast as you can pull the trigger, into the crowd. Anyone who has not dreamed of thus putting an end to the petty system of debasement and cretinization in effect has a well-defined place in the crowd with his belly at barrel level"87—there were limits beyond which he refused to follow Bataille's fascination with political transgression. This hesitancy certainly pertained to Bataille's advocacy of "fascist hetero-geneity."

Bataille's attraction toward fascism was consistent with a position he had articulated for some time, one epitomized by the epithet "left fascism." Like his brethren on the German right, Bataille was convinced of the bankruptcy of both bourgeois democracy and the communist alternative, which under Stalin's reign had degenerated into naked dictatorship. Like Germany's young conservatives, he sought out a "third way" beyond the equally disreputable politics of liberalism and communism.[88]

It seems that Bataille was already attracted to the left fascist worldview in the early 1930s. As early as 1934 he offered a remark-ably upbeat estimation of fascism's historical worth and import. Here was a force capable of restoring two elements that were desperately lacking in contemporary European society. Both com-ponents were quintessentially Durkheimian: a dimension of collec-tive solidarity that had disappeared with the advent of a society based on the division of labor, and the dimension of ritual-induced myth. In the face of a bourgeois order on the verge of disintegrative collapse, fascism, in Bataille's view, among its other attributes, restored scarce resources of social integration.[89] According to Bataille:

> The antagonisms expand from one day to the next and become too acute for society to survive without reabsorbing them. *Today, fascism represents the necessary labor of reabsorption.* It is *natural* that in the West the workers' movement, which is today moribund and miser-able, and which only knows how to do battle against itself, should be liquidated and disappear, *since it did not know how to win.* Per-haps there is no longer room for anything else on the earth other than societies transformed along the lines of monarchy, unified as much as the will of one man can be—that is, *room for great fascist societies.*[90]

In his study of France during the 1930s, Daniel Lindenberg has provided a felicitous account of Bataille's political evolution. Using a citation from Contre-Attaque as his point of departure ("The democratic regime, which finds itself in mortal contradictions, cannot be saved"), Lindenberg observes:

This is the credo that Bataille will develop, without ever distancing himself from it, from 1934 to the declaration of war [in 1939]. . . . Democracy is *against nature,* and the convulsions of our epoch prove this by demonstrating the true immutable and eternal nature of societies. . . . The "political" Bataille of the pre-war years wagered on a violent proletarian revolution; and, thereafter on Hitler's new order for the sake of founding a new tradition, to reestablish the rights of a tragic community. . . . But this does not prevent the fact that, as Jean-Michel Besnier has observed, "the refusal of history, the exaltation of origins and the valorization of mythology remain inscribed in the official philosophy of fascism."[91]

In hindsight Bataille himself was quick to acknowledge the disturbing nature of his prewar political orientation. Thus, in a series of critical reflections composed later in life, he avowed to having succumbed to a "paradoxical fascist tendency" during his Contre-Attaque period.[92]

Conclusion

The historical motivations behind the triumph of European fascism are complex. Moreover, they differ significantly according to specific national contexts. The central feature of Nazi ideology, the doctrine of race, has no parallel in the case of Italian fascism. Mussolini, who always emphasized the specificity of Italian traditions, stressed the preeminence of the state. This emphasis was foreign to the worldview of National Socialism, in which the state was often perceived as a bureaucratic impediment to the authenticity of the "movement."

But common features also unite the European fascist movements of the interwar period, and scrutinizing them will provide a better understanding of Bataille's political attitudes during the 1930s. His fascination with fascism was neither episodic nor accidental. Instead, it indicates how his work sought to articulate a widely shared "anticivilizational ethos" that was an integral part of the fascist sensibility.[93]

One of the generic features of fascism qua political movement was its attempt to roll back the achievements of the French Revolution—to efface the political ideas of 1789. As Goebbels opined shortly following Hitler's seizure of power, "The year 1789 is hereby eradicated from history." Commenting on the counterrevolutionary origins of European fascism, the historian Karl Dietrich Bracher has observed, "The intellectual forerunners on whom National Socialism drew in the development of its Weltanschauung were primarily ideologists fervently opposed to the ideas of democratic revolution, human rights, freedom, and equality."[94] In a similar vein, Zeev Sternhell has convincingly demonstrated the centrality of anti-Semitism in the ideology of counterrevolutionary worldview. For with its emergence in the latter decades of the nineteenth century, the condemnation of world Jewry became inextricably entwined with the desire to reverse the tide of democratic revolution, to dam the floodgate of egalitarian sentiment by virtue of which Jews emerged for the first time as the political equals of their Christian counterparts.[95] Whereas Bataille would certainly agree with socialist leader August Bebel's characterization of anti-Semitism as "the socialism of fools" (there are no traces of anti-Semitism in his work), his affinities with the ideologists of counterrevolution come to the fore precisely in his antipathy to the ideas of 1789.

Much has been written about the corollaries between fascism and "irrationalism" that remains conjectural and superficial.[96] It would be foolish to assert that all doctrines that radically question the primacy of reason exist in a symbiotic relation with forces of political reaction, let alone fascism.

Nevertheless, it would be equally misleading to deny that one of fascism's central ideological tenets entails a rejection of reason and all that it historically represents. In *Escape from Freedom*, Eric Fromm defined the fascist personality type in terms of a regressive character structure that yearns to be released from the demands of the ego autonomy. Such demands are felt to be burdensome to the weak ego identities produced in an era of managerial capitalism, in which socialization via large-scale organizations had become the rule. Social psychological regression takes the form of a defensive embrace of those ontogenetically prior components of the self, the id and the superego. The superego is embodied by the fascist leader, who sanctions the masses' longing to act out long repressed libidinal urges.

Hence, one of the primary means of escaping the demands of autonomy is an immersion of the self within the social collectivity, an approach to socialization common to both premodern and fascist communities. In *Group Psychology and the Analysis of the Ego* (1923), Freud presented the following observations concerning the regressive social psychological tendencies displayed by the masses, who play such an increasingly significant role in modern political life. The group

> respects force and can only be slightly influenced by kindness, which it regards merely as a form of weakness. What it demands of its heroes is strength, or even violence. It wants to be ruled and oppressed and to fear its masters. Fundamentally it is entirely conservative, and it has a deep aversion to all innovations and advances and an unbounded respect of tradition.

In sum, "When individuals come together in a group all their individual inhibitions fall away and all the cruel, brutal and destructive instincts, which lie dormant in individuals as relics of a primitive epoch, are stirred up to free gratifications."[97]

In light of Freud's analysis of the problem of group psychology, which has proved so fruitful for understanding fascist character structure, the basis for Bataille's infatuation with protofascist methods of socialization becomes clear. Such methods of socialization permit access to a realm of socially prohibited instinctual expression—a release of inhibitions, the emergence of cruel and destructive instincts, a sadomasochistic celebration of violence and mastery—on which, in many respects, Bataille's doctrine of transgression significantly draws. Needless to say, uninhibited instinctual expression is by no means inherently fascistic. Instead, only when this expression of pent-up libidinal urges is explicitly tied to the avowedly regressive sadomasochistic traits does the character type of associated with the "authoritarian personality" arise.

Bataille's uncritical glorification of elements and forces that have been repressed by civilization—"heterogeneous" experiences or the accursed share *(la part maudite)*—accounts for his troubling affinities with what Max Horkheimer has described as the "revolt of nature": the regressive channeling of anticivilizational urges undertaken by the authoritarian political regimes in our era.[98]

·5·

Maurice Blanchot: The Use and
Abuse of Silence

It [is] simply dishonest to praise piously the dimension of the
heterogeneous in the writings of one of the great writers of the century
. . . wholly deleting the most unassimilable fragment of his oeuvre.

—JEFFREY MEHLMAN, *Legacies of Anti-Semitism in France*

The Triumph of Nonphilosophy

If one examines the major developments in postwar French
thought, two phenomena stand out: first, sources drawn from the
realm of "nonphilosophy" contest the autonomy of philosophy —
above all, sources deriving from *literature* (in the case of thinkers
like Roland Barthes and Jacques Derrida) and the *social sciences* (in
the case of thinkers like Claude Lévi-Strauss and Michel Foucault);
second, a wide range of writers and thinkers engage in a generalized assault against the idea of "representation"—the notion that
mind is capable of portraying reality truthfully and objectively.
Thus, for thinkers like Barthes and Derrida, the traditional goal of
cognition, so-called objective knowledge, is impossible insofar as
discourse is pervaded by metaphor, and metaphor can only yield
"truths" that are inherently unstable. For if all language can do is
imply that one thing is like another thing, then the tasks of representation are infinite, and knowledge, which necessarily makes use
of language, is irremediably provisional and precarious.

Strikingly, these critiques are diametrically opposed to the main
developmental tendencies of French intellectual life, which, since
Descartes and the Enlightenment, have celebrated the values of

clarity, directness, lucidity, and transparency. According to these recent approaches, not only are traditional theories of knowledge deemed inadequate, they have been accused of producing results antithetical to the emancipatory aims originally intended. Instead of freeing men and women from immaturity and political bondage, Foucault, for example, alleges that "reason" inscribes them inexorably and inescapably in the trappings of "power." One result of this cynical take on knowledge is that the traditional relationship between insight and emancipation appears to be severed. Thus, in the work of Foucault "power" is elevated to the status of an impregnable prime mover. Its workings persist in defiance of the best-intentioned efforts to cast them off. Popular sovereignty and the virtues of public reason have a negligible effect on power's capacity to persevere and proliferate. The lure of intra-systemic change is precisely that: a mechanism of deception as a result of which the denizens of modern society find themselves more profoundly ensconced among the encumbrances of a "totally administered world" (Adorno). The recourse of those who seek to disentangle themselves from power's omnivorous maw remains highly circumscribed. A self-styled cenacle of postmodern aesthetes might engage in a set of alternative cultural practices—such as, following the lead of Nietzsche and Baudelaire, the choice of a beautiful life—that might temporarily outwit power's totalizing grasp.[1] But the emancipatory hopes of the vast majority of men and women seem consigned in advance to frustration and disappointment.

Today the radical theoretical current I have been describing—better known as poststructuralism—has become "historical." Its texts are still read and discussed. But the Nietzschean "transvaluation of values" it sought to herald never came to pass. Instead, ideas and concepts that were once deemed obsolete—democracy, truth, and human rights—merit a second look. These developments suggest the plausibility of attempting to situate poststructuralism historically. What were the social and political conditions that favored its emergence? What were the historical factors that facilitated its broad acceptance? What were the unstated presuppositions that enabled it to cohere as a "discourse" or a cohesive body of thought? Although scholars have frequently examined post-

structuralism's ideational patrimony, they have neglected its "historical" side—a partial reflection of its own antipathy to history, no
doubt.[2]

In this chapter, by examining the intellectual itinerary of one of
poststructuralism's pivotal forbears, the journalist and literary critic
Maurice Blanchot (1907–2003), I hope to shed light on French
theory's endemic mistrust of "representation." "Mistrust" differs
from "critique." Whereas critique operates with the intention of for-
tifying or strengthening the object of criticism, mistrust connotes a
latent hostility. Indeed, with the discourse in question, what begins
as "mistrust" quickly metamorphoses into "enmity." According to
the intellectual genealogy in question, the radical suspicion of representation begins in the 1930s and 1940s with "marginal" thinkers like
Blanchot and Bataille. Only during the 1960s, however, with the
breakthrough of renegade "antiphilosophers" like Derrida and Foucault, did it gain widespread acceptance, especially in North America—at the risk of becoming a new dogma. Thus, Derrida's early
texts on Husserl stress the "impossibility" of philosophy as "rigorous
science": the slippages, fissures, and instabilities of language perpetually render the ends of "first philosophy"—trustworthy and
reliable knowledge—null and void. According to the lexicon of
deconstruction, truth becomes "undecidable." In a kindred manner,
Foucault, explicitly relying on the intellectual precedents established
by Blanchot, celebrates the prospect of a "thought from outside": a
modality of expression that, like a time-bomb subtending the
"dynasty of representation," would explode the limits of "[rational]
discourse." According to Foucault, the result would be "an absolute
opening through which language endlessly spreads forth, while the
subject . . . fragments, disperses, [and] scatters, disappearing in that
naked space."[3]

By following the sinuous skein of Blanchot's early intellectual
path, I hope to shed light on the latent historical stakes involved in
the enmity toward representation. One of the neglected thematics
pertains to the so-called Vichy Syndrome: France's fitful postwar
effort to come to terms with the traumas of war, defeat, occupation, and collaboration. My supposition is that underlying the theoretical antipathy to "representation" as a figure for knowledge and

truth is a subconscious "will to nonknowledge": a desire to keep at bay an awareness of unsettling historical complicities, facts, and events.

Revolution from the Right

During the 1930s Maurice Blanchot was an engaged intellectual. A starker contrast to the *littérateur* and aesthete he would become in the postwar period could hardly be imagined.[4] In retrospect, however, Blanchot seems to have been "engaged" on the wrong side: instead of casting his lot with the antifascist alliance of the Popular Front, he wrote for and supported a dizzying array of far-right journals in whose eyes the Popular Front alliance between republicanism and godless communism was a pact brokered by the Antichrist. Though critics have scrutinized Blanchot's early political career (above all in two pathbreaking articles by Jeffrey Mehlman),[5] to date the full extent of his activities as an antirepublican ideologue have barely been treated.[6] For during the 1930s Blanchot's forays in the realm of far-right political journalism were anything but a passing dalliance. Instead, his literary output on behalf of a wide range of journals edited and funded by a prominent group of dissident Maurrasians—unconventional disciples of Action Française founder Charles Maurras—was by any standard prolific. Among the reviews to which he contributed were *La Revue française politique et littéraire*, *Réaction*, *Revue du siècle*, *Le Rempart*, *Combat*, *L'Insurgent*. While still in his mid-twenties, Blanchot was installed as foreign affairs editor of *Journal des débats*, an ultraconservative organ funded by France's legendary *deux cents familles* (the wealthiest families who reputedly controlled the nation's destiny from behind the scenes), in which capacity he penned a weekly column—on occasion, two.

From a contemporary vantage point, the political orientation of these far-right journals—not to mention the significance and import of Blanchot's participation in them—is difficult to discern. For although they display affinities with the predominant political orientations of the day—"fascination with fascism"—French writers like Blanchot brought a number of idiosyncratically Gallic features to an already exotic ideological brew that presents considerable retrospective interpretive difficulties.

Perhaps the thread uniting Blanchot and his fellow Maurrasian dissidents was an undying hatred of French republicanism and everything it represented: democracy, egalitarianism, civil liberties, universalism, the "rights of man and citizen." In the eyes of these circles, for over one hundred years the "ideas of 1789" had been responsible for sapping the nation of its integrity, honor, and virility. Since the Napoleonic era the nation's decline had progressed steadily until the debacle of 1870—the defeat at Sedan at the hands of Bismarck's Prussia (that France's defeat was brokered by a restored empire rather than a republic seemed to matter little in the eyes of critics like Ernst Renan and Hyppolite Taine).[7] That some thirty years later an alliance of socialists and republicans had in the course of the Dreyfus Affair triumphed at the expense of the forces of authority and order (army, church, and state) constituted an additional setback. At this juncture Action Française founder and far-right preceptor Charles Maurras coined his famous slogan "la politique d'abord!" ("politics above all!"). The Great War's favorable outcome accorded the hated republic a pyrrhic reprieve—at the cost of some 1.4 million dead and 3.6 million wounded. During the 1930s, however, the dam had burst, and whatever lukewarm support the embattled republic had enjoyed among French rightists rapidly dissipated. The economic effects of the Great Depression were slower to arrive in France, but when they did emerge circa 1932 they were acutely felt, and the latent ideological divides that had beset French politics in previous years suddenly seemed unbridgeable. As Blanchot would write in *Le Rempart*, "Today the signs of a general political crisis are everywhere. After having lived for many years with a feeling of security and order . . . we find ourselves confronted with a delegation of private interests jealously guarded by their representatives: *there is no state left.*"[8]

The 1933 Stavisky scandal embodied the ultimate confirmation of capitalism's endemic corruption, and was in many ways a replay of the Panama affair that had jolted the nascent republic some forty years earlier.[9] Before its foreign policy blunders later in the decade (the Abyssinian adventure and the ill-fated alliance with Hitler),

Fascist Italy had been admired by many on the French right as a model authoritarian state. In the 1930s Pétain expressed the opinion that in the event of a future war Italy would emerge fortified, since in Mussolini the Italians had a man who knew exactly what he wanted—as opposed to the democracies, whose vacillation and indecision were pitiable.[10] As the decade progressed it had become a commonplace among apostles of antirepublicanism that a similar regime—tailored to the peculiarities of hexagonal culture and traditions—would be appropriate for France. The search was on for an acceptable "fascist minimum" that would sanction the return of the state qua unyielding bastion of political authority—one that would put an end to the chaos and uncertainty of economic and political "liberalism."

Blanchot's political journalism dovetailed perfectly with this widespread, proto-fascist mentality. In his articles for *Le Rempart,* he polemicized against the "inhuman Declaration of the Rights of Man," which, in his view, disastrously redefined liberty as something "disengaged from its historical antecedents, freed from its natural ties." The only solution to a dysfunctional republicanism, observes Blanchot, is a fascist-type insurrection. "When the state has become incapable of working in favor of the state and in favor of the nation, the public weal can only be defended by resistance against the public powers . . . It becomes everyone's duty to denounce unjust laws and to remove themselves from their influence. Thus, the revolution begins." "The Italian and German adventures," Blanchot continues, "are, in this regard, full of promise. If they do not show us which revolution we should hope and prepare for, they show us nevertheless that we should hope for a revolution that will be our salvation."[11]

Hitler's ascent across the Rhine, accompanied by pledges to remilitarize and settle outstanding political scores, added a dimension of urgency to what was already a pressure-cooker political environment. Although the February 6, 1934 right-wing coup attempt staged at the Place de la Concorde was rebuffed by loyalists (two years later, in the pages of *Combat,* Blanchot would praise this revolt as "magnificent by virtue of its ardor, devotion, and sublime actions"), it appeared that, even among supporters, prorepublican sentiment was wearing thin.[12] When following a period of relative calm Léon Blum's Popular Front government came to power in 1936, it seemed as though the extreme right's worst nightmares had been confirmed: the Bolshevization of France appeared imminent; only a counterrevolution could stave off the impending apocalypse. When one surveys the degree of internecine political warfare that preoccupied France during the 1930s, it's little wonder that when the hour of truth came in May-June 1940, the hexagon succumbed to the Nazi Blitzkrieg in a mere six weeks.

For the apostles of the French *Jeune Droite* (Young Right), as they were collectively known—a movement that spawned journals such as Robert Aron and Arnaud Dandieu's *Ordre Nouveau* and Emmanuel Mounier's *Esprit*—Charles Maurras, who had once stood toe-to-toe with the hated Dreyfusards, was still revered as a *maître à penser*, albeit a mentor whose attitudes and positions possessed a faintly antiquarian whiff. Ultimately, for this group, including Blanchot, the distinctive combination of royalism, Catholicism, and classicism that characterized the Action Française worldview reeked of tradition. Whether this perspective could be updated for purposes of modern political combat was highly doubtful.

The Maurrasian dissidents were preoccupied with the question of where to turn for a viable political alternative to the despised republic. In the end, it would prove to be the group's Achilles' heel. For it was a fraternity that, in exemplary French fashion, excelled at stylized invective and literary disdain. But when it came to proposing concrete directives for France's political salvation, other than a perfunctory nod toward the virtues of "planning" and *étatisme*, their imagination failed miserably. They desired a France that would be glorious, virile, exalted, and potent. But the only means available to achieve such ends—means borrowed from the political repertoire of France's neighboring fascist dictatorships—seemed to rely on a crude mass politics; and this was a Rubicon that, in most cases, this coterie of well-born, nonconformist aesthetes, starry-eyed in their reverence for Nietzsche, refused to cross. A hesitation before the compromises of "mass politics" is what distinguished the political orientation of Blanchot and his fellow nonconformists from that of ardent fascists like Robert Brasillach, Pierre Drieu La Rochelle, Louis-Ferdinand Céline, and Lucien Rabatet—all of whom subscribed to the anti-Semitic ethos purveyed by Nazism.[13] Although Maurrasian dissidents like Blanchot were anything but philo-Semitic—Blanchot's 1930s journalism was suffused with a boilerplate, anti-Dreyfusard political demonology associating Jews with the evils of "capitalism" and "cosmopolitanism"—they balked at Nazism's uncouth, biological anti-Semitism.

As lapsed Catholics and ex-Maurrasians, one of the linchpins of their program for national renewal was the claim that their revolution would entail a prominent *spiritual* dimension—in this regard, Mounier's *Esprit* was prototypical. From an ideological standpoint, the emphasis on "spirit" and "things spiritual" accomplished several ends at once. It allowed Blanchot and his fellow nonconformists to distinguish *their* model of political authoritarianism from the rival, baser, *unspiritual* varieties flourishing on France's borders under guidance of Hitler and Mussolini. It also served to highlight the specificity of their revolutionary worldview vis-à-vis the competing ideologies of capitalism and socialism—both of which, in the eyes of right-wing youth, had succumbed to a craven materialism.

This point speaks to another peculiarity of Jeune Droite ideology: its adherents rarely bothered to distinguish between capitalism and socialism. In their eyes these rival political formations were only superficially opposed. On a more essential plane both capitalism and socialism shared a belief that the organization of economic life represented the central task of modern politics. Both systems alleged that the economic sphere represented the ne plus ultra of human fulfillment. Conversely, by according prominence to the spiritual dimension of politics, *French* fascism would rectify one of political modernity's fundamental ideological missteps.

Among this milieu of talented antidemocratic, right wing publicists, Nietzsche's tutelary presence loomed especially large. By the mid-1930s it even began to outstrip the influence of rival anti-Enlightenment contrarians such as Kierkegaard, Bergson, and Sorel, the intellectual beacons among first generation Maurrasians, such as Emmanuel Berl, Georges Bernanos, and Georges Valois.[14] As the editors of *Ordre Nouveau* proclaimed, "We must summon Nietzsche to the rescue. Nietzsche against the state, be it Hitlerite or Stalinist. Nietzsche for man against the masses, be they fascist, American, or Soviet. Nietzsche against rationalism, be it derived from Rome, Moscow, or the Sorbonne."[15] The Third Republic's rationalism and intellectualism had left it devoid of affective energies. Only a new infusion of vitality and instinct could redeem a moribund, republican France.

Since at this point Nietzsche's writings were not yet widely translated, much of the Jeune Droite's Nietzscheanism was imbibed second hand. Among renegade nationalists like Blanchot, Spenglerian declamations concerning the "decline of the West" were commonplace. As *Esprit* author Denis de Rougement declared in 1932, it had become all but impossible to identify with the "atrocious misery of an epoch where everything that a man could love and desire finds itself cut off from its living origins, tarnished, denatured, perverted, and sabotaged."[16] Neo-Nietzschean prophecies concerning the "twilight of white nations" and the advent of a "New Middle Ages" abounded. *Combat* editor Thierry Maulnier penned one of the first important French studies of Nietzsche. (One of Maulnier's other claims to fame was having written the introduction to the French edition of Arthur Moeller van den Bruck's 1923, proto-fascist diatribe, *The Third Reich*.) Ultimately, Blanchot and his fellow rightists were united by what they loathed: the democratic virtues of tolerance and equality that were the cornerstones of modern republicanism. Such abstractions were anathema to the brand of "integral nationalism" preached by Blanchot and his neo-Maurrasian cohorts.[17] Hence, this generation of French "spiritual reactionaries" shared a profound identification with German counterparts such as Spengler, Moeller van den Bruck, and Ernst Jünger.[18]

In their bestselling 1931 jeremiad, *Le Cancer américain, Ordre Nouveau* editors Aron and Dandieu bemoaned the fact that American influences had transformed French civilization into a soulless, technological Moloch. Kindred spirit Georges Duhamel invoked the "bestiality of United States civilization."[19] Building on these alarming diagnoses of the times, Blanchot advocated a "national spiritual revolution" that would be "severe, bloody, and unjust—our last chance for salvation."[20] In this way, the heritage of the 1789 would be swept away by a *counterrevolution,* a "revolution from the right."[21] This revolution would be, in every respect, the Great Revolution's sanguinary, diabolical equal, yet it would engender a diametrically opposed political result. In this way, Blanchot and his confreres stressed that by virtue of having become respectable parliamentarians, the left had betrayed the revolutionary credo whose mantel the right had newly inherited. During the 1930s this political conclusion was enthusiastically embraced by fascists and "national revolutionaries" throughout Europe, many of whom had been inspired by the model of Mussolini's 1922 March on Rome—the *Urszene* of the fascist political imaginary.

During the 1930s France, as was the case elsewhere in Europe, experienced an astonishing political turnabout: the left, which formed the backbone of the Popular Front, had become the "party of order." The right, conversely, proceeded to co-opt the language of revolution that the left had invented over a century earlier but, recently, had abandoned for tactical reasons.[22] Robespierre's messianic revolutionary rhetoric—for instance his infamous equation of "terror" with "virtue"—remained alive and well. But to the left's chagrin it had been appropriated and exalted by the forces of political reaction.

During the 1930s, Blanchot's journalism exemplified this ethos of protofascist, national revolutionary sedition. As he asserts in a 1933 article:

> There are still men who want neither a state that oppresses them, nor a world that enslaves them. There are still men for whom the true order must be the work of a revolution and for whom revolution is a combat and rejuvenation. It is this revolt made with wisdom and audacity that we are preparing today and that is the hope of today's youth.[23]

When Léon Blum's Popular Front government acceded to power in June 1936, it seemed that a threshold had been crossed: in the eyes of the French right, the specter of an imminent Bolshevik takeover was at hand. A year earlier France had signed the Franco-Soviet accords, setting off alarms among the antiparliamentary right. The fragile coalition of Radicals, Socialists, and Communists—headed by none other than a Jewish Dreyfusard—seemingly confirmed the rightists' worst paranoid fantasies about the existence of an international conspiracy of leftists and Semites. Led by figures like Drieu and Brasillach, the literary right had been long obsessed with French "decadence" and "effeminacy"—especially in contrast to the adjacent, bellicose and virile fascist regimes. From this point hence, their contempt for French republicanism knew no bounds. It was open season on Blum and the "Jew Republic."

From 1936 to 1939 Blanchot was a regular contributor to two far-right reviews, *L'Insurgé* and *Combat*. *Combat* was edited by Jean-Pierre Maxence, a wealthy, ultra-right financier, and Maurras disciple Thierry Maulnier. *L'Insurgé* was directed by Maulnier alone and possessed ties to one of the main right-wing terrorist organizations active during the 1930s, Eugène Deloncle's Cagoule (*L'Insurgé* offices were located in the Cagoule's former headquarters on the rue Caumartin).[24] Both reviews were a literary and political haven for apostles of a "third way" between capitalism and communism—which in practice meant that its contributors inclined toward fascism *à la française*. Between January and October 1937, when *L'Insurgé* ceased publication, Blanchot contributed sixty-seven articles. In March 1937 French authorities arrested Blanchot and five other *L'Insurgé* editors for incitement to murder (the would-be targets were Blum and communist leader Maurice Thorez) for having urged readers to avenge the recent deaths of two right-wing demonstrators. Since the republic was incapable of administering justice on its own, argued Blanchot and his fellow vigilantes, it was time for citizens to take matters into their own hands.

A recent biography of Blanchot identifies him as belonging to the "hard core of the extreme intellectual right."[25] And in his book on French fascism during the 1930s, *Neither Right, Nor Left,* Zeev Sternhell remarks that Blanchot consummately incarnated the "fascist spirit" of the era. According to Sternhell, Blanchot

> provided a perfect definition of the fascist spirit in claiming that it is
> a synthesis between a left that forsakes its original beliefs not to

draw closer to capitalist beliefs but to define the true conditions of the struggle against capitalism and a right that neglects the traditional forms of nationalism not to draw closer to internationalism but to combat internationalism in all its forms.[26]

Blum's victorious left-wing coalition inspired Blanchot to new heights of prolificness. Neither Drieu nor Brasillach surpassed his talent for antiparliamentary rhetorical vilification. The same year (1936) two major international crises erupted: Nazi troops reoccupied the Rhineland, in express violation of the Versailles accords; and the Spanish Civil War erupted. At last Blanchot found a political cause he could support: he became an enthusiastic backer of the Falangist cause, arguing fervently in favor of French intervention on behalf of Franco and his fellow insurgents. By supporting the antirepublican struggle militarily, reasoned Blanchot, France could reestablish its credentials as a major player on the international political stage. Otherwise the hexagon stood to lose even more ground to its geopolitical foe across the Rhine, which, by openly supporting Franco, had once again beaten the Gauls to the punch in what had traditionally been a French sphere of influence.[27]

For the antirepublican right the Popular Front raised the specter of a government dominated by "foreign" interests—Bolsheviks and Jews—and, hence, a further depletion of national substance. Moreover, it was a political era dominated by extraparliamentary "leagues" like Colonel François de la Rocque's Croix de Feu and Doriot's Parti populaire français. These organizations stood to profit politically by sowing fear of *métèques* or foreign immigrants—in most cases, eastern European Jews fleeing pre-Holocaust political persecution in Germany, the Balkans, and Poland.

Blanchot's political journalism during these years demonstrates that he had fully imbibed the anti-Semitic and xenophobic spirit of the times. As he wrote in a 1937 article, Blum "represents all that is most contemptible for the nation . . . a backwards ideology, a senescent mentality, a *foreign race.*"[28] A 1937 issue of *L'Insurgé,* for which Blanchot penned two weekly columns, prominently featured on its cover a crude, anti-Semitic caricature of Blum. The Socialist leader appeared with exaggerated Jewish features, brandishing a menorah atop a heap of coffins—an allusion to the five protesting workers who had been slain by the national guard in the course of an antifascist demonstration.

Two years later Pope Pius XII lifted the 1926 interdict on the Action Française, meaning that French Catholics could now read hate-filled Maurrasian organs such as *Je Suis Partout, Gringoire,* and *Action française* in good conscience. Around the same time Céline made his anti-Semitic debut in works such as *Bagatelles pour un massacre* and *L'École des cadavres.* "If you really want to get rid of the Jews," wrote Céline, "then, not thirty-six thousand remedies, thirty-six thousand grimaces: racism! That's the only thing Jews are afraid of: racism! And not a little bit, with the finger-tips, but all the way! Totally! Inexorably! Like complete Pasteur sterilization."[29] As Paxton and Marrus observe in *Vichy France and the Jews,* "Anti-Semitism was plainly an important focus for opposition to Blum's Popular Front government. Those years reshaped anti-Jewish sensibility into a political, economic, and social worldview, giving it a combative edge, the *cri de coeur* of an opposition movement attempting to defend France against revolutionary change."[30]

Blanchot's political journalism fits squarely within this trend. In an article written at the time of Germany's 1936 reoccupation of the Rhineland, he proclaimed one must be wary of Jews insofar as they were a people possessed of a "theological fervor." "Nothing is so perfidious," Blanchot continues, "as the propaganda of national honor promoted by suspicious foreigners in the offices of the Quai d'Orsay [the French foreign ministry] in order to force young Frenchmen into an immediate conflict in the name of Moscow or Israel."[31] Blanchot's underlying fear—one that was widespread among French rightists of the day—was that a successful military showdown with Germany would greatly strengthen the political hand of the much-hated republic.

His greatest journalistic offenses were perpetrated in a June 1936 *Combat* article (with an unmistakable nod towards Robespierre), "Terrorism as a Method of Public Safety." From the time of its February 1936 inaugural issue, *Combat* had displayed an almost perverse pride in distinguishing its own "reasonable anti-Semitism," predicated on "anticapitalism" (a brand of anti-Semitism the French right had assimilated from the political left), from the Nazis' race-based, "vulgar anti-Semitism." In other words, hatred of Jews was permissible—just as long as it was the right kind of hatred. When it came time for the 1942 *rafle des Juifs* or deportations, French authorities pitched in with alacrity: the "reasonable" anti-Semites of Vichy were none too proud to act as the facilitators of the Final Solution envisioned by their "vulgar" German brethren. Blanchot's essay recapitulated the pet themes of his 1930s political journalism: antirepublicanism, anti-Semitism, and an unbounded enthusiasm for the redemptive capacities of revolutionary violence, now yoked to the fortunes of the political right. Thus he speaks of the "detestable character of what is called with solemnity the Blum experiment . . . a splendid union, a holy alliance . . . of Soviet, Jewish, and capitalist interests." Alluding once more to the presumed international conspiracy of communists, Jews, and capitalists—a standard demonology on the part of the paranoid, far-right imagination—Blanchot continues,

> It is necessary that there be a revolution because one does not modify a regime *that controls everything, that has its roots everywhere*. One removes it, one strikes it down. It is necessary that that revolution be violent because one does not tap a people as enervated as our own for the strength and passions appropriate to a regeneration of decency, but through a series of bloody shocks, a storm that will overwhelm—and thus awaken—it. . . . That is why terrorism at present appears to us as a method of public salvation.[32]

Many of the Young Turks at *Combat* came to view France's "strange defeat" at the hands of the Nazis as a deliverance from the slackness and indecision of the bourgeois era they loathed. Echoing the verdict of Charles Maurras, French rightists perceived the German victory as a "divine surprise." In marked contrast with other nations the Nazis had conquered, the armistice terms granted to France were relatively favorable: the southern third of the country remained unoccupied (an approach that worked to the Germans' advantage, since it freed up tens of thousands of troops for the impending attack against the Soviet Union). In the eyes of many convinced antirepublicans, their hour had come: Pétain's "National

Revolution" offered a golden opportunity to realize the program of "integral nationalism" Maurrasian dissidents had been advocating for over a decade. Vichy's ministries hummed with bold plans for national rejuvenation. In many cases, the ideas for reform were culled directly from concepts and proposals that had been purveyed by far-right organs such as *Ordre Nouveau, Le Rempart, L'Insurgé, Combat,* and Mounier's *Esprit.*

The "new order" would be authoritarian, hierarchical, nativist, and corporatist. As Pétain declared in a July 1941 speech, "A people is not a determinate number of arbitrarily assembled individuals. A people is a hierarchy of families, professions, communities, and administrative responsibilities."[33] According to the Vichy political consensus, France needed a solidly authoritarian regime to keep the uncertainties and risks of political liberalism at bay. In the eyes of its supporters, by avoiding the twin extremes of "liberalism" and "totalitarianism," *L'État français* was destined to become a model of "third way" politics. It seemed that, at long last, the nonconformist "spirit of the 1930s" had found the political outlet it had been fecklessly seeking. As one French political historian has demonstrated, "Vichy can be explained much more readily as a result of themes developed in small [right-wing] journals of the 1930s than as a function of themes developed by the traditional right."[34]

Only after it became clear that despite tantalizing German promises France's role in a Nazi-dominated Europe would remain miniscule, did the illusions of "deliverance" dissipate. Thereafter, once-enthusiastic Vichyites like Emmanuel Mounier began to pass over to the resistance.

Several myths have arisen around the figure of Maurice Blanchot, myths that the writer has either consciously cultivated or helped perpetuate owing to his refusal to set the record straight. According to one such legend, between 1938, when he stopped writing for *Combat,* and 1940, Blanchot, recoiling from his previous, sanguinary rhetorical excesses, lapsed into literary silence. Although it makes for a nice story, it fails to measure up to the facts, since throughout this period Blanchot continued to produce a weekly literary column for the solidly Pétainist *Journal des débats.* Another fable has it that, despite his ardent antirepublicanism, Blanchot, having appreciated the follies of his youth following the fall of France, went on to join the resistance. Yet, having scoured French archives and interviewed surviving *résistants,* none of Blanchot's recent biographers has been able to identify a shred of evidence linking him to any active resistance groups. Blanchot may have known and fraternized with various individual résistants. But that seems to be about as far as things went.

In fact, not only are Blanchot's purported ties to the resistance apocryphal. It seems that during the early stages of the German occupation, he did everything within his power to lend his creative talents to the Pétainist cause. Blanchot was one of the key players of Jeune France, a cultural organization under the supervision of Vichy's Orwellian sounding Ministry of Youth *(Secrétariat Générale à la Jeunesse).*

Jeune France possessed close ideological ties to Uriage *(L'Ecole nationale des cadres),* an elite training ground for national revolutionary cadres modeled after a monastic order—owing in part to Catholic influences, talk of a "new Middle Ages" was rife under Vichy. Emmanuel Mounier, Uriage's ideological preceptor, frequently lectured Uriage recruits and helped formulate the curriculum for the school's rigorous, three-week leadership training course. The school's educational philosophy was based on Mounier's "personalism": a unique brand of communitarian social Catholicism that sought to transcend the risks and uncertainties of democratic pluralism. "Steeped in Catholic antiliberalism [Uriage] adopted the *Esprit* ideology as the conceptual framework of its educational program: anti-individualism, anti-liberalism, anti-Marxism, and a rejection of democracy, on the one hand, and, on the other, a cult of order, hierarchy and elitism, and reserved admiration for the German, Italian and Portuguese youth movements."[35]

As part of its effort to resurrect the precepts of authority and leadership, Uriage resembled a Pétainist cult: unquestioned reverence for the Maréchal and all he represented was one of its central pillars. Although Mounier's intentions were in certain respects admirable, the personalist ethos was colored by an anti-parliamentary outlook that made its supporters easy prey for both Vichy ideology as well as the fait accompli of a Nazi-ruled Europe. In August 1940

Mounier received permission from Vichy authorities to recommence publishing *Esprit*. Thereafter the journal professed a well-nigh phobic aversion to Nazism's enemies, the "decadent" Western democracies.

According to the Uriage credo, one of the reasons for France's ignominious military and political collapse had been a drastic failure of leadership. The Third Republic—commonly known as the "République des professeurs"—had been ruined by a sterile and effete intellectualism. By emphasizing the attributes of manliness, virility, labor, and community, the knight-monks of Uriage would train a future generation of leaders possessed of communitarian virtues that republican France lacked.[36] Since it was generally assumed that Europe's future would be fascist, it would be necessary to remake France along authoritarian lines so that the nation would be able to hold its own amid the new, predatory European political order. Thus Uriage's commission was to form "an aristocracy of French leaders, semi-military and semi-intellectual, activist, virile, solidary, armed with a burning faith against the vices of the Old Regime: individualism, hedonism, mercantilism, and capitalism."[37] Because of the retreat's self-professed monastic character, one French historian has suggested strong parallels between it and Bataille's College of Sociology.[38] Yet like many closely knit communities, Uriage was exclusionary: Jews were unwelcome, both as trainees and instructors. If republican France was liberal and democratic, the brand of communitarianism vaunted by Uriage and Vichy would be authoritarian and hierarchical. The Uriage experiment had one eye on Nazi Germany's Hitler-Schulen and Ordenburgen—elite SS training schools. Nevertheless, at Uriage Mounier sought to ensure that the programs for social reform were spoken with a French accent.

Uriage and its dreams of French cultural renewal collapsed in November 1942, when the Nazis invaded the unoccupied zone. Yet until this point, its knight-monks remained fully committed to the credo and goals of the National Revolution. As Mounier himself, reflecting on France's recent collapse, observed in November 1940, "Amid the dust that has been stirred by the collapse of a world, amid the inevitable confusion of what has already been born and what has died, certain conceptions of life emerge in which we can recognize the dominant traits of our heritage: the fight against individualism, sense of responsibility, sense of community, restoration of the role of leadership, renewed sense of the nation . . . restoration of the meaning of the state . . . sense of total man."[39] All of these factors, Mounier continues, constituted compelling reasons for *Esprit* followers to make peace with the new political order.

Yet those who pledged their support for the National Revolution tacitly sanctioned Vichy's draconian racial policies. And when it came to playing the anti-Semitic card—a presumed entry ticket to the Nazi-dominated New European Order—Pétain and company proved *plus royaliste que le roi.* A long-standing myth has held that Vichy's notorious *Statut des juifs,* proclaimed on October 3, 1940, had been promulgated at the behest of the Nazi occupiers. But nothing could be farther from the truth: the initiative was all Vichy's. As the authors of *Vichy France and the Jews* remind us, "Vichy measures against the Jews came from within, as part of the National Revolution. They were autonomous acts taken in pursuit of indigenous [political] goals."[40]

Already in August 1940—a mere two months after France's "strange defeat"—Vichy authorities revoked the Marchandeau Law, which had made it illegal to incite hatred against ethnic or religious groups. Thereafter, the floodgates burst and a wave of anti-Semitism—another legacy of the 1930s, antiparliamentary right—inundated the French press. Then, with one bold stroke, the *Statut des Juifs* codified the terms of Jewish de-emancipation. France, traditionally a haven for refugees and political exiles, became a bastion of repression. Jews were summarily excluded from public service, from the officer corps, and, later, from organs of public opinion such as journalism, radio, and film. A *numerus clausus* was established for Jewish physicians as well as the liberal professions like teaching and law. French officials eagerly undertook the task of registering the whereabouts of Jews throughout France. Although no one could know it at the time, in retrospect such measures served as a prelude to France's ignominious role in the Nazi Final Solution. The 1942 round up of Jews from the Unoccupied Zone was the only case during the war in which Jews were deported from a region that was not under the Nazis' direct administrative control. With the alacritous support of Vichy authorities, some 76,000 Jews residing on French soil would ultimately meet their death.

Conceived in a "personalist" spirit, Jeune France was charged with the mission of "promoting the arts and remaking men." Its political analogues seem to have been Mussolini's Dopo Lavoro program and Nazi Germany's Kraft durch Freude—state-sponsored recreation programs that tried to stamp leisure time with a fascist ideological imprint.[41] The idea of a Ministry of Youth was a Pétainist innovation. Like the neighboring fascist states, Vichy's program for national renewal placed a distinct stress on the regenerative capacities of "youth," who, presumably, had not yet been fully tainted by the corruptions of republicanism—no small irony given the fact that the État Français was led by an octogenarian. Whereas the Third Republic had been animated by an egalitarian ethos that trusted in human reason and the sensus communis, Vichy authoritarianism consciously strove to dismantle the outmoded assumptions of republican humanism. According to Pétain and company, men and women were fundamentally incapable of governing themselves; hence, one of the main goals of the new "tutelary state" would be to reintegrate the masses within a new, hierarchical network of authoritarian social and political structures, thereby relieving them of the burdens of self-government. To a large extent, the political tumult of the 1930s stemmed from a crisis of social integration. Under Vichy, "culture," divested of its liberal-republican, free-floating attributes, would play a central role in reintegrating men and women into the life of the national community. Thus, according to the Jeune France brain trust, culture would play a "functional" role in the future, compensating the denizens of modern society for the omnipresent risks of social disequilibrium. Its new raison d'être was as a vehicle of ideological indoctrination: the arts would be used as "a means of seduction and impregnation, [by way of] repetitive formulas, slogans, [and] ideological platitudes. . . . Art that emancipates, a culture that reinforces credulity, thus ally themselves with a totalitarian project: the captive spirit is constrained to work [in the service of] a collective conversion, to cement a new political regime and negate the effects of laic rationalism that was the philosophy of the defunct regime."[42] According to the Jeune France master plan, no sphere of cultural endeavor would remain unintegrated: cinema, radio, theater, music, and literature would be subordinated to the ends of cultural revolution. Needless to say, in this new, organic social order, the "Rights of Man and Citizen" would find no place. The liberal division between state and society would be surpassed by the National Revolution's communitarian ethos. In the eyes of one observer—Marc Fumaroli in *L'État Culturel*—the Jeune France experiment in national renewal left a profound imprint on Gaullist minister André Malraux's program of cultural reform during the early years of the Fifth Republic.

Among Jeune France's directors were figures with backgrounds similar to Blanchot's: right-wing literati who, like Blanchot, had been affiliated with the Jeune Droite during the 1930s and had written for organs such as *Ordre Nouveau, Esprit,* and *Combat.* All of these men believed that the Nazis had done France a service by abolishing the reviled republic. At Jeune France their intentions were to capitalize on the "divine surprise" of June 1940 and implement the program of right-wing "spiritual revolution" they had been assiduously promoting for the last decade.

According to historian Jean-Louis Loubet del Bayle, "Among [Jeune France's] principal collaborators [were] Maurice Blanchot in the occupied zone, Emmanuel Mounier . . . in the unoccupied zone."[43] Insofar as they were located in the Unoccupied Zone, the knight-monks of Uriage could at least claim they operated at safe remove from the compromises of collaboration. Blanchot, conversely, who received his commission directly from Vichy's Sécretariat Générale à la Jeunesse Georges Pelorson, was based in occupied Paris. Hence, he could harbor few illusions about the brutal realities entailed by the Nazi occupation.

Blanchot's commission was to edit a journal publicizing Jeune France's program for cultural renewal. In the end, however, the project was stillborn. It seems that Blanchot and his fellow Pétainistes were unable to convince the Gestapo that their intentions were primarily cultural rather than political. The French were welcome to collaborate, but the Nazis would define the terms.

Following nearly forty years of silence, Blanchot finally commented on his wartime activities in a letter to Jeffrey Mehlman, who in 1982 had exposed the compromising character of Blanchot's *Combat* articles in the pages of *Tel Quel*.[44] In the letter Blanchot relies on the classical collaborator's defense—in fact, the same defense that Maréchal Pétain himself had used at his 1945 trial, albeit to little avail (the 86-year-old Pétain was sentenced to death for treason, though de Gaulle commuted the sentence to life imprisonment; six years later, the Maréchal died in prison at age 91). Blanchot claimed that by joining with Vichy, he had been playing a *double game:* he had allowed himself to be co-opted by Vichy *all the better to combat Vichy from within.*

But in point of fact there was no double game. In Vichy, right-wing radicals like Blanchot saw a golden opportunity to realize the proto-fascist ideals of the "national revolution" they had been promoting journalistically for at least a decade. Given their visceral antipathy for the republic, they had few pangs of conscience when it came to accepting the idea of a Nazi-dominated, New European Order, regardless of its barbaric political implications. "Integral nationalism" was the wave of the future, and France had to do all that it could to adapt to the new political mandate established by Hitler and Pétain at Montoire in October 1940, when the Maréchal emerged proclaiming "the way of collaboration" as France's future. Pétain himself, of course, was fond of the "shield" metaphor, implying that Vichy offered the French protection against the German barbarism. But in truth collaboration was a shield for the Nazis: it offered them a much needed continental ally and freed up valuable manpower for the Wehrmacht and SS to continue their genocidal policies throughout occupied Europe.

"The Politics of Sainte-Beuve"

As late as 1942 Blanchot remained an active literary collaborationist. In March of that year he published a review essay entitled "La Politique de Sainte-Beuve" in the solidly Pétainist organ *Le Journal des débats.* Had Blanchot confined himself exclusively to literary themes, the article in question would in the context at hand be barely worth mentioning. As it turns out, however, "La Politique de Sainte-Beuve" is a compromising political allegory. Among his generational literary cohort, Sainte-Beuve was the only one to offer a craven defense of Louis Bonaparte's coup d'état of December 2, 1851. Hence, discerning Blanchot's sub rosa political agenda in seeking to draw analogies between the Second Empire and Vichy is not difficult. In both cases, tyrants had intervened to "redeem" France from the chaos of liberalism and return her to the path of political autocracy. Moreover, as Mehlman has pointed out, by praising Sainte-Beuve, Blanchot was following in the footsteps of his literary and political mentor, Action Française founder and Vichy enthusiast Charles Maurras. At the time of the Dreyfus Affair, Maurras had written his own political allegory, *Trois idées politiques: Chateaubriand, Michelet, Sainte-Beuve.* Anticipating Blanchot's argument of forty years hence, Maurras had similarly praised Sainte-Beuve for having resisted the blandishments of "sentiment" in favor of the imperatives of "order."[45]

The Writing of Silence

Blanchot's unsavory political past came to light rather belatedly: circa 1980, well after he was established as one of postwar France's leading writers and critics, especially among cognoscenti, who revered him as one of poststructuralism's principal progenitors. Since at the time France was in the throes of an immense controversy over the emergence of the Nouvelle Droite (New Right), a debate that coincided with a devastating synagogue bombing on rue Copernic, Blanchot's journalistic transgressions seemed paltry and dated. Hence, aside from an indignant newspaper commentary by "new philosopher" Bernard-Henri Lévy, they found little public echo.[46] Moreover, since Blanchot the author managed to turn self-effacement into an art form—his publications studiously avoided biographical hints or references; as a matter of principle, he eschewed interviews and all manner of publicity; one of his literary nicknames was "Blanchot, the obscure" (an allusion to his 1950 novel, *Thomas, l'obscur*)—his novels and essays never reached a broad public. The forbidding density of his texts—excessive even by French standards—has effectively precluded reception of his work by a more general readership.

What, then, was Blanchot's legacy to French literary theory?

Blanchot established the tone for much of French postwar criticism in a 1941 review essay—also published in *Le Journal des débats*—of Jean Paulhan's *Les Fleurs de Tarbes, ou la terreur dans la littérateur* (The Flowers of Tarbes, or Terror in Literature) entitled, "How is Literature Possible?" The subject of Paulhan's book was the transition in French letters from classicism to romanticism—a transformation that in Paulhan's view coincided with the Terror of 1793–94. The Jacobin dictatorship proved a fateful turning point from both a political and literary perspective. In both respects it signaled the death of the ancien regime. Paulhan's subtitle, "Terror in Literature," expressed his view that the Jacobins were to politics what the romantics were to literature. Both parties had abandoned classical considerations of "form" in favor of the nebulous, nonliterary ideal of "authenticity." At one point, Paulhan went so far as to brand the romantics "misologues" for having exposed language to the tyranny of "thought." In Paulhan's eyes, their original sin was to have subjected literature to a series extraneous, supra-literary ends—a process from which French literature had yet to recover. By having rashly abandoned the conventions and formalities proper to classicism, the romantics and their successors (Baudelaire, Rimbaud, the Surrealists) were in essence *terrorizing* literature in the name of a variety of ulterior personal and political agendas. Ultimately, Paulhan argued, the program of these literary "terrorists" was self-defeating. For it was constitutionally impossible for literature to escape its intrinsically literary nature, which pertained to the *being of language* rather than *things in the world*.

As Blanchot astutely points out in his review, at the heart of Paulhan's efforts stands a quixotic ambivalence. By attempting in *Les Fleurs de Tarbes* to return literature to its original concerns, Paulhan seems to be relying precisely on the instrumental, "terroristic," nonliterary means he otherwise condemns.

This caveat notwithstanding, Blanchot agrees wholeheartedly with Paulhan's critical program. He concedes that by taking a position, by trying to address worldly problems, literature has betrayed its original calling, its ontological raison d'être. What is literature about? It is about itself. It is about no-thing, or, in point of fact, "nothing." Therein lies its paradox, its beauty, and ultimately its futility—a suspicion from which literature, try as it might, will never succeed in freeing itself. In this sense, literature is "impossible": it is suffused with "negativity," permeated by "absence" as opposed to "presence." In relation to a modern civilization obsessively predisposed towards considerations of utility, literature signifies *la part maudite* (Bataille): an activity that, by virtue of its sheer uselessness, stands in defiance of predominant social codes.[47]

As Blanchot observes in another early essay, "From Dread to Literature," the writer's vocation is permeated with an equivalent emptiness, an analogous existential void. "The writer finds himself in the more and more comical condition of having nothing to write, of having no means of writing it, and of being forced by an extreme necessity to keep on writing." "Having nothing to say," Blanchot continues, "should be taken in the simplest sense. Whatever he wants to say, it is *nothing*. The world, things, knowledge, are for him only reference points across the void."[48] In Blanchot's criticism the literary void becomes a metaphor for the existential emptiness of the human condition, a predicament that Kierkegaard tried to capture via the concept of "dread." Paradoxically, only the writer who freely admits she has nothing to say remains true to the vocation of literature.

Already in the early 1940s Blanchot had anticipated all the essential elements of the poststructuralist vogue: "the need to account for the rhetorical dimension of language, the focus on the perplexing ambiguities in literary texts, the problematic nature of citations, and the transfer of linguistic structures to the study of literature, psychology, cultural phenomena, history, and metaphysics."[49]

In 1931 Heidegger's Freiburg University inaugural lecture, "What is Metaphysics?" was translated into French in the avant-garde literary journal *Bifur*. Thereafter it enjoyed remarkable currency among a prescient cenacle of writers and critics. Although Blanchot had been introduced to Heidegger's work during the late 1920s by

Emmanuel Levinas, this text undoubtedly played a major role in shaping his mature ideas about the vocation of literature.[50]

One of the lecture's main themes concerned the "nothing" or "nihilation" (das Nichts), to which Heidegger accorded a prominence exceeding the concept's relatively modest role in *Being and Time*. Heidegger thereby reprised the theme of the ontological "abyss": the *Ab-Grund*, which in German conveys the additional meaning of being "without ground" or "without reason." The "nothing" connotes the sheer arbitrariness of our Being-in-the-world: that our existence is not self-generated or self-willed, but the ungrounded result of events and circumstances that predate us and are beyond our control. "The essence of the originally nihilating nothing lies in this," remarks Heidegger, "that it brings Da-sein for the first time before beings as such. . . . Da-sein means: being held out into the nothing."[51] According to Heidegger, awareness of Being's precariousness distances Da-sein from its preoccupation with "worldliness" or "beings" and propels it towards an appreciation of the *Seinsfrage*, "the question of Being."

In his critical writings, Blanchot viewed literature through the prism of the uncanny that also motivated Heidegger's own confrontation with Being. The same notion of wholesale metaphysical estrangement had inspired Roquentin's epiphany concerning the Absurd in Sartre's 1938 novel, *Nausea*. Staring at the roots of a chestnut tree, Sartre's protagonist suddenly loses his grip on "things." Inexplicably, the world of entities seemed deprived of its necessity and familiarity. "I had found the key to Existence, the key to my Nausea, to my own life," muses Roquentin. "In fact, all that I could grasp . . . returns to this fundamental absurdity. . . . The essential thing is *contingency*. I mean that one cannot define existence as necessity. To exist is simply to be there."[52] As an astute young critic—Maurice Blanchot—commented at the time, "Nausea is the shattering experience that reveals to Roquentin what it is to exist without being, the pathetic illumination that puts him in contact, among existing things, not with the things, but with their sheer existence."[53]

At the same time, one cannot help but be struck by the historical context underlying Blanchot's reflections on the ends of literature in "How is Literature Possible?" These thoughts were penned at

France's—and Europe's—darkest hour. The United States had not yet entered the war, and Germany held England at bay and had recently opened a second front against the Soviet Union. To Nazi hegemony in Europe, there was no end in sight. The same events impelled Sartre (albeit, at a delay of several years) to formulate the doctrine of *"littérature engagée"*: never again, vowed Sartre, would literature sit on the sidelines while the world itself disintegrated.

For Blanchot, conversely, following Paulhan's lead in *Les Fleurs des Tarbes,* the vocation of literature led in the opposite direction: toward matters of literary form that precluded questions of reference. Was literature, then, a form of narcosis intended to extrude and repulse the real world? Was it essentially philosophical, an instance of "nihilation" in the Heideggerian sense, insofar as its own rhetorical and semiotic contingencies brought into relief the nonnecessity of being? What stands out about Blanchot's approach is that it endowed literary formalism with a philosophical dignity to which it had previously aspired—for instance, in the works of Proust, Valéry, and Gide—but never quite possessed.

In a series of pathbreaking essays during the 1940s and 1950s, Blanchot set forth his mature critical vision. Mallarmé's aestheticist ideal of *poésie pure* served as an indispensable touchstone. This was a very different Mallarmé than the apostle of *l'hasard* (chance) and semiotic delirium who had been apotheosized by the surrealists. Instead, Blanchot revered the poet who had theorized literature's "impossibility"—its sovereign lack of purpose from the standpoint of utilitarian ends. Paradoxically, the absence of meaning at the heart of literature was interpreted as a sign of its perfection. By celebrating the materiality of the word as an independent value, Mallarmé emancipated language from centuries of practical debasement and utilitarian servility. Whereas traditional doctrines of language wagered on the correspondence between words and things, Mallarmé theorized their incommensurability. Suddenly, literary language incarnated a type of pure negativity: like Plato's Ideas, it inhabited a superior ontological plane. As such, it enjoyed an absolute freedom denied to language yoked to the ends of sense.

Yet for Blanchot, writing at the height of *les années noires* or the occupation years, literature provided little solace. Instead, what consolation it might have dispensed was permeated with the acute ambivalence inherent in literature qua "impossible." Whereas inauthentic writing seeks solace in harmonious works or the external trappings of literary fame, genuine writers remain faithful to the ontological uncertainties of the vocation best captured by Kierkegaardian "dread": an uneasiness that pertains not to this or that facet of literary endeavor but to the *nonviability of literature in general*. For Blanchot, one of writing's central paradoxes is that its uselessness becomes a sign of its utter seriousness. Literature, declares Blanchot proudly, is fundamentally an exercise in "futility." It is the paragon of a *unsuccessful speech act*. For speech acts aim at a communicative transparency that literature seeks to avoid at all cost. Thus one might observe paradoxically that futility or failure is the sign of literature's "success." In an adage that could be interpreted as laying the groundwork for deconstruction, Blanchot remarks that for literature, "it is the impossibility of succeeding, of reaching the end . . . that makes it constantly possible."[54]

Conventional authors attempt to repress these vocational ambivalences by placing writing in the service of a positive moral, religious, or political program or end.[55] Authentic writing studiously resists such blandishments. Each time they put pen to paper, genuine writers risk "total debasement." According to Blanchot, literature's resolute lack of purposiveness risks disrupting the "totality of human relationships." For whereas social interaction is predicated on considerations of utility and exchange, writing self-consciously interrupts this flow. A literary cat is not a real cat, and a writer or critic who confuses the two is guilty of bad faith and hypocrisy. (Clearly, Blanchot intends such observations as an emphatic rejoinder to the missionary zeal of Sartrean "engagement.") For these reasons, literature bears marked affinities with the notion of "sacrifice" that loomed so large in Bataille's anthropological musings during the 1930s. Insofar as it is devoid of the teleological certainties that nourish conventional undertakings and practices, pure writing or *écriture* is an act of self-sacrifice—an expression of "creative destruction" that demolishes the language of common sense in favor of a nameless utopian idiom waiting to be born. As Blanchot phrases it, a work of art "is useful for something *precisely because it is not useful for anything;* its usefulness is to express that useless part without which civilization is not possible."[56] Literature's essential characteristics are *absence, silence, meaninglessness,* and *death*—themes that are stressed in another one of Blanchot's programmatic essays, "Literature and the Right to Death," where he maintains that *"silence and nothingness are the essence of literature."*[57] In Blanchot's criticism such themes attain a metaphysical dignity that leaves conventional, belletristic, sub-philosophical criticism lying in the dust.

Before concluding with some general reflections on the Vichy Syndrome as the historical unconscious of postwar French criticism, it may be useful to briefly trace the development of some parallel themes in the later work of Blanchot's fraternal spirit, Georges Bataille.

A Fraternal Spirit

In January 1962, a few months before his death, Bataille wrote a letter to his publisher outlining his thoughts concerning a new edition of a book he had issued in 1947 under the curious and provocative title *Hatred of Poetry* (La Haine de la poésie). The new title Bataille selected was *Impossible.* The former Surrealist had intended the original title in a quite literal sense, but it seems these noble intentions encountered little more than incomprehension among the French reading public. Bataille's "hatred of poetry"—which might as well have been called "hatred of literature"—was a longstanding conviction, going back to his halcyon days among the 1930s cultural avant-garde. It played a key role in his break with Surrealists, whom he accused of not hating poetry (and literature) enough.

In Bataille's view the Surrealists had betrayed their original revolutionary promise. The movement originated as a daring attempt to break with the pretense of bourgeois aestheticism. Their experimental approach—a veneration of automatic writing, dreams, séances, and "objective chance"—seemed promising, even if they conceded too much to then prominent "spiritualist" currents. Yet by the 1930s the Surrealists, with Breton at the helm, seemed content to cultivate the comforts of literary life—albeit, seasoned with the an occasional dash of Bohemian panâche.

Bataille's alternative title gave expression to his sense of futility: his concerted effort to transform literature into its opposite, into a product that was unassimilable from the standpoint of the bourgeois "culture industry," had foundered. Even Bataille's most execrable, Sadean, genre-defying experiments and forays, such as *Hatred of Literature's* opening chapter, "History of Rats," seemed grist for the literary mill.

In a subsequent letter Bataille explained the meaning of the Impossible by explicitly invoking the affinities between his approach and Blanchot's. "Philosophy is the meaning of the Impossible but . . . insofar as it is Impossible, it ceases to have anything in common with the dominant formal philosophy. In this sense the Impossible is expressed by Blanchot and me."[58] The Impossible connotes the idea of rupture, a wound that will not heal. It is revealed in a variety of nonutilitarian pursuits: sacrifice, defiant criminality, poetry as unbounded rapture, sexual ecstasy, frenzied political upheaval, and delirium. All of these tabooed experiences mock and overflow the bounds of sense. They lead us to a precipice where sanity and reason are subjected to the proverbial *mise en abîme* or suspension of meaning, to a series of limit experiences where the subject places itself *at risk*—a point at which, according to Bataille, "death becomes laughable."[59]

In the realm of philosophy Hegel was Bataille's bête noire.[60] Hegel's thought incarnated the values Bataille abhorred: idealism, intellectual high-mindedness, holism, "spirit" (Geist), totality—in sum, a naive confidence in the methods and goals of traditional systematic philosophy. Bataille subsumed Hegelianism under the pejorative rubric of the "homogeneous," which he and his fellow *poètes maudits* sought to disrupt and overturn. Bataille, who like Blanchot prided himself on his status as a philosophical outsider, developed a prescient critique of Hegelianism in conjunction with Alexandre Kojève's celebrated Hegel lectures.[61] Faced with the imperative of choosing between Hegel and Nietzsche, Bataille unhesitatingly opted for Zarathustra's ventriloquist, thereby anticipating a momentous sea-change in postwar French thought. In Bataille's view, Hegel's

polished dialectical syllogisms culminated in the intellectually sterile totality of Absolute Knowledge. As such, it was a barren philosophy of affirmation that marginalized and suppressed prospects
for "transgression": base matter, nonprocreative sexuality, sacrifice,
war, mourning, tears, laughter, and Kierkegaardian "dread" (l'an-
goisse). Whereas Absolute Idealism claimed to be a knowledge of
necessity ("the thoughts of God before He created the world," as
Hegel put it immodestly in the preface to the *Science of Logic*),
Bataille's unorthodox intellectual quest pursued the "Impossible"
qua "nonknowledge" (non-savoir): a realm of forbidden experience
that academic philosophy belittled as beneath the dignity of scholarly scrutiny.

Like Schelling before him, Bataille was convinced that the cognitive ideals of transcendental subjectivity were circular and self-
canceling.[62] By taking the epistemological subject as the *fons et origo*
of truth, post-Cartesian philosophy had excommunicated broad
swaths of experience merely because they failed to conform to the
distortions and prejudices of intellection. The questions it posed
and the responses it cultivated proved terminally self-referential.
Paradigmatic for this entire philosophical orientation was Hegel's attempt in the *Phenomenology of Spirit* to reduce Being to a
modality of "self-consciousness." The end result was a grotesque
mismeasure and falsification of Being. For according to this model,
the "unthought"—Being and experience—mattered only insofar as
it conformed to the predispositions and whims of self-positing
subjectivity.

The "Impossible" proved a felicitous trope for the intellectual
paradox that defined Bataille's oeuvre. For Bataille was interested in
promoting the virtues of *experience* rather than the capacities of an
austere and disembodied *ratiocination*. He made use of philosophical concepts to overturn them, as part of an attempt to accede to
the promised land of "nonphilosophy." As he remarks in the unpublished notes for *Impossible*, "When I say: 'The mildness of nudity
(the birth of the limbs or the breasts) brushed up against infinity,' I
thereby define the Impossible."[63]

Yet the only means at Bataille's disposal to articulate these concerns were conventional conceptual means—language, with its

attendant limitations and inadequacies. In a postwar lecture, "Holiness, Eroticism, and Solitude," Bataille urged his listeners to *"mistrust language."* His "impossible" preference, he continued, would be to *"speak a language equal to zero, a language that would be the equivalent of nothing, a language that returns to silence."*[64] Ultimately, the dilemma confronting Bataille was one familiar to mystics throughout the ages. As a profane means of communication, language falls short of the sacred in its ineffable sublimity. Sartre recognized this problem in an aptly titled 1947 essay on Bataille, "Un Nouveau Mystique" ("A New Mystic").

Bataille's dilemma—that linguistic concepts inherently falsify and distort Being and experience—would become poststructuralism's defining paradox. In an interview published two years after his death, Foucault, acknowledging the influence of "antiphilosophers" such as Nietzsche, Blanchot, and Bataille, addressed this problem directly in a rare lyrical outburst. "It is not while remaining within philosophy, by refining it to the maximum, by modifying it through its own discourse, that one frees oneself from it. No. It is by opposing to it a type of astonished and joyful lunacy, an uncomprehending burst of laughter."[65]

One of the major differences between Bataille and Blanchot was that whereas Bataille still hankered after the forbidden pleasures of "limit experience," his doppelganger Blanchot seemed satisfied with the sublimated joys of absolute literature. Nevertheless, both figures manifested a deep distrust of the representational capacities of language, which they believed inherently falsified life. In the end, both sought refuge in a paradoxical "language of silence." Their conclusions about the limitations of language and representation would become canonical for a subsequent generation of philosophers and critics, the poststructuralists. In an essay that became a methodological call-to-arms for poststructuralist criticism, "To Write: An Intransitive Verb," Roland Barthes forcibly reiterated Blanchot's contention that literature's raison d'être pertained to the sovereign claims of language.[66] Conversely, when language sought to communicate—when "to write" degenerated to the status of a *transitive* verb—language forfeited its autonomy. It became prosaic, functional, sullied by corruptions of sense.

The Vichy Syndrome and Epistemology

The critical stress on the virtues of "silence," the endemic suspicion of communication and meaning, raises a series of troubling and difficult questions. In Blanchot's case, the aversion to the communicative dimension of language poses few interpretive difficulties: it may plausibly be read as a reaction against his right-wing journalistic commitments during the1930s, the so-called Hollow Years. Having compromised himself politically during the prewar years, Blanchot sought refuge in literature as a repository of metaphysical nihilism.[67] He reinterpreted the failure of political meaning as a *failure of meaning in general*. His philosophical criticism during the 1940s rejected not only the virtues of literary "engagement"—a venerable French intellectual tradition dating back to Voltaire, Hugo, and Zola—but the referential capacities of literature as such. In the case of the next generation, the poststructuralists, this spirit of radical skepticism was extended to the totality of language. But the referential paralysis of language also portends an ethical and political paralysis. The risk in declaring meaning "undecidable" is the enthronement of doubt or uncertainty as ends in themselves.

The singularity of Blanchot's 1940s criticism is that, via timely references to Kierkegaard and Heidegger, he amalgamated literary formalism with an innovative metaphysical idiom, thereby infusing criticism with a philosophical depth-dimension that it previously lacked. When viewed in light of the conventions of literary history, Blanchot's stress on the pristine, nonutilitarian qualities of literary language seems uncontroversial: it was merely another way of affirming the virtues of *l'art pour l'art* or aestheticism, an ethos Blanchot transposed to literature. At a later point, poststructuralism's inordinate "textualism"—as represented by Derrida's celebrated maxim, *"il n' y a pas de hors texte"* (there is nothing outside the text) as well as Foucault's early focus on the "order of discourse"—developed into an analogue of these earlier French traditions as codified by Blanchot. From this vantage point the proximity between "modernism" and "poststructuralism" (the philosophical wing of postmodernism) stands out. Problems of language and textuality were already central for literary modernism; under the guise of "formalism," they also occupied center stage in modernist criticism.

Now that the poststructuralist vogue has passed, it seems legitimate to enquire after its historical depth-dimension. We know that certain political conjunctures are conducive to literary "disengagement." For example, in France the mood of political disillusionment following the failure of the revolutions of 1848 proved conducive to the flowering of art for art's sake.[68] One might in turn inquire why, for a time at least, did poststructuralism's claims about the ontological primacy of "misunderstanding" and communicative failure gain such widespread currency. At the level of the historical unconscious, there seems to be a significant correlation between the "Vichy Syndrome"—the repression of memories of occupation years during the 1950s and 1960s—and the functional role played by poststructuralism in postwar French intellectual life. The Third Republic's political and military failures, compounded with the ignominies of collaboration under Vichy, suggested that the totality of French intellectual and political traditions had been rendered dysfunctional. These circumstances implied that, in essence, the nation had been left without a "usable past." For a time, the deconstructionist *mise en abîme* or suspension of meaning functioned as a post hoc confirmation of this predicament; although, at a later point, a Derridean idiom was explicitly invoked to deal with the "inexpressible" nature of historical trauma—the twentieth century's genocidal mania as evidenced by Auschwitz and analogous tragedies.[69] In this respect, as discourses both structuralism and poststructuralism expressed the social psychological impasse associated with the Vichy Syndrome. Structuralism had, after all, denigrated the "event" in favor of timeless anthropological constants proper to the long durée. Poststructuralism, for its part, stressed the transcendental primacy of "miscommunication." In this respect, both discourses unwittingly perpetuated a specifically French refusal to "work through the past."

·6·

Down by Law: Deconstruction and
the Problem of Justice

*The strategy of deconstruction is the ruse that makes it possible to speak,
at the same time as there is, finally, nothing more to say.*

—Vincent Descombes, *Modern French Philosophy*

Deconstruction Conquers America

Following in Heidegger's footsteps, Derrida made his reputation as
critic of metaphysics. In *Being and Time* Heidegger spoke of the
need for a systematic *Destruktion* of Western metaphysics, which in
his view had forgotten the question of Being: the meaning of Being
in general as opposed to the being of specific entities or things. Yet
whereas Heidegger criticized the Western tradition to better establish the preconditions for "first philosophy" ("fundamental ontology"), this aspect of Heidegger's project could not be farther from
Derrida's own intentions. Viewed through a Derridean optic, Heidegger's thought betrays a residual "foundationalism" that res-
onates in the metaphors privileged by his philosophy of Being—a
nostalgia for "home," "place," and "authenticity." According to
Derrida, conversely, philosophy's original sin is to pretend that it is
in possession of something—truth qua "presence"—that, for compelling linguistic reasons, is impossible to possess. For philosophy
proceeds via language, and language, Derrida claims, inherently
operates at a twofold *temporal* and *spatial* remove from the objects it
seeks to represent. One could conceivably imagine a nonverbal,
mystical oneness between the "subject" and "truth." But beings that

use language are, in Derrida's view, condemned to a life of *cognitive futility:* the semiotic determinants of language mandate that our linguistic representations fail a priori in their efforts to provide an objective view of the way things really are. From a Derridean perspective, all language constitutes an object lesson in delayed gratification: it merely refers to things that in reality exist outside of it. Moreover, its claims and contentions betray what Freud might call a structural "posteriority" (Nachträglichkeit): they come into being after the fact, at a temporal remove vis-à-vis the objects they seek to depict.

Thus, as employers of language, we literally "Babel": we are the heirs to an epistemological Fall that mandates on the one hand an ontological abyss between the words we use, and on the other truth and meaning. For if truth has been cast to the winds of radical cognitive doubt, meaning, which Derrida has decreed inherently unstable, cannot be far behind.

For Derrida, the spatio-temporal delay inherent in language means that all truth-related claims made by and in language are in fact secondary and derivative. Primary in Derrida's estimation is the delay itself, which he famously baptized *"différance,"* a term that cleverly suggests the dual meaning of "to differ" and "to defer." In this respect, Derrida relies preponderantly on two claims by Ferdinand de Saussure: that language systems are constituted by a series of internal differences (rather than a direct correspondence with reality), and that the signifiers or phonemes we employ in speech stand in a relationship of utter contingency vis-à-vis questions of meaning (the dimension of the "signified")—the celebrated Saussurean thesis concerning the *arbitrariness of the signifier.* Hence, if "difference" is prior to "presence" and our signifiers are totally arbitrary, then the primordial goal of Western metaphysics—a systematic account of truth—is a linguistic and epistemological impossibility. For millennia philosophers have been making comprehensive claims about certainty, truth, meaning, and the ultimate nature of reality. Yet, until Derrida, they failed to undertake a systematic reflection on the constituents of language that underlie—and ultimately, undermine—all subsequent cognitive claims.

Ironically, one detects a lethal self-contradiction at the heart of the deconstructionist enterprise—Derrida's attempt to out-philosophize the history of philosophy. Like previous participants in the language game of Western metaphysics, he has decreed that *his* concepts (or "nonconcepts")—différance, dissemination, trace, hymen, grammatology—possess a status more primordial (and hence more "true") than those that have been proposed by his predecessors, from Plato to the historical present. A philosopher can, for any number of reasons one can imagine, cease philosophizing without the risk of falling into self-contradiction. Yet once philosophers decide to criticize the tradition by demonstrating its inherent inadequacies, they have, as it were, already taken the bait: the claims to truth or adequacy they raise can be criticized in turn.

Such claims can not only be criticized, but by proposing alternative accounts concerning the origins of truth and the nature of representation, as Derrida himself does with the concept of différance, all philosophy tends towards "realism." The thinker in question is implicitly staking claims about the relationship between cognition and the external world. Derrida a realist? Paradoxical as it may sound, for the author of anti-epistemological classics such as *Writing and Difference* and *Of Grammatology,* there is no getting around this dilemma. By seeking to provide an alternative account of the relationship between representation and reality, Derrida must argue—even if only implicitly—that his account is *more verisimilar* vis-à-vis the way things really are than the leading competing accounts. When viewed from this perspective, Derrida, whose philosophy seeks to unmask and eliminate the last residues of Western metaphysics, may in fact be its consummate practitioner—the "last metaphysician." The question as to whether his own foundationalist claims concerning the ontological abyss separating language and reality cohere transcends the scope of the present enquiry (although the problem of deconstruction's inherent "self-contradiction" raised above would seem to speak strongly against a verdict in deconstruction's favor). If deconstruction is to succeed in convincing philosophers that its methods and insights are superior to theirs, it must rely on practices and procedures that suggest a greater standard of generality—and thus a higher standard of "truth"—than metaphysics. Must it not, then, ultimately seek to outdo metaphysics on its own terms? In a nutshell, the problem with deconstruction is that if all previous truth-claims are vitiated by considerations of différance—the twofold spatio-temporal delay that afflicts all knowledge—then decostruction's claims are similarly vitiated. As one contemporary philosopher has observed, "It is usually a good strategy to ask whether a general claim about truth or meaning applies to itself'."[1] When judged according to this elementary criterion, deconstruction founders under the weight of its own cleverness.

Yet, assuming for the sake of argument that deconstruction's radical skepticism about meaning and morality hold water, where would this leave us? In the eyes of many readers and critics, the lack of a satisfactory response to this question constitutes one of deconstruction's major weaknesses. Under the sign of "undecidability," Derrida has repeatedly celebrated the indeterminacy of meaning. Meaning's insurmountable will-o'-the-wisp character represents an epistemic bulwark against the temptations of "logocentrism"—the tyranny of reason that has been one of the hallmarks of Western thought. As Derrida boldly declaims in *Of Grammatology*, "We want to reach the point of a certain exteriority with respect to the totality of the logocentric period."[2] On the same grounds, deconstruction has demonstrated an almost phobic aversion to formal logic and propositional truth, the sine qua non of discursive thought. Instead, Derridean texts revel in rhetorical tours de force, non sequiturs, puns, and abrupt linguistic jolts—techniques designed to upend the deceptive harmonies of narrative continuity. Yet this endemic mistrust of positive truth-claims seems to have undermined Derrida's own attempt to articulate a constructive critical standpoint. As Fredric Jameson has noted, deconstruction's status as a type of "negative hermeneutics"—one that privileges discontinuity and semiotic slippage rather than, like Gadamer, the "happening of tradition" in a positive sense—has not prevented it from congealing into merely another academic worldview, with acolytes and devotees, as well as the institutional trappings appropriate to a veritable postmodern scholarly cult.[3]

Thus as deconstructionists we seek to demonstrate ad infinitum how established claims to meaning and truth ultimately fail to cohere or the way texts are inherently at odd with themselves—but, ultimately, to what end? To the greater glory of the deconstructive enterprise as merely another corporate academic practice?[4] As one might expect, Derrida's responses to such queries have been evasive.[5] Yet he has always insisted that, contrary to appearances, deconstruction is not solely concerned with the interpretation of texts. It seeks to have a *practical effect.* As one devoted Derridean has optimistically written, "The literary and philosophical issues of deconstruction have had, among many other important academic effects, a political effect and outcome, in which reading—the reading of difference—arrived at working results far from the alleged effects of mere irony and play."[6] But once one peels away the rhetorical veneer and vague generalities of such assertions, one feels that the burden of proof concerning deconstruction's political benefits and viability remains very much with the claimants. Readers who have over the years followed deconstruction's studiously apolitical travails may be surprised upon encountering the philosopher's claim in *Specters of Marx* that "deconstruction has never had any sense or interest . . . except as a radicalization, which is to say also *in the tradition of* a certain Marxism, in a certain spirit of Marxism."[7] Yet even the favorably disposed editor of *Ghostly Demarcations,* the conference volume devoted to *Specters,* cannot help but avow, "If one comes to the book in the hope that now, at long last, Derrida's . . . relationship to Marxism will be profoundly clarified or definitively resolved, one will almost certainly be disappointed."[8] As another disillusioned contributor to the same tome laments, when all is said and done, Derrida's ethereal metapolitical musings offer us *Marx without Marxism*—a Marxism so divested of social, economic, and historical content as to be politically valueless.[9] As Michèle Lamont remarked in "How to Become a Dominant French Philosopher: The Case of Jacques Derrida," whereas Derrida's influence has been strong in countries lacking indigenous left-wing traditions such as the United States, conversely, in areas with a strong Marxist heritage—Germany, Italy, and Latin America—his impact has been negligible.[10]

In the realm of political critique in particular, deconstruction's "reality-deficit"—its endemic methodological aversion to extratextual concerns—returns to haunt it. When all is said and done, one suspects that Derrida's virtuoso dismantlings of logocentric philosophical prejudices have left interpretation frozen in an originary impotence in the stead of originary "presence." In his recent essays on "hospitality," "cosmopolitanism," and "forgiveness," Derrida, sounding very much like a liberal's liberal, has spoken out forcefully against a xenophobic "Fortress Europe" mentality and in favor of immigrants' rights.[11] Yet such appeals, while admirable, remain couched at such a pitch of meta-theoretical abstraction that it is difficult to discern what concrete policy implications, if any, the philosopher might have in mind. Earlier in his career, Derrida suggested in a Nietzschean vein that once we have been released from the straightjacket of Western metaphysics a Dionysian "joyous wisdom" would supplant the claims of reason; in consequence, we would presumably become—again, in a manner never clearly specified—citizens of a better world.[12]

Throughout his career, Derrida has been keen on exposing the integral relationship between "metaphysics" and "violence," leading one to believe—implausibly—that all injustice and oppression can be traced back to the history of metaphysics. Yet in the eighteenth century the "rights of man and citizen" evolved from the eminently metaphysical idea of modern natural law. One might reasonably conclude that metaphysics, in the guise of the "rights of man," provided the conceptual leverage necessary to overthrow the ancien régime.[13] Hegel arrived at this verdict in his *Lectures on the Philosophy of History* when, referring to modern natural law, he made the uncontroversial assertion that "the French Revolution received its first impulse from Philosophy."[14] Like Heidegger and Nietzsche before him, Derrida places an explanatory burden on metaphysics that the concept cannot bear. How, for example, would Derrida explain the prevalence of injustice and oppression in those parts of the world in which Western metaphysics has had a negligible impact? What role do nonmetaphysical sources of oppression— those attributable, say, to indigenous cultural factors—play in the deconstructionist worldview? And what about the *progressive* influence of metaphysics for contemporary ideas of human rights— ideas that played such a paramount role in the justly celebrated

"revolutions of 1989"?[15] In all of these respects, the habitual deconstructionist correlation between "violence" and "metaphysics" seems
to have been grossly exaggerated—if it ever existed at all.

If one traces the career of deconstruction in a French context,
one realizes the extent to which its history is a result of the "anxiety
of influence": like so much of French poststructuralism, it arose in
the shadow of—and in profound opposition to—Jean-Paul Sartre's
titanic presence. In "The Ends of Man" Derrida offered a polemical
indictment of Sartre's "metaphysics of subjectivity": the philosopher's antiquated attachment to the ideas of man, reason, humanism, and self-positing subjectivity. Much of Sartre's philosophical
backwardness, Derrida argued, could be traced to his misreading of
Heidegger. Whereas Heidegger's philosophical project aimed at the
"Overcoming of Metaphysics," Sartre misunderstood *Being and Time*
as consonant with the values of Western humanism. Thus, in *Being
and Nothingness* Sartre translated Dasein as "human reality" (la réal-
ité humaine)—in Derrida's view, a "monstrous translation" that prej-
udiced the French reception of Heidegger for decades to come.[16]

In a prefatory note appended to "The Ends of Man," Derrida
alludes to the fact that the text was written at the time of the May
1968 French student uprising, and obliquely suggests a secret relationship between the political upheavals of the 1960s and the deconstructionist project. Both the student revolt and deconstruction,
implies Derrida, shook the Eurocentric prejudices of Western society to their very foundations.

Ironically, however, Sartre seems to have had the last laugh. As
the philosopher Lucien Goldmann memorably proclaimed in the
heat of the May events, structures do not take to the streets to make
a revolution. Whereas for years the structuralist generation—Derrida
included—had been proclaiming the "end of history" and the "death
of man," May '68 appeared as a vindication of Sartre's faith in "subjectivity"—in the capacity of men and women to endow history
with meaning. As University of Nanterre psychologist Didier Anzieu
wrote in *The Ideas that Shook France*, alluding to Sartre's concept of
the "group-in-fusion," "The student revolt of May tried out its own
version of Sartre's formula, 'the group is the beginning of humanity.'" May '68, Anzieu continued, was not only a student revolution

but also "the death warrant of structuralism."[17] Hence, one of the slogans to appear on the walls of the University of Nanterre campus where the May events exploded: "Althusser is useless!"

Following ten stultifying years of Gaullist repression, with the student insurrection France experienced an unprecedented explosion of repressed subjectivity. Whereas the May revolt was populist and democratic, the students perceived structuralism as a resolutely mandarinate idiom: the very cant of hierarchy and privilege against which the students were rebelling. Whereas structuralists and post-structuralists had written off the "event" in favor of the *"longue durée"*—history's enduring depth dimension, in comparison with which short-term political and cultural changes paled in significance—Sartre's philosophy of subjectivity harbored a voluntaristic optimism about progressive historical change that came to the fore during May. Thus it was no accident that on the afternoon of May 10—the prelude to the famous "night of the barricades"—Sartre was the only French intellectual allowed to address the students who had assembled for a major rally in the large amphitheater at the Sorbonne. As François Dosse notes in *The History of Structuralism,* "Sartre's analysis of the alienation of individuals caught up in the practico-inert, and his insistence on the capacity of individuals to impose freedom by the actions of committed groups fused into a dialectic that made it possible to escape isolation and atomization, shed more light on May 1968 than did any structuralist position about structural chains, the subjected subject, or systems that reproduce or regulate themselves." Appropriately, Dosse entitles his chapter devoted to the May revolt "Jean-Paul Sartre's Revenge."[18] In *Structuralist Mornings,* a satiric, post-May lampoon of deconstruction's hermetic irrelevance, Clément Rosset subjected Derridean *écriture* to the following biting parody: "I write a first sentence, but in fact I should not have written it, excuse me, I will erase everything and I'll start over again; I wrote a second sentence, but, after thinking about it, I should not have written that one either."[19]

One of the peculiarities of deconstruction's reception is that its ramifications within American academic culture have far exceeded those in Derrida's native France. As a well-known statistical survey of Derrida's influence shows, as the philosopher's transatlantic

influence peaked circa 1984 (when fifty-nine English-language articles on his work appeared), secondary literature on Derrida in
French had leveled off to a feeble one or two articles per annum.[20]
Similarly, in an oft-cited poll conducted in 1980 by the cultural
weekly *Lire,* six hundred intellectual notables were asked to rate the
top three French intellectuals. The leading vote getters were (in
descending order) Lévi-Strauss, Raymond Aron, and Michel Foucault—all of whom, in addition to their status as academics, had
consciously cultivated a role as public intellectuals. Among the
thirty-six French intellectuals receiving votes in the poll, Derrida's
name was nowhere to be found.

How might one account for this disparity? Did American academics attempt to compensate for their theoretical inferiority complex by latching onto an abstruse and hermetic European idiom?
Was deconstruction's claim that all disciplines—indeed, all "writing"—were governed by considerations of "textuality" (the claims
of *différance*, the trace, and so forth) a way for literature departments to break out of their 1960s-induced marginalization, and
thus a failed grab at academic hegemony? (In this respect, it would
seem that the wheels of deconstruction's success had been greased
by New Criticism, which also focused on questions of textuality,
albeit in a very different respect.) After all, by reversing the traditional hierarchy between philosophy (as a "serious," truth-related
discipline) and literature (as one that was nonserious and playful),
and subsuming both under *écriture*, Derrida seemed to be providing
the field of literary theory with a much-needed shot-in-the-arm.[21]
Did deconstruction's "nihilism"—its trademark Nietzschean aversion to meaning, morality, and truth—strike an especially resonant
chord among post-1960s American youth, embittered and disillusioned by their failed efforts to foment political revolution? Did
deconstruction, then, become the ethos proper to *post-political
youth culture*—a generation that elected, consciously or uncon-
sciously, to sublimate its once robust revolutionary energies via theories of textuality? Or was America, with its seemingly limitless
geographical expanses, its hyper-modernism, its breathtaking social
mobility, its cultural fragmentation, and its resolute intellectual pluralism—in striking contrast with Derrida's tradition-bound, native

Europe—merely a natural home for an extraterritorial critical practice like deconstruction? Undoubtedly, a number of important affinities link the land of "unlimited possibilities" and a textual approach that stresses endless interpretation. In a parallel irony, since the deconstructionist approach is predicated on the ideas of dissemination, translation, and "grafting," the American rendition has become synonymous with deconstruction *simpliciter.* As Derrida himself has freely observed, "America *is* deconstruction—Amérique, mais *c'est* la deconstruction."[22] Paradoxically, the Master has not infrequently felt compelled to reinterpret his own theories in conformity with the version proffered by his North American acolytes and admirers.[23]

Deconstruction and the "Political"

The question of deconstruction's relationship to contemporary politics has always been somewhat of a sore point. Most are by now familiar with the criticisms leveled against it for its deficiencies in this regard. These critiques have mostly centered on the issue of deconstruction's inordinate focus on questions of textuality and reading—an issue best dramatized perhaps by Derrida's oft-cited, controversial maxim, "There is nothing outside the text"—"*il n'y a pas de hors texte.*"[24] Deconstruction's detractors have alleged that this well-nigh exclusive preoccupation with semiotic themes, with the figuration and involutions of texts, has functioned at the expense of more worldly and practical concerns. The world might be crumbling all around us, they charge, but Derrida seems more interested in the contingencies of this or that phoneme—the amusing fact that in French Hegel's name is the phonic equivalent of "eagle" ("aigle"). As those familiar with Derrida's work know, in *Glas* ("dirge") this chance homonymic equivalence gave rise to a rumination of some three hundred pages on analogous linguistic slippages and fissures.[25]

One of the first to raise such charges of practical-political irrelevance against Derrida's negative semiotics of reading was Michel Foucault. In his response to Derrida's unsparing critique of *Madness and Civilization,* Foucault pilloried deconstruction as nothing more than an idiosyncratic variant of the classical method of *"éxplication de texte."* As Foucault observes with palpable condescension, deconstruction practices an "historically determined little pedagogy" characterized by *"the reduction of discursive practices* [which for Foucault, of course, are sources of "power"—R.W.] to *textual traces:* the elision of the events produced therein and the retention only of marks for a reading; the invention of voices behind texts to avoid having to analyze the modes of implication of the subject in discourses; the assigning of the originary as said and unsaid in the text to avoid replacing discursive practices in the field of transformations where they are carried out." Thus, according to Foucault, Derrida offers us little more than an interpretive practice that "teaches the pupil that there is nothing outside the text" and "which conversely gives to the master's voice the limitless sovereignty which allows it to restate the text indefinitely."[26] As the progenitor of deconstruction, Derrida is the master ventriloquist who in sovereign fashion determines which textual meanings become unraveled and how. Foucault's major fear is that, in the hands of deconstruction, the critique of power and domination, one of the key outcomes of May '68, would be supplanted by an exclusive orientation toward politically pointless textual analysis.

Nor is Foucault the only critic to have challenged Derrida in this way. Edward Said has contended that Derrida's highly formalized obsession with the abstruse terms of "archewriting"—that is, with "nonconcepts" such as the trace, grammatology, supplement, différance, dissemination, and so forth—ends up by "muddling . . . thought beyond the possibility of usefulness." Said continues,

> The effect of [deconstructionist] logic (the *mise en abime*) is to reduce everything that we think of as having some extratextual leverage in the text to a textual function. . . . Derrida's key words . . . are unregenerate signs: he says that they cannot be made more significant than signifiers are. In some quite urgent way, then, there is something frivolous about them, as all words that cannot be accommodated to a philosophy of serious need or utility are futile or unserious.[27]

Said's reservations are akin to Foucault's. Derrida's preoccupation with an esoteric, negative semiotics of écriture remains self-referential to the point of otherworldliness: in his hands, the world itself is eclipsed in favor of acts of interpretive bravado that are meaningful only to a loyal coterie of devotees.

Other critics on the left have accused deconstruction of representing a linguistically sublimated version of 1960s radicalism. In their eyes it represents a form of *ersatz* praxis: instead of unmasking the ills of contemporary society, one exposes the traces of "metaphysics" or "presence" in the theoretical texts of Plato, Lévi-Strauss, Rousseau, Husserl, Levinas, J. L. Austin, and so forth. Nor has Derrida's well-nigh exclusive orientation toward the works of European male thinkers endeared him to proponents of multiculturalism.[28] Even former wholehearted supporters such as Gayatri Spivak have railed volubly against deconstruction's long-standing refusal "to open onto an 'outside' constituted by ethico-political contingencies."[29]

Needless to say, Derrida has not taken well to such criticisms. He believes that on the whole the political implications of his work have been seriously underestimated and misunderstood. Here, however, one might enquire as to how one could, from a strict deconstructionist standpoint, actually distinguish instances of misunderstanding from understanding in general. After all, when a theory is predicated on the maxims of dissemination and "iterability" (the implacable march of "signification"), claiming "all understanding is merely a species of misunderstanding," one would like to know on what basis the founder of deconstruction can plausibly claim to have been misunderstood.[30] In an era when the claims to "authorship" and other "transcendental signifieds" have been deconstructed, with what right can an author claim to have been misinterpreted?[31]

In his own defense Derrida has always insisted, "discourses on double affirmation, the gift beyond exchange and distribution, the undecidable, the incommensurable or the incalculable, or on singularity, difference and heterogeneity are also, through and through, at least obliquely discourses on justice, [ethics, and politics]."[32] And in response to one critic's accusation that "deconstruction is so obsessed with the play of difference that it ultimately ends up indifferent to everything," Derrida insists that "deconstruction is not an enclosure in nothingness but an *openness towards the other.*" Via such openness it seeks to "reevaluate the indispensable notion of responsibility" in ways that are fraught with ethical and political consequences.[33] Elsewhere he does not shy away from immodestly insisting, "Deconstruction is justice. . . . I know nothing more just than what I call deconstruction." And further: "Deconstruction is mad about this kind of justice. Mad about the desire for justice."[34]

Referring to recent debates in democratic theory involving thinkers such as John Rawls, Michael Sandel, Michael Walzer, and Jürgen Habermas, Derrida goes so far as to suggest that deconstruction offers a privileged vantage point. Rather than being *apolitical,* it stakes claims to a type of "hyper-politicization." In his words,

> Deconstruction is hyper-politicizing in following paths and codes which are clearly not traditional. . . . [It] permits us to think the political and think the democratic by granting us the space necessary in order not to be enclosed in the latter. In order to continue to pose the question of the political, it is necessary to withdraw something from the political and the same thing for democracy—which, of course, makes democracy a very paradoxical concept.[35]

With these remarks Derrida insinuates that existing democratic societies are incapable of self-reflection. Instead, they have an endemic tendency to fuse "empirical" and "normative" moments— a debatable claim. Such an interpretive approach as deconstruction is necessary, Derrida implies, to produce a critical space at a sufficient remove from the manifold failings of existing democratic practice.

Derrida's writing over the last decade has been replete with analogous reassurances concerning deconstruction's political relevance. What seems less convincing, however, given deconstruction's willful lexical abstruseness, are the practical implications of such avowals. For example, how can we be sure that Derrida's self-avowed fascination with discourses on the "double bind" and the "impossible"—the paradoxical challenge of relying on a discredited metaphysical vocabulary while at the same time fully recognizing its dysfunctionality—is not merely conducive to indecision and fence-straddling rather than to meaningful political engagement?[36] Moreover, in what ways might deconstruction's trademark "playfulness" be conducive to political earnestness? Lastly, since deconstruction qua political discourse seems to privilege the "negative" moments of "destabilization" and "dismantling," how might it counter the suspicion that it remains constitutionally incapable of fostering political solidarity: the democratic ideal of politics as an equitable and just framework for realizing collective goals and projects.

From his very first texts, Derrida has always emphasized the positional or contextual nature of deconstruction. His recent preoccupation with politics is no exception. Since the early 1990s, Derrida has sought to reposition his thought to counter charges of apoliticism, the widespread suspicion that deconstruction is interested in little more than the "free play of signification." Nevertheless, often his efforts have failed to go beyond a few rather abstract and perfunctory invocations of "responsibility" and "openness toward the other," as in the remarks quoted above. Thus, in lieu of a more concrete specification of the meaning of openness, of the particular "others" toward whom we should open ourselves, of how we should open ourselves to the other and why, and of how we might translate the ethical maxim of "openness" into forms of practical life conduct or everyday institutional settings, we are left with a directive that, in its generality and imprecision, seems more frustrating than illuminating. As one critic has remarked, despite its apparent merits, the inordinate stress on otherness seems indicative of an endemic "other-worldliness" that suffuses deconstructionist discussions of real world politics.[37]

In certain respects the problematic of "otherness"—a distinctly Levinasian inheritance—raises more questions than solves. This standpoint's criticism of the modern natural law tradition—the normative basis of the contemporary democratic societies—is sweeping and total to the point that democratic ideals themselves seem indefensible, and in this way undermines a politics of "reasonable democracy." Instead, we are left with a "political existentialism," in which, given the "groundless" nature of moral and political choice, one political "decision" seems almost as good as another.

Moreover, one can for example think of "others"—neo-Nazis, white supremacists, and other racists—who have forfeited their right to my openness. Should I remain open to *all* others—my wife, colleagues, friends, perfect strangers, enemies—in precisely the same way? Freud tried to address some of these dilemmas in *Civilization and Its Discontents* when he called into question the biblical injunction to "love thy neighbor as thyself." For him this maxim represented merely one more in a series of unattainable ideals and unrealistic demands erected by "civilization." Such commandments, which emanate from the social super ego, are a primary source of a neurotic discomfort with civilization, contended Freud. "My love is something valuable to me which I ought not to throw away without reflection," observed the founder of psychoanalysis. "On closer inspection . . . not merely is [the] stranger in general unworthy of my love; I must honestly confess that he has more claim to my hostility and even my hatred."[38]

In "The Force of Law: On the 'Mystical Foundation of Political Authority,'" Derrida discusses at length the problem of deconstruction's relationship to the ethics and politics. Along with *Specters of Marx* this text contains his most substantive and revealing reflections on such questions to date.

One of Derrida's major critical points in "The Force of Law" is that justice, as opposed to law, always pertains to the case at hand in its irreducible individuality. To count as just, it must transcend general maxims such as Kant's categorical imperative ("act such that your maxim for acting can become a universal law"). For Derrida such imperatives are deficient insofar as they are a species of what Kant called "determinant judgment": we know in advance the general law and subsume the particular case under this rubric. Those who observe this procedure, Derrida argues, can never do justice to the unique demands of the individual case. "[An] act of justice," Derrida remarks, "must always concern singularity, individuals, irreplaceable groups and lives, the other or myself as *other*." Law, conversely, "always seems to suppose the generality of a rule, a norm or a universal imperative." Hence, Derrida concludes, "if I were content to apply a just rule, without a spirit of justice and without in some way inventing the rule and the example for each case, I might be protected by law . . . but I would not be *just*."[39]

It is important, following Derrida's urging, to highlight the specificity of the individual case. When questions of judgment are at issue, a hiatus, a measure of indeterminacy, separates the general precepts (universal moral prescriptions, constitutional norms, declarations of rights, as well as parliamentary legislation) from the vagaries of a particular instance. It is also imperative—here, too, one can agree with Derrida's proposals—to emphasize the necessary, ineradicable tension between justice and positive law. In constitutional democracies, which are the main targets of Derrida's critical energies in "Force of Law," one can identify a fourfold division separating "first principles" of justice from specific legal instances. These are (in descending order): universalistic moral precepts (such as one finds in Kant and the modern natural law tradition), constitutional norms, parliamentary or congressional legislation, and, lastly, the adjudication of individual cases by the courts.

In the case of constitutional democracies, Derrida imputes a veritable ontological chasm between justice and law. This provides cause for concern. In his view, general maxims—be they moral, constitutional, or legal—are intrinsically incapable of doing justice to the specificity of the individual case; thus all attempts to narrow the gap between justice and positive law are consigned a priori to failure. Yet contrary to Derrida's rash supposition that justice and law are incompatible, one might alternatively argue that the uneasy balance between these two elements, which remains the cornerstone of the modern system of right, may be adjudged a qualified success. In a number of celebrated instances, the precarious equilibrium between justice and law has prevented positive law from congealing into something positivistically rigid, impervious to reinterpretation and changing historical needs. Here I am thinking of the paramount relationship between civil disobedience and political injustice in recent American history. The cases of the civil rights, women's and gay liberation, and anti-war movements were at least partly successful in provoking a sea change in political understanding. Stressing the moral imperatives of social equality, these protest movements effectively demonstrated that, in the case of numerous social groups, claims to democratic inclusion had been dishonored. In these and other cases, the existence of moral claims deemed higher than positive law, along with superordinate constitutional norms, underwrote instances of popular protest that sought to expose individual laws or policies that fell short of justice qua ethical ideal.[40] Such considerations form the core of the tradition of modern natural law: from the era of Locke and Rousseau, who provided the intellectual ammunition for the age of democratic revolutions, to the doctrines of Ronald Dworkin and John Rawls in our own day.

Yet Derrida systematically distrusts the modern natural law tradition insofar as it remains incurably logocentric. In expressing the hegemony of the logos, it fails to do justice to the claims of otherness and difference. Yet, *pace* Derrida, as the foregoing historical examples bear out, in many cases the dialectical tension between morality and law has prevented society from succumbing to the reign of an inflexible legal positivism—the tyranny of positive law.

As a critic of modern law, Derrida fails to strike a proper balance between the universal and the particular. As a critic of logocentrism and a philosopher of the "undecidable" (i.e., the indeterminacy of all truth claims), he glorifies the moment of particularity in a manner that is frankly *decisionistic*: that is, in a way that stresses the arbitrariness and contingency of all judgments and decisions. It is far from accidental, therefore, that Derrida cites with relish Kierkegaard's adage, "The moment of decision is madness." "This is particularly true," Derrida goes on to remark, "of the instant of the just decision that must rend time and defy dialectics."[41] From Derrida's perspective, general laws and maxims are downgraded as "logocentric": they are representative of the tyranny of the logos, which, instead of remaining open to the "otherness of the other"—Derrida's Levinasian approximation of justice—are more concerned with the imperatives of logical consistency and conceptual coherence.[42] As Derrida avows, "There is no justice except to the degree that some event is possible which . . . exceeds calculation, rules, programs, anticipations, and so forth. Justice as the experience of absolute alterity is *unpresentable.*"[43]

One suspects that given its marked aversion to "calculation, rules, and programs," Derrida's ideal of justice would be radically anti-institutional. This suspicion is borne out by his ensuing discussion of the ontological chasm separating justice and law. For Derrida positive law is intrinsically indigent insofar as it is empirical, institutional, normative, and embodied. The idea of a "just law," he claims, would be a contradiction in terms. In his view the deficiencies of positive law are counterbalanced neither by constitutional norms, nor by universalist maxims proper to modern natural right (Hobbes, Locke, Rousseau), nor by contemporary conceptions of human rights. Instead, for Derrida the counterpart to law that holds out prospects of justice is the idea of the *mystical*—thus his essay's subtitle, "'The Mystical Foundation of Authority,'" an allusion to Michel de Montaigne.[44] Via recourse to the mystical, Derrida suggests that in matters of adjudication we have something to rely on other than the facticity of positive law. As such the mystical is meant to account for the mysterious process—a virtual instance of transubstantiation—whereby something that is merely positive and factual (the law) becomes suffused with something supramundane and transcendent.

The alacrity with which Derrida is willing to dispense with universalistic criteria of judgment—a rejection he justifies philosophically in terms of Heidegger's critique of metaphysics—gives pause. He no longer regards such criteria as potentially useful heuristics or guidelines; instead, he views them simply as so many pernicious, atavistic, logocentric impediments to the attainment of justice qua mystical. For in Derrida's view, justice, in its utter singularity, its irreducibility to all formal calculations, programs, algorithms, procedures, and rules, resembles the wholly other, "absolute alterity," the eruption of transcendence in the midst of the profane order of things. "It is," says Derrida, "what I here propose to call the mystical."[45] With this phrase the philosopher pays homage to the "madness" of Kierkegaard's "moment of decision" as well as to the undecidability of judgment in general.

Derrida summarizes his position in the following revealing passage:

> The deconstruction of all presumption of a determinant certitude of a present justice itself operates on the basis of an infinite "idea of justice," infinite because it is irreducible, irreducible because owed to the other, owed to the other, before any contract, because it has come, the other's coming as the singularity that is always other. This "idea of justice" seems to me to be irreducible in its affirmative character, in its demand of gift without exchange, without circulation, without recognition or gratitude, without economic circularity, without calculation and without rules, without reason and without rationality. And so we can recognize in it, . . . identify a *madness*. And perhaps a sort of *mystique*.[46]

There is little doubt that in seeking to defend his position on the mystical authority of law, Derrida has drunk deeply from vitalist intellectual currents. Under the cover of the "undecidable," Derrida has already made a momentous and unequivocal decision: *for* "singularity," "madness," and the "mystical," *against* formal procedures, rules, and rationality. For someone who has staked so much on dismantling the binary oppositions of classical metaphysics, such a maneuver seems naive.

Nor do the intellectual precedents Derrida invokes to shore up this stratagem inspire confidence—Kierkegaard and the Nazi jurist Carl Schmitt. That these two thinkers would play a prominent role in a deconstructionist treatise on law is hardly coincidental. Both theorists regard law as something profoundly prosaic, routine, and unheroic. Both are theorists of the *exception* as opposed to the *norm*. In *Fear and Trembling* Kierkegaard's knight of faith becomes one of the elect only by transcending the prosaic character of the "ethical sphere," which he devalues as the realm of bourgeois convention.

Schmitt, like Derrida, an avowed enemy of legal positivism, contrasts the rigidity of law with the effervescence of "life." "The exception is more interesting than the rule," proclaims Schmitt in *Political Theology* (1922) with the zeal of a vitalist. "In the exception the power of *real life* breaks through the crust of a mechanism that has become torpid with repetition." Schmitt proceeds to quote approvingly from Kierkegaard: "The exception explains the general and itself. . . . It reveals everything more clearly than does the gen-

eral. Endless talk of the general is *boring*," concludes the Danish theologian in a manner that anticipates Schmitt's own disparagement
of the bourgeoisie as *die diskuttierende Klasse*—the class that knows
only how to discuss but not how to *decide*.[47]

As Theodor Adorno has demonstrated, Kierkegaard's embrace
of the exception (e.g., his rendition of the biblical tale of Abraham
and Isaac in *Fear and Trembling*) was confined to the sphere of bourgeois inwardness.[48] He equates the exception with the conversion
experience or "leap of faith" that propels the individual from the
ethical to the religious stage of existence.

Schmitt's reliance on the exception, however, was much less
innocuous. As an arch foe of the Weimar Republic, his fascination
with the state of emergency (Ausnahmezustand) as a key to the
problem of sovereignty translated into a glorification of emergency
powers and dictatorship.[49] Consequently, Schmitt had few difficulties in making the transition from the presidential dictatorship of
late Weimar to the German Revolution in 1933. Following the Nazi
seizure of power he eagerly participated in the drafting of *Gleichschaltung* legislation ensuring that Jews, communists, and other
undesirables were excluded from the National Socialist *Volksgemeinschaft*. In the pre-Nazi era he defended the imperatives of "racial
homogeneity" (Artgleichheit) as well as the need to annihilate the
domestic enemy.[50] In the 1930s, by virtue of his doctrine of *Gross-
raum* (a variation on the Nazi concept of Lebensraum), he achieved
renown as a theorist of German continental imperialism. Following the war he escaped prosecution as a war criminal by a hair's
breadth.[51]

Derrida mentions none of these troubling facts. Instead, he
glosses—glosses over would be a more apt characterization—
Schmitt's fascist past by referring to "his strange conversion to Hit-
lerism in 1933."[52] Yet in point of fact considerable continuity
marked Schmitt's authoritarian political doctrines of the 1920s and
his enthusiasm for Nazism in the decade that followed. Derrida further distorts Schmitt's political pedigree by misleadingly characterizing him as "that great conservative Catholic jurist" who at the
time of Weimar was "still a constitutionalist." Both insinuations are
misleading. Schmitt had ceased to be a conservative as of 1923 at

the very latest (the book on dictatorship dates from 1921). *The Crisis of Parliamentary Democracy,* published in 1923, concludes with a glowing encomium to Mussolini's March on Rome. With this act, according to Schmitt, the Duce was finally able to vanquish the "democracy of mankind" and replace it with a "conscious appeal to myth": specifically, the "irrational power of the national myth."[53] So much for "constitutionalism."

For Derrida Schmitt's theory of law is important insofar as Schmitt's decisionism foregrounds questions of "undecidability"—the arbitrary bases of decision and judgment—as does deconstruction. For Schmitt, as for Derrida, the legal system cannot be self-legitimating. At its basis lies a "groundless ground," the proverbial Heideggerian *Ab-grund* (abyss), that comes starkly into focus in the state of emergency, when questions of sovereignty arise—as in the case of Mussolini's March on Rome, where legality must be suspended and the mantle of legitimacy assumed by the sovereign or dictator. In point of fact, the similarities between Derridean undecidability and Schmitt's decisionism are uncanny. For Schmitt, as for Derrida, the norm fails to do justice to the specificity of the individual case in its existential immediacy. Since general rules are inherently inadequate for purposes of adjudication, instead of following a norm, we must simply *decide.* For Schmitt this means a decision ex nihilo, grounded in nothing but the abyss of sheer will. As he remarks, "The decision frees itself from all normative ties and becomes in the true sense *absolute.*" In contrast with the ontological inferiority of the norm, the exception yields an element of creative, purifying violence. As Schmitt avows enthusiastically, "The norm is *destroyed* in the exception."[54] "The decision becomes instantly independent of argumentative substantiation," declares Schmitt. "Looked at normatively, the decision emanates from nothingness."[55]

Schmitt's vitalist fascination with the exception as the basis of legitimacy parallels Derrida's belief in the "mystical foundation of authority." Schmitt's axiom that "the exception in jurisprudence is analogous to the miracle in theology" perfectly captures their intellectual kindredness.[56] For as we have seen, Derrida, too, describes justice as something that, akin to a miracle, emerges ex nihilo. In his view, a just decision is, strictly speaking, unaccountable. In its absolute purity, which is tied to the irreducible singularity of the individual case, it knows no precedent, nor may it be grounded in a higher instance or norm. Like the justice dispensed by Schmitt's sovereign, whose authority was once vouchsafed by divine right, Derrida's idea of justice as "mystical" has the structure of an epiphany. This is true in more than a metaphorical sense insofar as Derrida associates it with Walter Benjamin's political messianism.

The point is not that because Schmitt's glorification of the exception propelled him into the arms of fascism, Derrida runs similar risks. Instead it is that Derrida's theory of law, in its predilection for the mystical and the undecidable, and in its systematic denigration of traditional discursive approaches to adjudicating normative claims, remains, like Schmitt's, uncritically satisfied with an array of specious categories and precepts. He neglects to reflect critically on the dilemmas involved in trying to resolve normative questions decisionistically—dilemmas that leap to the eye in the case of a thinker like Schmitt. Instead, in his view such means become more adequate to the intractable dilemmas of bringing justice to bear on the particularity of the individual case. Thus, on the one hand we are presented with a caricature of modern jurisprudence as akin to Weber's bureaucratic image of the judge as "an automatic statute-dispensing machine, in which you insert the files together with the necessary costs and dues at the top, whereupon it will spit out the judgment together with the more or less cogent reasons for it at the bottom."[57] Needless to say, if legal verdicts are algorithmically predetermined, justice remains a sham. On the other hand, Derrida, relying on Levinas and Montaigne, purveys a naive celebration of extra-legal adjudication. Although these messianic allusions succeed in raising a number of tantalizing questions about the limitations of formal law, they simultaneously raise the specter of judgmental arbitrariness. What, one wonders, would be the institutional and political consequences of a system of adjudication in which general norms were jettisoned in favor of the criterion of "absolute alterity"?

Law and Violence

An additional aspect of Derrida's approach to law and justice raises concern: his uncritical reliance on Walter Benjamin's 1921 essay, "Critique of Violence." The entire second half of "The Force of Law" is preoccupied with this text.

Benjamin's essay establishes an antithesis between "law-creating" and "law-preserving violence" (rechtschaffende und rechtserhaltende Gewalt). Law-preserving violence is the hidden basis of the modern state. As such, it is oriented exclusively toward maintaining the status quo. Law-preserving violence is what Max Weber had in mind when he defined the modern state in terms of its "monopoly of the legitimate physical violence within a certain territory."[58] Benjamin's immediate historical point of reference was the failure of the German Revolution of 1918–19: the military suppression of the Bavarian Soviet Republic, whose leader, Kurt Eisner, was assassinated. Likewise, in the Berlin Spartacist League uprising of January 1919, Rosa Luxemburg and Karl Liebknecht had been brutally executed by Freikorps troops. In light of these bloody historical setbacks, Benjamin viewed law-preserving violence as the hidden essence of the bourgeois state. This element of frenzied vengeance lurks in waiting behind the civilized veneer of the bourgeois legal system, the system of positive law. In a spirit that is both *gauchiste* and *marxisant,* Derrida seems willing to accept many of Benjamin's formulations *tout court.*

By contrast, law-creating violence suggests the idea of a mystical, purifying violence. Instead of buttressing corrupt social institutions, as does law-preserving violence, law-creating violence sweeps them away in one fell swoop. In keeping with the imagery of Jewish Messianism to which Benjamin was partial during this period, law-creating violence signifies a type of divine violence—the violence one associates with the coming of the Messiah or the Last Judgment.[59] As such, law-creating violence is the diametrical opposite of the profane, instrumental, state-sponsored violence analyzed by Weber. It is a pure *noumenal violence,* a violence of ends—as though an avenging angel had swooped down from the heavens to right earthly wrongs, analogous to the violence that a wrathful biblical God visits on deserving enemies. In "Critique of Violence," Benjamin describes it as follows:

> The very task of destruction poses again . . . the question of a pure immediate violence. . . . Just as in all spheres God opposes myth, mythical violence is confronted by the divine. . . . If mythical violence is law-positing, divine violence is law-destroying; if mythical violence brings at once guilt and retribution, divine power expiates. . . . On the breaking of this cycle maintained by mythical forms of law, on the suspension of law with all the forces on which it depends as they depend on it, finally therefore on the abolition of state power, a new historical epoch is founded. . . . But if the existence of violence outside the law, as pure immediate violence, is assured, this furnishes the proof that revolutionary violence, the highest manifestation of unalloyed violence by man, is possible, and by what means. . . . All mythical law-positing violence . . . is pernicious. Pernicious, too, is the law-preserving, administrative violence that serves it. Divine violence. . . may be called *sovereign violence*.[60]

With the experiences of the German Revolution fresh in mind, Benjamin associated the law-destroying traits of divine violence with the purifying capacities of revolution. In support of such claims, he invoked Georges Sorel's notion of the proletarian general strike. For Sorel the general strike represented an absolute break with the timorous legalism and parliamentarism of bourgeois society and European social democracy. In an era when the European left had become social democratic, Sorel sought to restore a messianic dimension to revolutionary politics, even if this meant at times openly allying himself with Mussolini's fascist revolution.[61] Only a doctrine like Sorel's captured the element of uncompromising purity that Benjamin, as an apostle of political Messianism, had sought. Sorel desired a total break with the instrumentalist ethos of bourgeois society. Thus, in his thought the Marxist notion of revolution as a means to a given end (as in the well-known phrase, "Revolutions are the locomotive of history") disappeared. Instead, borrowing a page from the Russian anarchists, Sorel viewed the regenerative potential of revolutionary violence as a sacrosanct end in itself. In "Critique of Violence," Benjamin quotes Sorel approvingly:

> Taking up occasional statements by Marx, Sorel rejects every kind of program, of utopia—in a word, of law-positing—for the revolutionary movement: "With the general strike all these fine things disappear; the revolution appears as a clear, simple revolt, and no place is reserved either for the sociologists or for the elegant amateurs of social reform or for the intellectuals who have made it their profession to think for the proletariat."[62]

In "The Force of Law" Derrida is at pains to deepen the opposition between law and justice, to demonstrate in fact how these two realms are in so many crucial respects mutually exclusive. To find that he discovers considerable support for this view in the early Benjamin's antinomianism is hardly surprising. As Derrida, echoing Benjamin's reading of Sorel, observes,

> The general strike thus furnishes a valuable guiding thread, since it exercises the conceded right to contest the order of existing law and to create a revolutionary situation in which the task will be to found a new *droit*. . . . As this law to come will in return legitimate, retrospectively, the violence that may offend the sense of justice, its future anterior already justifies it. The foundation of all states occurs in a situation that we can thus call revolutionary. It inaugurates a new law, it always does so in violence.[63]

Although Derrida regrets the "sufferings, the crimes, [and] tortures" that accompany bloody revolutions, he nevertheless endorses this Benjaminian-Sorelian vision of purifying violence as akin to his notion of justice as "mystical."[64] In his view—and here the parallels with Schmitt's glorification of the state of emergency are striking— a violent act of revolutionary founding is somehow pristine. For such an act reveals the unwarranted originary violence—the "abyss" or "groundless ground"—that subtends all positive law. As such, it represents "the moment in which the foundation of law remains suspended in the void or over the abyss, suspended by a *pure performative act* that would not have to answer to or before anyone." Hence, according to Derrida, the origins of law are both "transcendent and theological."[65]

In remarks that may raise a few eyebrows, Derrida insists that an essential kindredness exists between the idea of the proletarian general strike and the interpretive enterprise of deconstruction. "For there is something of the general strike, and thus of the revolutionary situation, in every reading that founds something new and that remains unreadable in regard to established canons and norms of reading, that is to say the present state of reading or of what figures as the State." Why one might equate canonical readings of texts with "the State" is a point Derrida never clarifies. Nor can he resist the temptation, at least for a moment, of playing the salon revolutionary: "Today, the general strike does not need to demobilize or mobilize a spectacular number of people: it is enough to cut the electricity in a few privileged places, for example the services, public and private, of postal service and telecommunications, or to introduce a few efficient viruses into a well-chosen computer network or, by analogy, to introduce the equivalent of AIDS into the organs of transmission, into the hermeneutic *Gespräch*."[66] Here we have Derrida in the pose of a "third wave" anarchist, a cyberspace Bakunin.

The Re-Theologization of Politics: Derrida and Marx

One of the distinguishing features of Derrida's thought during the 1990s has been a flirtation with two doctrines usually deemed mutually antithetical: Marxism and theology. Since the red thread animating deconstruction over the years had been a steadfast aversion to self-realizing, metaphysical systems (whose totalizing claims Derrida has always sought to disrupt and undermine), his recent fascination with religion has caught many traditional supporters off guard. After all, during the 1960s and 1970s Derrida established his reputation as a critic of "onto-theology"—unwarranted claims to Absolute Knowledge that limit interpretive "play." Yet what could be more patently onto-theological than the unbridled flirtation with Messianism prominently on display in "Force of Law" and *Specters of Marx*? To be sure, the phrase Derrida uses to justify this fascination with the sacred, "the messianic without Messianism," is intended as a terminological hedge against the theology's potent redemptory lure; but how convincing this formulation really is remains to be seen.

Paradoxically, Derrida's interest in "religion without religion" is integrally related to deconstruction's belated political turn.[67] As thinkers like Benjamin knew well, Messianism offers a radical, otherworldly standpoint by virtue of which one might expose and denounce the indigence of the political present. But a reliance on Messianism to adjudicate secular ends, such as justice, entails two serious methodological risks: a tendency to discount in advance instances of incremental social progress or political reform as insufficiently radical, and the complementary danger of collapsing Messianism's normative and empirical dimensions by declaring prematurely that the Messiah has already arrived. One can appreciate the dilemmas presented by "false Messianism" in the politics of Israeli nationalism since the Six Day War.[68]

Ironically, the tenets of political Messianism also play a key role in Derrida's turn towards Marx, whose thought was resolutely atheological. For given Derrida's radical disenchantment with contemporary politics, which he disparages as an age of "global techno-capitalism," Messianism provides him with an important element of radical theoretical leverage (especially in comparison with the proponents of democratic theory such as Habermas and Rawls). In contrast to Derrida, democratic theorists remain "mired" in the realm of immanent criticism insofar as they believe that democratic societies retain an internal capacity for progressive political change. Derrida, conversely, seems to believe that qualitative change can only come from *without*—which helps to explain his need to legitimate political change in messianic terms. For these reasons Derrida, along with Benjamin and Schmitt, flirts with a "re-theologization of politics."

Earlier I hinted at a peculiar development in the history of ideas whereby a critique of the West formerly purveyed by thinkers on the German right during the 1920s became popular among the

French intellectual left in the 1960s. As set forth by conservative revolutionary theorists such as Oswald Spengler, Ernst Jünger, and Carl Schmitt, this critique took aim at a moribund and decadent bourgeois "civilization." These critics sought to replace the latter with a new form of Gemeinschaft or community that would prove capable of meeting the challenges of a technological age—especially with regard to the *ultima ratio* of war. The tenor of their views, which often crystallized around the idea of the "totalitarian" or "total state," was distinctly fascistic.[69]

In postwar France this critique of civilization took hold via the influence of Heidegger. In the years preceding Hitler's seizure of power, Heidegger had allied himself intellectually and politically with conservative revolutionaries such as Schmitt and Jünger. In the fateful year of 1933, Heidegger committed himself body and soul to the Nazi Revolution. As he remarked on one occasion, "Let not doctrines and ideas be the rules of your Being. The Fuhrer alone is the present and future German reality and its law."[70] Since the reception of Heidegger in France remained ahistorical and decontextualized, the ideological implications of his thought remained largely unremarked.[71] Nevertheless, during 1960s his philosophical antihumanism, as mediated through indigenous French theoretical traditions, became an obligatory right of passage for many intellectuals on the French left. Among this contingent, one would have to include the names of Lacan, Foucault, and Lyotard, as well as Derrida. This transposition of the conservative revolutionary critique of modernity from Germany to France gave rise to a phenomenon that might aptly be described as a *left Heideggerianism*. Thereby, a critique of reason, democracy, and humanism that originated on the German Right during the 1920s was internalized by the French left. The French philosophical left remained staunchly "post-Marxist," insofar as it believed that Marxism, too, was beholden to the foundationalist delusions of Western thought. After all, in Marx's work did not the proletariat function as the apotheosis of the Cartesian ideal of self-positing subjectivity?[72]

Derrida's reading of Marx is in part strategic: in an era marked by the collapse of communism and the triumph of global capitalism, we find ourselves at a point where, for the first time in almost two centuries, bourgeois society is without a major ideological competitor. By underlining the continued relevance of the Marxist tradition, Derrida is trying to reinscribe the events surrounding the fall of communism in a manner that leaves room for political alternatives. Moreover, a book on Marx allows Derrida to recertify his left-wing credentials at a time when, as we have already seen, deconstruction's adequacy for political purposes had been called into question, and when deconstruction's primacy in literature departments had been displaced by cultural studies and the Foucault-inspired paradigm of new historicism.

Some ironies are involved in Derrida's belated confrontation with Marx. Forty years ago, in the *Critique of Dialectical Reason*, Sartre, Derrida's intellectual bête noire, claimed, "Marxism is the unsurpassable horizon of our time."[73] At long last Derrida seems to agree. No thinker, he tells us, "seems as lucid concerning the way in which the political is becoming worldwide, concerning the irreducibility of the technical and the media." Few theorists "have shed so much light on law, international law, and nationalism."[74]

The problems that beset Derrida's attempt to grapple with Marx resemble those that afflicted his ruminations on the problem of justice. The title of Derrida's book, *Specters of Marx,* plays on the oft-cited first sentence of *The Communist Manifesto:* "A specter is haunting Europe—the specter of communism." In keeping with this preferred imagery of phantoms and specters, Derrida perceives Marxism—the critique of capitalism, of modern technology, of the nation-state, and so forth—as a "ghostly" presence whose theories continue to "haunt" modern bourgeois society despite the collapse of "really existing socialism." Thus, in *Specters of Marx,* Derrida offers us not an ontology but a "hauntology." Now that state socialism has (to continue Derrida's metaphorics) given up the ghost, the specter of Marx's critique of capitalism has become more necessary than ever. Otherwise, global capitalism threatens to become an all-consuming monolith, devoid of countervailing tendencies and otherness.

Yet the terms in which Derrida understands contemporary society are semi-apocalyptical. They rely on aspects of the Marxist tradition that have proved the most problematical and the least serviceable for the ends of radical criticism. These deficiencies pertain to a metatheoretical framework that stressed a non-falsifiable philosophy of history, a neo-Hegelian (hence, metaphysical) conception of the proletariat as the "universal class," and naiveté concerning the bureaucratic consequences related to the goal of socializing the means of production. Moreover, in Marxian theory one finds a fatal conflation of the values of economic and political liberalism. In practice, Marx cynically assumed that liberal democratic principles were little more than ideological window dressing for mechanisms of bourgeois class domination. In contrast to these assumptions, however, democratic norms often served as the basis for the progressive reform of inhuman levels of exploitation that existed under early capitalism.[75] Such conditions existed in blatant contradiction to the universalistic sentiments espoused by the intellectuals and philosophers who had laid the groundwork for the transition from feudal to modern democratic society.

In a recent attempt to offset the normative deficits of classical Marxism, a major effort has been underway to develop a critical theory of democracy. Such a theory would preserve Marx's original critique of the excesses of capitalist development with greater attention to the requirements for justice, fairness, and equity embodied in the modern democratic idea.[76] Derrida, for his part, takes virtually no interest in these developments. He situates himself *au delá* or beyond contemporary debates in democratic theory. Derrida adopts this standpoint not by accident, but for reasons of theoretical consistency. For, as we have seen, according to the logic of deconstruction, normative questions remain, strictly speaking, *undecidable*. Were deconstruction to reflect and debate in the idiom of normative political theory, it would succumb to a train of logocentric biases and illusions that, for decades, Derrida has been at pains to combat.

Instead, mirroring "Force of Law," in *Specters of Marx* we are presented with a set of Manichean extremes: on the one hand, the depredations of "world capitalism"; on the other, Derrida's own esoteric appeal to a messianic condition to come *(à venir)*. As Derrida affirms, it is a "matter of thinking another historicity—not a new history or still less a 'new historicism,' but another opening of event-ness as historicity that permitted one not to renounce, but on the contrary *to* open up access to an affirmative thinking of the messianic."[77] Marx's critique of capitalism, we are told, points in the direction of this messianic future, this specter or ghost of a utopia à venir.

What hinders Derrida's analysis is a dearth of mediating elements: concepts or terms that could bridge the gap between the two extremes he sets forth. In lieu of such mediating elements, one is left with a stark opposition between the perdition of the historical present and the sublimity of the messianic era to come. As one critic has pointed out, "In order to identify himself with a 'certain spirit of Marx' Derrida must not only strip Marxism of all its political practices and philosophical traditions but also then recoup it only in the indeterminacy of a 'messianic-eschatological' mode."[78] The later Heidegger once famously quipped that, so forlorn and hopeless are conditions in the modern world, "Only a god can save us."[79] By relying on a messianic idiom and a discourse of "negative theology" to ground social criticism, Derrida—true to the left Heideggerian legacy—follows closely in the Master's footsteps.[80]

In *Specters of Marx* Derrida degrades democracy and liberalism to expressions of capitalist hegemony. He rails against those "who find the means to puff out their chests with the good conscience of capitalism, liberalism, and the virtues of parliamentary democracy," thereby suggesting that the conceptual bases of all three phenomena are in essence the same.[81] Yet, historically, the liberal democratic ideals have often entered into sharp conflict with the capitalist ethos of profit maximization, a fact one notes time and again in the history of the labor, women's, and ecology movements. In the interstices of these various social spheres, with their conflicting normative claims, lie significant potentials for constructive social reform that Derrida excludes by virtue of his chosen apocalyptical discourse.

Previously Derrida, in neo-Heideggerian fashion, has condemned the social sciences in toto as a species of "techno-science"—in other words, they are irredeemably logocentric. "The term techno-science has to be accepted," observes Derrida, "and its acceptance confirms the fact that an essential affinity ties together objective knowledge, the principle of reason, and a certain metaphysical determination of the relation to truth."[82] As a result of this condemnation, however, Derrida's understanding of late capitalist society seems empirically impoverished. Throughout his text one finds tantalizing, yet superficial, allusions to new social tendencies that are threatening to break through. In the last analysis, such innuendoes possess a merely gestural or rhetorical function since they lack the type of empirical grounding that would provide them with the requisite cogency and power to convince. As one commentator has observed, *Specters of Marx* displays a "systematic . . . failure to engage genuinely with any of the social forces which [Derrida] is concerned to regulate through revised, 'inspired' laws."[83]

Ultimately, the inspired rhetoric of the text threatens to collapse amid the weight of a series of postmodernist banalities and clichés. "At a time when a new world disorder attempts to install its neocapitalism and neoliberalism," remarks Derrida, ". . . hegemony still organizes the repression and thus the confirmation of a haunting." "No one, it seems to me, can *contest* the fact," he continues, "that a dogmatics is attempting to install its worldwide hegemony."[84] Derrida polemicizes ineffectually against the triumph of "tele-technics," which he defines as "communications and interpretations, selective and hierarchized production of 'information' through channels whose power has grown in an absolutely unheard of fashion." In Derrida's view this postmodern techno-mediatic frenzy is supported by the proliferation of a "scholarly or academic culture, notably that of historians, sociologists and politologists, theoreticians of literature, anthropologists, philosophers, in particular political philosophers, whose discourse itself is relayed by the academic and commercial press, but also by the media in general."[85] Strangely, though conveniently, the one academic subculture that has been exempted from the foregoing list of the commercially compromised is deconstruction itself.

The "techno-mediatic power," as well as its "spectral effects," must be analyzed, Derrida claims, in terms of their "new speed of *apparition*": in terms of "the simulacrum, the synthetic or prosthetic image, the virtual event, cyberspace and surveillance," as well as "the speculations that today deploy unheard-of powers."[86] The aforementioned list—"simulacrum," "prosthetic image," "surveillance"—reads like a litany of post-Marxist buzzwords purveyed by the writings of Baudrillard, Foucault, and Guy Debord. We find ourselves, as it were, in the midst of a William Gibson novel ghostwritten by Jacques Derrida. Grasping at straws, Derrida at one point gratuitously lapses into an Althusserian discourse concerning "ideological state apparatuses": "In a given situation . . . a hegemonic force always seems to be represented by a dominant rhetoric and ideology, whatever may be the conflicts between forces, the principal contradiction or the secondary contradictions, the overdeterminations and the relays that may later complicate this schema."[87]

One would have hoped that by returning to Marx, Derrida would have broken new ground, that he would have pointed to a way of reinterpreting Marxism that would free it of some of its more dogmatic encumbrances. Instead, we are presented with a *Heideggerianized* Marx— hardly an improvement. Like Heidegger's doctrine of technology as an all-encompassing logic of "enframing" (das Gestell), Derrida's discussion of capitalism in an age of media technics suffers from an impoverishment of "action" categories. Thus, "surveillance," the "prosthetic image," and the "simulacrum," function as omnipotent unmoved movers. It contains no discussion of logics of socialization, of the complex process by virtue of which individuals internalize behavior patterns and norms. The methodological prejudices of philosophical antihumanism, a Heideggerian inheritance, categorically rule out such terms of social analysis. In Derrida's glib portrayal of information era capitalism, there are no "actors" left to speak of. They have been deconstructed along with the "subject." Only ghosts and phantoms remain.

These diagnostic incapacities correspond to those of Derridean archewriting in general. As a philosophy of language predicated on the logics of dissemination and the trace, grammatology is unable to account for mutual solidarity among actors. The process whereby norms are criticized or accepted by individuals is not merely a product of "iterability," nor is it merely an epiphenomenal blip set against the omnipotent backdrop of negative semiotics. It is rather the outcome of an intricate interweaving of ontogenesis and socialization. It is a process whereby persons become "social selves" via the internalization of roles, values, and norms. Yet such mechanisms of social integration remain dependent on a moment of autonomy: on the capacity of social actors to assent to or to reject collectively transmitted norms. Only a theory of socialization that can account for this capacity for refusal, for a moment of autonomous individuation, can simultaneously explain the ability of social actors to resist inherited constellations of power. For want of such perspectives, Derrida's negative hermeneutics of reading threatens to become merely a literary critical version of systems theory: trace, supplement, and différance become the prime movers, and the convictions of social actors are merely their effects—something merely inscribed by the endlessly churning, infernal machine of Derridean archewriting.

Following the lead of Debord and Baudrillard, there is a certain plausibility in understanding deconstruction as a form of theory appropriate to a neo-Orwellian age of semio-technics—an era in which a surfeit of signification simply overwhelms the "subject," leaving in its wake a substratum heteronomously fabricated rather than, as with the old liberal ideal, autonomous and self-positing. But this would mean the realization of a brave new world in which no contestation or oppositional praxis could take place, the potential addressees of the theory having been long cyberneticized out of existence.

Postscript

In December 1981, the proverbial "cunning of reason" caught up with Derrida. Until this point, Derrida had made his name as a critic of reason, humanism, and authorship—which he dismissed as logocentric atavisms. In one of his rare explicitly political forays, "Racism's Last Word," he subjected South African apartheid to deconstructionist scrutiny. Derrida concluded—predictably, yet erroneously—that as a product of European civilization apartheid was predicated on the classical, exclusionary logic and binary oppositions characteristic of Western metaphysics.[88] The only problem with this approach is that the progenitors of European racism, such as Arthur de Gobineau and H. Stewart Chamberlain, developed their ideology explicitly in opposition to the universalist spirit of the Enlightenment. The concept of "race" was intended as a particularistic antithesis to theories of modern natural right, according to which citizenship was determined by birth (jus soli) rather than ethnicity (jus sanguinis).[89] On another occasion, seeking to fathom the intellectual depths of Heidegger's Nazism, he argued counterintuitively that it was a surfeit of *humanism* that had propelled the Freiburg sage towards the lures of fascism, thereby implying that the Third Reich was in some way the consummation or apotheosis of Western humanism. According to Derrida, only when Heidegger *abandoned* the vestigial humanism still present in *Being and Time* (e.g., the anthropocentric implications of "Dasein") and became an avowed *antihumanist* (in the "Letter on Humanism" and other late works), did he free himself intellectually from the Nazi orbit.[90]

Although the events of December 1981 fell short of a proverbial "conversion experience," nevertheless, for Derrida, they shed an entirely new light on the meaning the humanistic tradition he had otherwise severely disparaged.

Derrida had been covertly holding philosophy seminars in Gustav Husek's Czechoslovakia and was suddenly and unexpectedly arrested. In an instant, the "rule of law" he had enjoyed as a French citizen was totally suspended. He found himself entirely at the mercy of an arbitrary and despotic political power. This, he reasoned, must be the predicament with which the citizens of Eastern Europe are confronted on an almost daily basis. He was released only after the direct intervention of President François Mitterrand. Derrida's contradictory intellectual reaction at the time is described by a fellow philosopher:

> I remember Derrida, at the [Ecole Normale Supérieur] on the rue d'Ulm, after having been arrested in Czechoslovakia. During his seminar, he said that he had been quite distressed because after having spent his life as a philosopher deconstructing humanism and saying that the idea of the author and of responsibility did not exist, he had one day been stripped naked in Czechoslovakia at a police sta-

tion. He had to admit that this was a serious infringement of human rights. On that day, Derrida demonstrated his great lucidity by saying that he was in a very bizarre intellectual situation. So he proposed a category of the intellectual baroque, because, according to him, the two levels did not intersect.[91]

Derrida chose to rationalize his experiences by relying on the notion of the "intellectual baroque," which expressed the dissonance between his (antihumanist) philosophy and a political reality in which the relevance of humanism seemed unarguable. Fortunately, there remain other intellectual options available to those of us who have not entirely given up on the humanist inheritance.

Designer Fascism: On the Ideology
of the French New Right

*The "positive nihilism" of Nietzsche has no other sense than this: one can
build only where the ground has been razed. . . . If we want to give birth
to a New Right, everything remains yet to be done. And given the delay
to be made up, we have about a century in which to succeed. Which
means there isn't a minute to lose.*

—ALAIN DE BENOIST, *Les Idées à l'endroit*

Le Pen's "April Surprise"

As recently as the late 1990s political commentators were en masse
composing schadenfreude-laced obituaries for *enfant terrible* Jean-
Marie Le Pen's National Front (FN). In early 1999 Le Pen had fallen
into a bitter dispute with FN heir apparent Bruno Mégret. "For Le
Pen," remarked *Nation* political columnist Daniel Singer, "it is probably the beginning of the end."[1] Attentive to the recent electoral
successes of fellow European rightists Jörg Haider and Gianfranco
Fini, Mégret felt that the FN's political prospects would be
enhanced by a feint toward the political mainstream. With Le Pen—
who was prone to calculated political gaffes—at the helm, alliances
with mainstream center-right parties were out of the question.
Whereas Le Pen's provocative racist taunts appealed greatly to hard-
core FN loyalists, they also facilitated the party's marginalization by
the political center. In a fit of pique Le Pen proceeded to expel
Mégret, who in turn started his own breakaway entity, the Mouvement National. Its leadership split, the FN displayed one of its poorest showings in years in the European parliamentary elections of

spring 1999. The old FN garnered a mere 6 percent—a net loss of 4.5 percent since the 1994 pan-European vote—while Mégret's Mouvement National hovered around the 3 percent mark, thereby failing to break the 5 percent qualification barrier.

Jump cut to April 21, 2002. Political commentators react in shock as Le Pen, defying pre-electoral polls and expert forecasts, edges out Socialist Prime Minister Lionel Jospin in the first round of presidential voting, thereby earning the right to face presidential incumbent Jacques Chirac two weeks later in the winner-take-all second round. Surely, prophecies of Le Pen's political "death" three years earlier had been premature. The hand wringing by leading French political analysts was something to behold. After all, in October 1999, when Haider's Austrian Freedom Party (FPÖ) attained an unprecedented political breakthrough by gaining 27 percent of the vote in national elections (thereafter entering into a coalition government with the Austrian People's Party), France, wary of the political "contagion effect," led the European Union's efforts at diplomatic quarantine. Now its own homegrown extremist, always something of a far-right political trendsetter, had apparently climbed to within a few percentage points of gaining national office. "Earthquake," "Shock," "Catastrophe," screamed the headlines of the leading Parisian dailies. Jospin abruptly resigned from politics, leaving the Socialist Party in a shambles—more or less the same shape in which he had found it upon becoming its standard-bearer in 1995. Conversely, the neo-Gaullist Chirac could now step into the political role he had been training for his whole life: that of France's political savior, thus aping de Gaulle's own Caeserist approach, which had been the founding act of the Fifth Republic.

Le Pen's remarkably strong showing was shocking indeed. Yet upon closer inspection, it seems that once again political commentators overreacted. After all, the 16.9 percent garnered by Le Pen in 2002 was only a slight, albeit disturbing, improvement upon his 15 percent total in the 1995 presidential elections. Moreover, Le Pen's admittedly strong showing was abetted by a number of contingencies that indicate the extent to which dissatisfaction with the political status quo conveniently played into the National Front's hands—a fact that suggests his triumph constituted less of an unambiguous endorsement of FN policies than an indictment of France's *classe politique.*

Thus, as far as the mainstream candidates (Chirac and Jospin) were concerned, French voters were confronted with the same choice they had been granted seven years earlier—which, in the eyes of many understandably disaffected citizens, signified essentially *no choice.* The comparative lack of genuine political alternatives meant that during the first round French voters stayed home in record numbers (an unprecedented 29 percent abstained), and voters were tempted as never before to opt for a number of "protest" candidates, including two Trotskyists who attracted a remarkable 11 percent of the vote. (The 2002 election represented an unambiguous swan song for the French Communists, who until the mid-1980s had been a major player in French electoral politics; their pitiful 3 percent total was inferior to that of a minor Trotskyite candidate, Arlette Laguiller.) Had 10 percent of the Trotskyite vote gone Jospin's way, he would have out-polled Le Pen.

Moreover, clearly, in retrospect, Chirac treacherously greased the wheels for Le Pen's stunning April breakthrough. With the French economy having recovered its steam after a lengthy fin-de-siècle slump, "crime" (*insecurité*) suddenly became the issue that most preoccupied hexagon voters. During the campaign, Chirac rarely missed an opportunity to raise this theme, traditionally one of the far right's bread-and-butter issues and widely perceived as a Socialist weakness. In March 2002—a month before the election—a deranged gunman murdered eight city council members in the Parisian suburb of Nanterre, an event that was followed by a series of high-profile, politically motivated attacks on prominent Jewish sites. In an election this close, with as many as eleven candidates (among them, feckless ex-*Frontiste* Bruno Mégret) vying for votes, a horrifying event like this, to which the French are so unaccustomed, could have easily tipped the scales.

Although no one doubted that Chirac would triumph in the second round, many feared that a strong showing by Le Pen would, à la Haider, boost the FN's status as a mainstream political contender—an entity with which the center-right parties would at long last be forced to deal. But these fears failed to materialize. A broad anti–Le Pen coalition quickly formed, turning the second round into a referendum on the FN itself. Sizeable anti–Le Pen rallies arose throughout France. The Socialists, for their part, duly instructed their voters to line up behind Chirac. The outpouring of anti–Le Pen sentiment had its desired effect—an electoral debacle for the FN. During the second round the party's totals were kept to 18 percent—slightly 1 percent more than the far-right candidate had accrued in April's first round.

At age 73, Le Pen's "April surprise" may well have been his political last hurrah; by the time the 2007 election rolls around, he will be an elderly 78. Yet there is no doubt that for some twenty years his FN has filled a dangerous void in French politics, raising concerns that traditional political elites have failed to address. Moreover, his brand of strident demagogic populism—as in his tirelessly repeated, demagogic claim of "three million unemployed means three million immigrants too many"—has clearly struck a chord throughout Europe: at the outset of the twenty-first century nearly every nation on the continent possesses a home-grown Le Pen clone, ranting against immigration, parliamentary government, the European Union, and a loss of national identity in a global age.

The Rise of Neofascism

Discussions of right-wing extremism in contemporary Europe often focus on comparisons with Weimar Germany. There exists a natural tendency to perceive parallels between the right-wing extremist movements making inroads across the contemporary European political landscape and "historical fascism": the first wave of fascist movements that swept across Europe in the 1920s and 1930s. Yet although neofascism bears important ideological affinities with the fascisms of yesteryear, it remains doubtful that in the foreseeable future it will either attain power or exercise a destabilizing effect analogous to that of historical fascism. In this respect we must understand that historical fascism was a political phenomenon highly specific to the interwar period, a response to a series of crises—political instability, economic catastrophe, and the Bolshevik threat—that emerged on the European scene following World War I. Its spirit of militarism and its imperialistic quest for living-space led to unprecedented dislocations and cataclysms—according to some estimates, 50 million persons, most of whom were civilians, lost their lives in the European theater alone during World War II. This is a phenomenon that very few Europeans—including many far-right leaders—are anxious to repeat. One might also recall that the leading fascist parties of the interwar period had at their disposal mass paramilitary organizations (the SA in Hitler's case, the *squadri* in Mussolini's), whose function was to foment disorder as well as to terrorize the opposition. Thus the orientation of the interwar fascist parties was avowedly extra- and antiparliamentary. In all these respects, the programmatic differences between historical fascism and the parties of the new European right are striking.[2] As Stanley Payne has observed, perhaps somewhat optimistically, in *A History of Fascism,* "The Western world has been inoculated against fascism, and all the cultural trends of the second half of the century have militated against it. Even a major new economic crisis will probably be inadequate to give it life, for its competitors are more sophisticated and it lacks any broad philosophical basis in terms credible to the ordinary population."[3] Lastly, the economic programs of most of today's European far-right parties are resolutely laissez-faire or "neoliberal"—a fact that contrasts sharply with the corporatist orientation of historical fascism.

Yet despite the fact that neofascism has taken root in a more stable political and economic context, there is little cause for complacency. On the contrary, far-right politics retains the capacity to exercise a distinctly destabilizing influence on the state of contemporary European democracy. Just because today's neofascists come outfitted in Italian suits rather than brownshirts and jackboots does not mean they should not be taken seriously. The European New Right has formulated a finely honed political program possessing considerable broad appeal. Thus, unlike the neofascist parties of the immediate postwar period, they cannot be easily dismissed as historical anachronisms or throwbacks. As one commentator has astutely noted, "Unlike the stodgy, splintered parties of the 1960s and 1970s, run by old Nazis and backward-looking nationalists, the streamlined New Right parties of western Europe . . . offer a far right ideology with a modern, democratic veneer."[4] Although they lack the mass electoral appeal of historical fascism, and while they have tried concertedly to distance themselves from the bellicose claims of interwar fascism, a number of their fundamental aims are similar: they seek to roll back as far as possible the egalitarian spirit of the contemporary democratic order and replace it with an ethnically homogeneous authoritarian state. As one of the European New Right's leading ideological benefactors, Alain de Benoist, has observed, "The enemy as I see it is not 'the left' or 'communism' or even 'subversion' but that egalitarian ideology, whose formulations, religious or lay, metaphysical or pseudo-scientific, have never cased to flourish for two thousand years [a reference to the birth of Christianity—R. W.], and in which 'the ideas of 1789' are nothing but a stage, and of which the current subversion and communism are the inevitable outcome."[5] The visceral antipathy towards the "ideas of 1789"—popular sovereignty, civil liberties, democratic equality—is perhaps the central element that unites contemporary right-wing extremists like de Benoist and company with the proponents of historical fascism. Although neofascism may be only a shadow of its former self, it casts a dark shadow across contemporary European society, "not least because it can reduce the overall level of tolerance and democratic pluralism in society as other parties try to contain the success of the extreme right by taking over some of its ideas, a development obvious both in France and Germany in the course of the 1980s and 1990s."[6]

Europe's Political Right Turn

A brief review of recent political developments will help illustrate the nature and extent of the extreme-right threat. In October 1994 Belgium's anti-immigrant Flemish Block Party (Vlaams Blok), led by Filip Dewinter, gained over 25 percent of the vote in Antwerp city elections. On the very same day, the FPÖ, led by the youthful and telegenic Jörg Haider, increased its electoral share to nearly a quarter of the country's vote in general elections. Commenting on these results, France's newspaper of record, *Le Monde,* remarked, "It is as if in one day the mythic gateways of the Ancient Continent—its North Sea port and the capital of Central Europe—had been swept away by a wave of extremism moving across Europe."[7] Le Pen, for his part, could barely conceal his glee: "The awakening of the European people has . . . translated into massive votes in favor of those who, despite demonization, rise against the dangers of cosmopolitanism and world-wide policies."[8] These results confirm that in European democracies up to 30 percent of the electorate has displayed a distinct preference for far-right parties whose programs are often characterized by an ethno-populist agenda—a tendency confirmed by Haider's shocking October 1999 breakthrough, resulting in the Freedom Party's incorporation within the governing coalition.

Far from being exceptions, the electoral results in Belgium and Austria confirm a disturbing trend. In Denmark and Norway, anti-immigrant parties have successfully pushed a far-right agenda, regularly attracting from 6 to 12 percent of the electorate. As we have seen, over the last twenty years Europe's most successful far-right party, Le Pen's FN, has become a permanent fixture on the French political landscape. In the 1988 French presidential elections Le Pen garnered an impressive 14.4 percent of the vote; in the 1995 presidential contest, he improved slightly to an even 15 percent.

In April 1994 Italy's National Alliance Party, formerly the neofascist MSI (Movimento Sociale Italiano), was incorporated into Prime Minister Silvio Berlusconi's first government, after having gained an unprecedented 13.5 percent of the vote in parliamentary elections. Although Berlusconi's government collapsed under the weight of corruption scandals ten months later, such developments do not seem to have adversely affected the future of National Alliance leader Gianfranco Fini, whom many are touting as a leading player in Italy's political future.[9]

At the same time, one should also take into account other less discouraging developments in far-right party politics. For example, over the last ten years German politics has been haunted by two extreme-right parties: the Republicans, led by former SS leader Franz Schönhuber, and the German People's Union (Deutsche

Volksunion). Both parties have surmounted the 5 percent threshold in city and regional elections in recent years. Yet in the national elections of October 1994, both the Republicans and the German People's Union failed to break the 5 percent barrier, and as a result are in disarray. Schönhuber has been ousted from Republican leadership, and, despite a much-discussed merger, both parties now seem to be of marginal importance on the German political scene.

But premature optimism in the German case would also be misplaced. For one of the key reasons for the electoral decline of the political right is that the mainstream political parties have steadily been incorporating key aspects of their program—above all, restrictions on immigration. Thus in June 1993 the Christian Democrats and Social Democrats joined together in a coalition of shame, transforming Germany's immigration law—formerly, the most liberal in Europe—into one of the most restrictive. This legislation, coming in the aftermath of several deadly and highly publicized attacks on foreign immigrants, seemed like an ex post facto endorsement of such xenophobic outbursts, the equivalent of blaming the victim. For German politicians, the perceived solution to neo-Nazi violence was, rather than to punish the perpetrators, to limit the influx of asylum seekers. The fecklessness of such measures soon became apparent. The 1993 arson attack in Solingen, in which five Turkish immigrants were killed, occurred well *after* the parliamentary agreement limiting asylum rights.

The process whereby mainstream parties broaden their platforms rightward for the sake of returning errant voters on the far right to the fold is one of the major consequences of the rise of a European New Right—a far-from-innocent development. Following such precedents, one discerns the European political spectrum shifting to the right on key questions concerning basic freedoms, tolerance, and civic openness.

A "Gramscism of the Right"

In the bulk of this chapter I will be concerned with the rise of the extreme right in France. This means addressing two separate though interrelated phenomena: the so-called New Right as it emerged in the late 1970s and its filiations to Jean-Marie Le Pen's FN.

The French Nouvelle Droite (New Right) bespeaks a shadowy assemblage of 1970s intellectuals, many of whom maintained ties to neofascist groups during the 1960s. Their agenda has been relatively straightforward: in a postwar era during which the extreme right had been delegitimated owing to the misdeeds of fascism and the taint of collaboration, they have sought to bring right-wing ideas into the political mainstream once again. While, qua intellectuals, many Nouvelle Droite leaders have remained politically marginal, in retrospect one would have to avow that they largely succeeded in their primary aims: to reestablish a discourse of xenophobia and racial hatred that has had a deleterious influence on French political culture of the 1980s and 1990s.

Originally, the French New Right consisted of two organizations: GRECE (Groupement de Recherches et d'Etudes pour une Civilisation Européene) and the Club de l'Horloge (named after the large clock gracing a seminar room at the Ecole Nationale d'Administration, the elite training ground for French political leaders). Although the Club de l'Horloge, founded in 1974, shared many positions with GRECE, unlike the latter, it maintained closer ties with the mainstream French conservative parties, the UDF (Union pour la Democratie Française) as well as Chirac's RPR. It also defended market capitalism in the tradition of "national liberalism" in a way that GRECE would never have countenanced. Moreover, it is worthy of note that in the early 1980s a number of the Club's prominent members—Jean-Yves Le Gallou, former secretary-general; Yvan Blot, the Club's President until 1985; and Bruno Mégret, who would later become the FN chairman prior to his histrionic 1999 break with Le Pen—abandoned their ties to the mainstream right and joined the FN.

GRECE was cofounded in 1968 by Alain de Benoist, who remains the theoretical mastermind behind the program of the Nouvelle Droite in France as well as the European New Right in general. Thus in 1994 de Benoist was warmly received by Alexander Dougine, the Russian nationalist leader and founder of a Russian New Right, a leading advisor to Vladimir Zhirinovsky; a Russian edition of one of Benoist's journals has recently begun publication. Benoist also maintains strong ties to representatives of the New European Right in Italy, Spain, Germany and Belgium.[10]

The 1960s and 1970s were the wilderness years for the extreme right in France. During this period the mainstream right, under the leadership of de Gaulle, Pompidou, and Giscard d'Estaing, enjoyed twenty-three continuous years of electoral success, keeping political extremists like Le Pen and others wholly on the margins. Paradoxically, however, during this period the left dominated France culturally and intellectually. To put an end to left-wing cultural hegemony, de Benoist and his disciples began to formulate a new program circa the late 1970s: a "Gramscism of the right," as de Benoist would baptize his strategy of replacing a left-wing cultural dominance with right-wing concepts and themes. This cultural political struggle was intended as a prelude to far-right political predominance. De Benoist would thus aptly characterize his efforts as a "metapolitical" struggle. In the words of political theorist Pierre-André Taguieff,

> GRECE's great innovation was to take cultural questions seriously from the standpoint of the right. The political right had abandoned the intellectual-cultural field to the Marxist left, while the radical nationalist movements (the "extreme right") were engaged in an anti-intellectual activism, which bore resemblances to the anti-intellectualism of *poujadisme* and which was linked to a type of populist revolt. In this respect GRECE reestablished links with the tradition of historian-writers of the *Action française*.[11]

In his attempt to revitalize the fascist ethos, de Benoist strove for a type of intellectual saturation effect: "the intellectual education of everyone in whose hands the power of decision will come to rest in the coming years." To facilitate this end, he established an international network of publications, study groups, and front organizations designed to ensure that French and European political elites would receive far-right ideas.

Originally, GRECE's program drew on the biological racism of fascist intellectuals such as Italy's Julius Evola—whose racial thinking was so extreme that during the early 1940s Mussolini considered having him arrested.[12] Over the last twenty years, however, GRECE has pursued a new line, minimizing the Nouvelle Droite's ties to a discredited historical fascism to facilitate more general acceptance. And while the Nouvelle Droite has gained a somewhat limited hearing among traditional right parties, Le Pen's FN has undoubtedly been the main beneficiary of its success in rehabilitating a politics of race that, following World War II, had remained confined to the political fringe. As one percipient critic has noted, "Heavily influenced by the ideas of various right-wing think tanks collectively known as the Nouvelle Droite, the National Front program began to emerge as a curious mix of in-vogue monetarism and traditional authoritarian values. Bolstered by the intellectual kudos of the various recruits from the Nouvelle Droite, Le Pen was able to counter the accusations of fascism and extremism leveled at his party."[13]

The filiations between the Nouvelle Droite and the FN are far from straightforward: Le Pen, a Poujadist deputy during the 1950s, espouses the values of an authoritarian national populism. De Benoist, conversely, is a confirmed elitist. The FN has sought to exploit the reactionary, antirepublican symbols of French Catholicism. De Benoist, following Nietzsche and historical fascism, advocates a new European paganism that harks back to mythological, pre-Christian, Indo-European traditions—clearly not a program destined to win a large following in contemporary Europe.[14] In fact, in 1982 de Benoist's endemic hostility to Catholicism and Christianity would cost him a major public outlet for his views as a regular contributor to one of Paris's leading daily papers, *Le Figaro*.

More generally, de Benoist's political sense and timing have left much to be desired. During the 1984 European elections, de Benoist, contemptuous of mainstream political parties on both the left and the right and enamored of his new media visibility, announced he would vote for the communists. Of course, this artless avowal was widely perceived as heretical by fellow rightists, who, unsurprisingly, proceeded to abandon GRECE in droves. Moreover, de Benoist's hyperbolic anti-Americanism (an understanding that doesn't seem to get much beyond Hollywood films and McDonald's hamburgers) and pseudo-militant third-worldism (he insists that the peoples of Europe have more in common with the freedom fighters of third world national liberation movements than with the United States) have not exactly endeared him to the cadres of the mainstream French right.[15]

The New Right's breakthrough came in 1978 when the editor of the *Figaro Magazine,* Louis Pauwels, began systematically publishing articles by de Benoist and like-minded intellectuals. Now a fixture in the Sunday supplement of one of France's leading conservative newspapers, de Benoist became a household name in a matter of months. Soon, nearly 2000 articles appeared about a figure who, until this point, had been a virtual unknown.[16] A major debate raged in the press as to whether Benoist's views were fascist, reactionary, conservative, or neofascist. Gallons of scholarly and journalistic ink were devoted to analyzing and dissecting this Nouvelle Droite phenomenon—much of it coming from the French left. After all, a new threat from the far right would (shades of the Popular Front) stand to enhance the political currency of the antifascist socialist and communist left.

In the last analysis, one senses that had the Nouvelle Droite not existed the left would have had to invent it. The Nouvelle Droite's ties to the conservative establishment represented a potential taint for the mainstream right, just as it embodied a galvanizing force for a left that had been excluded from political power for over twenty years. Moreover, these were the years of increased public awareness concerning the ignominies of Vichy. Hence, any hint of continuities between the contemporary French right and the occupation years was predestined to become a matter of intense national scrutiny.[17]

From Biological to Cultural Racism

What, then, is actually "new" about the Europe's New Right? A response to this question will help us to distinguish contemporary incarnations of the far right from the "antiquated" fascisms of the interwar period.

After flirting for many years with the more orthodox fascist concept of biological racism, in the early 1980s the Nouvelle Droite came up with a clever new strategy. Intended to help distance itself from an out-of-fashion historical fascism, this approach permitted it to convey an analogous racist message in a more acceptable guise. At this point the Nouvelle Droite shifted its emphasis from the concept of "race" to that of "culture." Abandoning outmoded arguments for biological racism, it moved in the direction of what might be called a cultural racism. Under the banner of preserving the sanctity and integrity of "cultures," the Nouvelle Droite argued against immigration, the mixing of cultures, and cosmopolitanism. For the sake of making its claims palatable to a wider audience, it cynically appropriated the universalistic values of tolerance and the "right to difference" for its own xenophobic agenda. Thus, argued de Benoist and company, it was the *cosmopolitans* who were the true racists, insofar as it was they who forced immigrants to submit to the brutal rites of assimilation. Further, the New Rightists claimed that "anti-racism itself is a form of racism, a witch-hunt used against individuals and intended to extinguish 'French' France to the benefit of a 'cosmopolitan' non-society."[18] Sounding like a liberal's liberal, de Benoist embraced what one might be best described as a nonhierarchical, "differentialist racism." No culture was intrinsically better than any other. Instead, they were all "different," and these differences should be respected and preserved.[19] Practically speaking, this meant that the place where Algerians should enjoy civil liberties was Algeria. "France for the French"—an old racist slogan dating from the Dreyfus Affair (and resurrected during the 1930s)—Europe for the Europeans, and so on. As de Benoist explained in the early 1980s, "The truth is that the people must preserve and cultivate their differences. . . . Immigration merits condemnation because it strikes a blow at the identity of the host culture as well as the immigrants' identity."[20]

Let us take a moment to compare Benoist's justification of ethnic particularism with a series of parallel claims made by Le Pen in the course of a 1984 interview: "Peoples cannot be summarily qualified as superior or inferior, they are different, and one must keep in mind these physical or cultural differences." "I love North Africans," continues Le Pen, "but their place is in the Maghreb. . . . I am not a racist, but a nationalist. . . . For a nation to be harmonious, it must have a certain ethnic and spiritual homogeneity." It is therefore necessary "to resolve, to France's benefit, the immigration problem, by the peaceful, organized return of immigrants."[21]

One element that facilitated a more general reception of de Benoist's and Le Pen's advocacy of differentialist racism was the climate of cultural relativism so widespread among Parisian intellectuals. During the 1960s French philosophers had radicalized the Marxist notion of ideology critique to the point where there seemingly remained few Western values worth saving. Marx, a child of the Enlightenment, had argued that bourgeois ideals were illusory and ultimately served class interests. Nevertheless, he remained enough of an Hegelian to believe that these ideals contained a "rational kernel" or "universal potential" that would be realized under socialism. The redemption of this "rational kernel" was the gist of the dialectical method of immanent criticism, which suggested that the "formal" universality implicit in bourgeois ideals must be made real or genuine.

The poststructuralists, conversely, who had replaced Marx with Nietzsche, no longer believed Western values were intrinsically worth redeeming. Instead, averse to the method of immanent criticism, they held, à la Nietzsche, that all values masked an unquenchable "will to power." Whereas Marx, following Hegel, had conceptualized history as "progress in the consciousness of freedom," French philosophers of the 1960s, such as Foucault, essentially stood this claim on its head: what we perceived as freedom—constitutions, civil liberties, humane punishment, and human rights—represented instead a more sophisticated and insidious process of social control. In this way, and in keeping with the spirit of Nietzsche's doctrines, there occurred a triumph of "cynical reason." In a resolutely anticolonial mood after the debacles of Vietnam and Algeria, French intellectuals wrote off "human rights" as colonial window-dressing, integral to the French *mission civilisatrice*—no more than an ideological ploy whereby Europeans justified their domination of the Third World. According to this logic, and in keeping with the anthropological relativism of the day, it followed that all cultures were equal except for those European formations that sought to employ their self-proclaimed superiority to dominate others.

This idea of cultural relativism, which had been canonized in the work of Claude Lévi-Strauss during the 1950s, was then epistemologically enshrined by the French philosophies of difference—Derrida, Deleuze, and Lyotard—that attained prominence during the 1960s. Yet once the much-emulated Third World Liberation movements in Vietnam, Cambodia, Cuba, and a variety of African nations (Mozambique, Uganda, Angola, the Central African Republic) turned despotic, the aforementioned philosophies of difference became increasingly difficult to defend. Instead, what was once presented as a solution now appeared to be part of the problem: in the name of these philosophies one could seemingly justify all manner of non-Western ethical and political excess—Foucault's strange fascination with Iran's "revolution of the Mullahs" offers an excellent case in point.[22] In light of these developments, the 1960s *gauchiste* ethos of Western self-hatred appeared increasingly misplaced. Then came the pièce de résistance: representatives of the European New Right such as Alain de Benoist began employing the claims of "differentialist racism" to justify cultural separatism—as epitomized by Le Pen's cynical claim, "I love North Africans but their place is in the Maghreb"—and discriminatory political legislation. At this point the vacuity of "difference" as an ethical paradigm became painfully apparent. Clearly, a more substantial theoretical bulwark against the new European racism was desperately needed. Suddenly, French thinkers rediscovered "human rights"—which their forbears had invented nearly two centuries earlier.

"Parliamentary Ethnic Cleansing"

Ideas have consequences. The upshot of the FN's advocacy of "cultural difference" has been the embrace of what might best be characterized as parliamentary ethnic cleansing.

In 1991 the FN went so far as to demand not only an end to French immigration but a review of the citizenship status of all immigrants since 1974—the first time since Vichy that ex post facto legislation had been publicly recommended. FN representatives have ominously proposed a "dismantling" of ethnic ghettoes, an end to the construction of mosques, and restrictions on the number of Islamic cultural centers and schools. Children of immigrants would no longer receive free education, and quotas would limit the number of immigrant children in classrooms. Acquisition of French citizenship would no longer be automatic for those born in France, but would instead be based on blood rights.[23]

The transition from a discourse of "race" to one of "culture" and the endorsement of an ideology of differentialist racism proved a crucial strategy in rehabilitating a far-right discourse of ethno-politics that had been long discredited. Though the rhetorical tactics were new, the argumentative strategy was, in truth, quite old. As Christopher Flood has remarked in *Fascism's Return,* "Ideologically, the roots of the extreme right in France can be traced back to the royalist counterrevolutionary theorists of the late eighteenth centuries, with their rejection of the Enlightenment heritage of rationalism, universalistic humanism, economic liberalism, and constitutionalism, which fed into the French Revolution."[24] The New Right political credo harks back to the antiuniversalist sentiment that emerged at the dawn of the European counterrevolution, famously embodied in Joseph de Maistre's claim that whereas there are Frenchmen, Italians, Russians, and even Persians, "humanity" as such does not exist.[25] Maistre's affirmation of the primacy of "ethnos" over "demos" is a direct precursor of Le Pen's notorious "concentric circle" theory of politics: "I like my daughters better than my cousins, my cousins better than my neighbors, my neighbors better than strangers, and strangers better than foes."[26] His unabashed chauvinism draws on anti-Dreyfusard Maurice Barrès's doctrine of "national egotism" (moi nationale) or cult of the "national self."[27] Whereas the idea of democratic citizenship that emerged in the course of the French Revolution stressed, in keeping with Rousseau's doctrine of the general will, the notion of *voluntary* belonging, the counterrevolutionary tradition to which Barrès belongs defines the nation as "community of fate" in which membership is predetermined by "la terre et les morts" (the land and the dead).

The emphasis on degeneracy's threatening a nation that succumbs to racial or cultural mixing (métissage) has been one of the linchpins of counterrevolutionary ideology from Comte Arthur de

Gobineau's *Essay on the Inequality of the Races* (1853–55) and Edouard Drumont's *La Libre parole* to the anti-Dreyfusards to the anti-Semitic legislation of Nuremberg and Vichy. In the late-nineteenth-century counterrevolutionary worldview, anti-Semitism assumed a well-nigh talismanic function: Jews are totemically identified as the source of all social ills; conversely, their total elimination from the body politic portends political salvation. As Drumont remarked in *La France Juive,* "Everything comes from the Jew, everything returns to the Jew."[28] In this context, the historian Saul Friedländer, alluding to modern anti-Semitism's Christian origins, has insightfully described politically motivated anti-Jewish sentiment as "redemptive anti-Semitism." According to this phantasmagorical logic—or "antilogic"—the eradication of Jewish influence heralds the nation's resurrection.

Unsurprisingly, Le Pen's xenophobic nationalism has drawn freely on the anti-Semitism that has been an historical trademark of the French and European right. In a gesture of solidarity with Holocaust deniers, Le Pen once remarked that the extermination of the Jews was no more than a mere "detail" in the overall course of World War II.[29] He is fond of referring to those with AIDS as "*sidaiques,*" recalling the derisory Vichy characterization of Jews as "judaiques." Of course, according to the classical texts of European racism, Jews, like AIDS patients, are also carriers of a "bacillus" or "virus." Nor does Le Pen ever tire of identifying prominent Jewish members of the Socialist Party as "Frenchmen of recent origin" (français de fraîche).

By claiming to support the existing constitutional order, and thus purportedly situating themselves within the lineage of French republicanism, Le Pen and the Nouvelle Droite can allege that the attempt to link them with the extreme right is merely a cynical maneuver on the part of left-wing critics to discredit them. But upon closer inspection, the FN's parliamentary allegiances appear paper-thin. Le Pen and his fellow *Frontistes* continue to regard the achievements of the French Revolution with skepticism. At the time of the bicentennial celebration, FN stalwarts went so far as to suggest that France should really celebrate the 1793 Vendée uprising rather than the Revolution itself. As we have seen, FN officials have frequently criticized the doctrine of jus soli—citizenship rights conferred automatically by birth—a doctrine that was one of the Revolution's key civic legacies. In its proposals for political reform, the FN has consistently vaunted the plebiscite—one of the standard mechanisms whereby authoritarian regimes have historically circumvented the checks and balances of parliamentary rule. Moreover, in interviews and speeches Le Pen himself has made no secret of his admiration for clerico-fascist dictatorships: Franco's Spain, Pinochet's Chile, and the Argentine junta. During the Gulf War, he stridently opposed Western military intervention, and went so far as to make a political embassy to Saddam Hussein (along with other rightist members of the European Parliament) that one might interpret as a gesture of solidarity with an admired fellow despot.

Although the risks of the FN gaining political power seem distant (because of the majoritarian system of voting, they are currently unrepresented in the French Chamber of Deputies, although from 1986 to 1988, under the system of proportional representation instituted under Mitterrand's presidency, they claimed as many as thirty-four delegates), they have been able to exercise an illiberal and debilitating influence on contemporary French political culture.

Since the FN has steadily attracted from 10 to 18 percent of the vote in presidential, European, and regional elections, mainstream parties on both left and right have vied to steal its thunder on the immigration issue. At one point the incentive for the center-right parties to ingratiate themselves with Le Pen's constituency became a mathematical imperative: Chirac's loss to Mitterrand in the 1988 presidential elections has frequently been attributed to the FN's erosion of the traditional right's electoral base. As Jonathan Marcus, author of *The National Front and French Politics,* has observed, "Problems were especially acute for the mainstream right, who during much of the 1980s . . . were motivated by one essential calculation: if the Front's backing, or that of its voters, was needed to secure electoral victory, then, in their view, it was better to deal with Le Pen's supporters than to suffer defeat at the hands of the left."[30] Having internalized the lessons of their 1988 defeat, both Chirac and Valéry

Giscard d'Estaing began pandering to Le Pen's supporters. In the summer of 1991 Chirac spoke of the plight of the French worker who sees a Muslim "family with a father, three or four wives, and about twenty kids, who without working, pull down $10,000 dollars in social benefits"; the smells emanating from their kitchens, he continued, were surely offensive to the average Frenchman.[31] For his part, Giscard d'Estaing suggested the need to abandon France's long-standing tradition of openness to immigrants, openly flirting with the idea of the need to base citizenship on the principle of jus sanguinis rather than jus soli.

In June 1993 the newly elected conservative parliamentary majority, borrowing a page from Le Pen's playbook, passed a new series of strict immigration laws. The measures included stop and search legislation on the basis of race, revoking a long-standing republican tradition of tolerance. Moreover, citizenship for those born on French soil ceased to be automatic; instead, one had to apply at age 17, with the outcome hardly a foregone conclusion.

Nor have the Socialists been immune from pandering, à la Le Pen, to the electorate's baser instincts. In summer 1991 Prime Minister Edith Cresson, in an attempt to outdo both Le Pen and Chirac, expressed her interest in repatriating prospective immigrants via government-sponsored "charter flights." Two years earlier, when the controversy concerning Arab women sporting Islamic headdress (the *foulard*) in the arch-secular French public school system erupted, a contingent of leading Socialists, including Mme. Mitterrand, signed a widely circulated petition supporting a ban. A book by three journalists, *La Main droite de Dieu,* has unmasked Mitterrand's behind-the-scenes machinations to aid Le Pen in gaining political credibility, anticipating the havoc FN prominence would wreak among the mainstream right.[32]

Throughout much of 1990s Le Pen's political competitors allowed him to set the tone and agenda for French political debate. Thus a good part of the FN's success has been attributable to the political void that resulted from the failure of the Socialist program in the 1980s, as well as the lack of alternatives offered by the traditional conservative parties. The FN succeeded with a vengeance in filling this political void. As the philosopher André Glucksmann has astutely noted,

We have a rather extraordinary phenomenon in France today, which is that 80 per cent of people who are neither communist nor supporters of Le Pen talk about nothing but Le Pen. I suggest that we in Europe are all in danger of talking about the fascist danger because we have nothing to say. . . . Words create things, and it is because of the absence of discussion about European integration, about the development of democracy in every country, that there is a fascist danger, not because of a few fascists.[33]

Until the mainstream parties on both left and right cease thinking in terms of political self-interest and instead unite in a stance of principled opposition to the mentality of hatred and fear that Le Pen has been so successful in sowing, the FN will remain a blot on the French political landscape for the foreseeable future.

Conclusion

What are the broader social and economic forces underpinning the emergence of the European New Right as a major force in contemporary European politics? Here, too, the differences with the fascism of the interwar period are instructive. Historical fascism was able to draw upon a fairly large middle-class electoral base: small town dwellers and farmers, small proprietors, the lower middle classes, and white-collar workers. Often, this group has been collectively characterized as the "losers of the modernization process": individuals most vulnerable and exposed to the social dislocations involved in industrialization. As political sociologist Seymour M. Lipset once expressed this thesis: the fascist movements appealed to

segments of the middle class displaced or threatened by the emergence of centralized, large-scale industry and the growing power and status of organized labor. Oppressed by developments fundamental to modern society, small entrepreneurs, small farm owners, and other insecure members of the middle strata were particularly prone to mobilization by fascist movements opposing both big labor and big capital. These developments represented in part a revolt against modernity.[34]

The constituency of the New European Right is also heavily comprised of *potential* "losers of the modernization process." Yet the nature of modernization itself has changed dramatically between the interwar period and today, a fact that at least in part accounts for the European New Right's more circumscribed mass base.

Since the early 1980s many Western European nations have experienced a structural mass unemployment in excess of 10 percent. This fact has given the lie to the traditional welfare state goal of full employment. Instead, recent commentators have begun referring to Europe as a *"civilisation du chomage"*—a "civilization of unemployment." To be sure, the predominant electoral constituency of the far-right parties does not appear to derive primarily from the ranks of the unemployed. Nevertheless, it correlates significantly with those social groups who feel in danger of being left behind by new developments in a globalized, postindustrial economy—an economy in which the values of education, cultural capital, and knowledge have become the primary determinants of salary, status, and social advancement. As one commentator has noted:

> The transition from industrial to postindustrial capitalism is in large part characterized by a process of dissolution, fragmentation, and differentiation [vis-à-vis the norms of class societies], which has its roots in a general acceleration of individualization process. These create new challenges to the individual's capability to adapt to rapidly changing circumstances. This, in turn, puts a premium on cultural capital, individual entrepreneurship, and flexibility.[35]

Postindustrial society has assumed an increasingly technocratic cast, in which positions of power and influence are occupied by elites possessing specialized knowledge or training. Correspondingly, many of those attracted to extreme right parties are young men of lower- or lower middle-class background whose prospects for upward social mobility appear blocked owing to lack of education or suitable training. The FN, for example, derives substantial support from "owners of small businesses, self-employed artisans and other traders, clerical workers, manual workers, and the unemployed."[36] They are the potential *losers of a postindustrial society.* Since the 1980s sociologists have forecast the advent of the "two-thirds society": a society in which two-thirds of the population lives in relative affluence, while the other third leads a quasi-marginal existence, more or less getting by. It is this group that makes up the reserve army of the chronically under- and unemployed: persons who are cut off from the glitz of consumption-oriented, postmodern lifestyles, and who instead perform menial, dead-end, low-paying "McJobs."[37] The New European Right has drawn its support predominantly from the forgotten lower echelons of the two-thirds society. Nor is it a coincidence that these parties have been able to cultivate a hard-core following among the young in a European Community in which youth unemployment has in recent years hovered around 15 percent. The aforementioned trends in occupational structure are likely to be exacerbated in the near future. The "technological elimination of unskilled and semiskilled jobs means that a great many people will be caught in a world of despair, lacking marketable skills or hope for the future."[38] The pronounced ideological emphasis in the discourse of the European New Right on "values" and questions of "collective identity"—be it ethnic, regional, or national—is consciously cultivated. It is intended to compensate for the instability and disorientation sensed by those who have become supernumeraries in a profoundly threatening global economy or "world society"—a highly impersonal, brave new cyber-technological order. Globalization has eroded and destabilized traditional networks of social solidarity on which individuals previously could rely as a source of normative integration: family and extended family, occupational groupings, neighborhoods, communities—even the hitherto sacrosanct autonomy of the traditional nation-state. Statistical breakdowns of the New Right's constituency abound with examples of how "feelings of anxiety and social isolation, political exasperation and powerlessness, loss of purpose in life, and insecurity and abandonment" provide social conditions conducive to the success of far-right political views.[39] New Right politicians are skilled at playing on such feelings and fears. Unfortunately, there is no reason to suspect that their demagogic tactics will not continue to reap a good measure of success.

CONCLUSION

"Site of Catastrophe": The Image
of America in Modern Thought

IMAGES OF AMERICA have always haunted the European psyche. Among Europeans America has often assumed the form of a nightmare vision, a degenerate image of Europe's own future. Such judgments, however, reveal much more about the state of the European mind than they do about America per se. They betray the anxieties and obsessions of European scholars and intellectuals confronted with modernity, "progress," and the discomfiting specter of democratization. Especially among advocates of Counter-Enlightenment, a harsh denunciation of things American would become stock-in-trade. For as the liberal aristocrat Alexis de Tocqueville realized, the success of political democracy in the New World sounded the death knell for the ancient régime. Thus proponents of European reaction firmly believed that by defaming the infant republic, they were simultaneously strengthening the cause of the Party of Order at home.

A century later, America's entry into World War I under the banner of Wilsonian internationalism presented a qualitatively new threat for the advocates of Counter-Enlightenment. It seemed as though a more self-confident and mature American democracy was intent on spreading its ideals militarily as well as by the ruses of international diplomacy. Leading critics of the Enlightenment—Oswald Spengler, Carl Schmitt, and Martin Heidegger—would soon rally around the banner of fascism, which had become the counterrevolutionary mindset's last best hope of staving off a society dominated by the "corrosive" precepts of liberalism, individualism, and freedom of thought.

Although the democracies emerged triumphant following the cataclysm of the Second World War, in many ways it remained a Pyrrhic victory. For, especially in Europe, the conflagration's primary site, the war dealt a mortal blow to the eighteenth century's assumptions about the necessary correlation between truth, reason, and progress. It was the first war in which civilian casualties outnumbered those among combatants, and it left an unfathomable fifty million dead in its wake. How, indeed, could such faith be maintained in the face of death camps, carpet bombing, and the specter of nuclear annihilation, all of which had emerged from the heart of the West? Followed by the traumas of the Cold War and decolonization, these events provided detractors of the Enlightenment with a new and compelling animus. During the 1960s a new generation of vociferous critics of democracy emerged, above all in France. There, the intellectual "event" of the postwar period was the rehabilitation of Nietzsche and Heidegger. Discredited in Germany owing to the taint of fascism, they emerged as the *maîtres penseurs* for poststructuralists such as Michel Foucault, Jacques Derrida, Jean-François Lyotard, and Jean Baudrillard. In this way, Counter-Enlightenment views that, heretofore, had been the exclusive preserve of the European right came to permeate the standpoint of the postmodern left. Whereas the left's previous targets had been social inequality and class injustice, the postmodernists, inspired by Nietzsche and Heidegger, adopted a neo-Spenglerian standpoint of "total critique." They aimed their sights unremittingly at "reason," "humanism," "modernity"—at the same targets that, for decades, had been privileged objects of scorn and derision among proponents of the counterrevolutionary right.

"Indians Can't Think"

In 1770 the naturalist Cornelius de Pauw published a three-volume treatise, *Recherches philosophiques sur les Américains.* Basing his views on the theory of climate popularized by Montesquieu in *Esprit des Lois,* according to which temperature and relative humidity were "destiny," De Pauw exulted in enumerating the grotesqueries of

North American biological life. He was convinced of the inferiority of American coffee beans (which no self-respecting European would deign to drink), the shortcomings of American sugar (grossly deficient in sweetness), and the manifest inadequacy of American wine (which derived from shriveled, insect-infested grapes).

Were genetic deficiencies of life in the New World confined to its agricultural specimens, things might not have been so bad. But with these criticisms de Pauw was just getting started. According to de Pauw, the animal species of the New World are "for the most part inelegantly shaped and . . . badly deformed." Many lacked tails; others suffered from a disproportion between the number of digits on their front and back feet. For vermin of all varieties, conversely, America was a kind of paradise: "The surface of the earth, covered with rot, is inundated by lizards, by snakes, and by reptiles and insects monstrous in their size and in the strength of their poison." Only in such a god-forsaken land might one find—as de Pauw reports—frogs that "weigh up to thirty-seven pounds and bellow like [European] calves."[1] For the taxonomist Buffon, too, it was self-evident that, owing to cooler temperatures and greater humidity, North American animal species were smaller, less variegated, and more lethargic compared to their transatlantic cousins.[2]

Unsurprisingly, the New World's human inhabitants fared little better in de Pauw's account. Take the Indians, for example. "Even today, after three hundred years (since the Europeans arrived), not one of them can think. Their fundamental characteristic is stupid insensibility. Their laziness prevents them from learning anything."[3] Native Americans "lacked vigor and endurance, were sexually frigid and perverted, unprolific, hairless, insensitive to pain, short-lived, and afflicted by a list of ills and perversions ranging from irregular menstruation to the eating of iguanas."[4]

So all encompassing was American environmental decrepitude that animals of European origin cease to grow. "Their size diminished, they lose a part of their instinct and capacity." Dogs mysteriously forget how to bark. European women are prone to become infertile. Is it any wonder, then, that, as de Pauw observes, "In all of America, from Cape Horn to the Hudson Bay, there has never appeared a philosopher, a scholar, an artist, or a thinker whose name merits being included in the history of science or who has served humanity"?[5]

It would be a serious error to dismiss de Pauw's characterizations as the nocturnal musings of an intellectual crank. His book was widely viewed as the most authoritative discussion of America of its day. It was rapidly translated into German and Dutch and won de Pauw a position of influence at the court of Frederick the Great. In *The Federalist* Alexander Hamilton took pains to refute de Pauw's "degeneration thesis," or, in Hamilton's words, the view that "all animals, and with them the human species, degenerate in America—that even dogs cease to bark after having breathed awhile our atmosphere."[6]

For the authors of *The Federalist,* moreover, the stakes were much greater than the honor of American crops and house pets. The issues raised by de Pauw's critique touched the very heart of their new undertaking of democratic government. For if natural history and biology were all determining, then free will was inconsequential and the New World experiment in political freedom was predestined to fail. In opposition to the reigning European view, which was profoundly shaped by taxonomists such as de Pauw and the Buffon, *The Federalist's* "Publius" insisted that it was not climate and heredity that were decisive for the formation of human societies; rather, it was the consciously willed elements of law, morality, and government. The peculiar virtue of human societies lay not with those aspects that have, as it were, been prescribed by nature. Instead, humanity's uniqueness—its capacity for political excellence—derived from its ability to *transcend* what was naturally given, to shape life according the designs of higher human ends. Against the biological determinism of de Pauw and his supporters, Publius argued that humankind is distinct from other forms of life insofar as it possesses the capacity to form politics on the basis of "reflection and choice."

The stakes of this methodological dispute between natural historians and political theorists concerned the viability of democratic government as such. Paradoxically, many philosophes, by rigidly adhering to a materialist epistemology, implicitly denied the reality of human freedom. Hence, the issues at stake possessed weighty policy implications. De Pauw, who believed both that heredity and environment were insurmountable and in the necessity of applying the laws of natural science to human affairs, became a leading spokesmen for European isolationism—thereby, Europeans might keep New World degeneracy at bay. As one commentator has observed, "Natural history could speak truth to power. By showing the pre-political causes that determine social life, science could expose the false claims of the 'political projectors' who had enticed European statesmen into their folly of investing in the New World."[7] By devoting considerable resources—both human and material—to America's colonization, the European powers were merely depleting themselves.

Moreover, colonization raised the specter of miscegenation, the mixing of two peoples who were in their essences unlike one another. Needless to say, arguments such as de Pauw's that questioned the basic humanity of Native Americans made it easier to justify their ill treatment. Such rough-hewn racial taxonomies were precursors to full-blown, nineteenth-century European biological racism.[8] In many respects modern racism was merely an extension of the eighteenth-century doctrine of "polygenesis": the view that there existed essential and unbridgeable differences among the various human races.

One could compile a fascinating compendium of misconceptions about America, expressions of European anxiety and paranoia that may be traced all the way up to the historical present. In the French debate over Euro-Disney during the early 1990s, Jean Cau, Sartre's former personal secretary turned right-wing pamphleteer, described the American theme park as a "cultural Chernobyl . . . a construction of hardened chewing gum and idiotic folklore written for obese Americans." Socialist Party spokesman Max Gallo was hardly more diplomatic, lamenting the fact that this "Trojan Mouse" would "bombard France with uprooted creations that are to culture what fast food is to gastronomy."[9] To judge by the rhetorical overkill that suffused the debate, one would think the Americans were attempting to install a battery of medium range nuclear missiles rather than a relatively harmless amusement park.

The idea of America as *Schreckbild*—as an image of horror—has been a staple of nineteenth- and twentieth-century European political thought. Progressives had been seduced by American promises of equal opportunity and democratic inclusion. Thus, for philosophes like Voltaire, the American colonies were tangible proof that humanity possessed the capacity to live in freedom. The colonists' successful experiment in self-rule inspired Enlightenment thinkers to recommend similar reforms at home. Conversely, leading apostles of Reaction—Joseph de Maistre, Louis de Bonald, Arthur de Gobineau, Oswald Spengler, and Martin Heidegger—viewed the American Revolution as a political sibling of the French, and, hence, as an extreme manifestation of political modernity—individualism, rights of man, liberalism—that deserved to be quashed via the purgative methods of counterrevolutionary violence.

The dystopian view of America is hardly a thing of the past. This vision informs a certain anti-intellectual spirit that pervades contemporary cultural life—a spirit best expressed by the fashionable view that Reason and the Enlightenment, instead of setting us free, are a curse. According to the reigning intellectual cant as embraced by proponents of academic postmodernism, Reason is essentially a form of repression. Its raison d'être is the suppression and marginalization of otherness or "difference." Reason and logic, allegedly, proceed by reducing the "other" to the "same"—to inherited norms of "coherence"—and in this respect prove intolerant of "difference," which is thereby (and problematically) elevated to the rank of a new first principle. The obvious risk in this approach (and, as we shall see, there are many more) is a systematic preference for "incoherence" over "coherence" or "non-sense" over "sense"—hence the taint of anti-intellectualism. To adjudicate differences discursively—be they intellectual, political, or cultural—is deemed illegitimate. For it goes without saying that methods of rational adjudication only serve further to suppress difference.

Riding the wave of academic postmodernism, the politics of difference has managed to entrench itself as a new intellectual orthodoxy. Although cultural differences must be respected, it is but a short step from the uncritical glorification of difference to a new intellectual tribalism. To celebrate cultures as windowless monads exalts ethnocentrism at the expense of cosmopolitanism. Worse still, it means surrendering prematurely the common ground necessary for productive cross-cultural dialogue. The politics of difference is relativist—all differences or standpoints should be treated equally—but only up to a point. The one standpoint *undeserving* of equal treatment is "Eurocentrism," the culture that gave us both Reason and the horrors of colonialism, the political corollary of Reason's endemic intolerance. Such intellectual tendencies—their glib denunciations of reason, their instinctual rejections of political liberalism as a sinister plot to level differences (on the basis of precepts such as "tolerance" and "equality before the law")—are troubling indeed.

What, then, is the connection between the "politics of difference"—the reigning form of radical intellectual chic—and the idea of America qua degeneracy that has haunted European thought for nearly two centuries? Ironically, images of America once a staple the European Counter-Enlightenment have been assimilated and recycled by the multicultural left. The subterranean affinities between these two intellectual traditions, European right and contemporary cultural left, reveal a disconcerting chapter in the history of political ideas—one that deserves to be recounted.

Maistre and "Multiculturalism"

Today the doctrines of Joseph de Maistre and Arthur de Gobineau are rarely studied. Yet, along with those of Maistre's contemporary and fellow aristocrat Louis de Bonald, they were the main sources of Counter-Enlightenment ideology. If one is interested in discerning the main lines of the right-wing critique of democracy—a tradition that would culminate in the visceral antiliberalism of European fascism—their writings remain an indispensable key.

It was the French Revolution that roused Maistre from the tranquil life of a provincial aristocrat. In 1792 the revolutionary armies invaded his native Savoy, forcing him into Swiss exile. Five years later he published his famous treatise, *Considerations on France*.

Along with the works of Edmund Burke, Benjamin Constant, and Madame de Stael, it still ranks as one of the landmark contemporary studies of the revolution's origins and significance.

Like the revolution's enthusiasts on the political left, Maistre was impressed by the sublimity of the momentous political tapestry that was unfolding before his eyes. For this reason he was convinced that no mere *historical* attempt to understand the events could do them justice. For Maistre, the revolution's apocalyptical scope indicated that the hand of Providence had played a decisive role. He concluded that only a *theological* understanding of the events could capture their real meaning.

Thus was born Maistre's thesis that the revolution was an act of divine vengeance visited upon France for her Enlightenment-driven apostasies. In his eyes the revolution signified providential retribution for France's sacrilegious flirtation with "enlightened" ideas: her wanton indulgence in atheism and materialism, culminating in the sin of regicide. The revolutionaries, trusting in the forces of progress and reason, flattered themselves that they were in control of the events they had unleashed. But Maistre knew better. As he famously remarked, "It is not men who lead the Revolution, it is the Revolution that employs men."[10] In this way alone could one explain the unprecedented levels of misery and chaos that revolutionary France had been forced to endure.

By interpreting the revolutionary events as a grandiose theological pageant, Maistre sought to underline the futility of all human efforts to endow history with intelligibility and meaning. By mocking the revolutionary actors, he wished to strike a deathblow against the Enlightenment faith in reason that had inspired them. Like Burke, he was convinced of the folly of trying to model human society according to the dictates of abstract reason. A devout Catholic and believer in original sin, Maistre held man to be an essentially foolish and wicked creature. Autocratic rule and fear of damnation were the only forces capable of saving humanity from the folly of its own schemes. In *Considerations* he gleefully pointed out the irony that it was a *dictatorship*—that of Robespierre and his fellow Jacobins—that had saved the Revolution during its most precarious hour. The eternal corruptions of human nature forced the revolutionaries—their enlightened, humanitarian sentiments notwithstanding—to rely on the time-honored means of despotism and the executioner's axe to secure their rule.

Maistre's view of human nature as fundamentally sinful, as well as his corresponding belief in the necessity of authoritarian rule, would become staples for all subsequent versions of Counter-Enlightenment doctrine. The conviction that humanity is incapable of rationally shaping its own destiny, and that, instead, mysterious, irrational forces are the ultimate determinants of human affairs, is a position shared by both reactionaries and postmodernists. Like his contemporary Bonald, Maistre believed it imperative that Enlightenment's course be reversed. He considered freedom of speech and "individualism" intrinsically destructive to the social fabric. Mankind's innate wickedness made it constitutionally incapable of self-rule. He lionized the Spanish Inquisition as providing the admixture of tyranny and cruelty appropriate to human sinfulness. In a famous witticism, he declared that authority of evidence must be replaced by the evidence of authority. Whereas the philosophes proclaimed a new faith in Reason, Maistre famously contended that "what we ought not to know is more important than what we ought to know."[11] Excessive faith in the powers of rational inquiry would erode the foundations of order and authority. Eventually, the entire social edifice would collapse—witness the chaos that ensued in the French Revolution's aftermath. Political sovereignty could never be rationally justified, let alone made the object of a social contract. Instead, it was a matter of unthinking obedience.

Heretofore, proponents of absolute monarchy had relied on either the divine right of kings or the authority of tradition. But with Maistre one detects an important shift. He was too sophisticated a thinker to deny the fact that, in the modern age, these traditional justifications were no longer tenable. Thus, stripped of its theological rhetoric, Maistre's theory of sovereignty bears important affinities with the modern concept of political dictatorship, whose most important exponent was the political philosopher Carl Schmitt. In the 1920s Schmitt realized that once one exposed political sovereignty to discussion and debate—to questions of "justification"—there was no hope of keeping liberal democracy at bay. In a manner reminiscent of Maistre, he suggested that sovereignty was ultimately a matter of "decision": "an absolute decision, created out of nothingness"—a matter of dictatorship.[12]

Unsurprisingly, Maistre was quick to dismiss the prospects of the American Revolution. Give it enough time, he argued, and it would succumb to the same debilities as the French. The American Constitution, he held, was a consummate expression of the hubris and ineptitude of human reason. As Maistre observes, "All that is truly new in their constitution, all that results from common deliberation, is the most fragile thing in the world; one could not bring together more symptoms of weakness or decay."[13] That the nascent republic endured as long as it did he attributed to the continuity of British traditions rather than the Framers' conscious design. Taking note of the bickering and infighting among the individual states, Maistre had few doubts that soon the entire edifice would collapse like a house of cards.

> Not only do I doubt the stability of the American government, but the particular establishments of English America inspire no confidence in me. The cities, for example, animated by a hardly respectable jealousy, have not been able to agree as to where the Congress should meet; none of them wanted to concede the honor to another. In consequence, they have decided to build a new city to be the capital. . . . Nevertheless, there is too much deliberation, too much *humanity* in this business, and one could bet a thousand to one that the city will not be built, that it will not be called *Washington,* and that the Congress will not meet there.[14]

In *Considerations on France* Maistre gives voice to a sentiment that would in the future have tremendous resonance among reactionaries of all stripes. "There is no such thing in the world as *man,*" he declares. "In my life I have seen Frenchmen, Italians, Russians, and so on. I even know, thanks to Montesquieu, that one can be Persian. But as for *man,* I declare I've never encountered him. If he exists, I don't know about it."[15]

According to the Enlightenment worldview, the essence of human dignity lay in the ability of men and women to transcend particular attachments, which were perceived as intrinsically limiting.

To accede to the promised land of Reason meant consciously abandoning all partial allegiances and elevating oneself to the standpoint of the "universal." Truth was one. With the universal, and with it alone, might truth to be found. This avowed prejudice in favor of the general over the particular was apparent in the Enlightenment idea of the *sensus communis*.[16] Particular truths come and go. Only those truths that could in principle find acceptance among *all* men and women—that is, by an ideal community of enlightened individuals—might be adjudged rational or universal truths.

Maistre's celebrated dictum, "as for *man,* I declare I've never encountered him," mocked Enlightenment universalism. On one level it gave voice to an unarguable empirical truth concerning the relationship between ethnicity and human identity. In the first instance, human attachments are always particular, allied to a specific family, clan, religion, or region. On another level, Maistre sought to demonstrate that "man in the abstract" was a chimera, a febrile—and ultimately dangerous—delusion of an unbridled philosophical imagination. Lastly, his remarks represent a forceful statement concerning the ineradicable nature of ethnic differences, in the face of which Enlightenment shibboleths concerning natural right paled.

Maistre's claims concerning the irreducibility of ethnic difference became an indispensable starting point for the Counter-Enlightenment assault against the philosophes' intellectual and political legacy. It informed Gobineau's mid-century critique of the revolutionary heritage and European liberalism. Thereafter, racism became a linchpin of counterrevolutionary thought. In the eyes of Isaiah Berlin, "Maistre's deeply pessimistic vision is the heart of the totalitarianisms, of both left and right, of the twentieth century."[17]

Viewed in light of the suggestive filiations between Counter-Enlightenment doctrine and postmodernism, Maistre's remarks about the ineffaceable nature of "difference" take on new meaning. When considered in these terms he appears as an important progenitor of the today's modish "politics of difference." Maistre was a multitalented intellect: Catholic, legitimist, essayist, and polemicist. But, ideologically speaking, he was, along with his German contemporary J. G. Herder, one of the first uncompromising multiculturalists. His theory of inalienable human difference, along with his scathing dismissal of the "rights of man," bequeathed a powerful and disturbing political legacy.

Gobineau: Race as a Master Key

Born in 1816, Gobineau, like Maistre, was a French aristocrat appalled by the political legacy of the French Revolution. The democratic radicalism unleashed by the Revolutions of 1848 convinced him that European civilization had reached a point of no return. Its final collapse was merely a question of time.

In the aftermath of the tumultuous events of 1848—the July monarchy was overthrown, a republic proclaimed, followed by a major working class insurrection—Gobineau decided to formalize his views on the forces responsible for European political decline. The end result was his mammoth *Essay on the Inequality of the Human Races,* which appeared in four volumes from 1853 to 1855.

Despite the distasteful character of his political views, with Gobineau, as with Maistre, one is unquestionably dealing with a figure of substance. In addition to the *Essay* for which he is best known, Gobineau was a talented novelist and had a distinguished career in the French diplomatic corps. When Tocqueville became France's foreign minister in 1849, he selected the young count, eleven years his junior, to serve as his personal secretary. Already in the mid-1830s the two had begun a lively correspondence that culminated in a contentious debate on the political implications of Gobineau's *Essay.* Tocqueville was the quintessential European liberal, Gobineau the archetypal reactionary. Their landmark exchange over Europe's future would foreshadow a century of political and ideological strife.

Both Maistre and Bonald proffered powerful indictments of political liberalism. But by the middle of the nineteenth century, their basic lines of attack—theological (Maistre) and traditionalist (Bonald)—seemed antiquated. The nineteenth century was the age of "scientism," and political convictions that failed to legitimate themselves before this new tribunal were destined to be ignored.

Gobineau's ingenious strategy was to reestablish the Counter-Enlightenment worldview on pseudoscientific foundations by employing the concept of *race* as a universal key to historical development. Racially based taxonomies of human types were already widely used by anthropologists and natural historians. But Gobineau was the first to apply race systematically to the study of history as a type of hidden master code. In advance of Nietzsche, Spengler, and Toynbee, he became the first significant prophet of European decline.

According to Gobineau the outcome of European history was genetically predetermined. Though he had no doubts about the ultimate superiority of European civilization, he was convinced that the Old Continent's glory days lay in the distant past. The tragedy of European development derived from the fact that whereas her racial preeminence made conquest of inferior peoples inevitable, in the process of lording over them, a mixing of the races was unavoidable, resulting in the necessary dilution of Europe's gene pool. In Gobineau's view the laws of genetic development were ironclad. They admitted of no exceptions. When noble races bred with those of inferior stock, the superior group suffered biological depletion. As he observes in the *Essay*, "A people will die definitively, and its civilization with it, the moment when its original ethnical element has become so subdivided or submerged by admixtures of foreign races that it can no longer give rise to sufficient impulse."[18]

It would be difficult to overestimate Gobineau's influence on the subsequent course of European political thought. He was a friend of Wagner and the primary source for the German composer's racist worldview. In 1900 Wagner's son-in-law, Houston Stewart Chamberlain, published *The Foundations of the Nineteenth Century*, the ur-text of Nazi racial theory. Chamberlain's elaborate arguments for Aryan superiority are of a distinctly Gobineauian provenance. The Nazis lionized Gobineau, and employed the *Essay* as a catechism for racial instruction. Hitler's one reservation concerned Gobineau's proto-Spenglerian thesis about the inevitability of racial decline. "How can we arrest racial decay? Must what Count Gobineau says come true?" mused the Führer in 1933.[19] As one scholar has astutely observed, "Implicit in Gobineau's thought were a style of historical myth-making, a theory of value, and a mode of reasoning that by its systematic abuse of logic showed the way for all subsequent racial theorists."[20]

Gobineau's opinions of America fluctuated. At first, he viewed it as a potential Aryan haven from European cultural decline. But as he became more familiar with American politics and customs, he arrived at a diametrically opposite view. The degeneracy of life in the New World, Gobineau argued, far outstripped that of Europe. For it was in America that the ills of democratic political culture—natural rights, social leveling, majority rule—were most advanced. American society was resolutely progressive and meritocratic. Such values were impossible to reconcile with the principles of aristocracy, according to which men and women were judged on the basis of who they were rather than what they did.

Moreover, as of the 1850s, a new wave of "non-Aryan" immigrants—Irish, Italians, and Germans of dubious racial patrimony—began flooding America's ports. In Gobineau's eyes, these new settlers were little more than "scum," Europe's detritus. Prospects for a racially pure sanctuary had been irretrievably squandered. Gobineau's view of the New World as a morass of racial impurity and "mongrelization" would henceforth become standard among intellectuals on the European right. For Oswald Spengler, too, writing in the mid-1930s, American cultural decay was a direct result of lax immigration policies leading to a diminution of the nation's Aryan core.[21]

Gobineau was an aristocratic racist. Entire nations could never be ethnically pure, only a racial elite. Like de Pauw, he was a harsh critic of European colonialism. The subjugation of inferior peoples would only encourage interbreeding and thereby accelerate the course of Europe's racial debasement. He disapproved of American slavery on similar grounds. Be that as it may, anti-abolitionists viewed the *Essay* as an eloquent justification of their cause and busily set about translating and distributing excerpts that suited them. Hitler, for one, fully sympathized with their perspective. He viewed the Confederacy as the lost "embryo of a future truly great America."[22]

In many respects Gobineau's racial doctrines constituted a rear-guard effort to defend his slipping class prerogative, even though he knew the battle was already lost. Talleyrand once observed that only those who had been alive during the ancien régime had tasted life in its full sweetness. An aristocratic latecomer, Gobineau would never forgive the bourgeoisie for having displaced his class from the pinnacle of the social hierarchy. His *Essay* was an elaborate labor of vengeance. Though the bourgeoisie may have triumphed politically, he did all he could to sully their victory by claiming they were chiefly responsible for Europe's irreversible cultural decline.

One of the most seductive aspects of Gobineau's position was its historical determinism. It proved a powerful ideological weapon to counter the progressivist Enlightenment view that human history could be consciously willed and controlled. In the nineteenth century, social scientific rationalism (e.g., Auguste Comte and his followers) was replete with optimistic prognoses concerning humanity's future once the forces of superstition and unreason had been vanquished. With his theory of biological determinism, Gobineau tried to show that the utopian dreams of the rising middle classes were essentially unrealizable.

This theory became the focus of Gobineau's celebrated debate with Tocqueville. Tocqueville always felt a certain affection for his protégé and fellow aristocrat. But the arguments he encountered in the *Essay* strained the terms of their friendship. Tocqueville, the intrepid champion of "liberty," began by challenging the empirical accuracy of Gobineau's claims. Admittedly, he argued, various human groups displayed different tendencies and capacities. But to contend that "these aptitudes cannot be overcome—not only has this assertion never been proved, but from its very nature it can never be. Whoever attempts it must have available to him not only the past but the future."[23]

Tocqueville went on to contest the ethical implications of Gobineau's doctrines. By alleging that social life was biologically predetermined, and that consciousness and will were powerless to effect meaningful historical change, Gobineau had sought to deprive humanity of one of its most precious attributes: hope. Tocqueville readily admitted that in the past social reformers had vastly overestimated humanity's ability to give shape to its own destiny. But this was no reason to jump to the opposite conclusion and rashly proclaim irremediable human impotence. Tocqueville rose to the occasion with rhetorical brilliance.

> You have chosen to support precisely that point of view which I have always considered most dangerous to our age. . . . The last century had an exaggerated and somewhat puerile confidence in man's power to control his destiny, both his own life and that of his society. This was the characteristic error of that period [the Enlightenment], but in the final analysis it was a noble error. While responsible for many follies, yet it produced many great achievements beside which posterity will find our age puny indeed. . . . After believing that we could transform ourselves, we now believe that even the slightest reform is impossible. After excessive pride, we have fallen into an equally excessive humility. Once we thought ourselves capable of everything; today we believe ourselves capable of nothing. It pleases us to believe that from now on struggle and effort are futile, that our blood, our bodies, and our nervous systems will always prevail over our will and capacity. This is the peculiar argument of our time. . . . No matter how you rearrange your argument, it will support rather than control this tendency: it will drive your contemporaries, who are already too weak, to an even greater weakness.[24]

In response, Gobineau sought refuge under the cover of scientific objectivity. There was nothing moral or immoral per se about his views. He likened his prognoses to those of a physician confronted with a dying patient. Should he console the patient by telling him there are better days ahead? Perhaps, but it would certainly be less honest.

> What I am saying to my readers is not, "You are guilty, or not guilty." Rather I tell them, "You are dying. . . . You have passed the age of youth, you approach that age which verges on decrepitude. . . . Winter

is coming on, and you have produced no heir to succeed you. You may found kingdoms, great empires, republics. . . . Go torture the Chinese, finish off the Turks, annex Persia—all this is possible and even inevitable. But while I do not interdict them, nevertheless the causes of your weakness continue to accumulate and are even aggravated by your activity."[25]

To his credit, Tocqueville refused to accept Gobineau's feeble self-justification. In truth, Gobineau's motivations were far from scientific: they were intensely ideological. In the *Essay* Gobineau desperately sought to inculpate one worldview (that of the rising middle classes) and to promote another (that of his own class). And it was all neatly packaged for intellectual mass consumption under the guise of "science."

In his correspondence with Tocqueville, Gobineau expressed the fear that his *Essay* was fated to be ignored in his native France. Perhaps so, the author of *Democracy in America* responded. Then, with uncanny prescience, Tocqueville went on to prophesy precisely where Gobineau's doctrine of Aryan supremacy was destined to find great favor: across the Rhine in Germany.

"Decline of the West"

In France counterrevolutionary doctrine found favor among political groupings such as the Action française, the militant "leagues," the anti-Dreyfusards, and supporters of Vichy. At the same time, since the days of the revolution, France remained a bulwark of republican traditions, which usually carried enough weight to keep the forces of reaction at bay. As Tocqueville understood, however, Germany was another case. There, liberal political traditions remained marginalized. And when national unity belatedly arrived in 1871, it was autocratically orchestrated from above by Bismarck instead of democratically from below.

Thus it was in Germany that counterrevolutionary ideology found greatest political favor. As Fritz Stern has observed, "From the 1870s on, conservative writers in imperial Germany expressed the fear that the German soul would be destroyed by 'Americanization,' that is by mammonism, materialism, mechanization and mass society."[26] A proverbial latecomer to modernity, the breathtaking pace of German industrialization produced shock waves of anxiety among traditional German elites: Junker aristocrats, mandarin intellectuals, not to mention rural inhabitants forced to migrate to the cities for work. A phobic preoccupation with the evils of modern industrial society became a hallmark of German social thought from the 1880s onward. More often than not, such fears were projected upon America, that upstart transatlantic colossus and apex of political liberalism.

Among postmodernists it has become fashionable to read Nietzsche as a poet, a stylist, an aesthete—as anything but a political thinker. Yet in Nietzsche's oeuvre there are extended discussions of "breeding," "hierarchy," "race," and war that have been conveniently excised from the postmodern canon. If one wants to understand the radicalization of Germany's right-wing intellectuals, an appreciation of Nietzsche's influence as a political thinker is indispensable. All the prejudices that existed among French prophets of counterrevolution one finds redoubled in Nietzsche.

According to Nietzsche, "The breathless haste with which [the Americans] work—the distinctive vice of the new world—is already beginning ferociously to infect old Europe and is spreading a spiritual emptiness over the continent." In America, observes Nietzsche, "one thinks with a watch in one's hand"; "prolonged reflection almost gives people a bad conscience." To their discredit, Americans have redefined the meaning of virtue. "Virtuousness now consists in doing something in less time than someone else." Perhaps things would not be so bad were such untrammeled philistinism confined to the New World alone. But, increasingly, such attitudes were manifesting themselves elsewhere. Thus, "the faith of the Americans today is more and more becoming the faith of the European as well."[27] If the modern age could aptly be described as an era of total nihilism, whose defining feature was the replacement of aristocratic values by the timorous, egalitarian mores of mass society, then it was America that was leading the charge. That Nietzsche had never set foot on American soil proved no obstacle to his judgmental self-confidence.

Such Nietzschean sentiments would inspire the worldview of Germany's "conservative revolutionary" thinkers, most of whom came of age during the interwar years. For this influential group of proto-fascist intellectuals—Ernst Jünger, Arthur Moeller van den Bruck, Carl Schmitt, and Oswald Spengler—several of whom would make their peace with the Nazi Party during the 1930s, "Americanization" symbolized a fate of thoroughgoing racial debasement and cultural degeneracy.

Though Spengler was perhaps the best known among this group, Moeller van den Bruck first popularized the idea of the Third Reich in a 1923 book that bore this title. For van den Bruck America was a one-dimensional society. "In America everything is a block, pragmatism, and the national Taylor System."[28] In his view the history of liberalism had obviously ended in failure. America's only hope was to shed the trammels of constitutional government in order to exploit to the hilt her industrial prowess and pioneer spirit.

In Spengler's writings the German preoccupation with technology was raised to the level of a major philosophical obsession. *Decline of the West* (1918, 1922) was significantly influenced by Gobineau's thesis concerning the inevitability of European decay and corresponded perfectly to Germany's postwar mood of despair and disorientation. Few books had a greater cultural impact on German society during the 1920s.

In 1931 Spengler published the equally influential *Man and Technology,* where he viewed the entire expanse of human history from the standpoint of man's struggle with the forces of "mechanization"—a confrontation that humanity was fated to lose. Inevitably, argued Spengler, the Faustian spirit of modern man was destined to recoil upon and consume its creator. "Civilization itself has become a machine that does, or tries to do, everything in mechanical fashion. We think only in horse-power now; we cannot look at a waterfall without mentally turning it into electric power; we cannot survey a countryside full of pasturing cattle without thinking of its exploitation as a source of meat-supply."[29] Spengler's rhetoric of apocalyptical imminence foreshadows contemporary environmentalist extremism:

> The mechanization of the world has entered on a phase of highly dangerous overextension. . . . In a few decades most of the great forests will have gone, to be turned into news-print, and climatic changes have been thereby set afoot which imperil the land-economy of whole populations. Innumerable animal species have been extinguished. . . . Whole races of humanity have been brought almost to a vanishing-point. . . . This machine-technology will end the Faustian civilization and one day will lie in fragments, forgotten—our railways and steamships as dead as the Roman roads and the Chinese wall.[30]

In Spengler's eyes such developments had reached their most extreme form in the United States. In his estimation, both Bolshevism and life in America were "organized exclusively from the economic side." In Spengler's view, "neither regime has a concern for man's spiritual side or his nobility, and both have abandoned themselves without understanding to the process of mechanization."[31] For Spengler, consequently, the two regimes represented twin variants of modern mass tyranny and, hence, were devoid of qualitative differences. "There is the same dictatorship of public opinion in America as in Russia (it does not matter that it is imposed by society instead of a party) that affects everything that is left in the West to the free option of individuals: flirtation and church-going, shoes and make-up, fashion in dance and novels, thinking, eating, and recreation."[32]

But the philosopher whose sweeping condemnation of America would have the greatest consequences for modern thought was Martin Heidegger. Moreover, Heidegger's impassioned ideological denunciation of "Americanism" would set the tone for most postmodernist criticisms of America—to the point where it becomes meaningful to characterize postmodernism as a type of "left Heideggerianism." As one critic has argued:

> No thinker in this century has had greater influence on the development of the idea of America than Martin Heidegger. Although he

borrowed much from his predecessors in Germany, particularly Spengler and Jünger, Heidegger went well beyond any of them in fashioning a symbol that has ever since connected the themes of desolation, horror, and homelessness to America. With Heidegger, America was transformed from a country to a major literary and philosophic category that intellectuals have since been unable to ignore.[33]

For Heidegger, as for Spengler, no essential differences marked Americanism and Bolshevism. "From a metaphysical point of view"—to which apparently Heidegger alone was privy—"Russia and America are the same, with the same dreary technological frenzy and the same unrestricted organization of the average man." Confirming the paranoid vision of Nietzsche, Moeller van den Bruck, and Spengler, Heidegger was convinced that, insofar as the world was becoming more and more Americanized, life was becoming increasingly mechanical, routinized, and insubstantial. As he observed in *An Introduction to Metaphysics* (1935):

> The lives of men began to slide into a world which lacked the depth from out of which the essential always comes. . . . The prevailing dimension became that of extension and number. Intelligence no longer meant a wealth of talent, lavishly spent, but only what could be learned by everyone, the practice of a routine, always associated with a certain amount of sweat and a certain amount of show. In America and in Russia this development grew into a boundless etcetera of indifference and always-the-sameness—so much so that quantity took on a quality of its own. . . . This is the onslaught of what we call *the demonic* (in the sense of destructive evil).[34]

Elsewhere, Heidegger simply insisted that America was "the site of catastrophe."[35] In his view, Germany alone—that embattled "nation in the middle"—offered the world hope for salvation. And the Germany from which Heidegger expected salvation was Hitler's Germany. In 1943, as the battle of Stalingrad raged, Heidegger could still proclaim, "The planet is in flames. The essence of man is out of joint. Only from the Germans can there come a world-historical reflection—if, that is, they find and preserve Germanness."[36] That the planetary devastation he described was a direct result of "Germanness" was a thought that, remarkably, never seemed to have crossed his mind.

Although Heidegger had strong opinions about "symbolic America"—that is, about America as the ultimate incarnation of modern decadence—the "real America" was unknown to him. For, as a matter of principle, Heidegger rarely traveled outside of his beloved *Heimat* in the German province of Baden.[37]

Heidegger's dystopian obsession with things American merely perpetuated a lineage of radical Kulturkritik dating back to the era of German Romanticism. For the romantics, America was in essence a *kulturlose Gesellschaft,* a society that was constitutionally incapable of culture (on which Europeans—and Germans in particular—held a monopoly). Since America was a land in which commerce proliferated, and since, as everyone knew, commerce and culture operated at cross-purposes, America was condemned condescendingly as a spiritually impoverished land. In his novel *Das junge Europa* Heinrich Laube, a friend of the poet Heinrich Heine, described America as "a business school that claims to be a world. . . . No history, no free science, no free art! Free trade is the total freedom; . . . anything that does not bring in money is useless, and that which is useless is unnecessary."[38] Heine's own views, while humorous, were hardly more sanguine. As he writes in *Romancero* (1851):

> I have sometimes thought to sail
> To America the Free
> to that Freedom Stable where
> All the boors live equally.
> But I fear a land where men
> Chew tobacco in platoons,
> There's no king among the pins,
> And they spit without spittoons."[39]

Twenty years earlier, Heine had described America as "that monstrous prison of freedom, where the invisible chains would oppress me even more heavily than the visible ones at home, and where the most repulsive of all tyrants, the populace, hold vulgar sway."[40]

Viewed from this perspective, the "real" America, or America "in itself," was beside the point, something of merely empirical interest. Imaginary America represented the cumulative sum of German fears about "the West": a stand-in for "capitalism," "democracy," "individualism," and "reason." Once Germany began industrializing in earnest during the latter third of the nineteenth century, anti-Semitism gained a permanent foothold in the German political psyche. From this point hence, the assumption that "capitalist" America must be dominated by Jews (its predominantly Anglo-Protestant cultural heritage notwithstanding) became commonplace. According to the new conventional wisdom, anti-Americanism blended indistinguishably with anti-Semitism—a development that began to careen out of control following Germany's humiliating treatment after the World War I armistice, which, in German eyes, turned Wilsonianism into a model of hypocrisy.

Before the war the image of America as a Jewish-dominated plutocracy had been assiduously cultivated by Werner Sombart in *The Jews and Modern Capitalism,* where the sociologist described the United States as a *Judenstaat*—a state monopolized by Jewish interests.[41] Sombart shunned all empirical validation of his claims. Instead, his thesis about the necessary connection between the Jews and capitalism possessed the status of an unfalsifiable, metaphysical deduction: where capitalism triumphed, Jews or the Jewish spirit must a fortiori play a prominent role. Whereas German character was rooted in the profundities of blood, Jews, like Americans, excelled at a superficial intellectualism. As Sombart concludes, "What we call Americanism is to a very great extent nothing other than *congealed Jewish spirit.*"[42] For the fascist intelligentsia during the 1930s, such associations would become commonplace. In *Bagatelles pour un massacre,* for example, Ferdinand-Louis Céline expressed the standard fascist view of the United States as an imperious capitalist state where world Jewry pulled the strings imperceptibly behind the scenes.[43]

Thus, in surveying the terrain of twentieth-century German Kulturkritik, in which an animus against Zivilisation—mechanistic, crass, and soulless—was a distinguishing leitmotif, it becomes impossible to dissociate such themes from the anti-Semitism that would reach fever pitch during the Third Reich. For, coincident with

Germany's traumatic defeat at the hands of the Triple Alliance, this potent thematic admixture, combining anticapitalism, anti-Americanism, and anti-Semitism, produced a noxious amalgam in which the aforementioned elements became fused and interchangeable. In the central European cultural imaginary, to invoke one of the terms immediately and metonymically conjured the other two. Thus throughout Heidegger's voluminous oeuvre one finds repeated references to the debilities of "technology," "liberalism," "America," and "Jews."[44] In a 1929 document Heidegger bemoaned the growing "Judaicization" (Verjudung) of German culture.[45] A few years later, in his capacity as Nazi rector of Freiburg university, he denounced Max Weber's nephew, Eduard Baumgarten, as excessively "Americanized" as well as for associating with Jews.[46] At a given point, clearly, any one of these terms could readily substitute for any other.

In light of these facts the anticivilizational rants of Heidegger, Spengler, et al., forfeit any claim to being an objective and nonpartisan diagnosis of the age. Moreover, when viewed in this optic their disturbing proximity to the worldview of National Socialism seems undeniable. It is no secret that Heidegger's lamentation concerning modernity's "forgetting of Being" and the consequent "flight of the gods" (stylized as *Seinsvergessenheit* and *Gottesverlassenheit*), along with his avowedly anti-intellectual contention that "reason is the most stiff-necked adversary of thought," constitute the philosophical inspiration behind the postmodern worldview.[47] The problem is less one of "guilt-by-association"—postmodernists may be any one of a number of things politically, but they are hardly "fascists"—than one of conceptual confusion and genealogical ignorance: an unwillingness or inability to squarely confront the political and intellectual implications of one's own theoretical standpoint.

"Desert of the Real"

What role does "America" play as a figure of the postmodern imagination? To begin with, one would do well to consult the writings of the French postmodernist sage Jean Baudrillard. Baudrillard is a theorist of the "simulacrum." In his view the postmodern era is characterized by a proliferation of copies or images—simulacra—without corresponding originals. In *Capital* Marx focused primarily on the sphere of production; he viewed the sphere of circulation as derivative or epiphenomenal. These assumptions, however, fail to do justice to the dynamics of late capitalism, where unprecedented economic affluence, along with demand artificially stimulated by Madison Avenue and the advertising industry, render Marx's original base/superstructure model obsolete. Instead, with the advent of consumer society, the superstructure—the circulation of cultural goods qua "commodities"—has become an independent source of influence and domination.

Before Baudrillard, the Frankfurt School tried to theorize this transformation under the rubric of the "reification of culture." Whereas Marx had limited the phenomenon of "commodity fetishism" or reification to the sphere of production, clearly by the 1930s the process had expanded exponentially. As Theodor Adorno remarked in "The Fetish Character of Music and the Regression of Listening," an early essay on the commodification of musical experience, "The consumer really worships the money that he himself has paid for the ticket to the Toscanini concert. . . . The liquidation of the individual is the real sign of the new musical situation."[48] Adorno's aperçu captures the fact that in consumer society "fetish value" increasingly supplants the capacity for authentic cultural experience. Western Marxism had always understood "culture" as a sphere of opposition or resistance. For Adorno and company, its commodification meant the advent of a society of "total integration"—a "one-dimensional society" (H. Marcuse) or "totally administered world" that individuals are powerless to resist.

Baudrillard takes "consumer society" (the title of one of his first books) as his point of departure but seeks to update the analysis for the information or media age. In his interpretive framework, the classical Marxian antithesis between basis and superstructure has been reversed. In essence, there is no infrastructure left to speak of. Instead, the theory of the simulacrum suggests that we live in an era in which models or copies spontaneously self-generate without any originals. "Hyperreality"—the media-generated proliferation of images and signs—has replaced what we once quaintly referred to as "reality." As Baudrillard observes:

> The territory no longer precedes the map, nor survives it. Henceforth, it is the map that precedes the territory—precession of simulacra. . . . In this passage to a space whose curvature is no longer that of the real, nor of truth, the age of simulation thus begins with a liquidation of all referentials. . . . It is no longer a question of imitation, nor of reduplication, not even of parody. It is rather a question of substituting signs of the real for the real itself. . . . Never again will the real have to be produced: this is the vital function of the model in a *system of death* . . . leaving room only for the orbital recurrence of models and the simulated generation of difference.[49]

In Baudrillard's optic America represents the furthest extreme of modern civilization qua simulationist wasteland—a veritable postmodern apocalypse. At history's end, civilization regresses to its aboriginal beginnings. In Baudrillard's view, the United States is "the only remaining primitive society"—"the desert of the real."[50] *"Utopia has been achieved here and anti-utopia is being achieved:* the anti-utopia of unreason, of deterritorialization, of the indeterminacy of the subject and of language, of the neutralization of all values, of the death of culture."[51] In postwar America, the "end of history" has passed from theoretical topos to reality. As Baudrillard observes, "History and Marxism are like fine wines and haute cuisine: they do not really cross the ocean."[52]

In 1991 Baudrillard authored a short book with the ingenious title, *The Gulf War Did Not Take Place,* in which he claimed that the real war paled in significance before the media-driven simulation of war. "So this military 'orgy' wasn't an orgy at all. It was an orgy of simulation, the simulation of an orgy." The "real war" was the battle for world opinion, whose "generals" were media consultants, spin doctors, and CNN "talking heads." Of course, if the real war did not take place, then why write a book about it? Given the death of "referentials," why add merely one more metacommentary (or metaobituary) to the hecatomb? At least Baudrillard lives up to the courage of his own convictions when he avows that his own study should be read "as a science fiction novel," akin to "Borges' chronicling of cultures that never existed."[53]

Once one understands Baudrillard's simulacrum thesis—not only have media-generated appearances become more important than reality, they have essentially *replaced* reality—one can anticipate his take on any number of subjects. His responses are algorithmic, virtually preprogrammed. This is certainly true for his short book on *America,* which has also been one of his most successful to judge by the amount of media attention it has received. After all, what other criteria are there in a postmodern universe where, according to Baudrillard, "there are no definitions possible. . . . It has all been done. . . . It has destroyed itself. It has deconstructed its entire universe. So all that are left are the pieces. *Playing with the pieces—that is postmodern"*?[54]

As a postmodernist, much of Baudrillard's theorizing is ironic. Yet once one penetrates the veneer of rhetorical playfulness, one finds a recycled, francophone version of the idea of America as degeneration incarnate—the same image proffered by Spengler and Heidegger, now outfitted with a French accent.

Baudrillard's analyses and observations thereby intersect with another pivotal Counter-Enlightenment thematic: the idea of the "end of history" or *posthistoire.*[55] According to this notion, democratic attempts to transcend the political culture of the ancien régime are predestined to failure. Such efforts will not merely founder, for although they consider themselves to be "progressive," in reality they will result in unprecedented misery and chaos—ultimately, in the advent of a new barbarism or "dark ages." Here, too, the fashionable assault on modernity proffered by postmodernism dovetails with the standpoint of earlier Counter-Enlightenment thinkers.

For Baudrillard America represents a negative utopia, the apogee of postmodern cultural suicide. From an historical and cultural point of view, America is a kind of tabula rasa: America "exorcises the question of origins, she does not cultivate the origins or mythical authenticity, she has neither a past nor a founding truth." At times Baudrillard almost seems envious of American superficiality and glibness. Americans embody a lack of self-consciousness and depth to which Europeans could never aspire no matter how hard they might try. The watchword of this shallow American character type seems to be "Smile if you have nothing to say, and don't hide above all that you have nothing to say. Show spontaneously the void, the profound indifference of your smile.... Illustrate the zero-degree of joy and pleasure, smile, smile!"[56] Baudrillard is obsessed with American obesity—that is, those Americans who are not anorexic. As one observer has aptly quipped, "The fact that Baudrillard calls Americans fat, dumb, and uncultured is surely no reason to think that he is anti-American."[57]

In America life no longer imitates art; instead, life and art—above all, cinematic art—have essentially exchanged places. Life itself now appears as an inferior incarnation of cinematic "hyperreality." As Baudrillard observes, "In America the cinema is true because . . . the whole mode of life is cinemagraphic: life is cinema." The same confusion of illusion and reality is true of America's gargantuan theme parks like Disneyland. According to Baudrillard, "Disneyland is presented as imaginary in order to make us believe that the rest is real, when in fact all of Los Angeles and America surrounding it are no longer real, but of the order of the hyperreal and of simulation."[58] In America qua Mecca of hyperreality, the relationship between image and reality has simply reversed itself.

Unlike Nietzsche and Heidegger, Baudrillard presumably *did* actually travel to the land he was describing. Yet one of the strange features of his narrative is that although he describes a myriad of tourist sites, he reproduces not a single conversation with a "real" American. But since Baudrillard's theoretical perspective on American life was fully worked out before he departed, perhaps such a conversation would have been in any event superfluous.

For all Baudrillard's predictability, there is no denying that, on occasion, he expresses a clever formulation or witty insight. But, ultimately, how seriously should we take a social philosopher who recommends that his books be treated like science fiction novels or Borgesesque *ficciones*? Very much so, insofar as Baudrillard's cliché-ridden view of American society has become standard issue among academic postmodernists. Like his precursors on the European right, Baudrillard believes that human actors are powerless to implement meaningful social change. The die has been cast. "Hyperrealilty"—the reign of the "simulacrum"—confronts us as an ineluctable fate, an inexorable, postmodern *condition humaine*. The *amor fati* celebrated by Germany's conservative revolutionaries has been updated and recycled, only to reemerge as one of the commonplaces of ivory tower radical chic. Yet as Baudrillard's critics have observed, his peculiar combination of epistemological skepticism and political nihilism accord with "a postmodern mood of widespread cynical acquiescence," resulting in a form of theory that is "ill-equipped to mount any kind of effective critical resistance."[59] There is no point in trying to combat today's "captains of consciousness," since all criticism and contestation end up recycled by the culture industry's vast semio-technological maw.

In the epitome of postmodern political fatalism, the only strategy Baudrillard has to recommend is "death": solely by aping the information society's own lifelessness and inertia—a practice he refers to as "crystal revenge"—does one stand a chance, argues Baudrillard, of escaping its enervating clutches.[60] Thus, according to Baudrillard, the implosions of media society portend the collapse of the emancipatory project in general. His verdict on the impossibility of progressive historical change reiterates one of the commonplaces of reactionary rhetoric: the so-called futility thesis, according to which attempts to transform society are condemned a priori to failure.[61]

The nihilistic implications of Baudrillard's approach have been confirmed by the unmitigated schadenfreude with which he responded to the September 11, 2001 terrorist attacks. In his view the assault represented a justified response to the challenge of American global hegemony. Although terrorist groups based in the Middle East may have been nominally responsible for executing the attacks, in truth it was an act that fulfilled the longings and aspirations of people all over the world. As Baudrillard observes, "haven't we dreamt of this event, hasn't the entire world, without exception, dreamt of it; no one could not dream of the destruction of a power that had become hegemonic to such a point. . . . In essence, it was [the terrorists] who committed the deed, *but it is we who wished for it*."[62]

A similar thesis informs Slavoj Zizek's Lacanian-psychoanalytic account of the attacks in "The Desert of the Real." The spectacular images of catastrophe radiating from lower Manhattan, he claims, were merely real-time reenactments of *The Towering Inferno* and countless other 1970s disaster films. As Lacanian social psychology has purportedly shown, the denizens of mass society project their hopes and fears via the images of mass culture. Thus, with the September 11 assaults, "America got what it fantasized about"—which, Zizek insinuates, echoing Baudrillard, is merely another way of saying that *America got what it had coming.* Thus, in his view, the terrorist attacks were merely a case of the West reaping what it had sowed: the disastrous consequences of American foreign policy had, at long last, merely boomeranged. According to Zizek, at issue is an "Hegelian lesson": "Whenever we encounter such a purely evil Outside . . . we should recognize *the distilled version of our own essence.*"[63]

What is striking about both interpretations is their absolute divorce from any discourse of morality or "right." With a self-defeating Nietzschean glibness, postmodernism has burned its bridges to a traditional rhetoric of moral evaluation. Hence, Baudrillard and Zizek pointedly fail to mention that the West, in addition to being an epicenter of imperialism (conveniently, instances of genocide or conquest that originate outside the West always go unmentioned), is also the birthplace of a moral discourse that has given birth to international law, the Universal Declaration of Human Rights, and the 1948 Convention against Genocide. For postmodernist hipsters like Zizek and Baudrillard, however, such precepts remain woefully "foundationalist" and are, consequently, simply irrelevant.

Amid the fog of postmodern relativism disseminated by Baudrillard, Zizek, and others, something essential is missing. Going back to the Thucydides' Melian Dialogue, the massacre of civilian innocents has been a touchstone of civilized moral judgment. It remains today the cornerstone of human rights law and just war theory. Yet for the cultural left, slavishly following the "genealogical" approach recommended by Nietzsche and Foucault, moral reasoning is merely another one of civilization's clever "normalizing" ruses—hence, an intellectual weakness to be avoided at all costs. Once again, postmodernism's right-wing intellectual pedigree— Nietzsche, Spengler, and Heidegger—has left it morally impotent and politically clueless.

For years the left has demonstrated a predilection to romanticize the "other"—Ho Chi Minh, Che, Fidel, as well as countless other apostles of Third World revolution—in the hope that the Wretched of the Earth would provide a remedy for the West's intractable political impasse. At a conference I attended recently, a friend with impeccable left-wing credentials who until communism's recent collapse had been an ardent champion of the proletarian cause, jumped on the pan-Arab bandwagon, reciting the names of obscure Muslim intellectuals who, he claimed, offered a promising political alternative to the debilities of Western liberalism. *Plus ça change* . . . The left can ignore the imperatives of morality and international law only at its own peril. By romanticizing the lifestyles and mores of non-Western peoples, it suspends critical judgment, destroys its own credibility, and guarantees its own political irrelevance.

Les extrêmes se touchent

On occasion, the European right's phobic view of America has often been matched by analogous sentiments among the European left. Thus, at various historical conjunctures (the height of the Cold War, Vietnam, the Euro-missile crisis of the 1980s), the same indictments of America qua technological Moloch that one finds in Spengler and Heidegger became common currency among the political left. Yet among leftists, invective concerning the predatory tendencies of modern capitalism usually substituted for abstract and suprahistorical indictments of "technology." The left perceived America as the pinnacle of capitalist exploitation, unrestrained by the mollifying influences of old-world traditions and *politesse*. As usual, in this connection, it is imperative to distinguish between justifiable and legitimate criticism of American foreign policy from the fever-pitch denunciations that characterize anti-Americanism proper.[64]

Take the case of Jean-Paul Sartre. As the Cold War intensified, Sartre renounced the more sanguine view of things American he had developed during the 1930s, when he was enamored of American literature and film. America had become, in his words, the land in which "the most odious form of capitalism had triumphed." For fellow existentialist Simone de Beauvoir Americans were, culturally speaking, "a people of sheep."[65] Italian Marxist philosopher Antonio Gramsci viewed America as the country in which "Fordism"—assembly-line mass production—had gained total ascendancy; it signified the consummate triumph of the capitalist rationalization of labor.[66] For the Frankfurt School's Max Horkheimer, America was the land in which "chewing gum"—as a figure for hedonistic mass consumption—had assumed metaphysical significance. "It is not that chewing gum undermines metaphysics but that it *is* metaphysics—this is what must be made clear."[67] Ironically, during the 1930s Horkheimer et al. seemed more traumatized by the New Deal's successes than its potential failures. One of the more humorous confirmations of this fear concerns Secretary of Agriculture Henry Foster Wallace's shibboleth, "There will be a pint of milk for every child." Instead of viewing this statement as related to the proto-socialist New Deal political idiom, Horkheimer and Adorno understood it as part of a Machiavellian capitalist scheme to sap the American proletariat's revolutionary ardor.

In the worldview of the European left, America's contributions to the history of political democracy—a constitutional commitment to popular sovereignty, a Bill of Rights, periodic creative upsurges of democratic populism—often fell beneath the radar screen. The requirements of ideological consistency mandated that all countervailing political evidence be expunged from the historical record. Put simply, America was the land of bourgeois class hegemony par excellence. Nowhere else—certainly nowhere in Europe—were the political and economic successes of the rising middle classes so dramatic and far-reaching. According to the left-wing catechism, since the political achievements of the bourgeoisie were, in essence, a form of class domination, they could be dismissed a priori. Yet even Marx, at least in his more lucid moments, conceived of socialism as the *realization* of bourgeois ideals (hence, "real" equality would replace formal equality) rather than as their abstract negation.

Is it surprising that the extreme left and extreme right would agree with respect to their perceptions of America? Hardly. Despite their political differences, both poles of the ideological spectrum share essential common terrain: an uncompromising rejection of political liberalism. For both political extremes, the liberal ideal of an independent civil society, legally secured against arbitrary governmental encroachments, remained politically insupportable, an insuperable obstacle to the authoritarian colonization of society by the state. In the cases of communism and fascism, therefore, both of which entail an ideologically charged rejection of liberalism, *les extrêmes se touchent*.

When communism collapsed in 1989, Central European politicians and intellectuals scrambled to obtain copies of the U.S. Constitution. They viewed the American founding—the Constitutional Convention, the Bill of Rights, the principle of judicial review—as an indispensable precedent on the road to political freedom. That same year France celebrated the bicentennial of the Great Revolution. But the only achievement deemed worthy of commemoration was the Declaration of Rights of Man and Citizen of August 20, 1789.[68] Thus after a fitful two-hundred year struggle to determine the revolution's ultimate scope and meaning, French political theorists and public opinion leaders decided to highlight the phase that approximated the ideals of political liberalism—that is, the aspect that bore the greatest affinities with the principles of the American Revolution. The collapse of communism coincided with unprecedented "waves of democratization" in Central and South America as well as South Africa.[69] What "lesson" might be construed from this unexpected political blessing? As the Italian democratic socialist Norberto Bobbio observed, not Marxism, but "political liberalism"—as a figure for the precepts of rule of law, human rights, and popular sovereignty—has become the unsurpassable political horizon of our time. That the American founding ushered in a set of fundamental and enduring political principles is a truth that is easily lost sight of.

In the background of these debates stands the postmodernist disavowal of Enlightenment reason. Although the contours and content of these disavowals vary, there is no mistaking their essence or crux: reason, instead of being a sine qua non of political freedom, has led to our progressive enslavement. To criticize reason is one thing. In truth, standards of rationality—scientific, political, and legal—could never "progress" (e.g., in the direction of greater inclusiveness) were it not for the constant criticisms to which they are exposed, on the part of experts as well as the reasoning public. Reasonable claims are ones that are subject to institutionalized procedures of refutation and verification. When two centuries ago the philosophes undertook an all-out assault against theological dogmatism and illegitimate political privilege, they laid the foundations for our modern conceptions of public reason and political fairness. In more ways than we realize or might conceivably enumerate, we are their direct heirs and beneficiaries.

Both the counterrevolutionaries and postmodernists are uninterested in mere *criticisms* of reason. As we have seen, both currents set their sights much higher. Instead, they seek to banish or dismantle the enterprise of reason in its entirety. Whereas philosophes such as Kant associated reason with the attributes of maturity and autonomy, their antagonists consider it responsible for all manner of social injustice and catastrophe. Postmodernist misology, or contempt for reason, is evidenced by Lyotard's equation of "consensus" with "terror," Foucault's portrayal of the semiotic coercion exercised by "discursive regimes" (epistemic "prison houses," as it were), and Derrida's fashionable critique of "logocentricism." (Significantly, this term was originally coined in the 1920s by the German reactionary philosopher Ludwig Klages.[70] Here, too, the affinities between postmodernism and the counterrevolutionary ideology speak volumes.) In all of the aforementioned cases, the operative assumption is that there exist cogent parallels between the philosophical longing for "totality" and political totalitarianism. Ironically, the attempt to account for totalitarianism via philosophical deduction harks back to the methods and procedures of "first philosophy"—an a priori and speculative approach to history and politics that postmodernists purportedly sought to move beyond.

The European counterrevolutionaries knew what they wanted as a replacement for liberal democracy: the "contrary of revolution," the restoration of the old regime. Their German heirs—Nietzsche, Spengler, Schmitt, and Heidegger—disillusioned denizens of modern society, knew that one could no longer turn back the clock. Instead, they decided to seize the bull by the horns. They embraced industrial society but only under the proviso that it be governed by a totalitarian dictatorship. Dictatorship was the most efficacious means with which to vanquish the debilities of political liberalism and reestablish the sublimity of "Great Politics" (Nietzsche).

The postmodernists, on the other hand, are inconsistent and confused. They bask in the freedoms of political liberalism—to whose institutions they are indebted for their brilliant academic careers—while biting the hand that feeds them. As philosophers of "difference," they present themselves as advocates of the politically marginalized. Yet the antiliberal rhetorical thrust of their arguments risks undermining the very norms of tolerance that, historically, have provided such groups with the greatest measure of political and legal protection.[71] Were the claims of "difference" to become the "norm," as postmodernists recommend, our inherited notions of selfhood and community would likely all but collapse. What kind of world would it be in which all forms of identity, both individual and collective, were anathematized to such an extent? In this and other respects the radical claims of difference risk becoming a recipe for epistemological, ethical, and political incoherence. As Michael Walzer observes succinctly, when all is said and done, "isn't the postmodern project . . . likely to produce increasingly shallow individuals and a radically diminished cultural life?"[72] Identities shorn of substantive ethical and cultural attachments would conceivably set a new standard of immateriality. It is unlikely that fragmented selves and Bataille-inspired ecstatic communities could mobilize the requisite social cohesion to resist political evil. Here, too, the hazards and dangers of supplanting the autonomous, moral self with an "aesthetic" self are readily apparent.

In the standard postmodernist demonology, the Enlightenment bears direct historical responsibility for the Gulag and Auschwitz. In the eyes of these convinced misologists, modern totalitarianism is merely the upshot of the universalizing impetus of Enlightenment reason. As Foucault proclaimed, "Raison, c'est la torture." According to the politics of "difference," reason is little more than the ideological window dressing for Eurocentrism and its attendant horrors. By making what is different the same or identical, reason, so the argument goes, is implicitly totalitarian. Conservatives hold postmodernists responsible for the latter-day "decline of the West," accusing them of promoting relativism by undermining the traditional concepts of reason and truth. But they seriously overestimate postmodernism's impact and influence, which has—happily—largely been confined to the isolated and bloodless corridors of academe.

Postmodernism's debilities lie elsewhere. In an era in which the values of tolerance have been forcefully challenged by the twin demons of integral nationalism and religious fundamentalism, postmodernism's neo-Nietzschean embrace of political agon remains at odds with democracy's normative core: the ever-delicate balancing act between private and public autonomy, basic democratic liberties and popular sovereignty.[73] Postmodernists claim they seek to remedy the manifest failings of really existing democracy. Yet, given their metatheoretical aversion to considerations of equity and fairness, accepting such de facto assurances at face value seems unwise. Paradoxically, their celebration of heterogeneity and radical difference risks abetting the neotribalist ethos that threatens to turn the post-communist world order into a congeries of warring, fratricidal ethnicities. Differences should be respected. But there are also occasions when they need to be bridged. The only reasonable solution to this problem is to ensure that differences are bounded and subsumed by universalistic principles of equal liberty. Ironically, then, the liberal doctrine of "justice as fairness" (Rawls) provides the optimal ethical framework by virtue of which cultural differences might be allowed to prosper and flourish. If consensus equals coercion and norms are inherently oppressive, it would seem that dreams of political solidarity and common humanity are from the outset nothing more than a lost cause.

An ignorance of history and a refusal to acknowledge the compromised legacy of its own intellectual genealogy proves postmodernism's undoing. The celebration of difference and rejection of reason were classical gambits of the counterrevolutionary ideologues. Maistre said it first and best: the rights of "man" are an unwarranted abstraction; concrete differences among the peoples are all there is. Carl Schmitt added the observation that "Whoever says humanity lies." In many respects, Maistre and Herder were the first multiculturalists. Following Nietzsche's prescriptions, their postmodern heirs profess an interest in intellectual "genealogy." But, to judge by all available evidence, they have not done their homework.

Notes to Introduction: Answer to the Question:
What Is Counter-Enlightenment?

1. On the *cahiers de doléances,* see Roger Chartier, "Culture populaire et culture politique dans l'Ancien Regime: quelques reflexions," in *The French Revolution and the Creation of Modern Political Culture,* vol. 1, *The Political Culture of the Old Regime,* ed. Keith Michael Baker (Oxford: Pergamon Press, 1987), 243–258.

Obviously, Rousseau's status qua philosphe is a matter of controversy. To judge by the *Discourse on the Arts and Sciences* or *Emile*—not to mention his antagonistic dealings with his fellow philosophes—he would seem to belong among the Enlightenment's harshest critics. Conversely, were one to judge by virtue of his political philosophy as set forth in the *Social Contract,* an ardent defense of popular sovereignty and modern natural law, he stands as an unequivocal advocate of political modernity.

2. Rivarol, cited in Jacques Godechot, *The Counter-Revolution: Doctrine and Action, 1789–1804,* trans. S. Attanasio (Princeton: Princeton University Press, 1981), 33.

For a transhistorical interpretation of Counter-Enlightenment—that is, one that understands it as a perennial challenge to the hubris and pretense of wisdom and knowledge that dates back to the Bible and Aristophanes—see Mark Lilla, "Was ist Gegenaufklaerung?" *Merkur* 566 (1996), 400–411.

3. Isaiah Berlin, "Counter-Enlightenment," in *Against the Current* (New York: Viking. 1980), 1–24. For an attempt to do justice to the complexities and ambivalences of Berlin's relationship to the Counter-Enlightenment, see Graeme Garrard, "The Counter—Enlightenment Liberalism of Isaiah Berlin," *Journal of Political Ideologies* 2(3) (1997), 281–296.

4. Goebbels, cited in Karl Dietrich Bracher, *The German Dictatorship* (Fort Worth: Holt, Rinehart, 1970), 10.

5. Darrin MacMahon, *Enemies of the Enlightenment: the French Counter-Enlightenment and the Making of Modernity* (New York: Oxford University Press, 2001), 12.

6. See Chantal Mouffe, "Radical Democracy," in *Universal Abandon: The Politics of Postmodernism,* ed. A. Ross (Minneapolis: University of Minnesota Press, 1988), 38–39. According to Mouffe, the commonalities between postmodernism and Counter-Enlightenment lie in the fact that "unlike liberalism and Marxism, both of which are doctrines of reconciliation and mastery, conservative thought is predicated upon human finitude, imperfection and limits." See also Mouffe, *The Democratic Paradox* (London: Verso, 2000).

7. See Seyla Benhabib, "Democracy and Difference: Reflections on the Metapolitics of Lyotard and Derrida," *Journal of Political Philosophy* 2(1) (1994), 3, an article that criticizes " postmodernist skepticism toward 'really existing western democracies.'" Poststructuralism began as a movement in philosophy and the "human sciences" that rejected the structuralist ideal of scientific closure in favor of an approach that emphasizes epistemological indeterminacy and openness. Nevertheless, as we shall see, despite their differences, both structuralism and poststructuralism share a number of key intellectual presuppositions that suggests a fundamental commonality.

8. Maistre, *Considerations on France,* trans. R. Lebrun (Montreal: McGill-Queens University Press, 1974), 97.

9. "Translator's Preface," François Dosse, *History of Structuralism,* vol. I, trans. D. Glassman (Minneapolis: University of Minnesota Press, 1997), xiv.

10. Lévi-Strauss, "Entretien avec Jean-Marie Benoist," *Le Monde* January 21–22, 1979, 14 (emphasis added).

11. Lévi-Strauss, *The Savage Mind* (Chicago: University of Chicago Press, 1966), 247 (emphasis added).

12. Foucault, *The Order of Things,* trans. A. Sheridan (New York: Pantheon, 1994), xxiii: "It is comforting, however, and a source of profound relief to think that man is only a recent invention, a figure not yet two centuries old, a new wrinkle in our knowledge, and that he will disappear again as soon as that knowledge has discovered a new form"; see also Nietzsche's indictment of "the last man" in *Thus Spoke Zarathustra,* trans. R. J. Hollingdale (New York: Vintage, 1961), 45–47.

13. For an excellent exploration and critique of these elements of Lévi-Strauss's oeuvre, see Tzvetan Todorov, *On Human Diversity* (Cambridge: Harvard University Press, 1992), 60–89.

14. For a fuller discussion of this problem, see chapter 4, "Designer Fascism."

15. *J. G. Herder on Social and Political Culture,* ed. F. Barnard (Cambridge: Cambridge University Press, 1969), 184, 186.

16. For Foucault's positions, see "Inutile de se soulever?" *Le Monde* May 11, 1979, 12; translated into English translation as "Is it Useless to Revolt?," *Philosophy and Social Criticism,* VIII(1) (Spring 1981), 1–9; "Iran: the Spirit of a World Without Spirit," in *Michel Foucault: Politics, Philosophy, Culture* (New York: Routledge, 1988), 211–226; "Una polveriera chiamata Islam," *Corriere della Sera,* 104 (36) (13 February 1979). See also Janet Afaray, "Sh'I Narratives of Karbala and Christian Rites of Penance: Michel Foucault and the Culture of the Iranian Revolution, 1978–1979," *Radical History Review* 86 (Spring 2003), 7–35.

17. See the conclusion to Lévi-Strauss, *Tristes Tropiques,* trans. J. Weightman and D. Weightman (New York: Penguin, 1992), 414, where, in opposition to the Enlightenment project, the anthropologist concludes with a paean to what he calls, *"the great religion of non-knowledge."*

18. Owen Bradley, *A Modern Maistre: The Social and Political Thought of Joseph de Maistre* (Lincoln: University of Nebraska Press, 1999), xi–xii. As Bradley goes on to observe, "Particularly contemporary is his belief that the key to the 'normal' functioning of society is to be sought in the "abnormality" of social excess and that social theory must therefore consider not only moments of stability but also moments of transformation and transgression. Equally fashionable is his thesis that the moorings of order are found in the spheres of language, the imaginary, and the symbolic."

19. For more on the affinities between postmodernism and political agonistics, see Mouffe, "For an Agonistic Pluralism," in *The Return of the Political* (London: Verso, 1993) 1–8; and Mouffe, "For an Agonistic Model of Democracy," in *The Democratic Paradox,* 80–107.

20. See also Russell Jacoby's remarks in *Dogmatic Wisdom: How the Culture Wars Divert Education and Distract America* (New York: Doubleday, 1994), 164. "In the 'culture wars' little is more striking than the ease with which the new professors defend professional reputations and language, sophisticated theories and distinguished friends, heaping contempt on journalists and critics as backward outsiders."

21. For background, see Luc Ferry and Alain Renaut, *French Philosophy of the Sixties,* trans. M. Cattani (Amherst: University of Massachusetts Press, 1989).

22. See, for example, Julian Bourg, *Forbidden to Forbid: Ethics in France, 1968–81* (Ph.D. Dissertation, University of California, Berkeley, 2001) and

Michael Christofferson, *French Intellectuals Against the Left: The Antitotalitarian Movement of the 1970s* (New York: Berghahn Books, 2004).

23. See Thomas Pavel, *The Feud of Language: A History of Structuralist Thought* (Cambridge, Mass.: Blackwell, 1992).

24. Cited in Jeffrey Mehlman, *Legacies of Anti-Semitism in France* (Minneapolis: University of Minnesota, 1982), 108.

25. I have discussed some of these questions in "Deconstruction at Auschwitz: Heidegger, de Man, and the New Revisionism," in *Labyrinths: Explorations in the Critical History of Ideas* (Amherst: University of Massachusetts Press, 1995).

26. Jacques Derrida, "Like the Sound of the Sea Deep Within a Shell: Paul de Man's War," *Critical Inquiry* 15(4) (Summer 1989), 647. See Dasenbrock, "Reading the Demanians Reading de Man," *South Central Review* 11(1) (Spring 1994), 37: "Derrida insists in "Limited Inc" on the openness of contexts, the necessary provisionality of any one reading. But there is nothing provisional in the least about Derrida's reading [of de Man] here. We are told that if we judge de Man, we are more than judges, we are censors, we are book burners, we are reproducing the exterminating gesture of the Holocaust. . . . In claiming interpretive privilege for his recontextualization and in ruling certain competing recontextualizations out of court, in claiming that his interpretation is privileged because it conforms to de Man's intentions, Derrida is here playing exactly the role of the policeman he is ascribing to unnamed others."

27. On this point, see Geoff Eley, *Forging Democracy: The History of the Left in Europe, 1850–2000* (New York: Oxford University Press, 2002).

28. Karen Arenson, "Cuts in Tuition Assistance Put College Education Beyond the Reach of Poorest Students," *New York Times* January 27, 1997, B1. See the debate between Judith Butler, "Merely Cultural," *New Left Review,* 227 (1998), 45–53, and Nancy Fraser, "Heterosexism, Misrecognition and Capitalism: A Response to Judith Butler," *New Left Review* 227 (1998), 140–49.

29. Foucault, *The History of Sexuality,* trans. R. Hurley (New York: Pantheon, 1990), 159.

30. Jean Cohen, "Democracy, Difference, and the Right to Privacy," in *Democracy and Difference: Contesting the Boundaries of the Political,* ed. S. Benhabib (Princeton: Princeton University Press, 1996), 188.

31. Christopher Lasch, *The Culture of Narcissism* (New York: Norton, 1978); Richard Sennett, *The Fall of Public Man* (New York: Norton, 1992).

32. Dosse, *History of Structuralism,* vol. I, xx.

33. See Steven Kaplan, *Farewell, Revolution: The Historians Feud: The French Revolution, 1789/1989* (Ithaca: Cornell University Press, 1995). See also Jean-Pierre Mathy, "The French Revolution at Two Hundred: The Bicentennial and the Return of Rights Liberalism," in *French Resistance: The French-American Culture Wars* (Minneapolis: University of Minnesota Press, 2001), 57–85.

34. See Political Excursus II, "Designer Fascism: On the Ideology of the French New Right," in part II of this book.

35. For a good example, see Susan Rowland, *Jung: A Feminist Revision* (New York: Routledge, 2002).

36. See, for example, the influential treatment of Gadamer in Richard Rorty's *Philosophy and the Mirror of Nature* (Princeton: Princeton University Press, 1979), 357–364. See also Mouffe, *The Democratic Paradox,* 34, who numbers Gadamer among a postmodernist, antifoundationalist pantheon that includes Derrida, Rorty, Wittgenstein, Heidegger, Lacan, and Foucault.

37. For more information about these two approaches, see Simon During, *The Cultural Studies Reader* (New York: Routledge, 1993) and Catherine Gallagher and Stephen Greenblatt, *Practicing New Historicism* (Chicago: University of Chicago Press, 2001).

38. Jean Baudrillard, "L'Esprit du terrorisme," *Le Monde,* November 3, 2001. Baudrillard, *The Spirit of Terrorism and Requiem for the Twin Towers,* trans. C. Turner (London: Verso, 2002).

Notes to Chapter One: Zarathrustra Goes to Hollywood

1. *Selected Letters of Friedrich Nietzsche,* ed. and trans. C. Middleton (Indianapolis: Hackett, 1996), 305.

2. Mussolini, *Opera omnia* (Florence: La Fireze, 1951–63), 17: 267–269.

3. *Selected Letters of Friedrich Nietzsche, 337.*

4. Ibid., 337.

5. Ibid., 339.

6. Ibid., 335.

7. Ibid., 341.

8. Ibid., 344.

9. Ibid.

10. Ibid., 346.

11. Nietzsche, "Why I Am So Wise," in *Ecce Homo,* trans. W. Kaufmann (New York: Vintage, 1967), 225. For discussions of Nietzsche's political

orientation, see Tracy Strong, *Nietzsche and the Politics of Transfiguration* (Berkeley: University of California Press, 1988), Mark Warren, *Nietzsche and Political Thought* (Cambridge: MIT Press, 1988), and Keith Ansell-Pearce, *An Introduction to Nietzsche as Political Thinker* (New York: Cambridge University Press, 1994).

12. Nietzsche, *The Will to Power*, trans. W. Kaufmann (New York: Vintage, 1967), 612.

13. Georg Lukács, *The Destruction of Reason*, trans. P. Palmer (Atlantic Heights, N. J.: Humanities Press, 1981).

14. Nietzsche, *The Twilight of the Idols, or How to Philosophize with a Hammer*, trans. R. Hollingdale (New York: Penguin, 1968).

15. Nietzsche, *The Genealogy of Morals*, trans. W. Kaufmann and R. J. Hollingdale (New York: Vintage, 1967), III, 12.

16. Nietzsche, *The Will to Power*, 272.

17. Nietzsche, *The Gay Science*, trans. W. Kaufmann (New York: Vintage, 1974), 232.

18. Nietzsche, *The Will to Power*, 419.

19. Descombes, *Modern French Philosophy*, trans. By L. Fox and J. Harding (New York: Cambridge University Press, 1980), 10.

20. Nietzsche, *Twilight of the Idols*, 31.

21. Foucault, letter to Pierre Klossowski, July 3, 1969, in *Cahiers pour un temps* (Paris: Centre Pompidou, 1985), 85–88.

22. Klossowski, *Nietzsche and the Vicious Circle* (Chicago: University of Chicago Press, 1997), xvii. For a more detailed look at the various stages of Nietzsche's reception in France, see Jacques Le Rider, *Nietzsche en France de la fin du XIXe siècle au temps present* (Paris: Presses Universitaires de France, 1999). See also, Douglas Smith, *Transvaluations: Nietzsche in France 1872–1972* (New York: Oxford University Press, 1997).

23. Klossowski, *Nietzsche and the Vicious Circle*, xix.

24. Ibid., 53.

25. Ibid., 54.

26. *Why We Are Not Nietzscheans*, ed. L. Ferry and A. Renaut, trans. R. de Loaiza (Chicago: University of Chicago Press, 1997), vii.

27. *The Foucault Reader*, ed. P. Rabinow (New York: Pantheon, 1987), 74.

28. Ibid., 95.

29. *Why We Are Not Nietzscheans*, 73.

30. Ibid., 106.

31. Alexander Nehamas, *Nietzsche: Life as Literature* (Cambridge: Harvard University Press, 1985), 8.

32. See Nietzsche, "Truth and Lies in an Extra-Moral Sense," in *Philosophy and Truth: Selections from Nietzsche's Notebooks of the Early 1870s*, ed. D. Brazeale (Atlantic Heights, N.J.: Humanities Press, 1979), 84: "Truths are illusions which we have forgotten are illusions."

33. Nehamas, *Nietzsche*, 9.

34. Take, for example, the case of one of his more elaborate specifications of perspectivism from *The Genealogy of Morals*, III, 12: "There is only a perspectival seeing, only a perspectival 'knowing'; and the more affects we allow to speak about one thing, the more eyes, different eyes, we can use to observe one thing, the more complete will our 'concept' of this thing, our 'objectivity,' be. But to eliminate the will altogether, to suspend each and every affect, supposing we were capable of this—what would that mean but to *castrate* the intellect?"

35. In trying to make sense of Nietzsche's perspectivism, yet another possibility presents itself that would allow him to avoid the doctrine's relativist implications: although human knowledge is incorrigibly perspectival, the accumulated sum of all perspectives—a standpoint inaccessible to human knowledge—would yield something like the truth. But this supposition seems to make Nietzsche's thinking reliant on the "two worlds" approach of traditional metaphysics (a world of appearances and a world of things-in-themselves), a view from which he took great pains to distance himself.

36. Nehamas, *Nietzsche*, 4. On page 6, Nehamas raises a similar objection, this time with reference to Nietzsche's celebrated confrontation with Christianity: "Can Nietzsche claim that he has revealed the most basic and objectionable features of Christianity and not also imply at the same time that both his revelations and his accusations are correct? And if he does so, does he not then violate his own perspectivism and fall back into the dogmatic tradition from which he wants to escape?"

For a good discussion of the problems raised by Nietzsche's perspectivism, see Maudemarie Clark, *Nietzsche on Truth and Philosophy* (New York: Cambridge University Press, 1990). For a rejoinder to Nehamas that questions his imputation of "aestheticism" to Nietzsche, see Brian Leiter, "Nietzsche and Aestheticism," *Journal of the History of Philosophy* 30 (1992), 275–290.

37. Nietzsche, *The Will to Power*, 427.

38. See M. S. Silk and J. P. Stern, *Nietzsche on Tragedy* (New York: Cambridge University Press, 1981).

39. For a properly skeptical view of the relationship between Nietzsche and postmodernism, see Robert Solomon, "Nietzsche, Postmodernism,

and Resentment," in *Nietzsche and Postmodernism: Essays Pro and Contra,* ed. C. Koelb (Albany: SUNY Press, 1990), 267–293.

40. Nietzsche, *The Will to Power,* 464.

41. Nietzsche, *Ecce Homo,* trans. W. Kaufmann and R. Hollingdale (New York: Vintage, 1967), 328.

42. Peter Berkowitz, *Nietzsche: The Ethics of an Immoralist* (Cambridge: Harvard University Press, 1995), 262.

43. Ibid., 21.

44. John Richardson, *Nietzsche's System* (New York: Oxford University Press, 1996), 290.

45. Nietzsche, *The Gay Science,* para. 344.

46. *Selected Letters,* 221.

47. Nietzsche, *Thus Spoke Zarathustra,* trans. R. Hollingdale (New York: Penguin, 1969), 299.

48. Nietzsche, *The Gay Science,* para. 341.

49. Nietzsche, *Thus Spoke Zarathustra,* 169.

50. Ibid., 296.

51. Ibid., 137.

52. Karl Löwith, *Nietzsche's Philosophy of the Eternal Recurrence of the Same,* trans. H. Lomax (Berkeley: University of California Press, 1997).

53. See Berkowitz, *Nietzsche,* 2.

54. Nietzsche, *Thus Spoke Zarathustra,* 75–77.

55. Nietzsche, *The Will to Power,* 458–459.

56. Cited in J. P. Stern, *A Study of Nietzsche* (New York: Cambridge University Press, 1979); see also Karl Löwith's remarks in *Nietzsche's Philosophy of Eternal Recurrence of the Same,* 195–196: "André Gide and Antoine de Saint-Exupéry, D. H. Lawrence and T. E. Lawrence, Stefan George and Rilke, Rudolf Pannwitz and Oswald Spengler, Robert Musil and Thomas Mann, Gottfried Benn and Ernst Jünger—they are all unthinkable without Nietzsche."

57. Nietzsche, *Ecce Homo,* 326–327.

58. Nietzsche, *The Will to Power,* 465.

59. Nietzsche, *Genealogy of Morals,* 76 (translation altered).

60. Nietzsche, *Beyond Good and Evil,* trans. Walter Kaufmann (New York: Vintage, 1966), 87.

61. Nietzsche, *The Will to Power,* 504.

62. Nietzsche, *Ecce Homo* (quoted in Nolte, *Nietzsche u. Nietzscheanism,* 193–194); emphasis added.

63. See George Lichtheim, *Europe in the Twentieth Century* (New York: Praeger, 1972), 186: "It is not too much to say that but for Nietzsche the SS—

Hitler's shock troops and the core of the whole movement—would have lacked the inspiration which enabled them to carry out their programme of mass murder in Eastern Europe." Also see the memoir written by Charlemagne Brigade propagandist Marc Augier, *Götter Dämmerung: Wende und Ende einer grossen Zeit* (Buenos Aires: Editorial Prometheus, 1950).

In his notebooks from the 1940s, Thomas Mann felt that a genuine Nietzschean sensibility pervaded the ethos of National Socialism: "Intellectual-spiritual fascism, throwing off of humane principle, recourse to violence, blood-lust, irrationalism, cruelty, Dionysiac denial of truth and justice, self-abandonment to the instincts and unrestrained 'Life' which in fact is death." Cited in T. J. Reed, *Thomas Mann: the Uses of Tradition* (Oxford: The Clarendon Press, 1996), 364.

64. Déat, *Pensée allemande et pensée française* (Paris: 1944), 97–98, cited in Zeev Sternhell, "Fascist Ideology," in *Fascism: A Reader's Guide*, ed. Walter Laqueur (Berkeley: University of California Press, 1976), 344.

65. Peters, *Zarathustra's Sister: the Case of Elisabeth and Friedrich Nietzsche* (New York: Crown, 1977), 221.

66. Aschheim, *The Nietzsche Legacy in Germany, 1890–1990* (Berkeley: University of California Press, 1992), 235–236.

67. Nolte, *Nietzsche und Nietzscheanismus* (Frankfurt and Berlin: Propyläen, 1990), 194–195.

68. F. Marinetti, "The Founding Manifesto of Futurism," in *Selected Writings* (New York: Farrar, Straus, Giroux, 1971), 42. For more on the link between futurism and Italian fascism, see Walter Adamson, *Avant-Garde Florence: From Modernism to Fascism* (Cambridge: Harvard University Press, 1993).

69. Mario Sznajder, "Hitler, Mussolini and Italian Fascism," in *Nietzsche: Godfather of Fascism?* (Princeton: Princeton University Press, 2002), 250. Mussolini also embraced Spengler's philosophy in a 1932 interview,

"Mussolini also recalled his admiration for and friendship with Oswald Spengler, whose work he perceived as a continuation of Nietzsche. Mussolini suggested that Spengler had found in Nietzsche the vision with which to counter scientific laws and the predictions of Marxism as they were acted out in contemporary reality and to propose a Caesarian alternative. The Duce went further and claimed that overcoming Spengler's prophecy of the downfall of the West was now a miraculous possibility—in Nietzschean 'Superhuman' terms—one currently being carried out by Mussolini and his followers as the creators of a new Europe" (255).

70. Mussolini, *Opere,* III, 66 (emphasis added).

71. Ibid., 206.

72. Mussolini, *Opere* II, 53.

73. Nolte, "Marx und Nietzsche im Sozialismus des jungen Mussolini," *Historische Zeitschrift* 191 (1960), 249–335.

74. Mussolini, "La filosofia dell forza: Postille alla conferenza dell' on. Treves," *Opere* I, 174–184.

75. In this respect Zeev Sternhell's controversial thesis that fascism was an outgrowth of the "crisis of Marxism" is technically correct. See Sternhell, *Neither Right Nor Left* (Princeton: Princeton University Press, 1996).

76. Benjamin, "The Work of Art, in the Era of Mechanical Reproduction," in *Illuminations,* ed. H. Arendt, trans. H. Zohn (New York: Schocken, 1969).

77. Mussolini, *Opere* V, 141–143.

Notes to Chapter Two: Prometheus Unhinged

1. For confirmation of these affinities, see Goodrick-Clarke, *The Occult Roots of Nazism: Secret Aryan Cults and Their Influence on Nazi Ideology: The Ariosophists of Austria and Germany, 1890–1935* (New York: New York University Press, 1994). See also Brigitta Hammann, *Hitler's Vienna: A Dictator's Apprenticeship* (New York: Oxford University Press, 1999).

2. Ernst Bloch, *The Heritage of Our Times,* trans. Neville Plaice and Stephen Plaice (Berkeley: University of California Press, 1990), 313.

3. Joseph Needham, *Science and Civilization in China* (New York: Cambridge University Press, 1983), vol. 4, 3.

4. *The Cambridge Companion to Jung,* ed. P. Young-Eisendrath and T. Dawson (Cambridge: Cambridge University Press, 1998), xii.

5. For a similar argument, see Christopher Hauke, *Jung and the Postmodern: the Interpretation of Realities* (New York: Routledge, 2000).

6. Susan Rowland, *Jung: A Feminist Revision* (New York: Routledge, 2002), 140.

7. See, for example, Samuels's introduction to *The Cambridge Companion to Jung,* "Jung and the Post-Jungians," where Jung is generously credited (too generously, in my opinion) with having anticipated almost all future developments in post-Freudian psychology.

8. John Kerr, *A Most Dangerous Method: The Story of Jung, Freud, and Sabina Spielrein* (New York: Vintage, 1993), 46–47.

9. Ibid., 46.

10. Jung, *Memories, Dreams, Reflections* (New York: Random House, 1961), 41.

11. Cited in Richard Noll, *The Jung Cult: Origins of a Charismatic Movement* (Princeton: Princeton University Press, 1994), 47.

12. Freud to Jung, 11 March 1908, *The Freud/Jung Letters: the Correspondence Between Sigmund Freud and C. G. Jung*, trans. R. Mannheim and R. F. C. Hull, ed. W. McGuire (Princeton: Princeton University Press, 1974), 134.

13. Linda Donn, *Freud and Jung: Years of Friendship, Years of Loss* (New York: Charles Scribner, 1998), 129. Freud would confide to the Swiss psychologist Ludwig Binswanger: "When the realm I have founded is orphaned, no one but Jung shall inherit it all."

14. Peter Homans, *Jung in Context: Modernity and the Making of Psychology* (Chicago: University of Chicago Press, 1995), 53.

15. Freud, *The Standard Edition of the Complete Psychological Works of Sigmund Freud*, trans. J. Strachey (London: Hogarth Press, 1953), vol. 2, 305.

16. *The Freud/Jung Letters*, 294.

17. Ibid., 295.

18. Cited in Kerr, *A Most Dangerous Method*, 58.

19. *The Freud/Jung Letters*, 289.

20. Noll, *The Jung Cult*, 129.

21. Cited in ibid.

22. Jung, "The State of Psychotherapy Today," in *Civilization in Transition, Collected Works*, vol. 10 (Princeton: Princeton University Press, 1970), 160.

23. Ibid., 165–166.

24. Jung, "Vom Werden der Persönlichkeit," in *Wirklichkeit der Seele* (Zurich: Rascher Verlag, 1934), 180n. In the English version, this last phrase is mistranslated. See *C. G. Jung Speaking: Interviews and Encounters* (Princeton: Princeton University Press, 1977), 65.

25. *C. G. Jung Speaking*, 59–66.

26. Jung, "Diagnosing the Dictators," *C. G. Jung Speaking*, 115–135.

27. Paul Roazen, "Jung and Anti-Semitism," in *Lingering Shadows: Jungians, Freudians, and Anti-Semitism*, ed. A. Maidenbaum and S. A. Martin (Boston and London: Shambhala, 1991), 218–219.

28. Cited in Noll, *The Aryan Christ*, 114.

29. Noll, *The Jung Cult*, 260–261.

30. *The Freud/Jung Letters*, 483–484.

31. Ernest Jones, *Free Associations: Memories of a Psychoanalyst* (New York: Basic Books, 1959), 172–173.

32. Ibid., 126.

33. For the best accounts of Gross, see Martin Green, *Mountain of Truth: The Counterculture Begins, Ascona, 1900–1920* (Hanover: University Press of New England, 1986), 17 and following, and *The von Richthofen Sisters: the Triumphant and Tragic Modes of Love* (New York: Basic Books, 1974), 31 and following.

34. *The Freud/Jung Letters*, 153.

35. Ibid., 156.

36. C. G. Jung, *Psychology of the Unconscious: A Study of the Transformations and Symbolisms of the Libido*, trans. B. Hinkle (Princeton: Princeton University Press, 1991), 326, para. 249.

37. Noll, *The Jung Cult*, 159.

38. Cited in ibid., 159.

39. Noll, *The Aryan Christ*, 84.

40. Ibid., 115.

41. Jung, *Analytical Psychology: Notes of the Seminar Given in 1925 by C. G. Jung*, ed. W. McGuire (Princeton: Princeton University Press, 1989), 96.

42. Ibid., 98.

43. *The Correspondence of Freud and Sandor Ferenczi*, vol. 1, ed. E. Brabant et al. (Cambridge: Harvard University Press, 1992), 399.

44. Noll, *The Jung Cult*, 128.

45. Noll, *The Aryan Christ*, 141.

46. Ibid., 133.

47. See Noll, *The Aryan Christ*, 269.

48. Sonu Shamdasani, "A Woman Called Frank," *Spring* 50 (1990), 40.

49. Jung, *Psychology of the Unconscious: A Study of the Transformations and Symbolisms of the Libido*, trans. B. Hinkle (New York: Moffat Yard, 1916), 109. Also see Noll, *The Aryan Christ*, 268ff.

50. Noll, *The Aryan Christ*, 270.

Notes to Chapter Three: Fascism and Hermeneutics

1. Michael Burleigh, *Germany Turns Eastwards: A Study of Ostforschung in the Third Reich* (New York: Cambridge University Press, 1988).

2. *Deutsche Historiker im Nationalsozialismus*, ed. Winfried Schulze and Otto G. Oexle (Frankfurt am Main: Fischer Verlg, 1999).

3. Frank-Rutger Hausmann, *Deutsche Geisteswissenchaft im Zweiten Weltkrieg: Die "Aktion Ritterbusch," 1940–1945* (Dresden-Munich: Dresden University Press, 1998).

4. See, for example, Eckhard Michels, *Das deutsche Institut im Paris: 1940–1944* (Stuttgart: Franz Steiner Verlag, 1993).

5. Martin Heidegger, *Reden und andere Zeugnisse eines Lebensweges 1910–1976* (Frankfurt am Main: Vittorio Klostermann, 2000). See also the summary by Ludger Lütkehaus, "Der Staat am Sterbebett," in *Die Zeit* 22, May 23, 2001.

6. See *Bekenntnis der Professoren an den deutschen Universitäten und hochschulen zu Adolf Hitler und dem nationalsozialistischen Staat* (Dresden: NS Lehrerbund Deutschland/Sachsen, 1933). Jean Grondin, *Hans-Georg Gadamer: Eine Biographie* (Tübingen: J.C.B. Mohr: 1999) (English translation: *Hans-Georg Gadamer: A Biography*, trans. J. Weinsheimer [New Haven: Yale University Press, 2003]). There are many failings to Grondin's approach—foremost among them, he proceeds in an unscholarly, hagiographic manner reminiscent of the George Kreis (e.g., Friedrich Gundolf's biography of Goethe or Ernst Kantorowicz's biography of Frederick the Great). For a more detailed discussion of Grondin's work, see my review in *Bookforum* 10(2) (Summer 2003), 4–6.

7. *Deutsche Historiker im Nationalsozialismus*, 32.

8. On the instability of Nazi ideology and the resultant interpretive problems that have arisen, see Jeffrey Herf, *Reactionary Modernism* (New York: Cambridge University Press, 1986).

9. Michael Grüttner, "Wissenschaft," in *Enzykopädie des Nationalsozialismus*, ed. W. Benz (Stutgartt: Klett-Cotta, 1997), 144.

10. Ibid., 145.

11. Wehler, *The German Empire* (Leamington Spa: Berg, 1985), 231.

12. Jan Ross, "Schmuggel: Gadamers Geheimnis," *Frankfurter Allgemeine Zeitung*, February 11, 1995, 27.

13. Hans-Georg Gadamer, "Reflections on My Philosophical Journey," in *Philosophical Apprenticeships*, trans. R. Sullivan (Cambridge: MIT Press, 1985), 2.

14. *The Philosophy of Hans-Georg Gadamer*, ed. L. E. Hahn (Chicago: Open Court Press, 1996), 6.

15. Gadamer, *Philosophical Apprenticeships*, 38.

16. Ibid., 50–51, 52, 71.

17. *The Philosophy of Hans-Georg Gadamer*, 9.

18. Gadamer, *Philosophical Apprenticeships*, 72.

19. Ibid., 75.

20. Ibid., 77, 76.

21. Ibid., 78, 79.

22. Hans-Georg Gadamer, "Die wirklichen Nazis hatten doch überhaupt kein Interesse an uns" (Interview with Dörte von Westernhagen), *Das Argument* 32(4) (July-August 1990), 551.

23. Gadamer, *Philosophical Apprenticeships,* 104.

24. Hans-Georg Gadamer, *Truth and Method* (New York: Seabury, 1975), 232, 234.

25. Ibid., 245.

26. Hans-Georg Gadamer, *Philosophical Hermeneutics,* trans. D. Linge (Berkeley: University of California Press, 1976), 9.

27. Gadamer, *Truth and Method,* 249.

28. Ibid., xvi, 258.

29. Jürgen Habermas, review of *Truth and Method,* in *The Hermeneutic Tradition,* ed. G. Ormiston and A. Schrift (Albany: SUNY Press, 1990), 238.

30. See his remarks in "The 1920s, the 1930s, and the Present: National Socialism, German History, and German Culture," in *Hans-Georg Gadamer on Education, Poetry, and History,* ed. D. Misgeld and G. Nicholson (Albany: SUNY Press, 1992), 140: "I have always been a liberal from early times until today, and I have always voted for the FDP [Free Democrat Party]."

31. Jaeger, "Der Humanismus als Tradition und Erlebnis," in *Humanistische Reden und Vorträge* (Berlin, 1937), 20 ff.

32. The competing, nonpolitically freighted option was merely to transliterate the Greek original, *Politea.*

33. See "The Republic," in *The Works of Plato,* ed. B. Jowett (New York: Tudor, 1936), 323–333. For a good short commentary on Plato's critique of democracy, see Ernest Barker, *Greek Political Theory: Plato and His Predecessors* (London: Methuen, 1960).

34. Jaeger, "Die Erziehung des politischen Menschen in der Antike," *Volk im Werden,* 1 (3) (1933), 46.

35. Ibid.

36. For indispensable background, see Beat Näf, *Von Perikles zu Hitler? Die athenische Demokratie und die deutsche Althistorie bis 1945* (Bern: Peter Lang, 1986). See also Teresa Orozco, "Die Platon-Rezeption in Deutschland um 1933," in *'Die besten Geister der Nation': Philosophie und Nationalsozialismus,* ed. I. Korotin (Wien: Picus Verlag, 1994), 146ff; Volker Losemann, *Nationalsozialismus und Antike: Studien zur Entwicklung des Faches Alte Geschichte, 1933–1945* (Hamburg: Historische Perspektive 7, 1977). For a good discussion of the role played by the idea of *Staatsgesinnung* in secur-

ing the loyalty of German classicists, as well as other intellectuals, to Nazism, see Markus Schmitz, "Plato and the Enemies of the Open Society," in *Antike und Altertumswissenchaft im Alter von Faschismus und Nationalsozialismus,* ed. Näf (Mandelbachtel, Cambridge: PUB, 2001), 465–485. On Jaeger, see Suzanne Marchand, *Down From Olympus: Arachaeology and Philhellenism in Germany, 1750–1970* (Princeton: Princeton University Press, 1996).

37. Cited in K. Vretska, "Introduction, Platon," *Der Staat* (Stuttgart: Reclam, 1980), 5.

38. G.W.F. Hegel, *The Philosophy of Right,* trans. T. M. Knox (Oxford: Oxford University Press, 1952), 257–258.

39. Heyse, *Die Idee der Wissenschaft und die deutsche Universität* (Königsberg: Königsberg Press, 1933), 12.

40. Näf, *Von Perikles zu Hitler?* 184–185.

41. *Das Humanistische Gymnasium* (1933), 209.

42. Jaeger, "Die Erziehung des politischen Mensch in der Antike," *Volk im Werden* I (3) (1933), 43.

43. All of these passages are recounted in William Calder and M. Braun, "Tell it Hitler, Ecco! Paul Friedländer on Werner Jaeger's *Paideia,*" *Quaderni di storia,* 22 (43) (1996), 211–248. For another discussion of Jaeger, Third Humanism, and Plato, see Donald White, "Werner Jaeger's 'Third Humanism' and the Crisis of Conservative Cultural Politics in Weimar Germany," in *Werner Jaeger Reconsidered,* ed. W. M. Calder III (New York/London: Illinois Classical Studies, Supplement 34, 1990), 267–288.

44. Gadamer, "Die wirklichen Nazis hatten doch überhaupt kein Interesse an uns," 549.

45. On this subject, see Leon Poliakov and Josef Wulf, *Das dritte Reich und seine Denker* (München, New York: K. G. Sauer, 1978); for the field of philosophy in particular, see T. Laugstien, *Philosophieverhältnisse im deutschen Faschismus* (Hamburg: Argument Verlag, 1990).

46. Hans-Georg Gadamer, "Plato and the Poets," in *Dialogue and Dialectic: Eight Hermeneutical Studies on Plato,* trans. C. Smith (New Haven: Yale University Press, 1980), 39. Subsequent references will appear parenthetically.

47. Ibid., 52.

48. Ibid., 57.

49. Ibid., 58.

50. Gadamer, "Reflections on My Philosophical Journey," 13.

51. Gadamer, "Plato and the Poets," 39.

52. Gadamer, "Die wirklichen Nazis," 549.

53. Gadamer, "Die wirklichen Nazis hatten doch überhaupt kein Interesse an uns," 546. For Gadamer's review of Hildebrandt (first published in 1935), see *Gesammelte Werke* V, 331–37.

54. Hitler, *Mein Kampf* (Boston: Houghton Mifflin, 1941), 423.

55. Volker Losemann, *Nationalsozialismus und die Antike* (Hamburg: Hoffman und Campe, 1977), 11.

56. Werner Maser, *Hitlers Briefe und Notizen. Seine Weltbild in handschriftlichen Dokumenten* (Düsseldorf: Econ, 1973), 295.

57. Hitler, *Sämtliche Aufzeichnungen 1905–1924*, ed. E. Jäckel (Stuttgart: Deutsche Verlags-Anstalt, 1980), 187.

58. Cited in Joachim Fest, *Hitler* (New York: Vintage, 1971), 382.

59. Näf, *Von Perikles zu Hitler?* 118.

60. Orozco, "Die Platon-Rezeption in Deutschland," 142; see also, Orozco, *Platonische Gewalt: Gadamers politische Hermeneutik der NS-Zeit* (Hamburg: Argument, 1995), 142.

61. As he remarks in "Yet Another Philosophy of History" (1774), "Each nation has its center of happiness within itself, just as every sphere has its center of gravity. . . . The Egyptian detests the shepherd and the nomad and despises the frivolous Greek. . . . But prejudice is good, in its time and place, for happiness may spring from it. It urges nations to converge upon their center, attaches the more firmly to their roots, causes them to flourish after their kinds." *Herder on Social and Political Culture*, ed. F. M. Barnard (Cambridge: Cambridge University Press, 1969), 186–187.

62. Benno von Wiese, *Herder: Grundzüge seines Weltbildes* (Leipzig: Meyer, 1939), 124; Friedrich Weinrich, *Herders deutsche Bezeugung des Evangeliums in den 'Christlichen Schriften'* (Weimar, 1937), 7.

63. Walter Kriewald, *Herders Gedanken über die Verbindung von Religion und Volkstum* (Ohlau i. Schlesien, 1935), 6.

64. Dahmen, *Die nationale Idee von Herder bis Hitler* (Köln: 1934), 62.

65. For an important survey of the appropriation of Herder during the Third Reich, see Bernhard Becker, "Herder in der nationalsozialistischen Germanistik," in *Herder im "Dritten Reich*," ed. J. Schneider (Bielefeld: Aisthesis Verlag, 1994).

66. See Orozco, *Platonische Gewalt*, 109.

67. Hans-Georg Gadamer, *Volk und Geschichte im Denken Herders* (Frankfurt: Klostermann, 1942), 5, 7 (emphasis added).

68. Ibid., 10, 12.

69. Ibid., 13.

70. Ibid., 20, 21, 22.

71. Ibid., 23.

72. Ibid., 24. For a systematic comparison of the different versions of Gadamer's Herder-*Schrift*, see Orozco, *Platonische Gewalt*, 235–249.

73. Hans-Georg Gadamer, *Gesammelte Werke*, vol. 4 (Tübingen: Mohr Verlag, 1987), 333.

74. Gadamer, *Philosophical Apprenticeships*, 99; "Reflections on My Philosophical Journey," 14. He also relates the following anecdote: "There is a particular reason why I am fond of this work [i.e., the Herder monograph]. I had dealt with this theme for the first time in a lecture given in French to French officers in a prisoner of war camp. In the question period and discussion afterwards I said that an empire that extends itself beyond measure, beyond moderation, is "auprès de sa chute—"near its fall." The French officers looked at each other meaningfully and understood."

75. Gadamer, "The 1920s, the 1930s, and the Present,"148.

76. Claus Grossner, *Verfall der Philosophie: Politik der deutschen Philosophen* (Reinbeck b. Hamburg: Christian Wegner Verlag), 234.

77. Letter from Gadamer, May 27, 1970, cited in Grossner, *Verfall der Philosophie*, 234. In "The 1920s, the 1930s, and the Present," 148, Gadamer offers the following, more forthright evaluation of his Paris lecture trip: "It is quite true: One accepted this kind of ambiguous assignment. Yes, I knew the Nazi regime wanted to show there still are those German professors who are not Nazis. That was what one was good for."

78. Gadamer, "On the Scope and Function of Hermeneutical Reflection," in *Philosophical Hermeneutics*, 21.

79. Habermas, "Review of Truth and Method," in *The Hermeneutic Tradition*, 239 (translation altered).

80. Gadamer, *The Philosophy of Hans-Georg Gadamer*, 97.

81. For the relevant texts, see Gadamer, "The Scope and Function of Hermeneutical Reflection," in *Philosophical Hermeneutics*, 18–44; and Habermas, "A Review of Gadamer's Truth and Method" and "The Hermeneutic Claim to Universality," in *The Hermeneutic Tradition*, 213–273.

82. Grossner, "Die Philosophie des Vorurteils," in *Verfall der Philosophie*, 53–63.

83. Hans-Georg Gadamer, *Truth and Method* (New York: Seabury, 1975), 239–240 (emphasis added).

84. See Hans Albert, "Critical Rationalism and Universal Hermeneutics," in *Gadamer's Century: Essays in Honor of Hans-Georg Gadamer*, ed. J. Malpas et al. (Cambridge: MIT Press, 2002), 17.

85. Wellmer, *Kritische Theorie und Positivismus* (Frankfurt: Suhrkamp Verlag, 1971), 48.

86. Gadamer, "The Universality of the Hermeneutical Problem," 16.

87. Ibid., 5.

88. Gadamer, "The 1920s, the 1930s, and the Present," 147, 148, 150.

89. Ibid., 150.

90. "Der 'Führer' und seine Denker: Zur Philosophie des 'Dritten Reiches,'" *Deutsche Zeitschrift für Philosophie* 47 (1999).

91. Hausmann, "Unwahrheit als Methode? Zu Hans Georg Gadamers Publikationen im 'Dritten Reich,' *Internationale Zeitschrift für Philosophie* 1 (November 2001).

92. Gereon Walters, "Der 'Führer' und seine Denker," 231.

93. Martin Heidegger, *Nietzsche: Europäischer Nihilismus, Gesamtausgabe 48* (Frankfurt: Klostermann, 1986), 205, 333.

94. See the texts assembled in *Internationale Zeitschrift für Philosophie* 1 (November 2001).

95. See, for example, Joachim Fest, *Das Gesicht des dritten Reiches: Profile eines totalitärischen Herrschaft* (Munich: Piper, 1988), 342.

96. See Herbert Marcuse, letter to Heidegger of May 12, 1948, in *The Heidegger Controversy: A Critical Reader,* ed. Richard Wolin (Cambridge: MIT Press, 1993), 152–164.

97. See, for example, the Richard Palmer's introduction to *Gadamer in Conversation: Reflections and Commentary* (New Haven: Yale University Press, 2001). Palmer's defense of Gadamer regresses behind the normal standards of critical scholarship insofar as it accepts all of Gadamer's own rationalizations of his political compromises during the 1930s and 1940s unquestioningly and systematically refuses to engage the vast literature on National Socialism and the humanities. Such literature offers an indispensable interpretive key to comprehending the nature and extent of the aforementioned political compromises.

For a general discussion of the relationship between intellectuals and tyranny, see Mark Lilla, *The Reckless Mind* (New York: New York Review Books, 2001).

98. Joseph Goebbels, *Tagebücher. Aus den Jahren 1942/43,* ed. L. P. Lorchner (Zürich: 1948), 186.

99. Michels, *Das Deutsche Institut in Paris,* 38.

100. Ibid., 223.

101. Ibid., 82.

102. Ibid., 261.

103. *Europa unter dem Hakenkreuz,* Dokument 7, 117.

104. On the Nazis' plans for European domination, see Robert Herzstein, *When Nazi Dreams Come True* (London: Abacus, 1982).

105. Hans-Georg Gadamer, *Volk und Geschichte im Denken Herders* (Frankfurt am Main: Vittorio Klostermann Verlag, 1942), 23.

Notes to Political Excursus I: Incertitudes Allemandes

1. Ernst Nolte and François Furet, *Fascism and Communism* (Lincoln: University of Nebraska Press, 2002).

2. Ernst Troeltsch, "The Ideas of Natural Law and Humanity in World Politics," in Otto von Gierke, *Natural Law and the Theory of Society,* ed. Ernest Barker (Cambridge: Cambridge University Press, 1950), 204, 211.

3. Ibid., 214.

4. Friedbert Pflüger, *Deutschland Driftet: Die konservative Revolution endeckt ihre Kinder* (Düsseldorf: Econ Verlag, n.d.).

5. Karl Heinz Bohrer, "Why We Are Not a Nation—and Why We Must Become One," *New German Critique* 52 (Winter 1991), 72–94.

6. Christian Meier, *Die Nation die keine sein will* (Munich: Hanser, 1991).

7. Jürgen Habermas, "Yet Again: German Identity—An Angry Nation of DM-Burghers," *New German Critique* 52 (Winter 1991), 84–101; Habermas, "The Normative Deficits of Reunification," *The Past as Future,* trans. M. Pensky (Lincoln: University of Nebraska Press, 1994), 55–73.

8. See Antonia Grunenberg, *Antifaschismus: Ein deutscher Mythos* (Reinbeck: Rowohlt, 1993).

9. See Joffe, "Mr. Heilbrunn's Planet," *Foreign Affairs* (March/April 1997), 152–161. Joffe's article was written in response to Jacob Heilbrunn, "Germany's New Right," *Foreign Affairs* (November/December 1996), 80–98.

10. For more on the French *Nouvelle Droite,* see, in this book, "Political Excursus II: Designer Fascism: On the French New Right."

11. See the contributions by Nolte and Stürmer in *Historikerstreit: Die Dokumentation der Kontroverse um dei Einzigartigekeit der natinalsozialistischen Judenvernichtung* (Munich: Piper, 1987); the Stürmer citation is from 37.

12. Zitelmann, cited in Maria Zens, "Vergangenheit verlegen," in H-M Lohmann, ed., *Extremismus der Mitte* (Frankfurt: Fischer Verlag, 1994), 116.

13. For a description of these events, see Elliot Neaman, *A Dubious Past: Ernst Jünger and the Politics of Literature after Nazism* (Berkeley: University of California Press, 1999), chapter 7.

14. *Westbindung: Chancen und Risiken für Deutschland,* ed. R. Zitelmann, K. Weissmann, and M. Grossheim (Frankfurt/Berlin: Propyläen, 1993), 10 (emphasis added).

15. Felix Stern, "Feminismus und Apartheid," in *Die Selbstbewusste Nation*, ed. Ulrich Schacht and Heimo Schwilk (Frankfurt am Main: Ullsetin, 1994), 291 (italics added).

16. Ernst Jünger, "Der Kampf um das Reich," cited in Pflüger, *Deutschland driftet*, 35–36.

17. Carl Schmitt, *The Concept of the Political*, trans. G. Scwhab (Chicago: University of Chicago Press, 1996), 67; see also the German edition, *Der Begriff des Politischen* (Berlin: Duncker und Humblot, 1963), 67: "Die Höhepunkte der grossen Politik sind zugleich die Augenblicke, in denen der Feind in konkreten Deutlichkeit als Feind erblickt wird." The English translation omits the allusion Nietzsche's concept of "great politics."

18. Jürgen Habermas, *The New Conservatism*, 249–268. According to Ernst Frankel, "Nothing better characterizes the change in German consciousness than the difference in overtones that surface today when discussion turns to 'the Western democracies'. . ." Cited in Klaus Naumann, "'Neuanfang ohne Tabus': Deutscher Sonderweg und politische Semantik," in *Extremismus der Mitte*, ed. H.-M. Lohmann, 70.

19. For a detailed discussion of Schmitt's influence on the New Right, see Klaus Kriener, "Plettenberg-Freiburg—Potsdam: Über den Einfluss Carl Schmitts auf die Junge Freiheit," in *Das Plagiat: Der völkische Nationalismus der Jungen Freiheit*, ed. H. Kellershohn (Duisberg: DISS, 1994), 181–212.

20. John Ely, "The *Frankfurter Allgemeine Zeitung* and National Conservativism," *German Politics and Society* 13(2) (Summer 1995), 83.

21. See Hans Magnus Enzensberger, *Aussichten auf dem Bürgerkrieg* (Frankfurt: Suhrkamp Verlag, 1993).

22. Botho Strauss, "Anschwellender Bockgesang," in *Die selbstbewusste Nation und weitere Beiträge zu einer deutschen Debatte*, ed. H. Schwilk and U. Schacht (Berlin: Ullstein, 1994), 26 (first published in *Der Spiegel* 46, 1993).

23. Cited in Klaus Naumann, "'Neuanfang ohne Tabus,'" 76.

24. Wolfgang Schäuble, *Und der Zukunft zugewandt* (Berlin: Siedler, 1994), 220ff.

25. Andrei Markovits and Simon Reich, *The German Predicament: Memory and Power in the New Europe* (Ithaca: Cornell University Press, 1997), 25.

26. Pflüger, *Deutschland Driftet*, 38.

27. "Ein historisches Recht Hitlers"? Der Faschismus-Interpret Ernst Nolte über den Nationalsozialismus, Auschwitz und die Neue Rechte. *Spiegel*-Gespräch mit Rudolf Augstein." *Der Spiegel*, Nr. 40 (Oct. 10, 1994), 83–103.

28. John Ely, "The *Frankfurter Allgemeine Zeitung* and National Conservatism," 106–107.

29. Cited in ibid., 88.

30. Willms, *Idealismus und Nation* (Paderborn: Schoningh, 1986), 17. Cited in ibid., 90ff. See also, Leonard Krieger, *The German Idea of Freedom* (Chicago: University of Chicago Press, 1957).

31. See Jeffrey Herf, *War By Other Means* (New York: Free Press, 1991); and Hans-Georg Betz, *Postmodern Politics in Germany* (New York: St. Martin's Press, 1991).

32. For more on National Bolshevism, see Herzinger and Stein, *Endzeit-Propheten*, 126–143; see also Louis Dupeux, *National Bolchevisme*, 2 vols. (Paris: Honoré Champion, 1979).

33. See David Pan, "Botho Strauss: Myth, Community, and Nationalism in Germany," *Telos* 105 (Fall 1995), 57: "Since the end of communism and the reunification of Germany, writers from both the former East and West Germany have sounded the alarm against the materialism of German culture, the dangers of capitalist homogenization, and the decline of values. An entire generation of 'left-wing' writers, including Heiner Müller, Botho Strauss, Hans Magnus Enzensberger, and Martin Walser have attempted to defend German culture against the perceived threat of American capitalism and Western rationalism."

34. Strauss, "Anschwellender Bockgesang," 31.

35. Strauss, *Beginnlosigkeit* (Munich: Carl Hanser Verlag, 1992), 107.

36. Nietzsche, *The Will to Power,* trans. W. Kaufmann (New York: Vintage, 1967), 796.

37. For an excellent treatment of this problem, see Hans Reiss, ed., *The Political Doctrines of German Romanticism;* and Josef Chytry, *The Aesthetic State* (Berkeley: University of California Press, 1989).

38. Strauss, "Anschwelleder Bockgesang," 39.

39. Ibid., 21.

40. Ibid., 28, 31, 34.

41. Ibid., 24 (emphasis added).

42. Syberberg, *Vom Unglück und Glück der Kunst im Deutschland nach dem letzten Kriege* (Munich: Matthes and Seitz, 1990), 114.

43. Ibid., 14.

44. Dieter Diederichsen, "Spiritual Reactionaries After German Reunification: Syberberg, Foucault, and Others," *October* 62 (Fall 1992), 66.

45. Cited in Pflüger, *Deutschland Driftet,* 11.

46. For a summary of the debate, see Roger Cohn, "Germany Searches for Normalization," *New York Times,* November 29, 1998, section 4, 10. At one point the dramatist Heiner Müller gleefully joined the chorus: "It has to do with a tragedy that has so far been completely covered up—the

tragedy of the German people and the end of the German nation. All of that has been suppressed. That is why there is no good German literature about the Second World War. The right is now pushing into this vacuum."

47. Saul Friedländer, "Die Metapher des Bösen," *Die Zeit* 49, November 26, 1998, 50.

48. Pflüger, *Deutschland driftet,* 89.

49. See Werner Bergmann, "Antisemitism and Xenophobia in Germany Since Unification," in *Antisemitism and Xenophobia in Germany Since Unification,* ed. H. Kurthen et al. (Cambridge: Cambridge University Press, 1998), 21–38.

50. Habermas, "1945 in the Shadow of 1989," in *A Berlin Republic* (Lincoln: University of Nebraska Press, 1996), 180–181. See also Habermas, "Die zweite Lebenslüge der Bundesrepublik: Wir sind wieder 'normal' geworden," *Die Zeit* 51 (December 18, 1992).

51. "Schröder Backs Design for a Vast Berlin Holocaust Memorial," *New York Times,* January 17, 1999, A6. For a good discussion of the controversial history of this project, see Michael Wise, *Capital Dilemma: Germany's Search for a New Architecture of Democracy* (Princeton: Princeton University Press, 1998).

52. Tocqueville, *Democracy in America,* trans. G. Lawrence (New York: Harper and Row, 1966), 703.

53. See Daniel Goldhagen, "Modell Budesrepublik: National History, Democracy, and Internationalization in Germany," *Common Knowledge* 6(3) (1997), 11: "Two parallel, indeed surprising, developments characterize the Federal Republic: the emergence of a relatively non-nationalist and remarkably self-critical, national history and a relatively non-nationalist, internationally responsible nation state."

Notes to Chapter Four: Left Fascism

1. Jürgen Habermas, "Die Moderne: Ein unvollendetes Projekt," in *Kleine Politische Schriften,* I–IV (Frankfurt: Suhrkamp, 1981), 444–464. The essay originated as a lecture delivered by Habermas on the occasion of his receipt of the Adorno prize awarded by the city of Frankfurt on September 11, 1980. It has appeared in English in *New German Critique* 22 (Winter 1981) under the title, "Modernity vs. Postmodernity," 3–14; as well as in *The Anti-Aesthetic: Essays on Postmodern Culture* (Port Townsend, Wash.: Bay Press, 1983), edited by Hal Foster, under the title, "Modernity: An

Incomplete Project" (which corresponds to the original German). The reference to "sovereignty" is an allusion to Bataille.

2. For an example of such confusion, see John Rajchman, "Habermas' Complaint," in *New German Critique* 45 (Spring 1988), 163–191. See my response to Rajchman, "On Misunderstanding Habermas," *New German Critique* 49 (Winter 1990), 139–154.

3. There is a substantial literature on this political grouping in German but relatively little in English. Schmitt's "membership" has been the object of some controversy. For one, unlike the others who worked as writers or *Publizisten,* Schmitt was a highly successful academic and jurist. For the terms of this debate over Schmitt's role among the Weimar intelligentsia, see my essay, "Carl Schmitt: the Conservative Revolutionary Habitus and the Aesthetics of Horror," *Political Theory* (20)3 (1992), 424–447. For a different view, see J. Bendersky, *Carl Schmitt: Theorist for the Reich* (Princeton: Princeton University Press, 1983).

4. I have explored these filiations in my book *The Politics of Being: The Political Thought of Martin Heidegger* (New York: Columbia University Press, 1990). See especially chapter 2, *"Being and Time* as Political Philosophy." In 1933 Heidegger urged Schmitt to join the Nazi Party. He later avowed that during this period his understanding of politics was largely shaped by Jünger's 1932 encomium to the totalitarian ideal, *Der Arbeiter: Gestalt und Herrschaft* (Hamburg: Hanseatische Verlanganstalt, 1932).

5. For an important discussion of this problem, see Kurt Sontheimer, "Anti-democratic Thought in the Weimar Republic," in *The Path to Dictatorship, 1918–1933* (Garden City, N.J.: Anchor, 1966), 32–49.

6. Manfred Frank, *Die Grenzen der Verständigung: Ein Geistergespräch zwischen Habermas and Lyotard* (Frankfurt: Suhrkamp, 1988), 20.

7. For substantiation of this claim, one should consult the important book by Luc Ferry and Alain Renaut, *French Philosophy of the Sixties* (Amherst: University of Massachusetts Press, 1990). The original French title of the book, *La Pensée '68,* is of course much more congenial from the standpoint of the argument I've just made.

8. "Créer une religion, voilà ce qu'il voulait. Une religion sans dieu." Cited in Bernard-Henri Lévy, *Les Aventures de la Liberté* (Paris: Grasset, 1991), 170.

9. See Jacques Derrida, "From Restricted to a General Economy: A Hegelianism without Reserve," *Writing and Difference,* trans. Alan Bass (Chicago: University of Chicago, 1978), 251–277; Michel Foucault, "A Preface to Transgression," *Language, Counter-Memory, Practice* (Ithaca:

Cornell University Press, 1977), 29–52. Derrida's attitudes toward Bataille are less unequivocally positive than are Foucault's.

10. "The logic developed by Bataille . . . Links the twenties' context to a later generation of radical critics, including Michele Foucault, Roland Barthes, Jacques Derrida, and the *Tel Quel* Group." James Clifford, *The Predicament of Culture* (Cambridge: Harvard University Press, 1988), 125, 127. See also the important number of the journal *Critique* (1963; the journal was founded by Bataille in the late 1940s), "Hommage à Georges Bataille," which contains contributions by Foucault, Derrida, Barthes, and Philippe Sollers.

11. See Friedrich Nietzsche, "European Nihilism," in *The Will to Power,* trans. W. Kaufmann and R. J. Hollingdale (New York: Vintage, 1968), pp. 9–82. "What does nihilism mean? That the highest values devaluate themselves. The aim is lacking; 'why?' finds no answer" (9).

12. Hans-Ulrich Wehler's *The German Empire* (Leamington Spa: Berg, 1973), remains one of the best historical accounts of this resistance. Wehler's argument concerning a German Sonderweg was called into question by Geoff Eley and Robin Blackbourn in *The Peculiarities of German History* (New York: Oxford University Press, 1984). The critics of the Sonderweg thesis have yet to explain how, if Germany's path to modernity was so "normal," the twelve year "detour" of National Socialism and then Auschwitz could have been possible.

13. Hannah Arendt, *The Origins of Totalitarianism* (New York: Meridian, 1958), 108.

14. "Déclaration," *Cahiers du Cercle Proudhon,* Jan.-Feb. 1912, 1.

15. See Zeev Sternhell, *Neither Right nor Left: Fascist Ideology in France* (Berkeley: University of California Press, 1986), an indispensable guide to the ideological genesis of the French right: "There can be no doubt: in large part, the emergence of the Faisceau was due to the deep need for action felt by the younger generation in the old ligues, and for that reason the fascist movement represented a danger both for the Action Française and for the other national ligues, headed by the oldest—Déroulède's Ligue des Patriotes" (101). In terms of its actual practice, the Faisceau sought to promote a convocation of the Estates General with the end in view of establishing a true corporative state.

16. Cited in ibid., 96.

17. See Philippe Burrin, *La Dérive fasciste: Bergery, Déat and Doriot* (Paris: Editions du Seuil, 1986).

18. Tony Judt, *Past Imperfect: French Intellectuals, 1944–1956* (Berkeley: University of California, 1993), 18.

19. Ibid.

20. Drieu La Rochelle, *Le Socialisme fasciste* (Paris: Gallimard, 1934).

21. For more on Proudhon, see K. Steven Vincent, *Pierre-Joseph Proudhon and the Rise of French Socialism* (New York: Oxford University Press, 1984).

22. A. Honneth, "An Aversion Against the Universal," *Theory, Culture and Society* 2(3) (1985).

23. See Richard Wolin, *The Politics of Being: The Political Thought of Martin Heidegger,* 28ff.; Martin Heidegger, "The Word of Nietzsche: 'God is Dead,'" in The *Question Concerning Technology and Other Essays,* ed. W. Lovitt (New York: Harper, 1977), 112 (emphasis added). What is equally striking is the extent to which the critique of modernity purveyed by the conservative revolutionaries—whose activities were largely journalistic—was largely shared by German academic mandarinate. In a key work, *The Decline of the German Mandarins* (Cambridge: Harvard, 1969), Fritz Ringer offers a thorough account of the *Kulturkritik* of the former group. The best book on the conservative revolutionaries is Jeffrey Herf's *Reactionary Modernism: Technology, Culture, and Politics in Weimar and the Third Reich* (New York: Cambridge University Press, 1984); although the typology Herf employs applies ideally to Jünger. In the cases of thinkers such as Spengler, Schmitt, and Heidegger, the enthusiasm for technology is either highly muted (Spengler and Schmitt) or nonexistent (Heidegger).

For another informative discussion of the conservative revolutionary worldview, with special reference to Heidegger's views, see Pierre Bourdieu, *Heidegger's Political Ontology* (Stanford: Stanford University Press, 1990). See also Jerry Z. Muller, *The Other God that Failed: Hans Freyer and the Deradicalization of German Conservatism* (Princeton: Princeton University Press, 1987).

For a general discussion of Bataille's philosophy in relationship to German thought, see Les Amis de Georges Bataille, *Georges Bataille et la pensée allemande,* (Paris: Amis de Georges Bataille, 1986).

24. Bataille, "The Sacred Conspiracy," in *Visions of Excess: Selected Writings, 1927–1929,* ed. A. Stoekl (Minneapolis: University of Minnesota Press, 1986), 179.

25. For a discussion of Bataille and his French theoretical heirs, see Martin Jay, *Downcast Eyes: The Denigration of Vision in Twentieth-Century French Thought* (Berkeley: University of California Press, 1993).

26. Oswald Spengler, *The Decline of the West,* vol. II, trans. C. F. Atkinson (New York: Alfred Knopf, 1950), 11.

27. One might also note that an analogous schema characterizes Ernst Bloch's early work, *Geist der Utopie* (a long chapter of which is devoted to philosophy of music), which appeared the same year (1918) as volume I of Spengler's opus.

28. Spengler, *The Decline of the West*, Vol. II, 8–9 (emphasis added).

29. Ibid., 440.

30. Jünger, *Der Kampf als inneres Erlebnis* (Berlin: E. S. Mittler, 1922), 57.

31. Bataille, "The Threat of War," *October 36* (Spring 1986), 28.

32. Jay, "The Reassertion of Sovereignty in a Time of Crisis: Carl Schmitt and Georges Bataille," in *Force Fields: Between Intellectual History and Cultural Critique* (New York: Routledge, 1992), 16.

33. Bataille, *The Accursed Share*, 74.

34. Ibid., 71.

35. Ibid., 54.

36. Walter Benjamin, "The Work of Art in the Age of Mechanical Reproduction, in *Illuminations,* ed. H. Arendt, trans. H. Zohn (New York: Schocken, 1969), 242. See also Benjamin's important statement on this theme in his review of Jünger's 1930 volume, *Krieg und Krieger,* in Benjamin, *Gesammelte Schriften* III (Frankfurt: Suhrkamp Verlag, 1972), 240: "The new theory of war . . . is nothing less than a transposition of the theses of *l'art pour l'art* to war."

37. Bataille, *The Accursed Share*, trans. R. Hurley (Cambridge: Zone Books, 1988), 38, 39.

38. Marcel Mauss, *The Gift: Forms and Function of Exchange in Archaic Societies,* trans. I Cunnison (New York: Norton, 1967), 1.

39. Bataille, "The Notion of Expenditure," in *Visions of Excess: Selected Writings,* 118 (emphasis added).

40. See, for example, the opening passages of *The Story of the Eye:*

I grew up very much alone, and as far back as I recall I was frightened of anything sexual. I was nearly sixteen when I met Simone, a girl my own age, at the beach in X. Our families being distantly related, we quickly grew intimate. Three days after our first meeting, Simone and I were alone in her villa. She was wearing a black pinafore with a starched white collar. I began realizing that she shared my anxiety at seeing her, and I felt even more anxious that day because I hoped she would be stark naked under the pinafore.

She had black silk stockings on covering her knees, but I was unable to see as far up as the cunt (this name, which I always used with Simone, is, I think, by far the loveliest of the names for the vagina). It merely struck me that by slightly lifting the pinafore from behind, I might see her private parts unveiled.

Now in the corner of a hallway there was a saucer of milk for the cat. "Milk is for the pussy, isn't it?" Said Simone. "Do you dare me to sit in the saucer?"

"I dare you," I answered, almost breathless.

The day was extremely hot. Simone put the saucer on a small bench, planted herself before me, and, with her eyes fixed on me, she sat down without my being able to see her burning buttocks under the skirt, dipping into the cool milk. The blood shot to my head, and I stood trembling, as she eyed my stiff cock bulging in my pants. Then I lay down at her feet without her stirring, and for the first time, I saw her "pink and dark" flesh cooling in the white milk. We remained motionless, on and on, both of us equally overwhelmed.

41. Judt, *Past Imperfect*, 73, 9.

42. See the interpretation of Foucault along these lines in James Miller, *The Passion of Michel Foucault* (New York: Random House, 1992). Miller views Foucault as faithful to the Nietzschean ethical legacy I have been describing, in which "self-overcoming" remains the highest value. See the critique of Miller's interpretation in Martin Jay, *Cultural Semantics: Keywords of Our Time* (Amherst: University of Massachusetts Press, 1998), chapter 5, "The Limits of Limit Experience: Bataille and Foucault."

43. See Maurice Blanchot, *La Communauté inavouable* (Paris: Minuit, 1983) and Jean-Luc Nancy *La Communauté désoeuvrée* (Paris: Galilée, 1986).

44. Bernard-Henri Lévy, *L'idéologie française* (Paris: Grasset, 1981), 220–221; emphasis added. For an article by one of Mauss's students that, relatively early on, perceived the problematic link between the new sociology of community and burgeoning fascism, see Svend Ranulf, "Scholarly Forerunners of Fascism," *Ethics* 50(1) (October 1939), 16–34.

45. E. E. Evans-Pritchard, "Introduction," to Mauss, *The Gift*, ix. See also Henri Hubert and Marcel Mauss, *Sacrifice: Its Nature and Function* (Chicago: University of Chicago, 1964).

46. Mauss, *The Gift*, 74.

47. Ibid., 70.

48. Ibid., 77 (emphasis added).

49. Bataille's relation to Hegelian dialectics is predominantly negative—he believes that they remain excessively indebted to the forces of modern rationality; as such, they partake of the order of the homogeneous—

which stands in stark contrast to his enthusiastic relation to Nietzsche. See "The Critique of the Foundations of the Hegelian Dialectic" in *Visions of Excess,* 105–115.

50. Bataille, "The Notion of Expenditure," 117–118.

51. Ibid., 118.

52. Ibid., 124, 125.

53. Bataille, *The Accursed Share,* 55–57.

54. Ibid., 59, 61.

55. Allan Stoekl, "Introduction," *Visions of Excess,* xiii.

56. Potlatch is most commonly practiced among Indian tribes of the Pacific Northwest and Canada, such as the Haida, Kwakiutl, and Tlinlgit.

57. Mauss, *The Gift,* 72 (emphasis added).

58. On this point, see Jean-Louis Loubet del Bayle, *Les Non-conformistes des années trentes* (Paris: Editions du Seuil, 1969).

59. Jean-François Fourny, *Introduction à la lecture de Georges Bataille* (New York: Peter Lang, 1988), 104. As Fourny goes on to observe, "This explains the fact that for the Bataille of this period the war signified hardly more than a sort of rumor that only began to matter when it penetrated his immediate universe." See also Fourny's excellent article, "Georges Bataille and Gaston Bergery: Sorcerer's Apprentices of the Thirties, *Clio* 18(3), 239–254.

60. Shortly before the fall of France, Caillois eloped to Argentina where he sat out the war with his paramour and sponsor, Victoria Ocampo. There he edited the prestigious literary journal, *Cahiers de Sud.* During the war, he also published *La Communion des Forts,* in which many of the troubling themes about leadership, the sacred, and sacrifice contained in "The Winter Wind" re-emerge. Although at this point in his career, Caillois is disillusioned with fascism, his fascination with fascist "elements" remained keen.

For the details of this strange intellectual odyssey, see Odile Felgine, *Roger Caillois* (Paris: Stock, 1992).

61. Surya's remarks are cited in Allan Stoekl's essay, "Truman's Apotheosis: Bataille, 'Planisme,' and Headlessness," *Yale French Studies* 78, "On Bataille" (1990), 181.

62. *La Critique Sociale* (Paris: La Découverte, 1983). It may be of interest to note in this connection that when Bataille published his "Theory of Expenditure" in Souvarine's review in 1933, the article appeared with a disclaimer to indicate that the point of view expressed in the essay were not necessarily shared by the editorial collective as a whole.

63. His charges have been rebutted by Maurice Blanchot in *Le Débat* 29 (March 1984), 20. Laure was Souvarine's *petite amie* before becoming enamored of Bataille, so there is also an *histoire d'amour* involved.

64. Bataille, "The Psychological Structure of Fascism," in *Visions of Excess*, 139.

65. For more on this distinction among various "action-types," see Jürgen Habermas, *The Theory of Communicative Action*, vol. 1. (Boston: Beacon Press, 1984).

66. Bataille, "The Psychological Structure of Fascism," 143.

67. Ibid.

68. Ibid., 145.

69. See supra, note 44.

70. Anthony Stephens, "Georges Bataille's Diagnosis of Fascism," *Thesis 11*, no. 24 (1989), 74, 85. In terms of the question I have raised concerning Bataille's affinities with the conservative revolutionaries, the same author has observed, Bataille "shows the same willingness to accept the Nazis as much nobler than all the facts suggested that determined, for varying lengths of time, the attitudes of Ernst Jünger, Gottfried Benn and Martin Heidegger."

71. Ernst Cassirer, *The Myth of the State* (New Haven: Yale University Press, 1946), 279, 280.

72. Bataille, "The Sorcerer's Apprentice," in *The College of Sociology*, ed. D. Hollier (Minneapolis: University of Minnesota, 1988), 22, 23.

73. Ibid., 42.

74. Ibid., 49.

75. Caillois, *La Communion des Forts* (Mexico City: Editions Quetzel, 1943). A French publication of *Communion des Forts* ensued the following year. Yet several key chapters were removed in anticipation of censorship. See Meyer Schapiro, "French Reaction in Exile," *Kenyon Review*, 7(1) (Winter 1945), 29–42.

76. Ginzburg, "Germanic Mythology and Nazism: On an Old Book by Georges Dumézil," in *Myths, Emblems, and Clues*, trans. John Tedeschi and Anne Tedeschi (London: Hutchinson Radius, 1990). As Ginzburg observes, "It is easy to identify the principal currents in Dumézil's research in the preoccupations (or obsessions) that dominated the leaders of the College, Bataille and Caillois. To simplify, we might say that for Bataille these were the connection between death (and sexuality) and the sacred; for Caillois, between the sacred and power. In both cases, these themes implied an extremely equivocal attitude towards Fascist and Nazi ideologies"

(142–143). Ginzburg's critique of Dumézil was first published in *Annales ESC* 4 (1985), 695–715. For Dumézil's response to Ginzburg, see "Science and Politique: Réponse à Carlo Ginzburg," *Annales ESC* 5 (September-October 1985), 985–989.

Dumézil had been Caillois's teacher at the Sorbonne and many of the mythological leitmotifs that appear in College texts may be attributable to his influence. In the aforementioned article, Ginzburg shows how the first edition of Dumézil's *Mythes et Dieux des Germains* was replete with proto-fascist elements and themes that had been carefully expurgated in the 1959 reprint. The first scholar to have criticized Dumézil in this vein, however, was Arnaldo Momigliano in "Georges Dumézil and the Trifunctional Approach to Roman Civilization," *History and Theory* 23(3) (1984), 312–330.

In contrast with Ginzburg, Denis Hollier has seized on the moment of political "equivocation" in Bataille's 1930s essays for purposes of exonerating him from the charge of fascism. Thus, in Hollier's view, since Bataille's attitudes towards fascism were "equivocal," he was not a genuine fascist. But in truth none of these critics argues that Bataille and his fellow Collegians were dyed-in-the-wool fascists; such an argument would be much too simplistic. Instead, they argue that Bataille and company exhibited a politically compromising "fascination with fascism"—a point which, given the massive evidence in support of such claims, seems undeniable. For Hollier's contribution, see "On Equivocation (Between Literature and Politics)," *October* 55 (Winter 1990) 3–22. Also see Hollier, *Absent without Leave: French Literature Under the Threat of War,* trans. C. Porter (Cambridge: Harvard University Press, 1997).

Following the publication of Surya's Bataille biography, there ensued a major scholarly debate over Bataille's relationship to fascism. One of the reasons for this debate is the fact that, Surya, in the second edition of *Georges Bataille,* went to great lengths to dispel insinuations that the College de Sociologie and other groups had flirted with fascism. In retrospect, this debate may be considered one of the aftereffects of the "Vichy Syndrome" discussed by Henry Rousso. See, for example, Marina Galletti, "*Masses:* A Failed College?" *Stanford French Review* (Spring 1988), 49–63; Bernard Sichère, "Bataille et les Fascistes," *La Règle du jeu,* 8(3) (September 1992), 153–178; Marc Simard, "Intellectuels, fascisme et antimodernité dans la France des années trente," *Vingtième Siècle* 18 (April-June 1988), 55–75; Michael Richardson, "Sociology on a Razor's Edge: Configurations of the Sacred at the College of Sociology," *Theory, Culture and Society* 9(3) (August 1992), 27–44; see also Jean Jamin, "Un Sacré College ou les

Apprentis Sorciers de la Sociologie," *Cahiers internationaux de sociologie* LXVIII (January-June 1980), 5–30.

77. Hollier, ed., *The College of Sociology*, 216–217. For more on the *Ordensburgen*, see Heinz Höhne, *The Order of the Death's Head*, trans. R. Barry (New York: Penguin, 2000).

78. Roger Caillois, "Entretien avec Roger Caillois," *La Quinzaine littéraire* (June 16–30, 1970).

79. Ibid.

80. Bataille, *Oeuvres complètes*, vol. 3, 521.

81. Breton, *Manifestoes of Surrealism* (Ann Arbor: University of Michigan Press, 1969). For more on the mercurial relations between Bataille and Breton, see Lévy, *Les Aventures de la liberté*, 164–166.

82. Bataille, *Oeuvres complètes*, vol. II, 380, 381, 382 (emphasis added).

83. See Bernd Mattheus, *Georges Bataille: Eine Thanatographie* (Munich: Matthes und Seitz, 1984), vol. 1, 296. For a discussion of Jünger's ideas in relation to Drieu La Rochelle, see Julien Hervier, *Deux individus contre l'histoire: Pierre Drieu la Rochelle et Ernst Jünger* (Paris: Klincksieck, 1978). See also, Elliot Neaman, *A Dubious Past: Ernst Jünger and the Politics of Literature After Nazism* (Berkeley: University of California Press, 1999).

84. Stoekl, Introduction to *Visions of Excess*, xviii.

85. Henri Dubief, "Témoignage sur Contre-Attaque," in *Textures* no. 6 (1970), 56–57.

86. Bataille, *Oeuvres complètes*, vol. 1, 398.

87. Breton, *Manifestos of Surrealism*, 125.

88. For more on German developments, see George Mosse, *Germans and Jews: The Right, the Left and the Search for a "Third Force" in Pre-Nazi Germany* (New York: Howard Fertig, 1970).

89. Bataille's essay was composed in the aftermath of the events of February 1934. Following the revelations concerning the Stavisky affair there occurred: riots on the part of right-wing paramilitary organizations, retaliatory actions by communist groups, and a successful general strike on 12 February organized by the forces that would later coalesce to form the Popular Front. The upshot of the "events of February," as one might expect, was a tremendous loss of confidence in the Third Republic.

90. Bataille, "Le Fascisme français," in *Oeuvres complètes*, vol. 2, 212; emphasis added.

91. Lindenberg, *Les Années souterraines* (Paris: Editions de la Découverte, 1993), 64, 62.

92. Bataille, *Oeuvres complètes*, vol. 7, 461.

93. Needless to say, but not to be omitted, is the fact that not all who shared the aforementioned "ethos" were fascist or even flirted with fascism. To wit, this ethos was also espoused by many on the left, for example, those thinkers subsumed by Lukacs under the designation "romantic anticapitalism": Theodor Adorno, Walter Benjamin, Ernst Bloch, and Herbert Marcuse. For more on this concept, see Michael Löwy, *Georg Lukacs: From Romanticism to Bolshevism* (London: New Left Books, 1977).

94. Cited in Karl Dietrich Bracher, *The German Dictatorship* (Fort Worth: Holt, Rinehart, 1970), 10.

95. See Sternhell, *Anti-Semitism and the Right in France* (Jerusalem: Shahar Library: 1988).

96. Perhaps the foremost offender remains Georg Lukacs, *The Destruction of Reason* (London: Merlin Press, 1980).

97. Freud, *Group Psychology and the Analysis of the Ego* (New York: Norton, 1959), 10–11. Freud goes on to describe the group as a manifestation of collective neurosis, insofar as it forsakes the reality principle in favor of a life of fantasy: "In the mental operations of the group the function for testing the reality of things falls into the background in comparison with the strength of wishful impulses with their affective cathexis" (12). See also the important study by Wilhelm Reich, *Character Analysis,* trans. V. Carfagno (New York: Noonday, 1980).

98. See Horkheimer, "The Revolt of Nature," in *The Eclipse of Reason* (New York: Seabury, 1974), 92.

Notes to Chapter Five: Maurice Blanchot

1. See *The Foucault Reader,* ed. P. Rabinow (New York: Pantheon, 1984), where in his later writings Foucault explicitly has recourse to the Nietzschean trope of an "aesthetics of existence" to extricate his theory from the apparent normative cul-de-sac of a seemingly omnipotent "biopower."

2. See, for example, Jürgen Habermas, *The Philosophical Discourse of Modernity,* trans. F. Lawrence (Cambridge: MIT Press, 1987); Manfred Frank, *What is Neostructuralism?* trans. S. Wilke and R. Gray (Minneapolis: University of Minnesota Press, 1989).

3. Foucault, *Maurice Blanchot: The Thought from Outside,* trans. B. Massumi (Cambridge: Zone Books, 1990), 11.

4. See Michel Foucault's characterization of Blanchot: "So far has he withdrawn into the manifestation of his work, so completely is he, not

hidden by his texts, but absent from their existence and absent by virtue of the marvelous force of their existence, that for us he is that thought [from outside] itself" (ibid., 19). See also Pierre Mesnard, *Maurice Blanchot: Le Sujet de l'engagement* (Paris: L'Harmatton, 1996), 9, who cites the following observation as a common mischaracterization of Blanchot's career: "Novelist and critic, born in 1907, his life is entirely devoted to literature."

5. See Mehlman, "Blanchot at *Combat:* of Literature and Terror," in *Legacies of Anti-Semitism in France* (Minneapolis: University of Minnesota Press, 1983), 6–22; and "Pour Sainte-Beuve: Maurice Blanchot, 10 March 1942," in *Genealogies of the Text* (New York: Cambridge University Press, 1995).

6. Two recent French biographies of Blanchot have helped to set the record straight. See Christophe Bident, *Maurice Blanchot: partenaire invisible* (Paris: Champ Vallon, 1998); and Mesnard, *Maurice Blanchot: Le sujet de l'engagement.* For a discussion of Blanchot's political positions during the 1930s that reaches conclusions different from those of Bident and Mesnard, see Gerald Bruns, *Maurice Blanchot: The Refusal of Philosophy* (Baltimore: Johns Hopkins University Press, 1997). See also, Steven Ungar, *Scandal and Aftereffect: Blanchot and France Since 1930* (Minneapolis: University of Minnesota Press, 1995).

7. For a good account of their views, see Roger Soltau, *French Political Thought in the Nineteenth Century* (New York: Russell and Russell, 1959), 203–250.

8. Maurice Blanchot, "Quand l'Etat est revolutionnaire," *Le Rempart,* April 24, 1933 (emphasis added).

9. Serge Stavisky, a Jewish financier with purported connections to France's leading politicians, sold stock in a municipal pawn shop near Biarritz. When the scheme collapsed late in 1933, he allegedly took his own life in his Swiss hideaway, though rumors persisted that he was killed by police in order to silence him.

10. Philippe Burrin, *France Under the Germans: Collaboration and Compromise,* trans. J. Lloyd (New York: The New Press, 1996), 61.

11. Blanchot, cited in Bident, *Maurice Blanchot,* 77.

12. Blanchot, "La Fin du 6 Février, 1934," *Combat* 2, February 1936, 2.

13. On this group, see David Carroll, *French Literary Fascism: Nationalism, Anti-Semitism, and the Ideology of Culture* (Princeton: Princeton University Press, 1995). Surprisingly, the book contains no sustained treatment of Blanchot's work. Nevertheless, during the 1930s Blanchot wrote primarily as a political critic, and his contributions to the realm of literary criticism took a back seat.

14. Berl was a Jew who always insisted he felt more French than Jewish. In 1938, as the Munich crisis peaked, he recommended that France adopt a *Statut des Juifs*—legislation limiting Jewish influence on French life—two years in advance of Vichy. As Berl claimed, "The xenophobic movement that is taking shape in the country can be contained within just limits only if no one misjudges its incontestable depth. A stature for foreigners is necessary—without—delay—if we are to avoid grave and graver conflicts between French and foreigners." Berl, *Les Pavés de Paris,* 21(4), November 4, 1938.

15. *Ordre Nouveau, 3* (July 1933), 3. In general, French Nietzscheanism is an underresearched phenomenon. Although his influence on poststructuralists like Foucault, Derrida, and Lyotard is well known, his prewar reception among proponents of the Jeune Droite have received much less attention. For an important corrective the important study by Jacques Le Rider, *Nietzsche en France: de la fin du XIXe siècle au temps présent.* (Paris: Presses Universitaires de France, 1999).

16. Denis de Rougement, *Nouvelle Revue Française* (December 1932).

17. For a good discussion of integral nationalism, see William C. Buthman, *The Rise of Integral Nationalism in France* (New York: Columbia University Press, 1939).

18. See Julien Hervier, *Deux individus contre l'histoire: Pierre Drieu la Rochelle, Ernst Jünger* (Paris: Klinck Sieck, 1978).

19. Mesnard, *Maurice Blanchot,* 20.

20. Blanchot, *Le Rempart,* June 22, 1933.

21. The title of a contemporaneous work by the German conservative revolutionary sociologist Hans Freyer. For more on Freyer, see Muller, *The Other God that Failed.*

22. On the left's contentious relationship to democracy and parliamentarism, see Geoff Eley, *Forging Democracy: The History of the Left in Europe, 1850–2000* (New York: Oxford University Press, 2001).

23. Blanchot, *La Revue du Siècle,* 6 (June 1933).

24. Etienne de Montety, *Thierry Maulnier: Biographie* (Paris: Julliard, 1994) 126–136.

25. Mesnard, *Maurice Blanchot,* 32.

26. Sternhell, *Neither Right, Nor Left: Fascist Ideology in France,* trans. D. Maisel (Princeton: Princeton University Press, 1996), 223. For a discussion of the ideological orientation of Maulnier and *Combat* that stresses the centrality of "spiritual revolution," see Carroll, *French Literary Fascism: Nationalism,* 222–247.

27. See Blanchot's article in *Le Rempart*, April 28, 1936.

28. Blanchot, *L'Insurgé*, January 27, 1937 (emphasis added).

29. Céline, *L'Ecole des cadavres* (Paris, 1938), 264.

30. Michael Marrus and Robert Paxton, *Vichy France and the Jews* (Stanford: Stanford University Press, 1995), 39.

31. Blanchot, "Après le coup de force allemande," *Combat*, 1(4), April 3, 1936.

32. Blanchot, "Terrorisme comme méthode du salut publique," *Combat*, 1(7), July 7, 1936 (emphasis added).

33. Cited in Jean-Louis Loubet del Bayle, *Les Non-Conformistes des années trentes: Une tentative de renouvellement de la pensée Française* (Paris: Editions du Seuil, 1968), 406. Although Loubet del Bayle's analysis remains useful in many respects, one of its major drawbacks is that his narrative ends in 1934.

34. Girardet, *Tendances politiques dans la vie Française depuis 1789* (Paris: Hachette, 1960), 131.

35. Sternhell, *Neither Right, Nor Left*, xvii. See also, Paxton, *Vichy France: Old Guard, New Order* (New York: Columbia University Press, 1972), 165. For more on Uriage, see John Hellman, *The Knight Monks of Vichy France: Uriage, 1940–45* (Montreal: McGill-Queens University Press, 1997).

36. See W. D. Halls, *The Youth of Vichy French* (New York: Oxford University Press, 1981), 313.

37. Marc Fumaroli, *L'Etat culturel: une religion moderne* (Paris: Editions de Fallois, 1991), 94.

38. Lindenberg, *Les Années souterrains, 1937–1947* (Paris: La Découverte, 1990).

39. Mounier, *Esprit,* (November 1940), 10.

40. Marrus and Paxton, *Vichy France and the Jews,* 13. See also Serge and Beate Klarsfeld, *Vichy-Auschwitz: le role de Vichy dans la solution finale de la question juive dans France* (Paris: Fayard, 1983–85).

41. Fumaroli, *L'Etat culturel,* 95.

42. Ibid., 99, 100.

43. Loubet del Bayle, *Les Non-Conformistes des années trentes,* 411–412.

44. Mehlman, "Blanchot à Combat: Littérature et Terreur," *Tel Quel* 92 (Summer 1982); reprinted in Mehlman, *Legacies of Anti-Semitism in France* (Minneapolis: University of Minnesota Press, 1983). Blanchot's 1979 letter is reprinted in Appendix II, 107–109.

45. Jeffrey Mehlman, *Genealogies of the Text* (New York: Cambridge University Press, 1995), 174–194.

46. See Mehlman, *Legacies of Anti-Semitism in France,* Appendix II, 107–109.

47. Blanchot and Bataille became friends in the early 1940s; clearly, the relationship had a transformative impact upon Blanchot's conception of criticism. For a good account of their mutual influence, see Mesndard, *Maurice Blanchot,* 70–83.

48. Blanchot, *The Gaze of Orpheus* (Barrytown: Station Hill, 1981), 5 (emphasis added).

49. Michael Syrotinski, "How is Literature Possible," in *A New History of French Literature,* ed. D. Hollier (Cambridge: Harvard University Press, 1989), 957.

50. See Blanchot's testimony in *Le Nouvel Observateur,* January 22, 1988, 79: "Thanks to Emmanuel Levinas, without whom, as of 1927 or 1928, I would not have begun to understand *Being and Time,* the reading of this book provoked a veritable intellectual shock. It produced an encounter of originary grandeur; even today, it is impossible for me to minimize the effect, even in memory."

51. Martin Heidegger, "What is Metaphysics," in *Basic Writings,* ed. D. Krell (New York: Harper Row, 1977), 105.

52. Jean-Paul Sartre, *Nausea,* trans. L. Alexander (New York: New Directions, 1964), 129, 131.

53. Cited in Jean-Paul Sartre, *Oeuvres romanesques* (Paris: Gallimard, 1981), 1708.

54. Blanchot, "From Dread to Literature," 19. For deconstruction's well-known claim that understanding is predicated on misunderstanding, see Jonathan Culler, *On Deconstruction: Theory and Criticism after Structuralism* (Ithaca: Cornell University Press, 1982).

55. See, for example, Blanchot's Aesopian diatribe against Sartre's notion of writing qua "engagement" in "Literature and the Right to Death," 27: "An author who is writing specifically for a public is not really writing. . . . [W]orks created to be read are meaningless: no one reads them. This is why it is dangerous to write for other people, in order to evoke the speech of others and reveal them to themselves: the fact is that other people do not want to hear their own voices; they want to hear someone else's voice, a voice that is real, profound, troubling like the truth." A few pages later in the same essay, Blanchot tries to turn the idiom of *Being and Nothingness* against Sartrean engagement by accusing the philosopher of "bad faith."

56. Blanchot, "From Dread to Literature," 8 (emphasis added).

57. Blanchot, "Literature and the Right to Death," 29 (emphasis added).

58. Bataille, *Oeuvres complètes*, III (Paris: Gallimard, 1971), 521 (emphasis added).

59. Bataille, *Oeuvres complètes*, V, 355.

60. For Bataille's criticisms of Hegel, see "The Critique of the Foundations of the Hegelian Dialectic," in *Visions of Excess: Selected Writings, 1927–1939*, ed. A. Stoekl (Minneapolis: University of Minnesota Press, 1986), and *Inner Experience*, trans. L. A. Boldt (Albany: SUNY Press, 1988), 109–111.

61. Bataille, *Oeuvres complétes*, VI, 416: "From 1933 to 1939 I attended Kojève's course on the *Phenomenology of Spirit*—a brilliant explication of the book. How many times did [Raymond] Queneau and I leave the room feeling suffocated—suffocated, riveted. Kojève's course broke me, crushed me, killed me ten times."

See John Heckman, "Introduction," Jean Hyppolite, *The Genesis and Structure of Hegel's Phenomenology of Spirit*, trans. S. Cherniak and J. Heckman (Evanston: Northwestern University Press, 1974); Michael Roth, *Knowing and History: Appropriations of Hegel in Twentieth Century France* (Ithaca: Cornell University Press, 1988).

62. See Schelling, *Sämtliche SchriftenU*, I/10 (Stuttgart and Augsburg: Cotta, 1856–1861), 10–11: "The *sum* that is enclosed in the *cogito* does not, therefore, have the meaning of an unconditioned "I am," but rather only the meaning of an 'I am *in a particular way*,' namely, as thinking, as being in the mode that is called thinking. Therefore, the *Ergo sum* cannot imply: 'I am in an unconditional way,' but only: 'I am in a particular way.'"

63. Bataille, *Oeuvres complètes*, III, 495.

64. Bataille, *L'Erotisme* (Paris: Editions de Minuit, 1957) (emphasis added).

65. Foucault, Interview with Roger-Pol Droit, *Le Monde*, September 6, 1986.

66. Barthes, "To Write: An Intransitive Verb," in, *The Structuralist Controversy*, ed. R. Macksey (Baltimore: Johns Hopkins University Press, 1972), 134–154.

67. Here, the parallels with Paul de Man's case are striking. Following his activities as a journalist-collaborator in Nazi-occupied Belgium, later in life de Man, too, reached the proto-deconstructionist conclusion that "meaning" is inherently unreliable and unstable. See my discussion of the de Man affair in "Deconstuction at Auschwitz: de Man, Heidegger, and the New Revisionism," in *Labyrinths: Explorations in the Critical History of Ideas* (Amherst: University of Massachusetts Press, 1995), 210–230.

68. See, for example, Arnold Hauser, *The Social History of Art*, vol. 4 (New York: Routledge, 1989), 17: "Until 1848 the most important and the

major part of the works of art belong to the activistic, after 1848 to the quietistic school. Stendahl's disillusionment is still aggressive, extroverted, anarchistic, whereas Flaubert's acquiescence is passive, egocentric and nihilistic." While I agree with Hauser descriptively, I am more averse to attempts to adjudicate questions of aesthetic merit in terms of art's "social function"—an orientation that is probably the greatest drawback of Hauser's "social history" approach.

69. See, for example, Shoshana Felman and Dori Laub, *Testimony: The Crisis of Witnessing in Literature, Psychoanalysis, and History* (New York: Routledge, 1991), and Felman, *The Juridical Unconscious: Trials and Traumas in the Twentieth Century* (Cambridge: Harvard University Press, 2002). See also Dominick Lacapra, *Representing the Holocaust: History, Theory, and Trauma* (Ithaca: Cornell University Press, 1994).

Notes to Chapter Six: Down by Law

1. Thomas Nagel, *The Last Word* (New York: Oxford University Press, 1997), 15.

2. Jacques Derrida, *Of Grammatology,* trans. G. Spivak (Baltimore: Johns Hopkins University Press, 1976), 12.

3. As Jameson observes, "Deconstruction is not the only example—but it is a particularly striking one—of the reification of a principle that wished to remain purely formal, its translation back against its own wishes into a philosophical worldview or conceptual thematics it set out to avoid being in the first place." Jameson, "Marx's Purloined Letter," in *Ghostly Demarcations: A Symposium on Jacques Derrida's Specters of Marx,* ed. M. Sprinker (New York: Verso, 1999), 35.

For a devastating critique of the ethical and political pitfalls of deconstruction as a theory that fetishizes "undecidability"—and, hence, indecision—see Richard Bernstein, "Serious Play: The Ethico-Political Horizon of Deconstruction," in *The New Constellation: The Ethical-Political Horizons of Modernity/Postmodernity* (Cambridge: MIT Press, 1993), 172–198.

For the disappointing encounter between Derrida and Gadamer (which, in retrospect, one might characterize as a "dialogue of the deaf"), see *Dialogue and Deconstruction: The Derrida-Gadamer Encounter,* ed. D. Michelfeld and R. Palmer (Albany: SUNY Press, 1989).

4. Of course, all academic practices and methods require a measure of institutional success to persevere and prosper. In deconstruction's case, however, there appears to be a performative contradiction at issue:

although it stakes claims to a potential political radicalism that would transcend the placid confines of academe, in point of fact its discursive esotericism and linguistic hermeticism would seem to militate quite effectively against deconstruction's prospect of having an extra-curricular "effect."

5. See, for example, Jacques Derrida, *Positions,* trans. A. Bass (Chicago: University of Chicago Press, 1982).

6. Anselm Haverkamp, "Introduction," *Deconstruction is/in America* (New York: New York University Press, 1995), 7–8.

7. Jacques Derrida, *Specters of Marx: The State of the Debt, the Work of Mourning, and the New International,* trans. P. Kamuf (New York: Verso, 1996), 92.

8. Michael Sprinker, "Introduction," *Ghostly Demarcations,* 1.

9. Terry Eagleton, "Marxism without Marxism," ibid., 83–87.

10. Michèle Lamont, "How to Become a Dominant French Philosopher: The Case of Jacques Derrida," *American Journal of Sociology* 93 (3) (1987), 607.

11. See Jacques Derrida, *On Cosmopolitanism and Forgiveness* (New York: Routledge, 2001), and "Hostipality" [sic] in *Acts of Religion,* ed. G. Anidjar (New York: Routledge, 2002), 356–420. In his chapter on Derrida's politics in *The Reckless Mind* (New York: New York Review Books, 2001), Mark Lilla has pointed out the contradiction between deconstruction's epistemological radicalism and the new liberal humanitarian guise it has assumed during the 1990s.

12. See Jacques Derrida, "Structure, Sign, and Play in the Discourse of the Human Sciences," in *Writing and Difference,* trans. A. Bass (Chicago: University of Chicago Press, 1978), 292, where Derrida speaks positively of the virtues of "Nietzschean affirmation."

13. See Jürgen Habermas, "Natural Law and Revolution," in *Theory and Practice,* trans. J. Viertel (Boston: Beacon Press, 1973), 82–120. See also the important book by Ernst Bloch, *Natural Law and Human Dignity,* trans. D. Schmidt (Cambridge: MIT Press, 1986).

14. Hegel, *The Philosophy of History,* trans. J. Sibree (New York: Dover Publications, 1956), 446.

15. See Andrew Arato, *Civil Society, Constitution, and Legitimacy* (Lanham, Maryland: Rowman and Littlefield, 2000); Ernest Gellner, *Conditions of Liberty: Civil Society and Its Rivals* (London: Hammish Hamilton, 1994); Ralf Dahrendorf, *Reflections on the Revolutions in Europe: In a Letter Intended to Be Sent to a Gentleman in Warsaw* (New York: Times Publishing, 1990).

16. Jacques Derrida, "The Ends of Man," *Margins of Philosophy,* trans. A. Bass (Chicago: University of Chicago Press, 1982), 115.

17. Epistémon (Didier Anzieu), *Ces Idées qui ont ébranlé la France* (Paris: Fayard, 1968), 83, 31 (emphasis added).

18. Dosse, *History of Structuralism* I, trans. D. Silverman (Minneapolis: University of Minnesota Press, 1967), 112–121.

19. Roger Crémont (Clément Rosset), *Les Matinées structuralistes* (Paris: Laffont, 1969), 32. For more on Derrida's (non) relation to the events of May '68, see Kristin Ross, *May '68 and Its Afterlives* (Chicago: University of Chicago Press, 2002).

20. Lamont, "How to Become a Dominant French Philosopher," 604.

21. As Derrida observed in a January 31, 1982 interview with Christian Descamps in *Le Monde:* "My first desire tended surely toward the point where the literary event traversed and even went beyond philosophy."

22. Jacques Derrida, *Memories for Paul de Man* (New York: Columbia University Press, 1986), 18.

23. See, for example, *Deconstruction is/in America,* cited in this chapter, note 6.

24. Derrida, *Of Grammatology,* 158.

25. Jacques Derrida, *Glas,* trans. J. Leavey (Lincoln: University of Nebraska Press, 1986); see also Richard Rorty's reflections on these questions in *Philosophical Papers,* vol. II, *Essays on Heidegger and Others* (New York: Cambridge University Press, 1990), 85–129.

26. Foucault, "My Body, This Paper, This Fire," *Oxford Literary Review* 4 (1979), 27 (emphasis added). See also, Jean-Philippe Mathy, *French Resistance: The French-American Culture Wars* (Minneapolis: University of Minnesota Press, 2000), 44:

> One of the most damaging criticisms from the Left presented post-structuralist theory as a sophisticated version of the traditional *commentaire de texte*—a brilliant example of continuity within change and a means of rejuvenating classical academic studies of canonical texts. After all, the French critics applied their interpretive skills to the consecrated authors of the national and continental traditions, seldom, if ever, dealing with nonwhite, non-European, or female writers, let alone with popular culture: Derrida deconstructed Valéry, Nietzsche, or Lévi-Strauss; de Man wrote on Proust, Rousseau, and the Romantics; and Barbara Johnson's early studies focused on Baudelaire and Mallarmé.

27. Edward Said, *The World, the Text, and the Critic* (Cambridge: Harvard University Press, 1983), 203, 204, 207.

28. See, for example, Russell Berman, "Troping To Pretoria: The Rise and Fall of Deconstruction," *Telos* 85 (1990), 4–16.

29. Cited in *Les Fins de l'homme: à partir du travail de Jacques Derrida* (Paris: Editions Galilée, 1981), 514.

30. See Jonathan Culler, *On Deconstruction* (Ithaca: Cornell University Press, 1983).

31. I have attempted to raise some of these questions in "Note on a Missing Text," *The Heidegger Controversy: A Critical Reader* (Cambridge: MIT Press, 1993) ix–xviii.

32. Jacques Derrida, "The Force of Law: The 'Mystical Foundation of Authority,'" in *Deconstruction and the Possibility of Justice,* ed. D. Cornell et al. (New York: Routledge, 1992). 7. For some critical observations on the translation and dissemination of Derrida's work, see Reed Way Dasenbrock, "Reading Demanians Reading de Man," *South Central Review* 11(1) (Spring 1994), 23–43; Dasenbrock, "Taking It Personally: Reading Derrida's Responses," *College English,* 56(3) (March 1994), 261–279. See also the excellent discussion in Ingrid Harris, "L'affaire Derrida: Business or Pleasure?" *Philosophy and Social Criticism* 19(3–4) (1994), 216–242.

For a work that argues for the importance of deconstruction as an ethical theory, see Simon Critchley, *The Ethics of Deconstruction: Derrida and Levinas* (Oxford: Blackwell, 1992).

33. Richard Kearney, "Deconstruction and the Other," in *Dialogues with Contemporary Thinkers* (Manchester, UK: Manchester University Press, 1984), 124, 125.

34. Derrida, "The Force of Law," 15, 21, 25.

35. Jacques Derrida, "Remarks on Deconstruction and Pragmatism," in Critchley et al., *Deconstruction and Pragmatism* (New York: Routledge, 1996), 85. Stephen K. White, *Political Theory and Postmodernism* (Cambridge: Cambridge University Press, 1991), 116: "Derrida, as usual, makes his point as provocatively as possible. But, after the effect wears off, one is left with a rather simple bipolar world: deconstructionists and other postmodernists who struggle for justice, and traditional ethical and political theorists who are the ideologues of unjust orders."

36. For a good discussion of the problems in Derrida, as they relate to the work of Bataille, see Jean-Michel Besnier, *La Politique de l'impossible* (Paris: La Découverte, 1988).

37. White, *Political Theory and Postmodernism,* 82. For a more sympathetic interpretation of Derrida's ethico-political demarche, one that argues that deconstruction offers a valuable space for political reflection that is otherwise lacking in political business-as-usual, see John McCormick, "Derrida

on Law; Or, Poststructuralism Gets Serious," *Political Theory* 29(3) (June 2001), 395–423.

38. Sigmund Freud, *Civilization and Its Discontents,* trans. J. Strachey (New York: Norton, 1962), 56–57.

39. Derrida, "The Force of Law," 17 (emphasis added).

40. Ronald Dworkin, "Civil Disobedience," in *Taking Rights Seriously* (Cambridge: Harvard University Press, 1978).

41. Derrida, "Force of Law," 26.

42. As Derrida (ibid., 22) remarks: "Levinas speaks of an infinite right: in what he calls 'Jewish humanism,' whose basis is not 'the concept of man,' but rather the other; 'the extent of the right of the other' is a practically infinite right'.... Here equity is not equality, calculated proportion, equitable distribution or distributive justice but rather absolute dissymetry."

43. Ibid., 27 (emphasis added).

44. See *The Complete Essays of Montaigne,* trans. D. Frame (Stanford: Standford University Press, 1948), 821.

45. Ibid., 14.

46. Ibid., 25,

47. Carl Schmitt, *Political Theology,* trans. G. Schwab (Cambridge: MIT Press, 1985), 15 (emphasis added).

48. Adorno, *Kierkegaard: The Construction of the Aesthetic,* trans. R. Hullot-Kentor (Minneapolis: University of Minnesota Press, 1989).

49. See, for example, Schmitt's *Die Diktatur* (Munich and Leipzig: Duncker und Humblot, 1921).

50. On this point, see his preface to the second edition of *The Crisis of Parliamentary Democracy,* trans. E. Kennedy (Cambridge: MIT Press, 1985), 1–17. For an excellent critique of Schmitt's doctrines, see William Scheuerman, *Between the Norm and the Exception: The Frankfurt School and the Rule of Law* (Cambridge: MIT Press, 1994).

51. "Interrogation of Carl Schmitt by Robert Kempner, 1-III," *Telos* 72 (1987), 97–129.

52. Derrida, "The Force of Law," 30.

53. Schmitt, *The Crisis of Parliamentary Democracy,* 75–76.

54. Schmitt, *Political Theology,* 12.

55. Ibid., 31–32.

56. Ibid., 36.

57. Max Weber, "The Parliament and Government of Germany under a New Regime," in *Political Writings* (Cambridge: Cambridge University Press, 1994), 148–49 (translation altered).

58. Weber, "Politics as a Vocation," in *Political Writings,* 310–311.

59. See, for example, the contemporaneous "Theological-Political Fragment," *Reflections* (New York: Harcourt Brace, 1978), 312–313.

60. Benjamin, "Critique of Violence," in *Reflections,* ed. P. Demetz (New York: Harcourt Brace, 1978), 297–300, and, "Zur Kritik der Gewalt," *Gesammelte Schriften* II (1), ed. R. Tiedemann (Frankfurt: Suhrkamp, 1977), 199–203. In the essay in question, Benjamin employs the term "critique" in the Kantian sense of establishing limits or "conditions of possibility."

61. For the best discussion of Sorel's ties to Mussolini, see Zeev Sternhell, *The Birth of Fascist Ideology* (Princeton: Princeton University Press, 1993).

62. Benjamin, "Critique of Force," 292, and "Zur Kritik der Gewalt," 194.

63. Derrida, "The Force of Law," 35. See the earlier text, "Declarations of Independence," *New Political Science* 15 (1986), 7–15, where Derrida sets forth similar arguments concerning acts of revolutionary founding as ex nihilo or groundless.

64. Derrida, "Force of Law," 35.

65. Ibid (emphasis added).

66. Ibid., 37, 37–38.

67. Jacques Derrida, *Acts of Religion* (New York: Routledge, 2001).

68. On this theme, see Gershom Scholem's classic study, *Sabbatai Sevi: The Mystical Messiah* (Princeton: Princeton University Press, 1976). For two articles that expose the problem of Messianic politics in Derrida's work, see Robert Bernasconi, "Different Styles of Eschatology: Derrida's Take on Levinas' Political Messianism," *Research in Phenomenology* (28) (1998), 3–17, and Mustapha Marrouchi, "Decolonizing the Terrain of Western Theoretical Productions," *College Literature,* 24 (2) (June 1997), 1–29. In *Derrida and the Political* (New York: Routledge, 1996), 156, Richard Beardsworth expresses the concern that Derrida's flirtation with political Messianism threatens to split deconstruction into two camps, right-wing and left-wing. According to Beardsworth, right-wing Derrideanism "would mobilize religious discourse and prioritize, for example, the radically 'passive' nature of the arts, following up on more recent work of Derrida on the absolute originarity of the promise and of his reorganization of religious discourse to think and describe it."

69. For the best account of the conservative revolutionaries in English, see Jeffrey Herf, *Reactionary Modernism: Technology, Culture and Politics in Weimar and the Third Reich* (New York: Cambridge University Press, 1984).

70. Cited in *The Heidegger Controversy: A Critical Reader,* ed. Richard Wolin (Cambridge: MIT Press, 1993), 47.

71. I have tried to chronicle these in my book, *The Politics of Being: The Political Thought of Martin Heidegger* (New York: Columbia University Press, 1990). I discuss Heidegger's ties to Schmitt and Jünger in chapter 2, "*Being and Time* as Political Philosophy." See also, Anson Rabinbach, "Heidegger's Letter on Humanisms as Text and Event," *New German Critique* 62 (Spring-Summer 1994), 3–38.

72. For a review of these developments, see Luc Ferry and Alain Renaut, *French Philosophy of the Sixties: An Essay on Antihumanism,* trans. M. Cattani (Amherst: University of Massachusetts Press, 1990). Also worth mentioning in connection with doctrines of left Heideggerianism are the works of Kostas Axelos, who in books such as *Horizons du monde* (Paris: Minuit, 1971), was one of the first thinkers on the French Left to attempt to fuse the doctrines of Heidegger and Marx.

73. Jean-Paul Sartre, *The Search for a Method,* trans. Hazel Barnes (New York: Vintage, 1963), 30 (translation altered).

74. Derrida, *Specters of Marx,* 13. A shortened version of Derrida's text appeared in *New Left Review* 205 (May-June 1994), 31–58.

75. For a convincing argument to this effect, see Geoff Eley, *Forging Democracy: The History of the Left in Europe* (New York: Oxford University Press, 2002).

76. See for example, J. Cohen and A. Arato, *Civil Society and Democratic Theory* (Cambridge: MIT Press, 1992). The literature on this theme has, of late, become enormous. For an attempt at synthesis, see Ernest Gellner, *Conditions of Liberty: Civil Society and Its Rivals.*

77. Derrida, *Specters of Marx,* 75.

78. Aijaz Ahmad, "Reconciling Derrida: 'Specters of Marx' and Deconstructive Politics," *New Left Review* (November-December 1994), 102.

79. Martin Heidegger, "Only a God Can Save Us," in *The Heidegger Controversy,* 107.

80. See *Derrida and Negative Theology,* ed. H. Coward and T. Foshay (Albany: SUNY Press, 1992).

81. Derrida, *Specters of Marx,* 15.

82. Derrida, "The Principle of Reason," *Diacritics* XIX (1983), 8.

83. Justin Barton, "Phantom Saviours, Phantom States," *Radical Philosophy* 65 (Autumn 1993), 63.

84. Derrida, *Specters of Marx,* 37, 51.

85. Ibid., 52–53.

86. Ibid., 54.

87. Ibid., 55.

88. Derrida, "Racism's Last Word," *Critical Inquiry* 12(1) (Autumn 1985), 290–299.

89. For more on Gobineau and Chamberlain, see this book's conclusion; see also George M. Fredrickson, *Racism: A Short History* (Princeton: Princeton University Press, 2001).

90. See Derrida, "Philosopher's Hell," in *The Heidegger Controversy*, 164–173.

91. Alain Renaut, quoted in Dosse, *History of Structuralism* I, 271. For a contemporary report of the events surrounding Derrida's arrest, see "Le philosophe Jacques Derrida serait détenu pour 'trafic de drogue,'" *Le Monde*, January 1, 1982, 1.

Notes to Political Excursus II: Designer Fascism

1. Singer, "France's Rival Fuhrers," *The Nation*, February 15, 1999, 6. See also Janice Valls-Russell, "Political Bickering in France," *The New Leader*, February 8, 1999 8.

2. For more on this point, see Roger Eatwell, "Why are Fascism and Racism Reviving in Western Europe?" *The Political Quarterly* 65(3) (July-September 1994), 323–325. See also, Robert O. Paxton, "Fascismes d'hier et d'aujourd'hui," *Le Monde*, June 17, 1994; and Roger Griffin, *The Nature of Fascism* (New York: Routledge, 1993), 161–169.

3. Stanley Payne, *A History of Fascism: 1914–1945* (Madison: University of Wisconsin Press, 1995), 511. In light of the political events of September 11, 2001, it is of interest to note Payne's observation (517), "There will probably never again be a reproduction of the Third Reich, but Saddam Hussein has come closer than any other dictator since 1945."

4. See Paul Hockenos, "Jörg Haider: Austria's Far Right Wunderkind," *World Policy Journal* (Fall 1995), 75.

5. Alain de Benoist, cited in Pierre Milza, *Facisme français: Passé et Présent* (Paris: Flammarion, 1987), 376. See also A.-M. Duranton-Crabol, *Visages de la Nouvelle Droite: La GRECE et son histoire* (Paris, 1988).

6. Geoffrey Harris, *The Dark Side of Europe* (Edinburgh: Edinburgh University Press, 1994), 15.

7. Cited in *The Economist*, October 15, 1994, 68.

8. Quoted in *The Independent* (London), October 11, 1994.

9. I have examined the events surrounding Fini's rise to power in "Mussolini's Ghost," *Tikkun* (June-July 1994), 11–16.

10. For an analysis of the pan-European dimensions of the new European right, see Mark Wegierski, "The New Right in Europe," *Telos* 98–99 (Winter 1993–Spring 1994), 55–70.

11. Pierre-André Taguieff, *Sur la Nouvelle droite* (Paris: Descartes & cie, 1994), 18. For more on GRECE, see 14–24; Ian R. Barnes, "The Pedigree of GRECE—Part II" in *Patterns of Prejudice* 15 (1980), 29–39.

12. For a good discussion of Evola's doctrines in relation to Benoist, see Thomas Sheehan, "Myth and Violence: The Fascism of Julius Evola and Alain de Benoist," *Social Research* (Spring 1981), 45–73.

13. Jim Wolfreys, "An Iron Hand in a Velvet Glove: The Programme of the French National Front," *Parliamentary Affairs* 46(3) (July 1993), 415. As another commentator (Geoffrey Harris, *The Dark Side of Europe: The Extreme Right Today* [Edinburgh: Edinburgh University Press, 1994], 89,) has remarked: "It is clear that Le Pen . . . has been strengthened by the work of the intellectuals of the *Nouvelle droite,* whose conscious aim has been to make the ideas of the extreme right dominant in French political life."

14. See Alain de Benoist, *Comment peut-on être paien?* (Paris: Albin Michel, 1981).

15. For Benoist's third worldism, see *Europe, Tiers Monde: Meme Combat* (Paris: R. Laffont, 1986).

16. This figure is given by Wolfreys, "The Iron Hand in the Velvet Glove," 417. One of the Nouvelle Droite's earliest supporters was ex-Vichyite and author of *Qu'est-ce que le fascisme* (1961) Maurice Bardèche. See his article, "Les Silences de la *Nouvelle droite,*" *Défense de l'Occident* (December 1979), 19. For a fascinating interview with Bardèche, see Alice Kaplan, *Reproductions of Banality* (Minneapolis: University of Minnesota, 1985), 161–192. Bardèche was the brother-in-law of fascist scribe Robert Brasillach, who was executed after the war for "intellectual collaboration."

For a good discussion of the at times tense relationship between the Nouvelle droite and the mainstream French right, see Pierre Milza, *Fascisme français: passé et présent, 373–375.

17. On this point see the standard work by Henry Rousso, *The Vichy Syndrome* (Cambridge: Harvard University Press, 1991).

18. D. S. Bell, "The French National Front," *History of European Ideas,* 18(2), 228.

19. For an excellent analysis of this phenomenon, see Pierre-André Taguieff, "De la race à la culture," *Sur la Nouvelle droite,* 7–106. See also, Taguieff, "The New Cultural Racism in France," *Telos* 83 (Spring 1990), 109–123. Taguieff is undoubtedly the leading political analyst of the

French Nouvelle Droite. For the best introduction to the ideas of the French New Right in English, see the double issue of the journal *Telos* 98-99 (Winter 1993–Spring 1994), "The French New Right: New Right, New Left, New Paradigm?" One of the focal points of the issue is Benoist's alleged "left turn" during the 1980s, as well as the collaboration between prominent figures on the French left (e.g., Jean Baudrillard) with the Nouvelle droite in its new, academically respectable guise, as embodied by the journal *Krisis* (founded by Benoist in 1988). See also Taguieff's earlier book, *The Force of Prejudice*, trans. H. Melehy (Minneapolis: University of Minnesota Press, 2001).

20. Robert de Herte [Alain de Benoist], "Avec les immigrés contre le nouvel esclavage," *Eléments pour la civilisation européene*, no. 45 (Spring 1983), 2.

21. Jean-Marie Le Pen, "Le Pen et L'Eglise" (interview), *National Hebdo*, 19 (44) (April 1985), 15.

22. For Foucault's writings on Iran, see "Iran: The Spirit of a World Without Spirit," in *Foucault: Politics, Philosophy and Culture* (New York: Routledge, 1988).

23. Wolfreys, "An Iron Hand in a Velvet Glove," 424.

24. Christopher Flood, "Organizing Fear and Indignation: The Front National in French Politics," in *Fascism's Return: Scandal, Revision, and Ideology Since 1980*, ed. R. Golsan (Lincoln: University of Nebraska Press, 1998), 20–21.

25. Joseph de Maistre, *Considerations on the French Revolution*, trans. R. Lebrun (Montreal: McGill-Queens University Press, 1974), 97.

26. Cited in M. Vaughan, "The Extreme Right in France: 'Lepénisme' or the Politics of Fear," in *Neo-Fascism in Europe*, ed. Luciano Cheles et al. (London and New York: Longman, 1991), 221.

27. For more on Barrès, see Zeev Sternhell, *Maurice Barrès et le nationalisme français* (Bruxelles: Editions Complexe, 1985); see also, Michel Winock, *Nationalisme, antisémitisme et fascisme en France* (Paris: Editions du Seuil, 1990).

28. Cited in Winock, *Nationalisme, antisémitisme et fascisme en France*, 44. See also Paul Massing, *Rehearsal for Destruction* (New York: Harper and Bros., 1949).

29. On Holocaust denial in France, see Pierre Vidal-Naquet, *The Assassins of Memory*, trans. J. Mehlman (New York: Columbia University Press, 1992).

30. Jonathan Marcus, *The National Front and French Politics* (New York: New York University Press, 1995), 171.

31. See *Encounters with the Contemporary Radical Right,* ed. P. Merkl and L. Weinberg (Boulder: Westview, 1993), 226.

32. Emmanuel Faux, Thomas Legrand, and Gilles Perez, *La Main Droite de dieu* (Paris: Le Seuil, 1994).

33. Evidence presented to the EP Committee of Inquiry, Annexe G. Cited in G. Harris, *The Dark Side of Europe,* 68.

34. Lipset, *Political Man* (Baltimore: Johns Hopkins, 1981), 489. Also see Thomas Childer's important study, *The Nazi Voter* (Chapel Hill: University of North Carolina Press, 1983).

35. Hans-Georg Betz, *Radical Right-Wing Populism in Western Europe* (New York: St. Martin's, 1994). For one of the best recent characterizations of the new postindustrial condition, see Ulrich Beck, *The Risk Society* (Newbury Park: SAGE, 1992).

36. Flood, "Organizing Fear and Indignation," 25.

37. See Richard Sennett, *The Corrosion of Character: The Personal Consequences of Work in the New Capitalism* (New York: Norton, 1998).

38. J. Hage and C. H. Powers, *Postindustrial Lives: Roles and Relationships in the 21st Century* (Newbury Park: SAGE, 1992), 41.

39. Betz, *Radical Right-Wing Populism,* 177.

Notes to Conclusion: "Site of Catastrophe"

1. Cornelius de Pauw, *Recherches philosophiques sur les Américains: Mémoires intéressants pour servir à l'histoire de l'espèce humaine,* 3 vols. (1770; reprint, Upper Saddle, N.J.: Gregg Press, 1968), 12, 7; cited in James Ceaser, *Reconstructing America: The Symbol of America in Modern Thought* (New Haven: Yale University Press, 1997), 24.

2. Buffon, *Histoire naturelle* (Paris: Imprimerie Royale, 1749–61).

3. De Pauw, *Recherches* I, 26.

4. Durand Echeverria, *Mirage in the West: A History of the French Image of American Society to 1815* (Princeton: Princeton University Press, 1957), 10.

5. De Pauw, *Recherches,* vol. 3, 10.

6. *Federalist,* 11.

7. Ceaser, *Reconstructing America,* 40.

8. George M. Fredrickson, *Racism: A Short History* (Princeton: Princeton University Press, 2001).

9. Alan Riding, "Only the French Elite Scorn Mickey's Debut," *New York Times,* April 13, 1992, A1, A13.

10. Cited in Massimo Boffa, "Maistre," *The Critical Dictionary of the French Revolution* (Cambridge: Harvard University Press, 1990), 966.

11. Ibid., 969.

12. See Schmitt, *Political Theology,* trans. G. Schwab (Cambridge: MIT Press, 1987).

13. Maistre, *Oeuvres complètes* (Geneva: Slatkine, 1979), vol. 1, 87; Maistre, *Considerations on France,* trans. R. Lebrun (Montreal: McGill-Queens University Press, 1974), 108.

14. Ibid., 109.

15. Ibid., 97.

16. For a discussion of Vico's employment of *sensus communis,* see Hans-Georg Gadamer, *Truth and Method* (New York, Seabury, 1975), 19–29; for a discussion of the relationship between the *sensus communis* and the "public opinion," see Jürgen Habermas, *Structural Transformation of the Public Sphere,* trans. F. Lawrence (Cambridge: MIT Press, 1989), 89–101.

In *The Critique of Pure Reason,* trans. N. K. Smith (London: MacMillan, 1929), A 738, B 766, Immanuel Kant offers an important clarification of the relationship between "reason" and "criticism."

"Reason must in all its undertaking subject itself to criticism; should it limit freedom of criticism by any prohibitions, it must harm itself, drawing upon itself a damaging suspicion. Nothing is so important through its usefulness, nothing so sacred, that it may be exempted from the searching examination, which knows no respect for persons. Reason depends on this freedom for its very existence. For reason has no dictatorial authority; its verdict is always simply the agreement of free citizens, of whom each one must be permitted to express, without intolerance, his objections or even his veto."

17. Berlin, *The Crooked Timber of Humanity* (New York: Vintage, 1992), 127. See also, Stephen Holmes, "Maistre and the Antiliberal Tradition," in *The Anatomy of Antiliberalism* (Cambridge: Harvard University Press, 1993), 13–36.

18. Gobineau, *Essai sur l'inégalité des races humaines,* ed. H. Juin (Paris: Pierre Belfond, 1967), 869. For a partial English translation, see Gobineau, *Selected Political Writings,* ed. Michael Biddiss (New York: Harper and Row, 1970). See also, Biddiss, *Father of Racist Ideology: The Political and Social Thought of Count Gobineau* (New York: Weybright and Talley, 1970).

19. Cited in Hermann Rauschning, *The Voice of Destruction* (New York: Putnam, 1940), 229.

20. Melvin Richter, "A Debate on Race: The Tocqueville-Gobineau Correspondence," *Commentary*, 160; see also Hannah Arendt, *The Origins of Totalitarianism* (New York: Meridian, 1958), 171: "Nobody before Gobineau thought of finding one single reason, one single force according to which civilization always and everywhere rise and falls."

21. As Spengler remarked in *The Year of Decision* (New York: Knopf, 1934), 70: "Quite apart from the Negroes, the immigrants during the twenty years before the War included—with only a small proportion of Germans, Czechs, Balkan Slavs, Eastern Jews, Greeks, inhabitants of Asia Minor, Spaniards, and Italians." For more on Spengler's racial views, see Ceaser, *Reconstructing America*, 120ff.

22. Cited in Rauschning, *Voice of Destruction*, 69.

23. Richter, "A Debate on Race," 154.

24. Ibid., 155.

25. Ibid., 156.

26. Stern, *The Politics of Cultural Despair: A Study in the Rise of Germanic Ideology* (Berkeley: University of California Press, 1961), 131.

27. Nietzsche, *The Gay Science*, trans. W. Kaufmann (New York: Vintage, 1974), 258–259, 303.

28. Cited in Ceaser, *Reconstructing America*, 174.

29. Spengler, *Man and Technics* (London: Allen and Unwin, 1932), 93–94.

30. Ibid., 94–95, 103.

31. Spengler, *Year of Decision*, 100; Ceaser, *Reconstructing America*, 179.

32. Spengler, *Year of Decision*, 68.

33. Ceaser, *Reconstructing America*, 187.

34. Martin Heidegger, *Introduction to Metaphysics* (New Haven: Yale University Press, 1959), 37.

35. Martin Heidegger, *Hölderlins Hymne 'Der Ister,'* Gesamtausgabe 58 (Frankfurt: Klostermann Verlag, 1985), 86. In *America*, trans. C. Turner (London: Verso, 1989), 7, Baudrillard uses the same exact phrase to describe the American "culture of speed." "Speed is not a vegetal thing. It is nearer to the mineral, to refraction through a crystal, and it is already the site of a catastrophe, of a squandering of time."

36. Martin Heidegger, *Heraklit*, GS 55 (Frankfurt: Klostermann Verlag, 1987), 123.

37. See, for example, the essay, "Creative Landscape: Why Do I Remain in the Provinces?" in the *Weimar Sourcebook*, ed. E. Dimendberg et al. (Berkeley: University of California, 1994), 426–428.

38. Cited in Günter Moltmann, "Deutscher Antiamerikanisumus heute und früher," in *Vom Sinn der Geschichte,* ed. Otmar Franz (Stuttgart: Seewald, 1976), 94.

39. *The Complete Poems of Heinrich Heine: A Modern English Version,* trans. Hal Draper (Boston: Suhrkamp, 1982), 633.

40. Heine, *The Romantic School and Other Essays,* ed. J. Hermand and R. Holub (New York: Continuum, 1985), 263.

41. See Klaus Schwabe, "Anti-Americanism within the German Right, 1917–1933," in *Amerikastudien* 21 (1) (1976), 97.

42. Sombart, *Die Juden und das Wirtschaftsleben* (Munich and Leipzig, 1918), xiii (emphasis added).

43. Céline, *Bagatelles pour un massacre* (Paris: Denoel, 1937). For a discussion of Céline's anti-Semitism, see David Carroll, *French Literary Fascism: Nationalism, Anti-Semitism, and the Ideology of Culture* (Princeton: Princeton University Press, 1995), 171–195.

44. For two good discussions of the systematic role that anti-Americanism and anti-Semitism play in Heidegger's thought, see Michael Ermarth, "Heidegger on Americanism: *Ruinanz* and the End of Modernity," *Modernism/Modernity* 7 (3) (2000), 379–400; and Heinz Kittsteiner, "Heidegger's Amerika als Ursprungsort der Weltverdüsterung," *Deutsche Zeitschrift für Philosophie* 45 (1997), 599–617.

45. See Ulrich Sieg, "Die Verjudung des deutschen Geistes: Ein unbekannter Brief Heideggers," *Die Zeit* 52, December 29, 1989, 19.

46. Victor Farias, *Heidegger et le nazisme* (Lagrasse: Editions Verdier, 1987), 235; see also Thomas Sheehan, "Heidegger and the Nazis," *New York Review of Books,* June 15, 1988, 40.

47. Heidegger, "The Word of Nietzsche: 'God is Dead,'" in *The Question Concerning Technology and Other Essays,* trans. W. Lovitt (New York: Harper and Row, 1977), 112.

See Stephen Holmes, *The Anatomy of Antiliberalism,* xi: "Why would some of America's leading intellects revile a tradition devoted, among other things, to freedom of thought? A generation ago, Martin Heidegger's subterranean but hypnotic influence prepared the way for this odd development. His harsh indictment of 'modernity' was adapted to the mental horizon of their new American audience by Hannah Arendt and Leo Strauss."

I have discussed some of these filiations in "Antihumanism in the Discourse of French Postwar Theory," in *Labyrinths: Explorations in the Critical History of Ideas* (Amherst: University of Massachusetts Press, 1995), 175–210.

48. Theodor Adorno, "The Fetish Character of Music and the Regression of Listening," in *The Essential Frankfurt School Reader,* ed. A. Arato and E. Gebhardt (Oxford: Blackwell, 1978), 278, 276.

49. Jean Baudrillard, "Simulacra and Simulations," in *Selected Writings,* ed. M. Poster (Stanford: Stanford University Press, 1988), 167 (emphasis added).

50. Baudrillard, *America,* (London: Verso, 1996), 7.

51. Ibid., 97–98.

52. Ibid., 79.

53. Jean Baudrillard, *The Illusion of the End,* trans. C. Turner (Stanford: Stanford University Press, 1994), 64; *The Gulf War Did Not Take Place,* trans. P. Patton (Bloomington: Indiana University Press, 1995).

54. Jean Baudrillard, "Game with Vestiges," in *On the Beach* 5 (Winter 1984), 24.

55. In *Posthistoire: Has History Come to an End?* trans. P. Camiller (New York: Verso, 1996), Lutz Niethammer also makes a strong case for the coalescence of reactionary and postmodern thought. Both intellectual currents, argues Niethammer, damn progressive historical change by relying on the "end of history" thesis.

56. Baudrillard, *America,* 34.

57. Ceaser, *Reconstructing America,* 236.

58. Jean Baudrillard, *Simulations* (New York: Autonomedia, 1984), 25.

59. Christoper Norris, *Uncritical Theory: Postmodernism, Intellectuals, and the Gulf War* (Amherst: University of Massachusetts Press, 1994), 27, 29. For some similar criticisms, see Steven Best and Douglas Kellner, *The Postmodern Turn* (New York: Guilford, 1997), 79–123.

60. See Jean Baudrillard, *Revenge of the Crystal* (London: Pluto Press, 1990).

61. See Albert O. Hirschman, *The Rhetoric of Reaction: Perversity, Futility, Jeopardy* (Cambridge: Harvard University Press, 1991). For a discussion of the "futility thesis"—the view that "the attempt at change is abortive, that in one way or another any alleged change is, was, or will be largely surface, façade, cosmetic, hence illusory, as the 'deep' structures of society remain wholly untouched"—see especially 43–80. For an informative discussion of the affinities between the German young conservatives and postmodernism—two camps whose approaches intersect in the ideology of *posthistoire* or the "end of history"—see Niethammer, *Posthistoire.*

62. Jean Baudrillard, "L'Esprit du terrorisme," *Le Monde,* November 3, 2001. For the English version of Baudrillard's article, see *The Spirit of Ter-*

rorism and Requiem for the Twin Towers, trans. C. Turner (London: Verso, 2002).

63. Zizek, *Welcome to the Desert of the Real: Five Essays on September 11 and Related Dates* (London: Verso, 2002).

64. This point constitutes an important guideline for two recent French studies of anti-Americanism: Jean-François Revel, *L'Obsession anti-américaine* (Paris: Plon, 2002), and Philippe Roger, *L'Ennemi américain* (Paris: Editions du Seuil, 2002). Revel's book possesses a more contemporary, journalistic focus, whereas Roger's study is more historically oriented.

65. Cited in Ceaser, *Reconstructing America,* 67.

66. See Antonio Gramsci, *Prison Notebooks* (New York: International Publishers, 1971).

67. Cited in Martin Jay, *The Dialectical Imagination* (Boston: Little and Brown, 1973), 173.

68. See Jean-Philippe Mathy, *French Resistance: The French American Culture Wars* (Minneapolis: University of Minnesota Press, 2000), especially chapter 2, "The French Revolution at Two Hundred: The Bicentennial and the Return of Rights-Liberalism," 57–85.

69. See Samuel Huntington, *The Third Wave: Democratization in the Late Twentieth Century* (Norman: University of Oklahoma Press, 1993).

70. See the discussion of this theme in chapter 6, "Down By Law: Deconstruction and the Problem of Justice."

71. On this subject, see the convincing documentary evidence compiled by Lynn Hunt in *The French Revolution and the Birth of Human Rights: A Brief Documentary History* (New York: Bedford/St. Martin, 1996).

72. See Michael Walzer, *On Toleration* (New Haven: Yale University Press, 1997), 91.

73. For one of the best statements of this problem, see Jürgen Habermas, *Between Facts and Norms: Contributions to a Discourse Theory of Law and Democracy,* trans. W. Rehg (Cambridge: MIT Press, 1996).

·INDEX·